THE GUINNESS
FORMULA 1
FACT BOOK

THE GUINNESS FORMULA 1 FACT BOOK

Ian Morrison

GUINNESS PUBLISHING

Copyright © Ian Morrison 1992

The right of Ian Morrison to be identified as the
Author of this Work has been asserted in accordance
with the Copyright, Design & Patents Act 1988.

Published in Great Britain by Guinness Publishing Ltd,
33 London Road, Enfield, Middlesex

Cover design: Ad Vantage Studios
Text design and layout: Steve Leaning

Typeset in Baskerville and Helvetica by
Ace Filmsetting Ltd, Frome, Somerset

Printed and bound in Great Britain by
The Bath Press, Bath

"Guinness" is a registered trademark of
Guinness Publishing Ltd

A catalogue record for this book is available from the
British Library

ISBN 0-85112-535-2

CONTENTS

INTRODUCTION

Motor racing encompasses far more than the thrilling world of Formula One. However, because the sport's premier division has such a worldwide appeal, this book is dedicated entirely to the World Formula One Championship which has been in existence since 1950.

The other branches of motor racing are not forgotten even though they may be neglected in this book, for all the present day Formula One drivers have progressed to their present status via the likes of kart racing, Formula Three, Formula Ford and so on. Without those branches of the sport there would be no Formula One drivers.

This book is filled with statistics about every aspect of the World Championship, including the Indianapolis 500 which formed part of the championship between 1950 and 1960 and is often ignored by some sources. It also contains histories of all the Grands Prix, accounts of some memorable races, biographies of drivers, a summary of each championship season, and much more. All records and statistics are up to and including the 1991 season.

I first enjoyed the thrill of Formula One in 1957 when I made the short journey from my Liverpool home to Aintree for the British Grand Prix. And what a day it was, with Stirling Moss taking the chequered flag in the Vanwall; the first British car to win a World Championship race. It is impossible to recreate the thrill, smell, and roar of Formula One racing in a book. I hope I have managed to do the next best thing.

Ian Morrison

ABBREVIATIONS

Countries

Arg	Argentina
Aus	Australia
Aut	Austria
Bel	Belgium
Bra	Brazil
Can	Canada
Chi	Chile
Col	Colombia
Fin	Finland
Fra	France
FRG	West Germany
GDR	East Germany
Ger	Germany (from 1990)
GB	Great Britain
Hol	Holland
Ire	Ireland
Ita	Italy
Jap	Japan
Mex	Mexico
Mon	Monaco
NZ	New Zealand
SRho	Southern Rhodesia
SAf	South Africa
Spa	Spain
Swe	Sweden
Swi	Switzerland
Uru	Uruguay
USA	United States of America
Ven	Venezuela

Other

CSI	Commission Sportive Internationale
FIA	Federation Internationale de l'Automobile
FISA	Federation Internationale du Sport Automobile
FOCA	Formula One Constructors Association
GP	Grand Prix
NASCAR	National Association for Stock Car Auto Racing (US)

ILLUSTRATIONS

Picture research by Image Select, Harrow
Black and white photographs courtesy of Farabolafoto, Milan; Allsport UK Ltd; Agence Vandystadt, Paris; Hulton-Deutsch Collection
Colour photographs courtesy of Allsport UK Ltd; Agence Vandystadt; Colorsport

ORIGINS OF THE WORLD CHAMPIONSHIP

The World Championship started on a sunny day at Silverstone in 1950, the culmination of more than 50 years of competitive motor racing. Now, for the first time, drivers had the chance to prove who was the best of all.

Manufacturers, notably the Italians in the early days, would use the championship as a means of gaining national pride and dominance, even though a championship for constructors was not officially conceived until 1958. But the roar of the Alfas, Ferraris and Maseratis in 1950 was a far cry from the machines the pioneers of the sport used to drive.

The first motorcar race using mechanical power was a 31km/19.3 mile race around Paris in 1887 and was won by Count Jules Philippe Albert de Dion at an average speed of 59kph/37mph. There are other claimants to having staged the world's first race, notably the Americans in 1878, but the Paris race is universally accepted as the first.

Towards the end of the 19th century, races from city to city became the most popular form of car and indeed bike racing, and in 1895 the race from Paris to Bordeaux was established as the first of these. It was won by Emile Levassor in a Panhard-Levassor which, unlike the De Dion steam quadricycle, was a 'real' motorcar and therefore *should* be regarded as the world's first motorcar race winner.

Manufacturers used these races as a means of promoting their cars. The motorcar was still in its infancy, and such was the prestige of these races that a win would guarantee sales for

One of the pioneers of the early World Championship races, Louis Chiron of Monte Carlo, at the wheel of his Bugatti at the start of a pre-war Italian Grand Prix.

Running repairs during the 1934 Mille Miglia. The fascist insignia worn by the driver and co-driver show how racing was used as an instrument of propaganda.

the likes of Panhard, Napier and Mercedes.

Rivalry became intense and the first set of motor racing rules were drawn up for the Paris–Amsterdam–Paris race of 1898. Because of that great desire to win, manufacturers were simply making bigger and more powerful cars; hence the curbs.

Grand Prix racing started at the beginning of the 20th century but first there was the Gordon Bennett series of races which was launched in 1900 and was a true test of a manufacturer's ability, because the rules of the series stipulated that all parts of a car had to be made in the manufacturer's country of origin.

The dangers of motor racing soon became apparent. The 1903 Paris to Madrid race was abandoned after many spectators were killed by the cars that made their way along open roads from the French capital to the Spanish border. Because of the accidents, road racing was immediately banned and this led to the construction of such enclosed circuits as Athy in Northern Ireland and Taunus in Germany. The Gordon Bennett series ended in 1905 and the following year saw the launch of the French Grand Prix, the first ever, at Le Mans. This was to be the start of a 44-year journey that ultimately led to the World Championship.

The cost of producing a racing machine had become prohibitive and motor racing declined as a sport in Europe a couple of years after the launch of the French Grand Prix, but when the Americans launched the Indianapolis 500 in 1911, interest picked up in Europe and the French Grand Prix was revived in 1912 after a three year lay-off. The European manufacturers simply didn't want the Americans to steal a march on them.

It was not until after the First World War that racing really took off in Europe, but by the mid-1920s competition was keen between drivers as well as manufacturers and Belgium, Germany, Spain, Monaco and Britain were soon staging Grands Prix. The British Grand

Prix was first held at the famous Brooklands circuit in 1926. Although known as the RAC Grand Prix at the time, it is still regarded as the first ever British Grand Prix.

The 1920s also saw the birth of two of the sport's best known races, the Le Mans 24 Hour race and the Mille Miglia in 1923 and 1927 respectively. It was certainly a boom time for the sport as manufacturers like Bugatti, Alfa Romeo and Mercedes-Benz all proved themselves with outstanding racing machines, while behind the wheel there emerged some great drivers like Louis Chiron, Lord Howe, and Rudi Caracciola.

As the sport went into the next decade, other great drivers like Tazio Nuvolari, Hermann Lang, Luigi Fagioli, and

Jean-Marie Balestre, for 13 years the President of FISA, Formula One's administrative body.

Giuseppe Farina emerged. But the real battle for supremacy was still among the manufacturers, and with war clouds looming, the German and Italian manufacturers in particular saw the sport as a propaganda machine and were anxious to out-do each other.

The Italians, through Alfa Romeo, originally held sway in the early 1930s, but for the second half of the decade the German Mercedes and Auto Unions took control. Then Enzo Ferrari, one of the greatest names in the sport, developed the Alfa Romeo 158 and it dethroned the Germans in 1938; and in the closing months before the Second World War the Italians were holding on to their dominance on the track. The last race before the war was at Tripoli; Mercedes had secretly developed a new car which now left the Alfas in its wake. So Germany went into the

war with the upper hand on the racetrack.

The German manufacturers were missing when Grand Prix racing resumed at the Bois de Boulogne in 1945 as Jean-Pierre Wimille won the *Grand Prix de Liberation* in a Bugatti. Because the sport was in a state of uncertainty, all races were run to the *Formula Libre* rules with sports cars and Grand Prix cars running side by side. A new Grand Prix formula was launched in 1946 and the following year international Grand Prix racing returned with the Italian manufacturers Alfa and Maserati taking advantage of the Germans' absence.

Then in October 1947 it was announced at the annual general meeting of the FIA (*Federation Internationale de l'Automobile*) that from the following season there would be two formulae, FI.1 and FI.2; effectively, it was on that day that Formula One was born. However, it was not called Formula One at first but the Grand Prix Formula. Some sources simply called the two formulae A and B.

The World Championship was not far away. Racing had taken on a whole new look, and outlook. Formula Three was created in 1949 and in Britain there were many club enthusiasts taking up the sport. It was this activity at grass roots level that was to form the base of a pyramid that pinnacled with Formula One. The situation is no different today.

The FIA announced plans for a World Championship at a meeting in February 1950, and on 10 April Juan Manuel Fangio, in a Maserati, won the Pau Grand Prix, the first race to be labelled 'International Formula One race'. A month later Silverstone hosted the first World Championship race. The rest of the story can be found on the following pages.

ARGENTINE GP

All races at Buenos Aires

Grand Prix racing first came to Buenos Aires in 1947 when the inaugural Buenos Aires Grand Prix was raced. The city often staged two races per year under the *Formula Libre* regulations and with its new home at the Buenos Aires autodrome, the race was included in the Grand Prix calendar for the first time in 1953 when it became the opening race of the season. For the first time, Grand Prix drivers took to competitive racing in the winter months. But there is no resem-blance to 'winter' in Buenos Aires in January and the race was often run in sweltering heat which made it a testing start to the new season for driver and car alike.

The inaugural World Championship race, which was renamed the Argentine Grand Prix, was won by Alberto Ascari in his Ferrari but the race, in front of a huge crowd, was marred by one of the sport's worst tragedies. A spectator strolled across the track in front of Giuseppe Farina's Ferrari on lap 32. Farina tried to avoid the spectator but could not maintain control over his car and he went into a slide before catapulting into the crowd. Farina was not badly injured, but 15 spectators lay dead and many more seriously injured.

Financial problems almost cost the Argentine Grand Prix its place on the calendar in 1958, but the following year it had to be cancelled. It returned in 1960 for one year only and did not reappear until 1972. The last Argentine Grand Prix was in 1981 and South America's only Grand Prix is now the Brazilian.

1953

18 January, 379.46km/235.79 miles
1 Alberto Ascari (Ita) Ferrari
2 Luigi Villoresi (Ita) Ferrari
3 José Froilán González (Arg) Maserati
4 Mike Hawthorn (GB) Ferrari
5 Oscar Galvez (Arg) Maserati
6 Jean Behra (Fra) Gordini
Winner's speed: 125.73kph/78.14mph
Fastest lap: Ascari 129.93kph/80.74mph
Pole position: Ascari

1954

17 January, 340.34km/211.48 miles
1 Juan Manuel Fangio (Arg) Maserati
2 Giuseppe Farina (Ita) Ferrari
3 José Froilán González (Arg) Ferrari
4 Maurice Trintignant (Fra) Ferrari
5 Elie Bayol (Fra) Gordini
6 Harry Schell (USA) Maserati
Winner's speed: 112.84kph/70.13mph
Fastest lap: Gonzalez 129.95kph/80.76mph
Pole position: Farina

1955

16 January, 375.55km/233.36 miles
1 Juan Manuel Fangio (Arg) Mercedes-Benz

2 José Froilán González (Arg)/Giuseppe Farina (Ita)/
  Maurice Trintignant (Fra) Ferrari
3 Giuseppe Farina (Ita)/Umberto Maglioli (Ita)/Maurice
  Trintignant (Fra) Ferrari
4 Hans Herrmann (FRG)/Karl Kling (FRG)/Stirling Moss
  (GB) Mercedes-Benz
5 Roberto Mieres (Arg) Maserati
6 Harry Schell (USA)/Jean Behra (Fra) Maserati
Winner's speed: 124.74kph/77.51mph
Fastest lap: Fangio 130.05kph/80.81mph
Pole position: Gonzalez

1956

22 January, 383.38km/238.22 miles
1 Luigi Musso (Ita)/Juan Manuel Fangio (Arg) Lancia-
  Ferrari
2 Jean Behra (Fra) Maserati
3 Mike Hawthorn (GB) Maserati
4 Chico Landi (Bra)/Gerino Gerini (Ita) Maserati
5 Olivier Gendebien (Bel) Lancia-Ferrari
6 Alberto Uria (Uru)/Oscar Gonzalez (Uru) Maserati
Winner's speed: 127.76kph/79.39mph
Fastest lap: Fangio 133.74kph/83.11mph
Pole position: Fangio

1957

13 January, 391.20km/243.08 miles
1 Juan Manuel Fangio (Arg) Maserati

2 Jean Behra (Fra) Maserati
3 Carlos Menditeguy (Arg) Maserati
4 Harry Schell (USA) Maserati
5 José Froilán González (Arg)/Alfonso de Portago (Spa) Lancia-Ferrari
6 Cesare Perdisa (Ita)/Wolfgang von Trips (FRG)/Peter Collins (GB) Lancia-Ferrari
Winner's speed: 129.73kph/80.61mph
Fastest lap: Stirling Moss (GB) Maserati 134.51kph/83.58mph
Pole position: Moss

1958

19 January, 312.96km/194.46 miles
1 Stirling Moss (GB) Cooper-Climax
2 Luigi Musso (Ita) Ferrari
3 Mike Hawthorn (GB) Ferrari
4 Juan Manuel Fangio (Arg) Maserati
5 Jean Behra (Fra) Maserati
6 Harry Schell (USA) Maserati
Winner's speed: 134.56kph/83.61mph
Fastest lap: Fangio 138.34kph/85.96mph
Pole position: Fangio

1960

7 February, 312.96km/194.46 miles
1 Bruce McLaren (NZ) Cooper-Climax
2 Cliff Allison (GB) Ferrari
3 Maurice Trintignant (Fra)/Stirling Moss (GB) Cooper-Climax
4 Carlos Menditeguy (Arg) Cooper-Maserati
5 Wolfgang von Trips (FRG) Ferrari
6 Innes Ireland (GB) Lotus-Climax
Winner's speed: 133.18kph/82.77mph
Fastest lap: Moss 142.36kph/88.48mph
Pole position: Moss

1972

23 January, 317.77km/197.45 miles
1 Jackie Stewart (GB) Tyrrell-Ford
2 Denny Hulme (NZ) McLaren-Ford
3 Jacky Ickx (Bel) Ferrari
4 Clay Regazzoni (Swi) Ferrari
5 Tim Schenken (Aus) Surtees-Ford
6 Ronnie Peterson (Swe) March-Ford
Winner's speed: 161.61kph/100.42mph
Fastest lap: Stewart 163.48kph/101.58mph
Pole position: Carlos Reutemann (Arg) Brabham-Ford

1973

28 January, 321.12km/199.53 miles
1 Emerson Fittipaldi (Bra) Lotus-Ford
2 François Cevert (Fra) Tyrrell-Ford
3 Jackie Stewart (GB) Tyrrell-Ford
4 Jacky Ickx (Bel) Ferrari
5 Denny Hulme (NZ) McLaren-Ford
6 Wilson Fittipaldi (Bra) Brabham-Ford
Winner's speed: 165.69kph/102.95mph
Fastest lap: E Fittipaldi 169.11kph/105.08mph
Pole position: Clay Regazzoni (Swi) BRM

1974

13 January, 316.30km/196.54 miles
1 Denny Hulme (NZ) McLaren-Ford
2 Niki Lauda (Aut) Ferrari
3 Clay Regazzoni (Swi) Ferrari
4 Mike Hailwood (GB) McLaren-Ford
5 Jean-Pierre Beltoise (Fra) BRM
6 Patrick Depailler (Fra) Tyrrell-Ford
Winner's speed: 187.85kph/116.72mph
Fastest lap: Regazzoni 191.66kph/119.09mph
Pole position: Ronnie Peterson (Swe) Lotus-Ford

1975

12 January, 316.30km/196.54 miles
1 Emerson Fittipaldi (Bra) McLaren-Ford
2 James Hunt (GB) Hesketh-Ford
3 Carlos Reutemann (Arg) Brabham-Ford
4 Clay Regazzoni (Swi) Ferrari
5 Patrick Depailler (Fra) Tyrrell-Ford
6 Niki Lauda (Aut) Ferrari
Winner's speed: 190.86kph/118.60mph
Fastest lap: Hunt 193.72kph/120.37mph
Pole position: Jean-Pierre Jarier (Fra) Shadow-Ford *(did not start)*

1977

9 January, 316.30km/196.54 miles
1 Jody Scheckter (SAf) Wolf-Ford
2 Carlos Pace (Bra) Brabham-Alfa Romeo
3 Carlos Reutemann (Arg) Ferrari
4 Emerson Fittipaldi (Bra) Fittipaldi-Ford
5 Mario Andretti (USA) Lotus-Ford
6 Clay Regazzoni (Swi) Ensign-Ford
Winner's speed: 189.44kph/117.71mph
Fastest lap: James Hunt (GB) McLaren-Ford 193.46kph/120.21mph
Pole position: Hunt

1978

15 January, 316.30km/196.54 miles
1 Mario Andretti (USA) Lotus-Ford
2 Niki Lauda (Aut) Brabham-Alfa Romeo
3 Patrick Depailler (Fra) Tyrrell-Ford
4 James Hunt (GB) McLaren-Ford
5 Ronnie Peterson (Swe) Lotus-Ford
6 Patrick Tambay (Fra) McLaren-Ford
Winner's speed: 191.82kph/119.19mph
Fastest lap: Gilles Villeneuve (Can) Ferrari 195.75kph/121.63mph
Pole position: Andretti

1979

21 January, 316.30km/196.54 miles
1 Jacques Laffite (Fra) Ligier-Ford
2 Carlos Reutemann (Arg) Lotus-Ford
3 John Watson (GB) McLaren-Ford
4 Patrick Depailler (Fra) Ligier-Ford
5 Mario Andretti (USA) Lotus-Ford
6 Emerson Fittipaldi (Bra) Fittipaldi-Ford

Winner's speed: 197.59kph/122.78mph
Fastest lap: Laffite 200.97kph/124.88mph
Pole position: Laffite

1980

13 January, 316.30km/196.54 miles
1 Alan Jones (Aus) Williams-Ford
2 Nelson Piquet (Bra) Brabham-Ford
3 Keke Rosberg (Fin) Fittipaldi-Ford
4 Derek Daly (Ire) Tyrrell-Ford
5 Bruno Giacomelli (Ita) Alfa Romeo
6 Alain Prost (Fra) McLaren-Ford
Winner's speed: 183.44kph/113.99mph
Fastest lap: Jones 194.53kph/120.87mph
Pole position: Jones

1981

12 April, 316.30km/196.54 miles
1 Nelson Piquet (Bra) Brabham-Ford
2 Carlos Reutemann (Arg) Williams-Ford
3 Alain Prost (Fra) Renault
4 Alan Jones (Aus) Williams-Ford
5 René Arnoux (Fra) Renault
6 Elio de Angelis (Ita) Lotus-Ford
Winner's speed: 200.63kph/124.67mph
Fastest lap: Piquet 204.07kph/126.81mph
Pole position: Piquet

MOST WINS

Drivers
4 Juan Manuel Fangio
2 Emerson Fittipaldi
Manufacturers
2 Cooper, Lotus, Maserati, McLaren

MOST FASTEST LAPS

Drivers
3 Juan Manuel Fangio
2 James Hunt, Stirling Moss
Manufacturers
4 Ferrari
2 Maserati

MOST POLE POSITIONS

Drivers
2 Juan Manuel Fangio, Stirling Moss
Manufacturers
3 Ferrari
2 Brabham, Lotus, Maserati

AUSTRALIAN GP

All races at Adelaide

Although the Australian Grand Prix did not gain World Championship status until 1985, the race has been in existence since 1928 and has been won by some of the great names of Grand Prix racing: Jack Brabham, Jim Clark, Stirling Moss, Jackie Stewart, Graham Hill and Bruce McLaren, for example.

The winner of the first ever race was Arthur Waite, an executive of the Austin Motor Company who was married to Lord Austin's daughter. Waite's Austin Seven took the chequered flag averaging 56.3 mph.

While the race has always been popular and regarded as the most prestigious in Australasia, it received an added boost in 1964 when the Tasman Cup series was launched and the world's top Formula One drivers took part. During the days of the Cup, Sandown Park, Longford, Lakeside, and Warwick Farm all played host to the Australian Grand Prix.

The Tasman Cup series ended in 1976 and the race became the Grand Prix that everyone forgot, but it was granted World Championship status in 1985 and is traditionally the last Grand Prix of the season. In its short existence it has seen some exciting finishes to the championship.

There was that great battle between the two McLaren teammates, Senna and Prost, in 1988 when Senna just had to stay within sight of Prost to clinch his first title. Prost did everything right and won the race but he couldn't do anything about Senna who came home in second place. But there had been even greater drama two years earlier – and the story of that race is told on the next page.

MOST WINS

Drivers
2 Alain Prost
Manufacturers
3 McLaren
2 Williams

MOST FASTEST LAPS

Drivers
2 Gerhard Berger
Manufacturers
2 Ferrari, Williams, McLaren

MOST POLE POSITIONS

Drivers
5 Ayrton Senna
Manufacturers
4 McLaren

1985

3 November, 309.86km/192.54 miles
1 Keke Rosberg (Fin) Williams-Honda
2 Jacques Laffite (Fra) Ligier-Renault
3 Philippe Streiff (Fra) Ligier-Renault
4 Ivan Capelli (Ita) Tyrrell-Renault
5 Stefan Johansson (Swe) Ferrari
6 Gerhard Berger (Aut) Arrows-BMW
Winner's speed: 154.03kph/95.71mph
Fastest lap: Rosberg 162.38kph/100.90mph
Pole position: Ayrton Senna (Bra) Lotus-Renault

1986

26 October, 309.86km/192.54 miles
1 Alain Prost (Fra) McLaren-TAG
2 Nelson Piquet (Bra) Williams-Honda
3 Stefan Johansson (Swe) Ferrari
4 Martin Brundle (GB) Tyrrell-Renault
5 Philippe Streiff (Fra) Tyrrell-Renault
6 Johnny Dumfries (GB) Lotus-Renault
Winner's speed: 163.55kph/101.63mph
Fastest lap: Piquet 168.34kph/104.60mph
Pole position: Nigel Mansell (GB) Williams-Honda

HE GREAT RACES

1986 Australian GP

In 1976 the final race of the season, the Japanese Grand Prix, turned into a memorable occasion for Britain's last world champion James Hunt, because it was there that he clinched his title. Ten years later Nigel Mansell was hoping to become Britain's next champion when he went to Adelaide for the final race of the season but what a different ending it was for Mansell.

The Briton led the championship going into the 16th and final race of the season by seven points from Alain Prost and Nelson Piquet. A third place or better would guarantee Mansell the title, no matter whether either of the other two won the race or not.

The McLaren pair of Keke Rosberg and one of the title contenders, Alain Prost, dominated the race but Prost had to go into the pits and his mechanics took the opportunity to check out his tyres. They were happy with what they saw, and that indicated to them that Rosberg's would be fine as well.

But while leading at the three-quarter stage, the Finn lost part of his tread coming down the fast Brabham straight. Seeing what had happened, the Williams camp thought they had better pull Mansell and team-mate Nelson Piquet in for tyre checks. But Mansell never made it to the pits. The left rear tyre of his Williams exploded. The result could have been disastrous but Nigel handled the car superbly and took it into a run-off area. The car was damaged but Mansell was unhurt, externally that is. Inside it must have been a different story as he stood and watched Prost take the chequered flag and with it the nine points that won him – and denied Mansell – the title.

Utter dejection for Nigel Mansell after being denied the world title by his accident in Adelaide.

1987

15 November, 309.86km/192.54 miles
1 Gerhard Berger (Aut) Ferrari
2 Michele Alboreto (Ita) Ferrari
3 Thierry Boutsen (Bel) Benetton-Ford
4 Jonathan Palmer (GB) Tyrrell-Ford
5 Yannick Dalmas (Fra) Lola-Ford (*)
6 Roberto Moreno (Bra) AGS-Ford
Ayrton Senna (Bra) finished 2nd but subsequently disqualified.
(*) Dalmas not a regular competitor and therefore received no points
Winner's speed: 164.63kph/102.30mph
Fastest lap: Berger 169.18kph/105.12mph
Pole position: Berger

1988

13 November, 309.96km/192.62 miles
1 Alain Prost (Fra) McLaren-Honda
2 Ayrton Senna (Bra) McLaren-Honda
3 Nelson Piquet (Bra) Lotus-Honda
4 Riccardo Patrese (Ita) Williams-Judd
5 Thierry Boutsen (Bel) Benetton-Ford
6 Ivan Capelli (Ita) March-Judd
Winner's speed: 164.23kph/102.07mph
Fastest lap: Prost 167.52kph/104.12mph
Pole position: Senna

1989

5 November, 264.60km/164.41 miles
1 Thierry Boutsen (Bel) Williams-Renault
2 Alessandro Nannini (Ita) Benetton-Ford

3 Riccardo Patrese (Ita) Williams-Renault
4 Satoru Nakajima (Jap) Lotus-Judd
5 Emanuele Pirro (Ita) Benetton-Ford
6 Pierluigi Martini (Ita) Minardi-Ford
Winner's speed: 131.98kph/82.01mph
Fastest lap: Nakajima 138.18kph/85.62mph
Pole position: Ayrton Senna (Bra) McLaren-Honda

1990

4 November, 306.02km/190.11 miles
1 Nelson Piquet (Bra) Benetton-Ford
2 Nigel Mansell (GB) Ferrari
3 Alain Prost (Fra) Ferrari
4 Gerhard Berger (Aut) McLaren-Honda
5 Thierry Boutsen (Bel) Williams-Renault
6 Riccardo Patrese (Ita) Williams-Renault
Winner's speed: 167.40kph/104.02mph
Fastest lap: Mansell 174.01kph/108.12mph
Pole position: Ayrton Senna (Bra) McLaren-Honda

1991

3 November, 52.92km/32.88 miles
1 Ayrton Senna (Bra) McLaren-Honda
2 Nigel Mansell (GB) Williams-Renault
3 Gerhard Berger (Aut) McLaren-Honda
4 Nelson Piquet (Bra) Benetton-Ford
5 Riccardo Patrese (Ita) Williams-Renault
6 Gianni Morbidelli (Ita) Ferrari
Race stopped after 16 laps but positions as at 14 laps taken into consideration. Half points awarded.
Winner's speed: 129.17kph/80.26mph
Fastest lap: Berger 134.55kph/83.60mph
Pole position: Senna

AUSTRIAN GP

Formula One racing was first seen in Austria in 1963 and the following year the Austrian Grand Prix formed a round of the World Championship. It was held around the military aerodrome at Zeltweg where the circuit was very bumpy and totally unsuitable, and the race was taken off the calendar until 1970. Making his World Championship debut in the inaugural race was the future world champion, and local hero, Jochen Rindt.

In the six years it was off the World Championship rota the Austrian Grand Prix was run as a sports car race. But hopeful of regaining its Formula One status, the Austrian Automobile Club set about building a new permanent home for the race, and in 1969 the Österreichring was opened not far from the old Zeltweg circuit. The following year the organisers were granted their wish and the race returned to the calendar, and it was a great success as an estimated 100 000 packed into the new circuit.

Despite being one of the best circuits from a spectating point of view, the narrow pit straight was the scene of chaos in 1987 and consequently Austria lost its Grand Prix again the following year.

MOST WINS

Drivers
3 Alain Prost
2 Alan Jones, Ronnie Peterson
Manufacturers
4 Lotus
3 McLaren
2 Ferrari, Renault, Williams

MOST FASTEST LAPS

Drivers
2 René Arnoux, Alain Prost
Manufacturers
4 McLaren
3 Brabham, Renault
2 Ferrari

MOST POLE POSITIONS

Drivers
3 René Arnoux, Niki Lauda, Nelson
  Piquet
2 Emerson Fittipaldi
Manufacturers
5 Lotus   3 Renault
4 Ferrari   2 Brabham, BRM, McLaren

1964 Zeltweg

23 August, 336.00m/208.78 miles
1 Lorenzo Bandini (Ita) Ferrari
2 Richie Ginther (USA) BRM
3 Bob Anderson (GB) Brabham-Climax
4 Tony Maggs (SAf) BRM
5 Innes Ireland (GB) BRP-BRM
6 Jo Bonnier (Swe) Brabham-Climax
Winner's speed: 159.62kph/99.20mph
Fastest lap: Dan Gurney (USA) Brabham-Climax
163.46kph/101.57mph
Pole position: Graham Hill (GB) BRM

1970 Österreichring

16 August, 354.66km/220.38 miles
1 Jacky Ickx (Bel) Ferrari
2 Clay Regazzoni (Swi) Ferrari
3 Rolf Stommelen (FRG) Brabham-Ford
4 Pedro Rodriguez (Mex) BRM
5 Jackie Oliver (GB) BRM
6 Jean-Pierre Beltoise (Fra) Matra-Simca
Winner's speed: 208.04kph/129.27mph
Fastest lap: Ickx/Regazzoni 211.95kph/131.70mph
Pole position: Jochen Rindt (Aut) Lotus-Ford

1971 Österreichring

15 August, 319.20km/198.34 miles
1 Jo Siffert (Swi) BRM
2 Emerson Fittipaldi (Bra) Lotus-Ford
3 Tim Schenken (Aus) Brabham-Ford
4 Reine Wisell (Swe) Lotus-Ford
5 Graham Hill (GB) Brabham-Ford
6 Henri Pescarolo (Fra) March-Ford
Winner's speed: 211.86kph/131.64mph
Fastest lap: Siffert 216.10kph/134.28mph
Pole position: Siffert

1972 Österreichring

13 August, 319.19km/198.34 miles
1 Emerson Fittipaldi (Bra) Lotus-Ford
2 Denny Hulme (NZ) McLaren-Ford
3 Peter Revson (USA) McLaren-Ford
4 Mike Hailwood (GB) Surtees-Ford
5 Chris Amon (NZ) Matra-Simca
6 Howden Ganley (NZ) BRM
Winner's speed: 214.52kph/133.30mph
Fastest lap: Hulme 216.43kph/134.48mph
Pole position: Fittipaldi

1973 Österreichring

19 August, 319.19km/198.34 miles
1 Ronnie Peterson (Swe) Lotus-Ford
2 Jackie Stewart (GB) Tyrrell-Ford
3 Carlos Pace (Bra) Surtees-Ford
4 Carlos Reutemann (Arg) Brabham-Ford
5 Jean-Pierre Beltoise (Fra) BRM
6 Clay Regazzoni (Swi) BRM
Winner's speed: 215.64kph/133.99mph
Fastest lap: Pace 218.72kph/135.91mph

Pole position: Emerson Fittipaldi (Bra) Lotus-Ford

1974 Österreichring

18 August, 319.19km/198.34 miles
1 Carlos Reutemann (Arg) Brabham-Ford
2 Denny Hulme (NZ) McLaren-Ford
3 James Hunt (GB) Hesketh-Ford
4 John Watson (GB) Brabham-Ford
5 Clay Regazzoni (Swi) Ferrari
6 Vittorio Brambilla (Ita) March-Ford
Winner's speed: 215.80kph/134.09mph
Fastest lap: Regazzoni 218.88kph/136.01mph
Pole position: Niki Lauda (Aut) Ferrari

1975 Österreichring

17 August, 171.42km/106.52 miles
1 Vittorio Brambilla (Ita) March-Ford
2 James Hunt (GB) Hesketh-Ford
3 Tom Pryce (GB) Shadow-Ford
4 Jochen Mass (FRG) McLaren-Ford
5 Ronnie Peterson (Swe) Lotus-Ford
6 Niki Lauda (Aut) Ferrari
Half points only awarded because insufficient distance covered
Winner's speed: 177.50kph/110.29mph
Fastest lap: Brambilla 186.83kph/116.09mph
Pole position: Lauda

1976 Österreichring

15 August, 319.14km/198.30 miles
1 John Watson (GB) Penske-Ford
2 Jacques Laffite (Fra) Ligier-Matra
3 Gunnar Nilsson (Swe) Lotus-Ford
4 James Hunt (GB) McLaren-Ford
5 Mario Andretti (USA) Lotus-Ford
6 Ronnie Peterson (Swe) March-Ford
Winner's speed: 212.43kph/132.00mph
Fastest lap: Hunt 221.81kph/137.83mph
Pole position: Hunt

1977 Österreichring

14 August, 320.87km/199.38 miles
1 Alan Jones (Aus) Shadow-Ford
2 Niki Lauda (Aut) Ferrari
3 Hans Stuck (FRG) Brabham-Alfa Romeo
4 Carlos Reutemann (Arg) Ferrari
5 Ronnie Peterson (Swe) Tyrrell-Ford
6 Jochen Mass (FRG) McLaren-Ford
Winner's speed: 197.93kph/122.99mph
Fastest lap: John Watson (GB) Brabham-Alfa Romeo
211.89kph/131.66mph
Pole position: Lauda

1978 Österreichring

13 August, 320.87km/199.38 miles
1 Ronnie Peterson (Swe) Lotus-Ford
2 Patrick Depailler (Fra) Tyrrell-Ford
3 Gilles Villeneuve (Can) Ferrari
4 Emerson Fittipaldi (Bra) Fittipaldi-Ford

5 Jacques Laffite (Fra) Ligier-Matra
6 Vittorio Brambilla (Ita) Surtees-Ford
Winner's speed: 189.95kph/118.03mph
Fastest lap: Peterson 207.45kph/128.91mph
Pole position: Peterson

1979 Österreichring

12 August, 320.87km/199.38 miles
1 Alan Jones (Aus) Williams-Ford
2 Gilles Villeneuve (Can) Ferrari
3 Jacques Laffite (Fra) Ligier-Ford
4 Jody Scheckter (SAf) Ferrari
5 Clay Regazzoni (Swi) Williams-Ford
6 René Arnoux (Fra) Renault
Winner's speed: 219.71kph/136.52mph
Fastest lap: Arnoux 223.82kph/139.08mph
Pole position: Arnoux

1980 Österreichring

17 August, 320.87km/199.38 miles
1 Jean-Pierre Jabouille (Fra) Renault
2 Alan Jones (Aus) Williams-Ford
3 Carlos Reutemann (Arg) Williams-Ford
4 Jacques Laffite (Fra) Ligier-Ford
5 Nelson Piquet (Bra) Brabham-Ford
6 Elio de Angelis (Ita) Lotus-Ford
Winner's speed: 223.20kph/138.69mph
Fastest lap: René Arnoux (Fra) Renault 231.20kph/
143.66mph
Pole position: Arnoux

1981 Österreichring

16 August, 314.93km/195.69 miles
1 Jacques Laffite (Fra) Talbot-Matra
2 René Arnoux (Fra) Renault
3 Nelson Piquet (Bra) Brabham-Ford
4 Alan Jones (Aus) Williams-Ford
5 Carlos Reutemann (Arg) Williams-Ford
6 John Watson (GB) McLaren-Ford
Winner's speed: 215.70kph/134.03mph
Fastest lap: Laffite 219.14kph/136.17mph
Pole position: Arnoux

1982 Österreichring

15 August, 314.93km/195.69 miles
1 Elio de Angelis (Ita) Lotus-Ford
2 Keke Rosberg (Fin) Williams-Ford
3 Jacques Laffite (Fra) Talbot-Matra
4 Patrick Tambay (Fra) Ferrari
5 Niki Lauda (Aut) McLaren-Ford
6 Mauro Baldi (Ita) Arrows-Ford
Winner's speed: 222.10kph/138.01mph
Fastest lap: Nelson Piquet (Bra) Brabham-BMW
228.32kph/141.88mph
Pole position: Piquet

1983 Österreichring

14 August, 314.93km/195.69 miles
1 Alain Prost (Fra) Renault

2 René Arnoux (Fra) Ferrari
3 Nelson Piquet (Bra) Brabham-BMW
4 Eddie Cheever (USA) Renault
5 Nigel Mansell (GB) Lotus-Renault
6 Niki Lauda (Aut) McLaren-Ford
Winner's speed: 223.49kph/138.87mph
Fastest lap: Prost 227.66kph/141.47mph
Pole position: Patrick Tambay (Fra) Ferrari

1984 Österreichring

19 August, 303.04km/188.30 miles
1 Niki Lauda (Aut) McLaren-Porsche
2 Nelson Piquet (Bra) Brabham-BMW
3 Michele Alboreto (Ita) Ferrari
4 Teo Fabi (Ita) Brabham-BMW
5 Thierry Boutsen (Bel) Arrows-BMW
6 Marc Surer (Swi) Arrows BMW
Winner's speed: 223.88kph/139.12mph
Fastest lap: Lauda 230.31kph/143.11mph
Pole position: Piquet

1985 Österreichring

18 August, 308.98km/191.99 miles
1 Alain Prost (Fra) McLaren-TAG
2 Ayrton Senna (Bra) Lotus-Renault
3 Michele Alboreto (Ita) Ferrari
4 Stefan Johansson (Swe) Ferrari
5 Elio de Angelis (Ita) Lotus-Renault
6 Marc Surer (Swi) Brabham-BMW
Winner's speed: 231.13kph/143.62mph
Fastest lap: Prost 239.70kph/148.95mph
Pole position: Prost

1986 Österreichring

17 August, 308.98km/191.99 miles
1 Alain Prost (Fra) McLaren-TAG
2 Michele Alboreto (Ita) Ferrari
3 Stefan Johansson (Swe) Ferrari
4 Alan Jones (Aus) Lola-Ford
5 Patrick Tambay (Fra) Lola-Ford
6 Christian Danner (FRG) Arrows-BMW
Winner's speed: 227.80kph/141.56mph
Fastest lap: Gerhard Berger (Aut) Benetton-BMW
238.90kph/148.46mph
Pole position: Teo Fabi (Ita) Benetton-BMW

1987 Österreichring

16 August, 308.98km/191.99 miles
1 Nigel Mansell (GB) Williams-Honda
2 Nelson Piquet (Bra) Williams-Honda
3 Teo Fabi (Ita) Benetton-Ford
4 Thierry Boutsen (Bel) Benetton-Ford
5 Ayrton Senna (Bra) Lotus-Honda
6 Alain Prost (Fra) McLaren-TAG
Winner's speed: 235.42kph/146.28mph
Fastest lap: Mansell 242.21kph/150.50mph
Pole position: Piquet

BELGIAN GP

The Belgian Grand Prix was first held in 1925 and has been part of the World Championship since its inaugural year, 1950. It has only failed to appear on four occasions.

Most races have been at the fast Spa-Francorchamps circuit, south of Liege, and some of the quickest ever Grands Prix have been on this circuit, the fastest race being in 1970 when Pedro Rodriguez won in his BRM at an average speed of 241.31 kph/149.94mph. On lap 28 Chris Amon covered the 14.10 km/8.76 mile circuit at an average speed of 244.74kph/152.08mph.

The 1961 Belgian Grand Prix at Spa saw one of the most dramatic finishes in Formula One history when Phil Hill beat Wolfgang von Trips by seven tenths of a second. In the previous Grand Prix at Zandvoort three weeks earlier the roles had been reversed with von Trips winning by less than a second.

Sadly, it was also at Spa the previous year that Grand Prix racing witnessed one of its most tragic races when the British pair of Chris Bristow and Alan Stacey both lost their lives. And it was while practising at Zolder in 1982 that the popular French-Canadian Gilles Villeneuve lost his life. But tragedy is nothing new to the once perilous Spa circuit because it was here in 1939 that Dick Seaman

Gilles Villeneuve, pictured shortly before his tragic death at Zolder in 1982.

was killed when his Mercedes skidded into a tree and burst into flames

---

1950 Spa-Francorchamps

18 June, 494.20km/307.08 miles
1 Juan Manuel Fangio (Arg) Alfa Romeo
2 Luigi Fagioli (Ita) Alfa Romeo
3 Louis Rosier (Fra) Lago-Talbot
4 Giuseppe Farina (Ita) Alfa Romeo
5 Alberto Ascari (Ita) Ferrari
6 Luigi Villoresi (Ita) Ferrari
Winner's speed: 177.07kph/110.03mph
Fastest lap: Farina 185.68kph/115.40mph
Pole position: Farina

1951 Spa-Francorchamps

17 June, 508.32km/316.85 miles
1 Giuseppe Farina (Ita) Alfa Romeo
2 Alberto Ascari (Ita) Ferrari
3 Luigi Villoresi (Ita) Ferrari
4 Louis Rosier (Fra) Lago-Talbot
5 Yves Giraud-Cabantous (Fra) Lago-Talbot
6 André Pilette (Bel) Lago-Talbot
Winner's speed: 183.94kph/114.30mph
Fastest lap: Juan Manuel Fangio (Arg) Alfa Romeo
93.94kph/120.51mph
Pole position: Fangio

1952 Spa-Francorchamps

22 June, 508.32km/316.85 miles
1 Alberto Ascari (Ita) Ferrari
2 Giuseppe Farina (Ita) Ferrari
3 Robert Manzon (Fra) Gordini
4 Mike Hawthorn (GB) Cooper-Bristol
5 Paul Frére (Bel) HWM
6 Alan Brown (GB) Cooper-Bristol

Winner's speed: 165.94kph/103.13mph
Fastest lap: Ascari 172.89kph/107.44mph
Pole position: Ascari

1953 Spa-Francorchamps

21 June, 508.32km/316.85 miles
1 Alberto Ascari (Ita) Ferrari
2 Luigi Villoresi (Ita) Ferrari
3 Onofre Marimon (Arg) Maserati
4 Emmanuel de Graffenried (Swi) Maserati
5 Maurice Trintignant (Fra) Gordini
6 Mike Hawthorn (GB) Ferrari
Winner's speed: 180.96kph/112.47mph
Fastest lap: José Froilán González (Arg) Maserati
185.50kph/115.27mph
Pole position: Juan Manuel Fangio (Arg) Maserati

1954 Spa-Francorchamps

20 June, 508.32km/316.85 miles
1 Juan Manuel Fangio (Arg) Maserati
2 Maurice Trintignant (Fra) Ferrari
3 Stirling Moss (GB) Maserati
4 José Froilán González (Arg)/Mike Hawthorn (GB) Ferrari
5 André Pilette (Bel) Gordini
6 'B Bira' (Siam) Maserati
Winner's speed: 185.16kph/115.08mph
Fastest lap: Fangio 191.46kph/118.97mph
Pole position: Fangio

1955 Spa-Francorchamps

5 June, 508.32km/316.85 miles
1 Juan Manuel Fangio (Arg) Mercedes-Benz
2 Stirling Moss (GB) Mercedes-Benz

3 Giuseppe Farina (Ita) Ferrari
4 Paul Frére (Bel) Ferrari
5 Roberto Mieres (Arg)/Jean Behra (Fra) Maserati
6 Maurice Trintignant (Fra) Ferrari
Winner's speed: 191.24kph/118.83mph
Fastest lap: Fangio 195.05kph/121.21mph
Pole position: Eugenio Castellotti (Ita) Lancia

1956 Spa-Francorchamps

3 June, 508.32km/316.85 miles
1 Peter Collins (GB) Lancia-Ferrari
2 Paul Frére (Bel) Lancia-Ferrari
3 Cesare Perdisa (Ita)/Stirling Moss (GB) Maserati
4 Harry Schell (USA) Vanwall
5 Luigi Villoresi (Ita) Maserati
6 André Pilette (Bel) Lancia-Ferrari
Winner's speed: 190.61kph/118.44mph
Fastest lap: Moss 199.58kph/124.01mph
Pole position: Juan Manuel Fangio (Arg) Lancia-Ferrari

1958 Spa-Francorchamps

15 June, 338.40km/210.27 miles
1 Tony Brooks (GB) Vanwall
2 Mike Hawthorn (GB) Ferrari
3 Stuart Lewis-Evans (GB) Vanwall
4 Cliff Allison (GB) Lotus-Climax
5 Harry Schell (USA) BRM
6 Olivier Gendebien (Bel) Ferrari
Winner's speed: 209.09kph/129.92mph

Fastest lap: Hawthorn 213.01kph/132.36mph
Pole position: Hawthorn

1960 Spa-Francorchamps

19 June, 507.60km/315.41 miles
1 Jack Brabham (Aus) Cooper-Climax
2 Bruce McLaren (NZ) Cooper-Climax
3 Olivier Gendebien (Bel) Cooper-Climax
4 Phil Hill (USA) Ferrari
5 Jim Clark (GB) Lotus-Climax
6 Lucien Bianchi (Bel) Cooper-Climax
Winner's speed: 215.06kph/133.63mph
Fastest lap: Brabham, P Hill, Innes Ireland (GB) Lotus-Climax 218.89kph/136.01mph
Pole position: Brabham

1961 Spa-Francorchamps

18 June, 423.00km/262.84 miles
1 Phil Hill (USA) Ferrari
2 Wolfgang von Trips (FRG) Ferrari
3 Richie Ginther (USA) Ferrari
4 Olivier Gendebien (Bel) Ferrari
5 John Surtees (GB) Cooper-Climax
6 Dan Gurney (USA) Porsche
Winner's speed: 206.24kph/128.15mph
Fastest lap: Ginther 211.68kph/131.53mph
Pole position: Hill

THE GREAT RACES

1961 Belgian GP

There cannot have been two closer races than the 1961 Dutch and Belgian Grands Prix and for them to be back-to-back races, and with the same men involved, makes them even more memorable.

Wolfgang von Trips had beaten his Ferrari teammate Phil Hill by nine tenths of a second at Zandvoort a month earlier, and now the third race of the 1961 season, staged at the fast Spa circuit in Belgium, would give the American his opportunity to gain revenge – which he did by an even smaller margin.

A Ferrari trio of Hill, von Trips and, this time, Olivier Gendebien, again occupied the front row of the grid and by the fourth lap the Italian team had, once more, showed their dominance and started to pull away. As the race went into the 25th lap such was their pace that the four Ferraris were amongst just eight cars still on the same lap.

Gendebien and another Ferrari team-mate Richie Ginther were battling it out for third place, which Ginther eventually captured by 26 seconds, but for the second successive race all eyes were again on Hill and von Trips as the chequered flag

beckoned, and as they went across the line it was the American who took first place by just seven tenths of a second and thus avenged his defeat at Zandvoort.

The two men not only engaged in two exciting races in Holland and Belgium but were to enjoy an intense battle for the championship. Hill was to go on and become the first North American world champion but, sadly, his team-mate never saw the season out. He was tragically killed in a accident at Monza when leading the championship.

1962 Spa-Francorchamps

17 June, 451.20km/280.36 miles
1 Jim Clark (GB) Lotus-Climax
2 Graham Hill (GB) BRM
3 Phil Hill (USA) Ferrari
4 Ricardo Rodriguez (Mex) Ferrari
5 John Surtees (GB) Lola-Climax
6 Jack Brabham (Aus) Lotus-Climax
Winner's speed: 212.27kph/131.90mph
Fastest lap: Clark 215.45kph/133.87mph
Pole position: G Hill

1963 Spa-Francorchamps

9 June, 451.20km/280.36 miles
1 Jim Clark (GB) Lotus-Climax
2 Bruce McLaren (NZ) Cooper-Climax
3 Dan Gurney (USA) Brabham-Climax
4 Richie Ginther (USA) BRM
5 Jo Bonnier (Swe) Cooper-Climax
6 Carel Godin de Beaufort (Hol) Porsche
Winner's speed: 183.63kph/114.10mph
Fastest lap: Clark 213.19kph/132.47mph
Pole position: G Hill (GB) BRM

1964 Spa-Francorchamps

14 June, 451.20km/280.36 miles
1 Jim Clark (GB) Lotus-Climax
2 Bruce McLaren (NZ) Cooper-Climax
3 Jack Brabham (Aus) Brabham-Climax
4 Richie Ginther (USA) BRM
5 Graham Hill (GB) BRM
6 Dan Gurney (USA) Brabham-Climax
Winner's speed: 213.68kph/132.79mph
Fastest lap: Gurney 221.47kph/137.61mph
Pole position: Gurney

1965 Spa-Francorchamps

13 June, 451.20km/280.36 miles
1 Jim Clark (GB) Lotus-Climax
2 Jackie Stewart (GB) BRM
3 Bruce McLaren (NZ) Cooper-Climax
4 Jack Brabham (Aus) Brabham-Climax
5 Graham Hill (GB) BRM
6 Richie Ginther (USA) Honda
Winner's speed: 188.54kph/117.16mph
Fastest lap: Clark 200.71kph/124.72mph
Pole position: Hill

1966 Spa-Francorchamps

12 June, 394.80km/245.32 miles
1 John Surtees (GB) Ferrari
2 Jochen Rindt (Aut) Cooper-Maserati
3 Lorenzo Bandini (Ita) Ferrari
4 Jack Brabham (Aus) Brabham-Repco
5 Richie Ginther (USA) Cooper-Maserati
Only five classified.
Winner's speed: 183.36kph/113.93mph
Fastest lap: Surtees 196.21kph/121.92mph
Pole position: Surtees

1967 Spa-Francorchamps

18 June, 394.80km/245.32 miles
1 Dan Gurney (USA) Eagle-Westlake
2 Jackie Stewart (GB) BRM
3 Chris Amon (NZ) Ferrari
4 Jochen Rindt (Aut) Cooper-Maserati
5 Mike Spence (GB) BRM
6 Jim Clark (GB) Lotus-Ford
Winner's speed: 234.95kph/145.99mph
Fastest lap: Gurney 239.55kph/148.85mph
Pole position: Clark

1968 Spa-Francorchamps

19 June, 394.80km/245.32 miles
1 Bruce McLaren (NZ) McLaren-Ford
2 Pedro Rodriguez (Mex) BRM
3 Jacky Ickx (Bel) Ferrari
4 Jackie Stewart (GB) Matra-Ford
5 Jackie Oliver (GB) Lotus-Ford
6 Lucien Bianchi (Bel) Cooper-BRM
Winner's speed: 236.80kph/147.14mph
Fastest lap: John Surtees (GB) Honda 241.14kph/
149.84mph
Pole position: Chris Amon (NZ) Ferrari

1970 Spa-Francorchamps

7 June, 394.80km/245.32 miles
1 Pedro Rodriguez (Mex) BRM
2 Chris Amon (NZ) March-Ford
3 Jean-Pierre Beltoise (Fra) Matra- Simca
4 Ignazio Giunti (Ita) Ferrari
5 Rolf Stommelen (FRG) Brabham-Ford
6 Henri Pescarolo (Fra) Matra- Simca
Winner's speed: 241.31kph/149.94mph
Fastest lap: Amon 244.74kph/152.08mph
Pole position: Jackie Stewart (GB) March-Ford

1972 Nivelles-Baulers

4 June, 316.54km/196.69 miles
1 Emerson Fittipaldi (Bra) Lotus-Ford
2 François Cevert (Fra) Tyrrell-Ford
3 Denny Hulme (NZ) McLaren-Ford
4 Mike Hailwood (GB) Surtees-Ford
5 Carlos Pace (Bra) March-Ford
6 Chris Amon (NZ) Matra- Simca
Winner's speed: 182.42kph/113.35mph
Fastest lap: Amon 185.89kph/115.51mph
Pole position: Fittipaldi

1973 Zolder

20 May, 295.40km/183.55 miles
1 Jackie Stewart (GB) Tyrrell-Ford
2 François Cevert (Fra) Tyrrell-Ford
3 Emerson Fittipaldi (Bra) Lotus-Ford
4 Andrea de Adamich (Ita) Brabham-Ford
5 Niki Lauda (Aut) BRM
6 Chris Amon (NZ) Tecno
Winner's speed: 173.38kph/107.74mph
Fastest lap: Cevert 177.85kph/110.51mph
Pole position: Ronnie Peterson (Swe) Lotus-Ford

1974 Nivelles-Baulers

12 May, 316.54km/196.69 miles
1 Emerson Fittipaldi (Bra) McLaren-Ford
2 Niki Lauda (Aut) Ferrari
3 Jody Scheckter (SAf) Tyrrell-Ford
4 Clay Regazzoni (Swi) Ferrari
5 Jean-Pierre Beltoise (Fra) BRM
6 Denny Hulme (NZ) McLaren-Ford
Winner's speed: 182.02kph/113.10mph
Fastest lap: Hulme 188.00kph/116.82mph
Pole position: Regazzoni

1975 Zolder

25 May, 298.34km/185.38 miles
1 Niki Lauda (Aut) Ferrari
2 Jody Scheckter (SAf) Tyrrell-Ford
3 Carlos Reutemann (Arg) Brabham-Ford
4 Patrick Depailler (Fra) Tyrrell-Ford
5 Clay Regazzoni (Swi) Ferrari
6 Tom Pryce (GB) Shadow-Ford
Winner's speed: 172.29kph/107.05mph
Fastest lap: Regazzoni 176.85kph/109.89mph
Pole position: Lauda

1976 Zolder

16 May, 298.34km/185.38 miles
1 Niki Lauda (Aut) Ferrari
2 Clay Regazzoni (Swi) Ferrari
3 Jacques Laffite (Fra) Ligier-Matra
4 Jody Scheckter (SAf) Tyrrell-Ford
5 Alan Jones (Aus) Surtees-Ford
6 Jochen Mass (FRG) McLaren-Ford
Winner's speed: 173.98kph/108.10mph
Fastest lap: Lauda 178.45kph/110.88mph
Pole position: Lauda

1977 Zolder

5 June 298.34km/185.38 miles
1 Gunnar Nilsson (Swe) Lotus-Ford
2 Niki Lauda (Aut) Ferrari
3 Ronnie Peterson (Swe) Tyrrell-Ford
4 Vittorio Brambilla (Ita) Surtees-Ford
5 Alan Jones (Aus) Shadow-Ford
6 Hans-Joachim Stuck (FRG) Brabham-Alfa Romeo
Winner's speed: 155.53kph/96.64mph
Fastest lap: Nilsson 175.63kph/109.13mph
Pole position: Mario Andretti (USA) Lotus-Ford

1978 Spa-Francorchamps

21 May, 298.34km/185.38 miles
1 Mario Andretti (USA) Lotus-Ford
2 Ronnie Peterson (Swe) Lotus-Ford
3 Carlos Reutemann (Arg) Ferrari
4 Gilles Villeneuve (Can) Ferrari
5 Jacques Laffite (Fra) Ligier-Matra
6 Didier Pironi (Fra) Tyrrell-Ford
Winner's speed: 179.24kph/111.38mph
Fastest lap: Peterson 184.57kph/114.69mph
Pole position: Andretti

1979 Zolder

13 May, 298.34km/185.38 miles
1 Jody Scheckter (SAf) Ferrari
2 Jacques Laffite (Fra) Ligier-Ford
3 Didier Pironi (Fra) Tyrrell-Ford
4 Carlos Reutemann (Arg) Lotus-Ford
5 Riccardo Patrese (Ita) Arrows Ford
6 John Watson (GB) McLaren-Ford
Winner's speed: 179.02kph/111.24mph
Fastest lap: Gilles Villeneuve (Can) Ferrari 184.66kph/
114.74mph
Pole position: Laffite

1980 Zolder

4 May, 306.86km/190.68 miles
1 Didier Pironi (Fra) Ligier-Ford
2 Alan Jones (Aus) Williams-Ford
3 Carlos Reutemann (Arg) Williams-Ford
4 René Arnoux (Fra) Renault
5 Jean-Pierre Jarier (Fra) Tyrrell-Ford
6 Gilles Villeneuve (Can) Ferrari
Winner's speed: 186.40kph/115.82mph
Fastest lap: Jacques Laffite (Fra) Ligier-Ford 189.70kph/
117.88mph
Pole position: Jones

1981 Zolder

17 May, 230.15km/143.01 miles
1 Carlos Reutemann (Arg) Williams-Ford
2 Jacques Laffite (Fra) Talbot-Matra
3 Nigel Mansell (GB) Lotus-Ford
4 Gilles Villeneuve (Can) Ferrari
5 Elio de Angelis (Ita) Lotus-Ford
6 Eddie Cheever (USA) Tyrrell-Ford
Winner's speed: 180.45kph/112.13mph
Fastest lap: Reutemann 184.19kph/114.45mph
Pole position: Reutemann

1982 Zolder

9 May, 298.34km/185.38 miles
1 John Watson (GB) McLaren-Ford
2 Keke Rosberg (Fin) Williams-Ford
3 Eddie Cheever (USA) Talbot-Matra
4 Elio de Angelis (Ita) Lotus-Ford
5 Nelson Piquet (Bra) Brabham-BMW
6 Chico Serra (Bra) Fittipaldi-Ford
*Niki Lauda (Aut) McLaren-Ford finished 3rd but was
subsequently disqualified; car underweight.*
Winner's speed: 188.09kph/116.88mph
Fastest lap: Watson 192.39kph/119.55mph
Pole position: Alain Prost (Fra) Renault

1983 Spa-Francorchamps

22 May, 278.62km/173.13 miles
1 Alain Prost (Fra) Renault
2 Patrick Tambay (Fra) Ferrari
3 Eddie Cheever (USA) Renault
4 Nelson Piquet (Bra) Brabham-BMW
5 Keke Rosberg (Fin) Williams-Ford
6 Jacques Laffite (Fra) Williams-Ford

Winner's speed: 191.73kph/119.14mph
Fastest lap: Andrea de Cesaris (Ita) Alfa Romeo
196.22kph/121.93mph
Pole position: Prost

1984 Zolder

29 April. 298.34km/185.38 miles
1 Michele Alboreto (Ita) Ferrari
2 Derek Warwick (GB) Renault
3 René Arnoux (Fra) Ferrari
4 Keke Rosberg (Fin) Williams-Honda
5 Elio de Angelis (Ita) Lotus-Renault
6 Ayrton Senna (Bra) Toleman-Hart
Stefan Bellof (FRG) Tyrrell-Ford finished 6th but all Tyrrell points for drivers and manufacturers were deducted because of rule infringement.
Winner's speed: 185.43kph/115.23mph
Fastest lap: Arnoux 193.50kph/120.24mph
Pole position: Alboreto

1985 Spa-Francorchamps

15 September. 298.42km/185.43 miles
1 Ayrton Senna (Bra) Lotus-Renault
2 Nigel Mansell (GB) Williams-Honda
3 Alain Prost (Fra) McLaren-TAG
4 Keke Rosberg (Fin) Williams-Honda
5 Nelson Piquet (Bra) Brabham-BMW
6 Derek Warwick (GB) Renault
Winner's speed: 189.81kph/117.95mph
Fastest lap: Prost 205.24kph/127.54mph
Pole position: Prost

1986 Spa-Francorchamps

25 May, 298.42km/185.43 miles
1 Nigel Mansell (GB) Williams-Honda
2 Ayrton Senna (Bra) Lotus-Renault
3 Stefan Johansson (Swe) Ferrari
4 Michele Alboreto (Ita) Ferrari
5 Jacques Laffite (Fra) Ligier-Renault
6 Alain Prost (Fra) McLaren-TAG
Winner's speed: 203.55kph/126.48mph
Fastest lap: Prost 209.44kph/130.15mph
Pole position: Nelson Piquet (Bra) Williams-Honda

1987 Spa-Francorchamps

17 May, 298.42km/185.43 miles
1 Alain Prost (Fra) McLaren-TAG
2 Stefan Johansson (Swe) McLaren-TAG
3 Andrea de Cesaris (Ita) Brabham-BMW
4 Eddie Cheever (USA) Arrows-Megatron
5 Satoru Nakajima (Jap) Lotus-Honda
6 René Arnoux (Fra) Ligier-Megatron
Winner's speed: 205.68kph/127.80mph
Fastest lap: Prost 213.25kph/132.51mph

Pole position: Nigel Mansell (GB) Williams-Honda

1988 Spa-Francorchamps

28 August. 298.42km/185.43 miles
1 Ayrton Senna (Bra) McLaren-Honda
2 Alain Prost (Fra) McLaren-Honda
3 Ivan Capelli (Ita) March-Judd
4 Nelson Piquet (Bra) Lotus-Honda
5 Derek Warwick (GB) Arrows-Megatron
6 Eddie Cheever (USA) Arrows-Megatron
Thierry Boutsen (Bel) Benetton-Ford, and Alessandro Nannini (Ita) Benetton-Ford finished 3rd and 4th respecitvely but were subsequently disqualified for fuel irregularities.
Winner's speed: 203.45kph/126.42mph
Fastest lap: Gerhard Berger (Aut) Ferrari 206.87kph/128.54mph
Pole position: Senna

1989 Spa-Francorchamps

27 August. 298.42km/185.43 miles
1 Ayrton Senna (Bra) McLaren-Honda
2 Alain Prost (Fra) McLaren-Honda
3 Nigel Mansell (GB) Ferrari
4 Thierry Boutsen (Fra) Williams-Renault
5 Alessandro Nannini (Ita) Benetton-Ford
6 Derek Warwick (GB) Arrows-Ford
Winner's speed: 181.58 kph/113.49 mph
Fastest lap: Prost 189.89 kph/118.68 mph
Pole position: Senna

1990 Spa-Francorchamps

26 August. 305.36km/189.74 miles
1 Ayrton Senna (Bra) McLaren-Honda
2 Alain Prost (Fra) Ferrari
3 Gerhard Berger (Aut) McLaren-Honda
4 Alessandro Nannini (Ita) Benetton-Ford
5 Nelson Piquet (Bra) Benetton-Ford
6 Mauricio Gugelmin (Bra) Leyton House-Judd
Winner's speed: 211.73kph/131.57mph
Fastest lap: Prost 217.09kph/134.89mph
Pole position: Senna

1991 Spa-Francorchamps

25 August. 305.36km/189.74 miles
1 Ayrton Senna (Bra) McLaren-Honda
2 Gerhard Berger (Aut) McLaren-Honda
3 Nelson Piquet (Bra) Benetton-Ford
4 Roberto Moreno (Bra) Benetton-Ford
5 Riccardo Patrese (Ita) Williams-Renault
6 Mark Blundell (GB) Brabham-Yamaha
Winner's speed: 209.89kph/130.42mph
Fastest lap: Moreno 216.95kph/134.81mph
Pole position: Senna

MOST WINS

Drivers		Manufacturers
5 Ayrton Senna	3 Juan Manuel Fangio	8 Ferrari, Lotus, McLaren
4 Jim Clark	2 Alberto Ascari, Emerson Fittipaldi, Niki Lauda, Alain Prost	2 Alfa Romeo, Williams

MOST FASTEST LAPS

Drivers
5 Alain Prost
3 Jim Clark, Juan Manuel Fangio
2 Chris Amon, Dan Gurney, John Surtees

Manufacturers
11 Ferrari
6 Lotus, McLaren
3 Alfa Romeo, Maserati

MOST POLE POSITIONS

Drivers
4 Juan Manuel Fangio, Ayrton Senna
3 Graham Hill, Alain Prost
2 Mario Andretti, Niki Lauda

Manufacturers
9 Ferrari
5 Lotus, McLaren
4 Williams
3 BRM
2 Alfa Romeo, Lancia, Maserati, Renault

BRAZILIAN GP

Held continuously since 1973, the Brazilian Grand Prix is currently the only World Championship race in South America and all races have been held over either the twisting Interlagos circuit at São Paulo or the Rio de Janeiro circuit at Jacarepagua, 30 kilometres south of Rio.

It was appropriate that the 1973 race should be won by the first of the great Brazilian drivers, Emerson Fittipaldi; and the country's other two world champions, Nelson Piquet and Ayrton Senna, have also both won their home Grand Prix, Senna eventually doing so for the first time in 1991.

Brazil followed Argentina onto the Grand Prix calendar after successfully staging a non-championship Formula One race in 1972 and getting the seal of approval from the drivers. So it was across the Argentinian border and into Brazil for the second race of the season in 1973. The Brazilian round of the championship is now the curtain raiser to the season.

Ayrton Senna racing in front of his home crowd in Rio, 1988. The Brazilian public would have to wait another three years, though, for a Senna home victory.

1973 Interlagos

11 February, 318.40km/197.85 miles
1 Emerson Fittipaldi (Bra) Lotus-Ford
2 Jackie Stewart (GB) Tyrrell-Ford
3 Denny Hulme (NZ) McLaren-Ford
4 Arturo Merzario (Ita) Ferrari
5 Jacky Ickx (Bel) Ferrari
6 Clay Regazzoni (Swi) BRM
Winner's speed: 183.82kph/114.22mph
Fastest lap: Fittipaldi/Hulme 184.88kph/114.88mph
Pole position: Ronnie Peterson (Swe) Lotus-Ford

1974 Interlagos

27 January, 254.72km/158.28 miles
1 Emerson Fittipaldi (Bra) McLaren-Ford
2 Clay Regazzoni (Swi) Ferrari
3 Jacky Ickx (Bel) Lotus-Ford
4 Carlos Pace (Bra) Surtees-Ford
5 Mike Hailwood (GB) McLaren-Ford
6 Ronnie Peterson (Swe) Lotus-Ford
Winner's speed: 180.62kph/112.23mph
Fastest lap: Regazzoni 183.63kph/114.10mph
Pole position: Fittipaldi

1975 Interlagos

26 January, 318.40km/197.85 miles
1 Carlos Pace (Bra) Brabham-Ford
2 Emerson Fittipaldi (Bra) McLaren-Ford
3 Jochen Mass (FRG) McLaren-Ford
4 Clay Regazzoni (Swi) Ferrari
5 Niki Lauda (Aut) Ferrari
6 James Hunt (GB) Hesketh-Ford
Winner's speed: 182.49kph/113.39mph
Fastest lap: Jean-Pierre Jarier (Fra) Shadow-Ford
185.88kph/115.50mph
Pole position: Jarier

1976 Interlagos

25 January, 318.40km/197.85 miles
1 Niki Lauda (Aut) Ferrari
2 Patrick Depailler (Fra) Tyrrell-Ford
3 Tom Pryce (GB) Shadow-Ford
4 Hans-Joachim Stuck (FRG) March-Ford
5 Jody Scheckter (SAf) Tyrrell-Ford
6 Jochen Mass (FRG) McLaren-Ford
Winner's speed: 181.47kph/112.76mph
Fastest lap: Jean-Pierre Jarier (Fra) Shadow-Ford
184.80kph/114.83mph
Pole position: James Hunt (GB) McLaren-Ford

1977 Interlagos

23 January, 318.40km/197.85 miles
1 Carlos Reutemann (Arg) Ferrari
2 James Hunt (GB) McLaren-Ford
3 Niki Lauda (Aut) Ferrari
4 Emerson Fittipaldi (Bra) Fittipaldi-Ford
5 Gunnar Nilsson (Swe) Lotus-Ford
6 Renzo Zorzi (Ita) Shadow-Ford
Winner's speed: 181.73kph/112.92mph
Fastest lap: Hunt 185.43kph/115.22mph
Pole position: Hunt

1978 Rio de Janeiro

29 January, 316.95km/196.95 miles
1 Carlos Reutemann (Arg) Ferrari
2 Emerson Fittipaldi (Bra) Fittipaldi-Ford
3 Niki Lauda (Aut) Brabham-Alfa Romeo
4 Mario Andretti (USA) Lotus-Ford
5 Clay Regazzoni (Swi) Shadow-Ford
6 Didier Pironi (Fra) Tyrrell-Ford
Winner's speed: 172.89kph/107.43mph
Fastest lap: Reutemann 175.72kph/109.19mph
Pole position: Ronnie Peterson (Swe) Lotus-Ford

1979 Interlagos

4 February, 314.96km/195.71 miles
1 Jacques Laffite (Fra) Ligier-Ford
2 Patrick Depailler (Fra) Ligier-Ford
3 Carlos Reutemann (Arg) Lotus-Ford
4 Didier Pironi (Fra) Tyrrell-Ford
5 Gilles Villeneuve (Can) Ferrari
6 Jody Scheckter (SAf) Ferrari
Winner's speed: 188.67kph/117.23mph

Fastest lap: Laffite 190.55kph/118.40mph
Pole position: Laffite

1980 Interlagos

27 January, 314.96km/195.71 miles
1 René Arnoux (Fra) Renault
2 Elio de Angelis (Ita) Lotus-Ford
3 Alan Jones (Aus) Williams-Ford
4 Didier Pironi (Fra) Ligier- Ford
5 Alain Prost (Fra) McLaren-Ford
6 Riccardo Patrese (Ita) Arrows-Ford
Winner's speed: 188.93kph/119.57mph
Fastest lap: Arnoux 192.42kph/117.40mph
Pole position: Jean-Pierre Jabouille (Fra) Renault

1981 Rio de Janeiro

29 March, 311.92km/193.82 miles
1 Carlos Reutemann (Arg) Williams-Ford
2 Alan Jones (Aus) Williams-Ford
3 Riccardo Patrese (Ita) Arrows-Ford
4 Marc Surer (Swi) Ensign-Ford
5 Elio de Angelis (Ita) Lotus-Ford
6 Jacques Laffite (Fra) Talbot-Matra
Winner's speed: 155.45kph/96.60mph
Fastest lap: Surer 158.45kph/98.46mph
Pole position: Nelson Piquet (Bra) Brabham-Ford

1982 Rio de Janeiro

21 March, 316.95km/196.95 miles
1 Alain Prost (Fra) Renault
2 John Watson (GB) McLaren-Ford
3 Nigel Mansell (GB) Lotus-Ford
4 Michele Alboreto (Ita) Tyrrell-Ford
5 Manfred Winkelhock (FRG) ATS-Ford
6 Didier Pironi (Fra) Ferrari
Nelson Piquet (Bra) Brabham-Ford and Keke Rosberg
(Fin) Williams-Ford finished 1st and 2nd but were
subsequently disqualified for having underweight cars.
Piquet also established the fastest lap at 187.52kph/
116.52mph but this does not stand because of his
disqualification.
Winner's speed: 181.89kph/113.02mph
Fastest lap: Prost 186.69kph/116.00mph
Pole position: Prost

1983 Rio de Janeiro

13 March, 316.95km/196.95 miles
1 Nelson Piquet (Bra) Brabham-BMW
2 –
3 Niki Lauda (Aut) McLaren-Ford
4 Jacques Laffite (Fra) Williams-Ford
5 Patrick Tambay (Fra) Ferrari
6 Marc Surer (Swi) Arrows-Ford
Keke Rosberg (Fin) Williams-Ford finished 2nd but was
later disqualified for receiving a push start in the pits. Other
drivers not promoted.
Winner's speed: 175.33kph/108.93mph
Fastest lap: Piquet 181.43kph/112.74mph
Pole position: Rosberg

1984 Rio de Janeiro

25 March, 306.89km/190.69 miles
1 Alain Prost (Fra) McLaren-Porsche
2 Keke Rosberg (Fin) Williams-Honda
3 Elio de Angelis (Ita) Lotus-Renault
4 Eddie Cheever (USA) Alfa Romeo
5 Patrick Tambay (Fra) Renault
6 Thierry Boutsen (Bel) Arrows-Ford
Martin Brundle (GB) Tyrrell-Ford finished 5th but all Tyrrell points deducted at end of season following rule infringements.
Winner's speed: 179.51kph/111.55mph
Fastest lap: Prost 187.69kph/116.63mph
Pole position: de Angelis

1985 Rio de Janeiro

7 April, 306.89km/190.96 miles
1 Alain Prost (Fra) McLaren-TAG
2 Michele Alboreto (Ita) Ferrari
3 Elio de Angelis (Ita) Lotus-Renault
4 René Arnoux (Fra) Ferrari
5 Patrick Tambay (Fra) Renault
6 Jacques Laffite (Fra) Ligier-Renault
Winner's speed: 181.53kph/112.80mph
Fastest lap: Prost 187.29kph/116.38mph
Pole position: Alboreto

1986 Rio de Janeiro

23 March, 306.89km/190.69 miles
1 Nelson Piquet (Bra) Williams-Honda
2 Ayrton Senna (Bra) Lotus-Renault
3 Jacques Laffite (Fra) Ligier-Renault
4 René Arnoux (Fra) Ligier-Renault
5 Martin Brundle (GB) Tyrrell-Renault
6 Gerhard Berger (Aut) Benetton-BMW
Winner's speed: 184.97kph/114.94mph
Fastest lap: Piquet 193.74kph/120.39mph
Pole position: Senna

1987 Rio de Janeiro

12 April, 306.89km/190.69 miles
1 Alain Prost (Fra) McLaren-TAG
2 Nelson Piquet (Bra) Williams-Honda
3 Stefan Johansson (Swe) McLaren-TAG
4 Gerhard Berger (Aut) Ferrari
5 Thierry Boutsen (Bel) Benetton-Ford
6 Nigel Mansell (GB) Williams-Honda
Winner's speed: 184.59kph/114.70mph
Fastest lap: Piquet 192.96kph/119.90mph
Pole position: Mansell

1988 Rio de Janeiro

3 April, 301.86km/187.57 miles
1 Alain Prost (Fra) McLaren-Honda
2 Gerhard Berger (Aut) Ferrari
3 Nelson Piquet (Bra) Lotus-Honda
4 Derek Warwick (GB) Arrows-Megatron
5 Michele Alboreto (Ita) Ferrari
6 Satoru Nakajima (Jap) Lotus-Honda
Winner's speed: 188.44kph/117.09mph
Fastest lap: Berger 194.88kph/121.09mph
Pole position: Ayrton Senna (Bra) McLaren-Honda

1989 Rio de Janeiro

26 March , 306.89km/190.69 miles
1 Nigel Mansell (GB) Ferrari
2 Alain Prost (Fra) McLaren-Honda
3 Mauricio Gugelmin (Bra) March-Judd
4 Johnny Herbert (GB) Benetton-Ford
5 Derek Warwick (GB) Arrows-Ford
6 Alessandro Nannini (Ita) Benetton-Ford
Winner's speed: 185.56kph/115.30mph
Fastest lap: Riccardo Patrese (Ita) Williams-Renault 195.79kph/121.66mph
Pole position: Ayrton Senna (Bra) McLaren-Honda

1990 Interlagos

25 March, 307.08km/190.78 miles
1 Alain Prost (Fra) Ferrari
2 Gerhard Berger (Aut) McLaren-Honda
3 Ayrton Senna (Bra) McLaren-Honda
4 Nigel Mansell (GB) Ferrari
5 Thierry Boutsen (Bel) Williams-Renault
6 Nelson Piquet (Bra) Benetton-Ford
Winner's speed: 189.19kph/117.56mph
Fastest lap: Berger 194.87km/121.09mph
Pole position: Senna

1991 Interlagos

24 March, 307.08km/ 190.78miles
1 Ayrton Senna (Bra) McLaren-Honda
2 Riccardo Patrese (Ita) Williams-Renault
3 Gerhard Berger (Aut) McLaren-Honda
4 Alain Prost (Fra) Ferrari
5 Nelson Piquet (Bra) Benetton-Ford
6 Jean Alesi (Fra) Ferrari
Winner's speed: 187.11kph/116.26mph
Fastest lap: Nigel Mansell (GB) Williams-Renault 193.58kph/120.28mph
Pole position: Senna

MOST WINS

Drivers	Manufacturers
6 Alain Prost	6 McLaren
3 Carlos Reutemann	5 Ferrari
2 Emerson Fittipaldi, Nelson Piquet	2 Brabham, Renault, Williams

MOST POLE POSITIONS

Drivers
5 Ayrton Senna
2 James Hunt, Ronnie Peterson
Manufacturers
7 McLaren
4 Lotus
2 Renault, Williams

MOST FASTEST LAPS

Drivers		Manufacturers	
4	Nelson Piquet	5 McLaren	3 Ferrari
2	Gerhard Berger, Jean-Pierre Jarier, Alain Prost	4 Williams	2 Brabham, Shadow

BRITISH GP

It was the British Grand Prix at Silverstone on 13 May 1950 that heralded the start of the Formula One World Championship. But the history of the British Grand Prix dates back to the 1920s.

The first race to carry the British Grand Prix tag was at Silverstone in 1948, but a forerunner, the RAC Grand Prix was inaugurated at Brooklands in 1926 and won by Senechal and Wagner in a Delage. The race was repeated in 1927 but lapsed until it was revived as the Donington Grand Prix in 1935. It survived four years until the outbreak of the war. It resumed in 1948 when Gigi Villoresi in his Maserati won at Silverstone in front of 120 000 spectators. The following year Toulo de Graffenried took the chequered flag, also in a Maserati.

Since it became part of the World Championship, Silverstone, Brands Hatch and Aintree have all played host to the British Grand Prix, and it was at Aintree in 1957 that Stirling Moss and Tony Brooks shared victory in a Vanwall to end a drought of more than 30 years for British cars in major Grands Prix. Two years earlier Moss had become the first home winner of the British Grand Prix, but in a Mercedes. It was the first of 16 Grand Prix wins for Moss. Jim Clark and Jack Brabham have uniquely won the race at all three circuits, Brabham's three wins being his only three in the race.

In recent years the British trio of James Hunt, John Watson and Nigel Mansell have all been cheered on to victory by the vast army of loyal fans at the British Grand Prix, a memorable moment indeed in any British driver's career.

Nigel Mansell waves to jubilant fans after capturing his third British Grand Prix in six years, 1991.

1950 Silverstone

13 May, 325.46km/202.23 miles
1 Giuseppe Farina (Ita) Alfa Romeo
2 Luigi Fagioli (Ita) Alfa Romeo
3 Reg Parnell (GB) Alfa Romeo
4 Yves Giraud-Cabantous (Fra) Lago-Talbot
5 Louis Rosier (Fra) Lago-Talbot
6 Bob Gerard (GB) ERA
Winner's speed: 146.39kph/90.95mph
Fastest lap: Farina, 151.34kph/94.04mph
Pole position: Farina

1951 Silverstone

14 July, 418.45km/260.01 miles
1 José Froilán González (Arg) Ferrari
2 Juan Manuel Fangio (Arg) Alfa Romeo
3 Luigi Villoresi (Ita) Ferrari
4 Felice Bonetto (Ita) Alfa Romeo
5 Reg Parnell (GB) BRM
6 Consalvo Sanesi (Ita) Alfa Romeo
Winner's speed: 154.68kph/96.11mph
Fastest lap: Giuseppe Farina (Ita) Alfa Romeo 160.92kph/99.99mph
Pole position: González

1952 Silverstone

19 July, 400.40km/248.90 miles
1 Alberto Ascari (Ita) Ferrari
2 Piero Taruffi (Ita) Ferrari
3 Mike Hawthorn (GB) Cooper-Bristol
4 Dennis Poore (GB) Connaught
5 Eric Thompson (GB) Connaught
6 Giuseppe Farina (Ita) Ferrari
Winner's speed: 146.32kph/90.92mph
Fastest lap: Ascari 151.41kph/94.08kph
Pole position: Farina

1953 Silverstone

18 July, 423.45km/263.43 miles
1 Alberto Ascari (Ita) Ferrari
2 Juan Manuel Fangio (Arg) Maserati
3 Giuseppe Farina (Ita) Ferrari
4 José Froilán González (Arg) Maserati
5 Mike Hawthorn (GB) Ferrari
6 Felice Bonetto (Ita) Maserati
Winner's speed: 149.63kph/92.97mph
Fastest lap: González & Ascari 154.16kph/95.79kph
Pole position: Ascari

1954 Silverstone

17 July, 423.95km/263.43 miles
1 José Froilán González (Arg) Ferrari
2 Mike Hawthorn (GB) Ferrari
3 Onofre Marimon (Arg) Maserati
4 Juan Manuel Fangio (Arg) Mercedes-Benz
5 Maurice Trintignant (Fra) Ferrari
6 Roberto Mieres (Arg) Maserati

Winner's speed: 144.34kph/89.69mph
Fastest lap: González, Hawthorn, Marimon, Fangio, Stirling Moss (GB) Maserati, Alberto Ascari (Ita) Maserati, & Jean Behra (Fra) Gordini 154.16kph/95.79mph
Pole position: Fangio

1955 Aintree

16 July, 434.52km/270.00 miles
1 Stirling Moss (GB) Mercedes-Benz
2 Juan Manuel Fangio (Arg) Mercedes-Benz
3 Karl Kling (FRG) Mercedes-Benz
4 Piero Taruffi (Ita) Mercedes-Benz
5 Luigi Musso (Ita) Maserati
6 Mike Hawthorn (GB)/Eugenio Castellotti (Ita) Ferrari
Winner's speed: 139.16kph/86.47mph
Fastest lap: Moss 144.36kph/89.70mph
Pole position: Moss

1956 Silverstone

14 July, 475.77km/295.63 miles
1 Juan Manuel Fangio (Arg) Lancia-Ferrari
2 Alfonso de Portago (Spa)/Peter Collins (GB) Lancia-Ferrari
3 Jean Behra (Fra) Maserati
4 Jack Fairman (GB) Connaught
5 Horace Gould (GB) Maserati
6 Luigi Villoresi (Ita) Maserati
Winner's speed: 158.76kph/98.65mph
Fastest lap: Stirling Moss (GB) Maserati 164.32kph/102.10mph
Pole position: Moss

THE GREAT RACES

1950 *British GP*

Of the 500-plus races that have counted towards the World Championship, the 1950 British Grand Prix at Silverstone probably doesn't figure too highly amongst those races regarded as 'memorable' in the true sense of the word. But because it was this race that on 13 May 1950 started it all off, it holds a special place in Formula One history and for that reason is memorable, not to mention nostalgic.

Held on a sunny day, it was a Royal occasion with the King and Queen present; along with Princess Margaret they watched the race from the Royal Box. Sadly they were not to witness a home victory because the Italian Alfas were vastly superior and after occupying the four places on the front row of the grid they went on to take the first three places. And it was an Italian driver, Giuseppe 'Nino' Farina, who took the chequered flag nearly three seconds ahead of his fellow Italian Luigi Fagioli with Britain's Reg Parnell third, but in one of the Italian cars. The other Alfa from the front row of the grid was driven by the Argentinian Juan Manuel Fangio. He led at one stage but was forced out of the race on lap 62. But his day was certainly to come and he went on to become one of the true stars of the Formula one World Championship which all started at Silverstone on that day in May.

1957 Aintree

20 July, 434.52km/270.00 miles
1 Tony Brooks (GB)/Stirling Moss (GB) Vanwall
2 Luigi Musso (Ita) Lancia-Ferrari
3 Mike Hawthorn (GB) Lancia-Ferrari
4 Maurice Trintignant (Fra)/Peter Collins (GB) Lancia-Ferrari
5 Roy Salvadori (GB) Cooper-Climax
6 Bob Gerard (GB) Cooper-Bristol
Collins did not receive any points because he drove for only three laps and was therefore ineligible for points.
Winner's speed: 139.68kph/86.79mph
Fastest lap: Moss 145.81kph/90.60mph
Pole position: Moss

1958 Silverstone

19 July, 353.29km/219.52 miles
1 Peter Collins (GB) Ferrari
2 Mike Hawthorn (GB) Ferrari
3 Roy Salvadori (GB) Cooper-Climax
4 Stuart Lewis-Evans (GB) Vanwall
5 Harry Schell (USA) BRM
6 Jack Brabham (Aus) Cooper-Climax
Winner's speed: 164.23kph/102.05mph
Fastest lap: Hawthorn 168.23kph/104.53mph
Pole position: Stirling Moss (GB) Vanwall

1959 Aintree

18 July, 362.10km/225.00 miles
1 Jack Brabham (Aus) Cooper-Climax
2 Stirling Moss (GB) BRM
3 Bruce McLaren (NZ) Cooper-Climax
4 Harry Schell (USA) BRM
5 Maurice Trintignant (Fra) Cooper-Climax
6 Roy Salvadori (GB) Aston Martin
Winner's speed: 144.65kph/89.88kph
Fastest lap: Moss/McLaren 148.56kph/92.31mph
Pole position: Brabham

1960 Silverstone

16 July, 362.71km/225.38 miles
1 Jack Brabham (Aus) Cooper-Climax
2 John Surtees (GB) Lotus-Climax
3 Innes Ireland (GB) Lotus-Climax
4 Bruce McLaren (NZ) Cooper-Climax
5 Tony Brooks (GB) Cooper-Climax
6 Wolfgang von Trips (FRG) Ferrari
Winner's speed: 174.93kph/108.69mph
Fastest lap: G Hill (GB) BRM 179.64kph/111.62mph
Pole position: Brabham

1961 Aintree

15 July, 362.10km/225.00 miles
1 Wolfgang von Trips (FRG) Ferrari
2 Phil Hill (USA) Ferrari
3 Richie Ginther (USA) Ferrari
4 Jack Brabham (Aus) Cooper-Climax
5 Jo Bonnier (Swe) Porsche
6 Roy Salvadori (GB) Cooper-Climax

Winner's speed: 135.02kph/83.91mph
Fastest lap: Tony Brooks (GB) BRM-Climax 147.54kph/91.68mph
Pole position: P Hill

1962 Aintree

21 July, 362.10km/225.00 miles
1 Jim Clark (GB) Lotus-Climax
2 John Surtees (GB) Lola-Climax
3 Bruce McLaren (NZ) Cooper-Climax
4 Graham Hill (GB) BRM
5 Jack Brabham (Aus) Lotus-Climax
6 Tony Maggs (SAf) Cooper-Climax
Winner's speed: 148.46kph/92.25mph
Fastest lap: Clark 151.14kph/93.91mph
Pole position: Clark

1963 Silverstone

20 July, 386.27km/240.01 miles
1 Jim Clark (GB) Lotus-Climax
2 John Surtees (GB) Ferrari
3 Graham Hill (GB) BRM
4 Richie Ginther (USA) BRM
5 Lorenzo Bandini (Ita) BRM
6 Jim Hall (USA) Lotus-BRM
Winner's speed: 172.75kph/107.35mph
Fastest lap: Surtees 176.65kph/109.76mph
Pole position: Clark

1964 Brands Hatch

11 July, 341.18km/212.00 miles
1 Jim Clark (GB) Lotus-Climax
2 Graham Hill (GB) BRM
3 John Surtees (GB) Ferrari
4 Jack Brabham (Aus) Brabham-Climax
5 Lorenzo Bandini (Ita) Ferrari
6 Phil Hill (USA) Cooper-Climax
Winner's speed: 151.51kph/94.14mph
Fastest lap: Clark 155.40kph/96.56mph
Pole position: Clark

1965 Silverstone

10 July, 376.84km/234.16 miles
1 Jim Clark (GB) Lotus-Climax
2 Graham Hill (GB) BRM
3 John Surtees (GB) Ferrari
4 Mike Spence (GB) Lotus-Climax
5 Jackie Stewart (GB) BRM
6 Dan Gurney (USA) Brabham-Climax
Winner's speed: 180.28kph/112.02mph
Fastest lap: Hill 183.90kph/114.29kph
Pole position: Clark

1966 Brands Hatch

16 July, 341.18km/212.00 miles
1 Jack Brabham (Aus) Brabham-Repco
2 Denny Hulme (NZ) Brabham-Repco
3 Graham Hill (GB) BRM
4 Jim Clark (GB) Lotus-Climax
5 Jochen Rindt (Aut) Cooper-Maserati

6 Bruce McLaren (NZ) McLaren- Serenissima
Winner's speed: 153.66kph/95.48mph
Fastest lap: Brabham 158.28kph/98.35mph
Pole position: Brabham

1967 Silverstone

15 July, 376.84km/243.16 miles
1 Jim Clark (GB) Lotus-Ford
2 Denny Hulme (NZ) Brabham-Repco
3 Chris Amon (NZ) Ferrari
4 Jack Brabham (Aus) Brabham-Repco
5 Pedro Rodriguez (Mex) Cooper-Maserati
6 John Surtees (GB) Honda
Winner's speed: 189.33kph/117.64mph
Fastest lap: Hulme 194.92kph/121.12mph
Pole position: Clark

1968 Brands Hatch

20 July, 341.18km/212.00miles
1 Jo Siffert (Swi) Lotus-Ford
2 Chris Amon (NZ) Ferrari
3 Jacky Ickx (Bel) Ferrari
4 Denny Hulme (NZ) McLaren-Ford
5 John Surtees (GB) Honda
6 Jackie Stewart (GB) Matra-Ford
Winner's speed: 168.70kph/104.83mph
Fastest lap: Siffert 171.16kph/106.35mph
Pole position: Graham Hill (GB) Lotus-Ford

1969 Silverstone

19 July, 395.64km/245.87 miles
1 Jackie Stewart (GB) Matra-Ford
2 Jacky Ickx (Bel) Brabham-Ford
3 Bruce McLaren (NZ) McLaren-Ford
4 Jochen Rindt (Aut) Lotus-Ford
5 Piers Courage (GB) Brabham-Ford
6 Vic Elford (GB) McLaren-Ford
Winner's speed: 204.79kph/127.25mph
Fastest lap: Stewart 208.58kph/129.61mph
Pole position: Rindt

1970 Brands Hatch

8 July, 341.18km/212.00 miles
1 Jochen Rindt (Aut) Lotus-Ford
2 Jack Brabham (Aus) Brabham-Ford
3 Denny Hulme (NZ) McLaren-Ford
4 Clay Regazzoni (Swi) Ferrari
5 Chris Amon (NZ) March-Ford
6 Graham Hill (GB) Lotus-Ford
Winner's speed: 174.91kph/108.69mph
Fastest lap: Brabham 178.73kph/111.06mph
Pole position: Rindt

1971 Silverstone

17 July, 320.32km/199.04 miles
1 Jackie Stewart (GB) Tyrrell-Ford
2 Ronnie Peterson (Swe) March-Ford
3 Emerson Fittipaldi (Bra) Lotus-Ford
4 Henri Pescarolo (Fra) March-Ford

5 Rolf Stommelen (FRG) Surtees-Ford
6 John Surtees (GB) Surtees-Ford
Winner's speed: 209.99kph/130.48mph
Fastest lap: Stewart 212.24kph/131.88mph
Pole position: Clay Regazzoni (Swi) Ferrari

1972 Brands Hatch

15 July, 324.12km/201.40 miles
1 Emerson Fittipaldi (Bra) Lotus-Ford
2 Jackie Stewart (GB) Tyrrell-Ford
3 Peter Revson (USA) McLaren-Ford
4 Chris Amon (NZ) Matra-Simca
5 Denny Hulme (NZ) McLaren-Ford
6 Arturo Merzario (Ita) Ferrari
Winner's speed: 180.34kph/112.06mph
Fastest lap: Stewart 182.78kph/113.57mph
Pole position: Jacky Ickx (Bel) Ferrari

1973 Silverstone

14 July, 315.61km/196.11 miles
1 Peter Revson (USA) McLaren-Ford
2 Ronnie Peterson (Swe) Lotus-Ford
3 Denny Hulme (NZ) McLaren-Ford
4 James Hunt (GB) March-Ford
5 François Cevert (Fra) Tyrrell-Ford
6 Carlos Reutemann (Arg) Brabham-Ford
Winner's speed: 212.03kph/131.75mph
Fastest lap: Hunt 215.75kph/134.06mph
Pole position: Peterson

1974 Brands Hatch

20 July, 319.86km/198.75 miles
1 Jody Scheckter (SAf) Tyrrell-Ford
2 Emerson Fittipaldi (Bra) McLaren-Ford
3 Jacky Ickx (Bel) Lotus-Ford
4 Clay Regazzoni (Swi) Ferrari
5 Niki Lauda (Aut) Ferrari
6 Carlos Reutemann (Arg) Brabham-Ford
Winner's speed: 186.26kph/115.74mph
Fastest lap: Lauda 189.31kph/117.63mph
Pole position: Lauda

1975 Silverstone

19 July, 264.24km/164.19 miles
1 Emerson Fittipaldi (Bra) McLaren-Ford
2 Carlos Pace (Bra) Brabham-Ford
3 Jody Scheckter (SAf) Tyrrell-Ford
4 James Hunt (GB) Hesketh-Ford
5 Mark Donohue (USA) March-Ford
6 Vittorio Brambilla (Ita) March-Ford
Winner's speed: 193.15kph/120.02mph
Fastest lap: Clay Regazzoni (Swi) Ferrari 209.97kph/130.47mph
Pole position: Tom Pryce (GB) Shadow-Ford

1976 Brands Hatch

18 July, 319.72km/198.66 miles
1 Niki Lauda (Aut) Ferrari
2 Jody Scheckter (SAf) Tyrrell-Ford
3 John Watson (GB) Penske-Ford

4 Tom Pryce (GB) Shadow-Ford
5 Alan Jones (Aus) Surtees-Ford
6 Emerson Fittipaldi (Bra) Fittipaldi-Ford
*James Hunt (GB) McLaren-Ford finished 1st and set
fastest lap at 189.71kph/117.88mph but was disqualified
for illegally participating in the restarted race following a
shunt. The disqualification came two months after the
race.*
Winner's speed: 183.87kph/114.23mph
Fastest lap: Lauda 189.52kph/117.74mph
Pole position: Lauda

1977 Silverstone

16 July, 320.87km/199.38 miles
1 James Hunt (GB) McLaren-Ford
2 Niki Lauda (Aut) Ferrari
3 Gunnar Nilsson (Swe) Lotus-Ford
4 Jochen Mass (FRG) McLaren-Ford
5 Hans-Joachim Stuck (FRG) Brabham-Alfa Romeo
6 Jacques Laffite (Fra) Ligier-Matra
Winner's speed: 209.79kph/130.35mph
Fastest lap: Hunt 213.40kph/132.60mph
Pole position: Hunt

1978 Brands Hatch

16 July, 319.72km/198.66 miles
1 Carlos Reutemann (Arg) Ferrari
2 Niki Lauda (Aut) Brabham-Alfa Romeo
3 John Watson (GB) Brabham-Alfa Romeo
4 Patrick Depailler (Fra) Tyrrèll-Ford
5 Hans-Joachim Stuck (FRG) Shadow-Ford
6 Patrick Tambay (Fra) McLaren-Ford
Winner's speed: 187.69kph/116.61mph
Fastest lap: Lauda 192.69kph/119.71mph
Pole position: Ronnie Peterson (Swe) Lotus-Ford

1979 Silverstone

14 July, 320.87km/199.38 miles
1 Clay Regazzoni (Swi) Williams-Ford
2 René Arnoux (Fra) Renault
3 Jean-Pierre Jarier (Fra) Tyrrell-Ford
4 John Watson (GB) McLaren-Ford
5 Jody Scheckter (SAf) Ferrari
6 Jacky Ickx (Bel) Ligier-Ford
Winner's speed: 223.37kph/138.80mph
Fastest lap: Regazzoni 228.31kph/141.87mph
Pole position: Alan Jones (Aus) Williams-Ford

1980 Brands Hatch

13 July, 319.72km/198.66 miles
1 Alan Jones (Aus) Williams-Ford
2 Nelson Piquet (Bra) Brabham-Ford
3 Carlos Reutemann (Arg) Williams-Ford
4 Derek Daly (Ire) Tyrrell-Ford
5 Jean-Pierre Jarier (Fra) Tyrrell-Ford
6 Alain Prost (Fra) McLaren-Ford
Winner's speed: 202.32kph/125.69mph
Fastest lap: Didier Pironi (Fra) Ligier-Ford 209.28kph/
130.02mph
Pole position: Pironi

1981 Silverstone

18 July, 320.87km/199.38 miles
1 John Watson (GB) McLaren-Ford
2 Carlos Reutemann (Arg) Williams-Ford
3 Jacques Laffite (Fra) Talbot-Matra
4 Eddie Cheever (USA) Tyrrell-Ford
5 Hector Rebaque (Mex) Brabham-Ford
6 Slim Borgudd (Swe) ATS-Ford
Winner's speed: 221.51kph/137.65mph
Fastest lap: René Arnoux (Fra) Renault 226.29kph/
140.62mph
Pole position: Arnoux

1982 Brands Hatch

18 July, 319.72km/198.66 miles
1 Niki Lauda (Aut) McLaren-Ford
2 Didier Pironi (Fra) Ferrari
3 Patrick Tambay (Fra) Ferrari
4 Elio de Angelis (Ita) Lotus-Ford
5 Derek Daly (Ire) Williams-Ford
6 Alain Prost (Fra) Renault
Winner's speed: 200.74kph/124.71mph
Fastest lap: Brian Henton (GB) Tyrrell-Ford 207.38kph/
128.85mph
Pole position: Keke Rosberg (Fin) Williams-Ford

1983 Silverstone

16 July, 316.15km/196.44 miles
1 Alain Prost (Fra) Renault
2 Nelson Piquet (Bra) Brabham-BMW
3 Patrick Tambay (Fra) Ferrari
4 Nigel Mansell (GB) Lotus-Renault
5 René Arnoux (Fra) Ferrari
6 Niki Lauda (Aut) McLaren-Ford
Winner's speed: 224.05kph/139.22mph
Fastest lap: Prost 228.90kph/142.24mph
Pole position: Arnoux

1984 Brands Hatch

22 July, 298.69km/185.59 miles
1 Niki Lauda (Aut) McLaren-Porsche
2 Derek Warwick (GB) Renault
3 Ayrton Senna (Bra) Toleman-Hart
4 Elio de Angelis (Ita) Lotus-Renault
5 Michele Alboreto (Ita) Ferrari
6 René Arnoux (Fra) Ferrari
Winner's speed: 200.30kph/124.46mph
Fastest lap: Lauda 206.91kph/128.57mph
Pole position: Nelson Piquet (Bra) Brabham-BMW

1985 Silverstone

21 July, 306.71km/190.58 miles
1 Alain Prost (Fra) McLaren-TAG
2 Michele Alboreto (Ita) Ferrari
3 Jacques Laffite (Fra) Ligier-Renault
4 Nelson Piquet (Bra) Brabham-BMW
5 Derek Warwick (GB) Renault
6 Marc Surer (Swi) Brabham-BMW
Winner's speed: 235.40kph/146.28mph

Fastest lap: Prost 243.07kph/151.04mph
Pole position: Keke Rosberg (Fin) Williams-Honda

1986 Brands Hatch

13 July, 315.51km/196.05 miles
1 Nigel Mansell (GB) Williams-Honda
2 Nelson Piquet (Bra) Williams-Honda
3 Alain Prost (Fra) McLaren-TAG
4 René Arnoux (Fra) Ligier-Renault
5 Martin Brundle (GB) Tyrrell-Renault
6 Philippe Streiff (Fra) Tyrrell-Renault
Winner's speed: 208.85kph/129.78mph
Fastest lap: Mansell 217.60kph/135.22mph
Pole position: Piquet

1987 Silverstone

12 July, 310.58km/192.99 miles
1 Nigel Mansell (GB) Williams-Honda
2 Nelson Piquet (Bra) Williams-Honda
3 Ayrton Senna (Bra) Lotus-Honda
4 Satoru Nakajima (Jap) Lotus-Honda
5 Derek Warwick (GB) Arrows-Megatron
6 Teo Fabi (Ita) Benetton-Ford
Winner's speed: 235.30kph/146.21mph
Fastest lap: Mansell 246.33kph/153.06mph
Pole position: Piquet

1988 Silverstone

10 July, 310.58km/192.99 miles
1 Ayrton Senna (Bra) McLaren-Honda
2 Nigel Mansell (GB) Williams-Judd
3 Alessandro Nannini (Ita) Benetton-Ford
4 Mauricio Gugelmin (Bra) March-Judd
5 Nelson Piquet (Bra) Lotus-Honda
6 Derek Warwick (GB) Arrows-Megatron
Winner's speed: 199.78kph/124.14mph
Fastest lap: Mansell 206.47kph/128.30mph
Pole position: Gerhard Berger (Aut) Ferrari

1989 Silverstone

16 July, 305.90km/190.08 miles
1 Alain Prost (Fra) McLaren-Honda
2 Nigel Mansell (GB) Ferrari
3 Alessandro Nannini (Ita) Benetton-Ford
4 Nelson Piquet (Bra) Lotus-Judd
5 Pierluigi Martini (Ita) Minardi-Ford
6 Luis Sala (Spa) Minardi-Ford
Winner's speed: 231.25kph/143.69mph
Fastest lap: Nigel Mansell 238.93kph/148.465mph
Pole position: Ayrton Senna (Bra) McLaren-Honda

1990 Silverstone

15 July, 305.90km/190.08 miles
1 Alain Prost (Fra) Ferrari
2 Thierry Boutsen (Bel) Williams-Renault
3 Ayrton Senna (Bra) McLaren-Honda
4 Eric Bernard (Fra) Lola-Lamborghini
5 Nelson Piquet (Bra) Benetton-Ford
6 Aguri Suzuki (Jap) Lola-Lamborghini
Winner's speed: 233.76kph/145.25mph
Fastest lap: Nigel Mansell (GB) Ferrari 241.36kph/
149.98mph
Pole position: Mansell

1991 Silverstone

14 July, 308.31km/191.57 miles
1 Nigel Mansell (GB) Williams-Renault
2 Gerhard Berger (Aut) McLaren-Honda
3 Alain Prost (Fra) Ferrari
4 Ayrton Senna (Bra) McLaren-Honda
5 Nelson Piquet (Bra) Benetton-Ford
6 Bertrand Gachot (Bel) Jordan-Ford
Winner's speed: 211.19kph/131.23mph
Fastest lap: Mansell 217.78kph/135.33mph
Pole position: Mansell

MOST WINS

Drivers
5 Jim Clark
4 Alain Prost
3 Jack Brabham, Niki Lauda, Nigel
   Mansell
2 Alberto Ascari, Emerson Fittipaldi,
   José Froilán González, Stirling
   Moss, Jackie Stewart
Manufacturers
9 Ferrari, McLaren
8 Lotus
5 Williams
2 Cooper, Tyrrell

MOST FASTEST LAPS

Drivers
6 Nigel Mansell
5 Stirling Moss
4 Niki Lauda
3 Alberto Ascari, Jackie Stewart
2 Jack Brabham, Jim Clark, Giuseppe
   Farina, José Froilán González, Mike
   Hawthorn, Graham Hill, James Hunt,
   Alain Prost, Clay Regazzoni
Manufacturers
11 Ferrari
 5 Maserati, Williams
 4 Brabham, BRM
 3 Lotus, McLaren, Tyrrell
 2 Alfa Romeo, Mercedes-Benz,
   Renault

MOST POLE POSITIONS

Drivers
5 Jim Clark
4 Stirling Moss
3 Jack Brabham, Nelson Piquet; René
   Arnoux, Giuseppe Farina, Niki
   Lauda, Nigel Mansell, Ronnie
   Peterson, Jochen Rindt, Keke
   Rosberg
Manufacturers
11 Ferrari
10 Lotus
 6 Williams
 2 Brabham, Cooper, McLaren,
   Mercedes-Benz, Vanwall

CANADIAN GP

A near ever-present on the World Championship list since it made its bow at the Mosport circuit close to the shores of Lake Ontario in 1967, the Canadian Grand Prix was first run in 1961 as a sports car race but was accorded Grand Prix status in 1967 as part of Canada's centenary celebrations. The last race at Mosport was in 1977 when the drivers felt it had fallen a long way behind the European circuits.

A new circuit was constructed in just three months on the Expo '67 site along the St Lawrence seaway in Montreal. It became known as the Ile Notre Dame circuit and was later renamed the Gilles Villeneuve Circuit in memory of the great French-Canadian driver who won the Canadian Grand Prix in a Ferrari in 1978 and lost his life at Zolder four years later. In that same year, 1982, the Italian driver Ricardo Paletti lost his life at Montreal.

A third circuit at Mont Tremblant-St Jovite, in skiing country north of Montreal, has also been used to host the Canadian Grand Prix.

1967 Mosport

27 August, 356.16km/221.31 miles
1 Jack Brabham (Aus) Brabham-Repco
2 Denny Hulme (NZ) Brabham-Repco
3 Dan Gurney (USA) Eagle-Weslake
4 Graham Hill (GB) Lotus-Ford
5 Mike Spence (GB) BRM
6 Chris Amon (NZ) Ferrari
Winner's speed: 133.01kph/82.65mph
Fastest lap: Jim Clark (GB) Lotus-Ford 171.44kph/106.54mph
Pole position: Clark

1968 St Jovite

22 September, 383.83km/238.50 miles
1 Denny Hulme (NZ) McLaren-Ford
2 Bruce McLaren (NZ) McLaren-Ford
3 Pedro Rodriguez (Mex) BRM
4 Graham Hill (GB) Lotus-Ford
5 Vic Elford (GB) Cooper-BRM
6 Jackie Stewart (GB) Matra-Ford
Winner's speed: 156.47kph/97.22mph
Fastest lap: Jo Siffert (Swi) Lotus-Ford 161.44kph/100.31mph
Pole position: Jochen Rindt (Aut) Brabham-Repco

1969 Mosport

20 September, 356.16km/221.31 miles
1 Jacky Ickx (Bel) Brabham-Ford
2 Jack Brabham (Aus) Brabham-Ford
3 Jochen Rindt (Aut) Lotus-Ford
4 Jean-Pierre Beltoise (Fra) Matra-Ford
5 Bruce McLaren (NZ) McLaren-Ford
6 Johnny Servoz-Gavin (Fra) Matra-Ford
Winner's speed: 178.93kph/111.18mph
Fastest lap: Ickx & Brabham, 182.41kph/113.35mph
Pole position: Ickx

1970 Mosport

20 September, 383.83km/238.50 miles
1 Jacky Ickx (Bel) Ferrari
2 Clay Regazzoni (Swi) Ferrari
3 Chris Amon (NZ) March-Ford
4 Pedro Rodriguez (Mex) BRM
5 John Surtees (GB) Surtees-Ford
6 Peter Gethin (GB) McLaren-Ford
Winner's speed: 162.97kph/101.27mph
Fastest lap: Regazzoni 166.51kph/103.47mph
Pole position: Jackie Stewart (GB) Tyrrell-Ford

1971 Mosport

19 September, 253.27km/157.38 miles
1 Jackie Stewart (GB) Tyrrell-Ford
2 Ronnie Peterson (Swe) March-Ford
3 Mark Donohue (USA) McLaren-Ford
4 Denny Hulme (NZ) McLaren-Ford
5 Reine Wisell (Swe) Lotus-Ford
6 François Cevert (Fra) Tyrell-Ford
Winner's speed: 131.88kph/81.95mph
Fastest lap: Hulme 137.64kph/85.52mph
Pole position: Stewart

1972 Mosport

24 September, 316.59km/196.72 miles
1 Jackie Stewart (GB) Tyrrell-Ford
2 Peter Revson (USA) McLaren-Ford
3 Denny Hulme (NZ) McLaren-Ford
4 Carlos Reutemann (Arg) Brabham-Ford
5 Clay Regazzoni (Swi) Ferrari
6 Chris Amon (NZ) Matra-Simca
Winner's speed: 183.90kph/114.27mph
Fastest lap: Stewart 189.17kph/117.57mph
Pole position: Revson

1973 Mosport

23 September, 316.59km/196.72 miles
1 Peter Revson (USA) McLaren-Ford
2 Emerson Fittipaldi (Bra) Lotus-Ford
3 Jackie Oliver (GB) Shadow-Ford
4 Jean-Pierre Beltoise (Fra) BRM
5 Jackie Stewart (GB) Tyrrell-Ford
6 Howden Ganley (NZ) Williams-Ford
Winner's speed: 159.53kph/99.13mph
Fastest lap: Fittipaldi 188.71kph/117.26mph
Pole position: Ronnie Peterson (Swe) Lotus-Ford

1974 Mosport

22 September, 316.59km/196.72 miles
1 Emerson Fittipaldi (Bra) McLaren-Ford
2 Clay Regazzoni (Swi) Ferrari
3 Ronnie Peterson (Swe) Lotus-Ford
4 James Hunt (GB) Hesketh-Ford
5 Patrick Depailler (Fra) Tyrrell-Ford
6 Denny Hulme (NZ) McLaren-Ford
Winner's speed: 189.13kph/117.52mph
Fastest lap: Niki Lauda (Aut) Ferrari 193.41kph/120.18mph
Pole position: Fittipaldi

1976 Mosport

3 October, 316.59km/196.72 miles
1 James Hunt (GB) McLaren-Ford
2 Patrick Depailler (Fra) Tyrrell-Ford
3 Mario Andretti (USA) Lotus-Ford
4 Jody Scheckter (SAf) Tyrrell-Ford
5 Jochen Mass (FRG) McLaren-Ford
6 Clay Regazzoni (Swi) Ferrari
Winner's speed: 189.65kph/117.84mph
Fastest lap: Depailler 193.00kph/119.92mph
Pole position: Hunt

1977 Mosport

9 October, 316.59km/196.72 miles
1 Jody Scheckter (SAf) Wolf-Ford
2 Patrick Depailler (Fra) Tyrrell-Ford
3 Jochen Mass (FRG) McLaren-Ford
4 Alan Jones (Aus) Shadow-Ford
5 Patrick Tambay (Fra) Ensign-Ford
6 Vittorio Brambilla (Ita) Surtees-Ford
Winner's speed: 189.95kph/118.03mph
Fastest lap: Mario Andretti (USA) Lotus-Ford 194.36kph/120.77mph
Pole position: Andretti

1978 Montreal

8 October, 315.00km/195.73 miles
1 Gilles Villeneuve (Can) Ferrari
2 Jody Scheckter (SAf) Wolf-Ford
3 Carlos Reutemann (Arg) Ferrari
4 Riccardo Patrese (Ita) Arrows-Ford
5 Patrick Depailler (Fra) Tyrrell-Ford
6 Derek Daly (Ire) Ensign-Ford
Winner's speed: 160.40kph/99.67mph
Fastest lap: Alan Jones (Aus) Williams-Ford 165.18kph/102.64mph
Pole position: Jean-Pierre Jarier (Fra) Lotus-Ford

1979 Montreal

30 September, 317.52km/197.30 miles
1 Alan Jones (Aus) Williams-Ford
2 Gilles Villeneuve (Can) Ferrari
3 Clay Regazzoni (Swi) Williams-Ford
4 Jody Scheckter (SAf) Ferrari
5 Didier Pironi (Fra) Tyrrell-Ford
6 John Watson (GB) McLaren-Ford
Winner's speed: 169.93kph/105.59mph

Fastest lap: Jones 173.94kph/108.08mph
Pole position: Jones

1980 Montreal

28 September, 308.70km/191.82 miles
1 Alan Jones (Aus) Williams-Ford
2 Carlos Reutemann (Arg) Williams-Ford
3 Didier Pironi (Fra) Ligier-Ford
4 John Watson (GB) McLaren-Ford
5 Gilles Villeneuve (Can) Ferrari
6 Hector Rebaque (Mex) Brabham-Ford
Pironi finished 1st but was penalised one minute for jumping the start and was classified 3rd.
Winner's speed: 173.49kph/107.80mph
Fastest lap: Pironi 178.85kph/111.13mph
Pole position: Nelson Piquet (Bra) Brabham-Ford

1981 Montreal

27 September, 277.83km/172.64 miles
1 Jacques Laffite (Fra) Talbot-Matra
2 John Watson (GB) McLaren-Ford
3 Gilles Villeneuve (Can) Ferrari
4 Bruno Giacomelli (Ita) Alfa Romeo
5 Nelson Piquet (Bra) Brabham-Ford
6 Elio de Angelis (Ita) Lotus-Ford
Winner's speed: 137.29kph/85.31mph
Fastest lap: Watson 145.02kph/90.12mph
Pole position: Piquet

1982 Montreal

13 June, 308.70km/191.82 miles
1 Nelson Piquet (Bra) Brabham-BMW
2 Riccardo Patrese (Ita) Brabham-Ford
3 John Watson (GB) McLaren-Ford
4 Elio de Angelis (Ita) Lotus-Ford
5 Marc Surer (Swi) Arrows-Ford
6 Andrea de Cesaris (Ita) Alfa Romeo
Winner's speed: 173.70kph/107.94mph
Fastest lap: Didier Pironi (Fra) Ferrari 179.75kph/111.70mph
Pole position: Pironi

1983 Montreal

12 June, 308.70km/191.82 miles
1 René Arnoux (Fra) Ferrari
2 Eddie Cheever (USA) Renault
3 Patrick Tambay (Fra) Ferrari
4 Keke Rosberg (Fin) Williams-Ford
5 Alain Prost (Fra) Renault
6 John Watson (GB) McLaren-Ford
Winner's speed: 170.66kph/106.05mph
Fastest lap: Tambay 174.75kph/108.59mph
Pole position: Arnoux

1984 Montreal

17 June, 308.70km/191.82 miles
1 Nelson Piquet (Bra) Brabham-BMW
2 Niki Lauda (Aut) McLaren-Porsche
3 Alain Prost (Fra) McLaren-Porsche
4 Elio de Angelis (Ita) Lotus-Renault

5 René Arnoux (Fra) Ferrari
6 Nigel Mansell (GB) Lotus-Renault
Winner's speed: 174.09kph/108.18mph
Fastest lap: Piquet 178.86kph/111.14mph
Pole position: Piquet

1985 Montreal

16 June, 308.70km/191.82 miles
1 Michele Alboreto (Ita) Ferrari
2 Stefan Johansson (Swe) Ferrari
3 Alain Prost (Fra) McLaren-TAG
4 Keke Rosberg (Fin) Williams-Honda
5 Elio de Angelis (Ita) Lotus-Renault
6 Nigel Mansell (GB) Williams-Honda
Winner's speed: 174.69kph/108.55mph
Fastest lap: Ayrton Senna (Bra) Lotus-Renault 181.55kph/
112.82mph
Pole position: de Angelis

1986 Montreal

15 June, 304.29km/189.08 miles
1 Nigel Mansell (GB) Williams-Honda
2 Alain Prost (Fra) McLaren-TAG
3 Nelson Piquet (Bra) Williams-Honda
4 Keke Rosberg (Fin) McLaren-TAG
5 Ayrton Senna (Bra) Lotus-Renault
6 René Arnoux (Fra) Ligier-Renault
Winner's speed: 179.26kph/111.39mph
Fastest lap: Piquet 186.88kph/116.13mph
Pole position: Mansell

1988 Montreal

12 June, 302.91km/188.22 miles
1 Ayrton Senna (Bra) McLaren-Honda
2 Alain Prost (Fra) McLaren-Honda
3 Thierry Boutsen (Bel) Benetton-Ford
4 Nelson Piquet (Bra) Lotus-Honda
5 Ivan Capelli (Ita) March-Judd
6 Jonathan Palmer (GB) Tyrrell-Ford
Winner's speed: 182.15kph/113.19mph
Fastest lap: Senna 186.00kph/115.60mph
Pole position: Senna

1989 Montreal

18 June, 302.91km/188.22 miles
1 Thierry Boutsen (Bel) Williams-Renault
2 Riccardo Patrese (Ita) Williams-Renault
3 Andrea de Cesaris (Ita) Dallara-Ford
4 Nelson Piquet (Bra) Lotus-Judd
5 René Arnoux (Fra) Ligier-Ford
6 Alex Caffi (Ita) Dallara-Ford
Winner's speed: 149.70kph/93.02mph
Fastest lap: Jonathan Palmer (GB) Tyrrell-Ford 171.93kph/
106.83mph
Pole position: Alain Prost (Fra) McLaren-Honda

1990 Montreal

10 June, 307.31km/190.96 miles
1 Ayrton Senna (Bra) McLaren-Honda
2 Nelson Piquet (Bra) Benetton-Ford
3 Nigel Mansell (GB) Ferrari
4 Gerhard Berger (Aut) McLaren-Honda
5 Alain Prost (Fra) Ferrari
6 Derek Warwick (GB) Lotus-Lamborghini
*Berger finished 1st but penalised one minute for jumping
the start and was classified 4th.*
Winner's speed: 180.16kph/111.95mph
Fastest lap: Berger 192.55kph/119.65mph
Pole position: Senna

1991 Montreal

2 June, 305.67km/188.93 miles
1 Nelson Piquet (Bra) Benetton-Ford
2 Stefano Modena (Ita) Tyrrell-Honda
3 Riccardo Patrese (Ita) Williams-Renault
4 Andrea de Cesaris (Ita) Jordan-Ford
5 Bertrand Gachot (Bel) Jordan-Ford
6 Nigel Mansell (GB) Williams-Renault
Winner's speed: 185.52kph/115.28mph
Fastest lap: Mansell 193.58kph/120.28mph
Pole position: Patrese

MOST WINS

Drivers
3 Nelson Piquet
2 Jacky Ickx, Alan Jones, Ayrton
  Senna, Jackie Stewart
Manufacturers
6 McLaren
4 Brabham, Ferrari, Williams
2 Tyrrell

MOST FASTEST LAPS

Drivers
2 Alan Jones, Nelson Piquet, Didier
  Pironi, Ayrton Senna
Manufacturers
5 Lotus, McLaren
4 Ferrari
3 Tyrrell, Williams
2 Brabham

MOST POLE POSITIONS

Drivers
3 Nelson Piquet
2 Ayrton Senna, Jackie Stewart
Manufacturers
6 McLaren
5 Brabham, Lotus
3 Williams
2 Ferrari, Tyrrell

DALLAS GP

At Fir Park

1984

8 July, 261.37km/162.41 miles
1 Keke Rosberg (Fin) Williams-Honda
2 René Arnoux (Fra) Ferrari
3 Elio de Angelis (Ita) Lotus-Renault
4 Jacques Laffite (Fra) Williams-Honda
5 Piercarlo Ghinzani (Ita) Osella-Alfa Romeo
6 Nigel Mansell (GB) Lotus-Renault
Winner's speed: 129.22kph/80.30mph
Fastest lap: Niki Lauda (Aut) McLaren-Porsche 133.30kph/82.83mph
Pole position: Mansell

The one and only Dallas Grand Prix replaced the United States Grand Prix (West) in 1984, but so dangerous was the surface of the Fir Park circuit that its Grand Prix life did not survive to a second year.

It was a tight and bumpy circuit and concrete walls around the track resulted in several crashes in practice. Britain's Martin Brundle broke his ankle in one such accident and there were doubts that the race itself would be staged.

DETROIT GP

All races at Detroit

The backdrop of the skyscrapers; common landmarks on the street circuit at Detroit.

When it was first held in 1982 the Detroit Grand Prix was known as the United States Grand Prix (East) and was one of three World Championship races in the United States that year. A street circuit similar to Monaco, it did, like its European counterpart, utilise a tunnel as part of the circuit, but it did not have the appeal of Monaco because of concrete walls which made it a tough circuit for the drivers.

It remained as part of the World Championship for five years and when the United States Grand Prix was revived in 1987 the Detroit circuit became its new home.

MOST WINS

Drivers
No driver has won the race twice
Manufacturers
No manufacturer has won the race twice

MOST FASTEST LAPS

Drivers
No driver has registered two fastest laps
Manufacturers
2 Renault

MOST POLE POSITIONS

Drivers	Manufacturers
2 Ayrton Senna	2 Lotus

1982

6 June, 248.75km/154.57 miles
1 John Watson (GB) McLaren-Ford
2 Eddie Cheever (USA) Talbot-Matra
3 Didier Pironi (Fra) Ferrari
4 Keke Rosberg (Fin) Williams-Ford
5 Derek Daly (Ire) Williams-Ford
6 Jacques Laffite (Fra) Talbot-Matra
Winner's speed: 125.75kph/78.14mph
Fastest lap: Alain Prost (Fra) Renault 130.80kph/81.28mph
Pole position: Prost

1983

5 June, 241.40km/150.00 miles
1 Michele Alboreto (Ita) Tyrrell-Ford
2 Keke Rosberg (Fin) Williams-Ford
3 John Watson (GB) McLaren-Ford
4 Nelson Piquet (Bra) Brabham-BMW
5 Jacques Laffite (Fra) Williams-Ford
6 Nigel Mansell (GB) Lotus-Ford
Winner's speed: 130.41kph/81.04mph
Fastest lap: Watson 134.53kph/83.60mph
Pole position: René Arnoux (Fra) Ferrari

1984

24 June, 253.47km/157.50 miles
1 Nelson Piquet (Bra) Brabham-BMW
2 Elio de Angelis (Ita) Lotus-Renault
3 Teo Fabi (Ita) Brabham-BMW
4 Alain Prost (Fra) McLaren-Porsche
5 Jacques Laffite (Fra) Williams-Honda
Only five classified.

Martin Brundle (GB) Tyrrell-Ford finished 2nd but all Tyrrell points for drivers and manufacturers deducted because of rule infringement.
Winner's speed: 131.45kph/81.68mph
Fastest lap: Derek Warwick (GB) Renault 136.36kph/84.73mph
Pole position: Piquet

1985

23 June, 253.47km157.50 miles
1 Keke Rosberg (Fin) Williams-Honda
2 Stefan Johansson (Swe) Ferrari
3 Michele Alboreto (Ita) Ferrari
4 Stefan Bellof (FRG) Tyrrell-Ford
5 Elio de Angelis (Ita) Lotus-Renault
6 Nelson Piquet (Bra) Brabham-BMW
Winner's speed: 131.49kph/81.71mph
Fastest lap: Ayrton Senna (Bra) Lotus-Renault 137.13kph/85.21mph
Pole position: Senna

1986

22 June, 253.47km/157.50 miles
1 Ayrton Senna (Bra) Lotus-Renault
2 Jacques Laffite (Fra) Ligier-Renault
3 Alain Prost (Fra) McLaren-TAG
4 Michele Alboreto (Ita) Ferrari
5 Nigel Mansell (GB) Williams-Honda
6 Riccardo Patrese (Ita) Brabham-BMW
Winner's speed: 136.75kph/84.97mph
Fastest lap: Nelson Piquet (Bra) Williams-Honda 143.07kph/88.90mph
Pole position: Senna

DUTCH GP

All races at Zandvoort

In its 30 years as a World Championship race, the Dutch Grand Prix has had just one home, Zandvoort. Opened in 1948 for the Zandvoort Grand Prix, it was situated along the sand dunes at Haarlem. The race became the Dutch Grand Prix in 1950 but remained a non-championship event until 1952.

The circuit offered the drivers plenty of variety with its fast straights and mixture of fast and very tight corners. Sand blowing across the track was probably the biggest problem the drivers faced on what was not a very demanding circuit.

Zandvoort has claimed the lives of two British Formula One drivers over the years: Piers Courage in 1970 and Roger Williamson who perished in his car in 1973 despite the brave effort of his close friend David Purley to pull him from his blazing car.

Because the track started to break up during the 1985 race it was removed from the Grand Prix calendar. Niki Lauda won the final race, his 25th and final Grand Prix victory. Graham Hill (1962) and James Hunt (1975) both had their first Grand Prix successes at Zandvoort.

MOST WINS

Drivers
4 Jim Clark
3 Niki Lauda, Jackie Stewart
2 Alberto Ascari, Jack Brabham, James Hunt, Alain Prost
Manufacturers
8 Ferrari
6 Lotus
3 McLaren
2 Brabham, BRM, Matra

MOST FASTEST LAPS

Drivers
5 Jim Clark
3 René Arnoux, Niki Lauda, Stirling Moss
2 Jackie Ickx, Ronnie Peterson
Manufacturers
10 Ferrari
8 Lotus
2 Brabham, Cooper, Matra

MOST POLE POSITIONS

Drivers

3 René Arnoux
2 Mario Andretti, Alberto Ascari, Graham Hill, Niki Lauda,
  Ronnie Peterson, Nelson Piquet, Alain Prost, Jochen
  Rindt

Manufacturers

8 Lotus	4 Brabham, Renault
7 Ferrari	2 BRM

1952

17 August, 377.37km/234.49 miles
1 Alberto Ascari (Ita) Ferrari
2 Giuseppe Farina (Ita) Ferrari
3 Luigi Villoresi (Ita) Ferrari
4 Mike Hawthorn (GB) Cooper-Bristol
5 Robert Manzon (Fra) Gordini
6 Maurice Trintignant (Fra) Gordini
Winner's speed: 130.57kph/81.15mph
Fastest lap: Ascari 137.48kph/85.43mph
Pole position: Ascari

1953

7 June, 377.37km/234.49 miles
1 Alberto Ascari (Ita) Ferrari
2 Giuseppe Farina (Ita) Ferrari
3 Felice Bonetto (Ita)/José Froilán González (Arg)
  Maserati
4 Mike Hawthorn (GB) Ferrari

5 Emmanuel de Graffenried (Swi) Maserati
6 Maurice Trintignant (Fra) Gordini
Winner's speed: 130.43kph/81.04mph
Fastest lap: Luigi Villoresi (Ita) Ferrari 133.82kph/83.15mph
Pole position: Ascari

1955

19 June, 419.30km/260.54 miles
1 Juan Manuel Fangio (Arg) Mercedes-Benz
2 Stirling Moss (GB) Mercedes-Benz
3 Luigi Musso (Ita) Maserati
4 Roberto Mieres (Arg) Maserati
5 Eugenio Castellotti (Ita) Ferrari
6 Jean Behra (Fra) Maserati
Winner's speed: 144.21kph/89.60mph
Fastest lap: Mieres 149.60kph/92.96mph
Pole position: Fangio

1958

26 May, 314.48km/195.41 miles
1 Stirling Moss (GB) Vanwall
2 Harry Schell (USA) BRM
3 Jean Behra (Fra) BRM
4 Roy Salvadori (GB) Cooper-Climax
5 Mike Hawthorn (GB) Ferrari
6 Cliff Allison (GB) Lotus-Climax
Winner's speed: 151.16kph/93.95mph
Fastest lap: Moss 154.66kph/96.10mph
Pole position: Stuart Lewis-Evans (GB) Vanwall

THE GREAT RACES

1961 Dutch GP

The 1961 Dutch Grand Prix was one of the many races which have produced exciting and close finishes, with Phil Hill of America and Wolfgang von Trips, the German driver, being the central characters on this occasion.

The 1961 championship was a long way from being decided – the Zandvoort race was only the second of the season. But on their showing in practice it was obvious that the Ferrari duo of Hill and von Trips were likely to be the main championship con-

tenders throughout the season. They occupied the front row of the grid, along with team-mate Richie Ginther, another American.

The race was dominated by Hill and von Trips. The German led the race from start to finish, and in second place for all the race – except a brief period on the 17th lap when Jim Clark in the Lotus overtook him – was Hill. But although von Trips ultimately held on to the lead all the way, the outcome was not decided until the chequered flag

came down. Von Trips held on despite a charge from his team-mate and won by less than one second in a race that was unique because not one of the 15 starters made a pit stop and all 15 were running at the end of the 195 mile race.

So von Trips won one of Zandvoort's most exciting races. Four weeks later the two Ferrari drivers were the central characters again at Spa and it was the turn of Hill to reverse the roles in an even closer contest.

1959

31 May, 314.48km/195.41 miles
1 Jo Bonnier (Swe) BRM
2 Jack Brabham (Aus) Cooper-Climax
3 Masten Gregory (USA) Cooper-Climax
4 Innes Ireland (GB) Lotus-Climax
5 Jean Behra (Fra) Ferrari
6 Phil Hill (USA) Ferrari
Winner's speed: 150.41kph/93.46mph
Fastest lap: Stirling Moss (GB) Cooper-Climax 156.09kph/
96.99mph
Pole position: Bonnier

1960

6 June, 314.48km/195.41 miles
1 Jack Brabham (Aus) Cooper-Climax
2 Innes Ireland (GB) Lotus-Climax
3 Graham Hill (GB) BRM
4 Stirling Moss (GB) Lotus-Climax
5 Wolfgang von Trips (FRG) Ferrari
6 Richie Ginther (USA) Ferrari
Winner's speed: 154.93kph/96.27mph
Fastest lap: Moss 160.93kph/99.99mph
Pole position: Moss

1961

22 May, 314.48km/195.41 miles
1 Wolfgang von Trips (FRG) Ferrari
2 Phil Hill (USA) Ferrari
3 Jim Clark (GB) Lotus-Climax
4 Stirling Moss (GB) Lotus-Climax
5 Richie Ginther (USA) Ferrari
6 Jack Brabham (Aus) Cooper-Climax
Winner's speed: 154.83kph/96.21mph
Fastest lap: Clark 158.06kph/98.21mph
Pole position: Hill

1962

20 May, 335.44km/208.43 miles
1 Graham Hill (GB) BRM
2 Trevor Taylor (GB) Lotus-Climax
3 Phill Hill (USA) Ferrari
4 Giancarlo Baghetti (Ita) Ferrari
5 Tony Maggs (SAf) Cooper-Climax
6 Carel Godin de Beaufort (Hol) Porsche
Winner's speed: 153.60kph/95.44mph
Fastest lap: Bruce McLaren (NZ) Cooper-Climax
159.88kph/99.36mph
Pole position: John Surtees (GB) Lola-Climax

1963

23 June, 335.44km/208.43 miles
1 Jim Clark (GB) Lotus-Climax
2 Dan Gurney (USA) Brabham-Climax
3 John Surtees (GB) Ferrari
4 Innes Ireland (GB) BRP-BRM
5 Richie Ginther (USA) BRM
6 Ludovico Scarfiotti (Ita) Ferrari
Winner's speed: 156.96kph/97.53mph

Fastest lap: Clark 161.10kph/100.10mph
Pole position: Clark

1964

24 May, 335.44km/208.43 miles
1 Jim Clark (GB) Lotus-Climax
2 John Surtees (GB) Ferrari
3 Peter Arundell (GB) Lotus-Climax
4 Graham Hill (GB) BRM
5 Chris Amon (NZ) Lotus-BRM
6 Bob Anderson (GB) Brabham-Climax
Winner's speed: 157.74kph/98.02mph
Fastest lap: Clark 162.64kph/101.01mph
Pole position: Dan Gurney (USA) Brabham-Climax

1965

18 July, 335.44km/208.43 miles
1 Jim Clark (GB) Lotus-Climax
2 Jackie Stewart (GB) BRM
3 Dan Gurney (USA) Brabham-Climax
4 Graham Hill (GB) BRM
5 Denny Hulme (NZ) Brabham-Climax
6 Richie Ginther (USA) Honda
Winner's speed: 162.33kph/100.87mph
Fastest lap: Clark 166.61kph/103.53mph
Pole position: Hill

1966

24 July, 377.37km/234.49 miles
1 Jack Brabham (Aus) Brabham-Repco
2 Graham Hill (GB) BRM
3 Jim Clark (GB) Lotus-Climax
4 Jackie Stewart (GB) BRM
5 Mike Spence (GB) Lotus-BRM
6 Lorenzo Bandini (Ita) Ferrari
Winner's speed: 161.11kph/100.11mph
Fastest lap: Denny Hulme (NZ) Brabham-Repco
166.61kph/103.53mph
Pole position: Brabham

1967

4 June, 377.37km/234.49 miles
1 Jim Clark (GB) Lotus-Ford
2 Jack Brabham (Aus) Brabham-Repco
3 Denny Hulme (NZ) Brabham-Repco
4 Chris Amon (NZ) Ferrari
5 Mike Parkes (GB) Ferrari
6 Ludovico Scarfiotti (Ita) Ferrari
Winner's speed: 168.09kph/104.44mph
Fastest lap: Clark 171.38kph/106.49mph
Pole position: Graham Hill (GB) Lotus-Ford

1968

23 June, 377.37km/234.49 miles
1 Jackie Stewart (GB) Matra-Ford
2 Jean-Pierre Beltoise (Fra) Matra
3 Pedro Rodriguez (Mex) BRM
4 Jacky Ickx (Bel) Ferrari
5 Silvio Moser (Swi) Brabham-Repco

6 Chris Amon (NZ) Ferrari
Winner's speed: 136.25kph/84.66mph
Fastest lap: Beltoise 142.52kph/88.56mph
Pole position: Amon

1969

21 June, 377.37km/234.49 miles
1 Jackie Stewart (GB) Matra-Ford
2 Jo Siffert (Swi) Lotus-Ford
3 Chris Amon (NZ) Ferrari
4 Denny Hulme (NZ) McLaren-Ford
5 Jacky Ickx (Bel) Brabham-Ford
6 Jack Brabham (Aus) Brabham-Ford
Winner's speed: 178.71kph/111.04mph
Fastest lap: Stewart 182.00kph/113.09mph
Pole position: Jochen Rindt (Aut) Lotus-Ford

1970

21 June, 335.44km/208.43 miles
1 Jochen Rindt (Aut) Lotus-Ford
2 Jackie Stewart (GB) March-Ford
3 Jacky Ickx (Bel) Ferrari
4 Clay Regazzoni (Swi) Ferrari
5 Jean-Pierre Beltoise (Fra) Matra-Simca
6 John Surtees (GB) McLaren-Ford
Winner's speed: 181.78kph/112.95mph
Fastest lap: Ickx 190.52kph/118.38mph
Pole position: Rindt

1971

20 June, 293.51km/182.38 miles
1 Jacky Ickx (Bel) Ferrari
2 Pedro Rodriguez (Mex) BRM
3 Clay Regazzoni (Swi) Ferrari
4 Ronnie Peterson (Swe) March-Ford
5 John Surtees (GB) Surtees-Ford
6 Jo Siffert (Swi) BRM
Winner's speed: 151.38kph/94.06mph
Fastest lap: Ickx 158.98kph/98.78mph
Pole position: Ickx

1973

29 July, 304.27km/189.07 miles
1 Jackie Stewart (GB) Tyrrell-Ford
2 François Cevert (Fra) Tyrrell-Ford
3 James Hunt (GB) March-Ford
4 Peter Revson (USA) McLaren-Ford
5 Jean-Pierre Beltoise (Fra) BRM
6 Gijs van Lennep (Hol) Williams-Ford
Winner's speed: 184.03kph/114.35mph
Fastest lap: Ronnie Peterson (Swe) Lotus-Ford 189.44kph/
117.71mph
Pole position: Peterson

1974

23 June, 316.95km/196.94 miles
1 Niki Lauda (Aut) Ferrari
2 Clay Regazzoni (Swi) Ferrari
3 Emerson Fittipaldi (Bra) McLaren-Ford
4 Mike Hailwood (GB) McLaren-Ford
5 Jody Scheckter (SAf) Tyrrell-Ford

6 Patrick Depailler (Fra) Tyrrell-Ford
Winner's speed: 184.63kph/114.72mph
Fastest lap: Ronnie Peterson (Swe) Lotus-Ford 186.81kph/
116.08mph
Pole position: Lauda

1975

22 June, 316.95km/196.94 miles
1 James Hunt (GB) Hesketh-Ford
2 Niki Lauda (Aut) Ferrari
3 Clay Regazzoni (Swi) Ferrari
4 Carlos Reutemann (Arg) Brabham-Ford
5 Carlos Pace (Bra) Brabham-Ford
6 Tom Pryce (GB) Shadow-Ford
Winner's speed: 177.80kph/110.48mph
Fastest lap: Lauda 186.58kph/115.93mph
Pole position: Lauda

1976

29 August, 316.95km/196.94 miles
1 James Hunt (GB) McLaren-Ford
2 Clay Regazzoni (Swi) Ferrari
3 Mario Andretti (USA) Lotus-Ford
4 Tom Pryce (GB) Shadow-Ford
5 Jody Scheckter (SAf) Tyrrell-Ford
6 Vittorio Brambilla (Ita) March-Ford
Winner's speed: 181.34kph/112.68mph
Fastest lap: Regazzoni 184.21kph/114.46mph
Pole position: Ronnie Peterson (Swe) March-Ford

1977

28 August, 316.95km/196.94 miles
1 Niki Lauda (Aut) Ferrari
2 Jacques Laffite (Fra) Ligier-Matra
3 Jody Scheckter (SAf) Wolf-Ford
4 Emerson Fittipaldi (Bra) Fittipaldi-Ford
5 Patrick Tambay (Fra) Ensign-Ford
6 Carlos Reutemann (Arg) Ferrari
Winner's speed: 186.87kph/116.12mph
Fastest lap: Lauda 190.19kph/118.18mph
Pole position: Mario Andretti (USA) Lotus-Ford

1978

27 August, 316.95km/196.94 miles
1 Mario Andretti (USA) Lotus-Ford
2 Ronnie Peterson (Swe) Lotus-Ford
3 Niki Lauda (Aut) Brabham-Alfa Romeo
4 John Watson (GB) Brabham-Alfa Romeo
5 Emerson Fittipaldi (Bra) Fittipaldi-Ford
6 Gilles Villeneuve (Can) Ferrari
Winner's speed: 188.16kph/116.91mph
Fastest lap: Lauda 191.20kph/118.81mph
Pole position: Andretti

1979

26 August, 316.95km/196.94 miles
1 Alan Jones (Aus) Williams-Ford
2 Jody Scheckter (SAf) Ferrari
3 Jacques Laffite (Fra) Ligier-Ford
4 Nelson Piquet (Bra) Brabham-Alfa Romeo

5 Jacky Ickx (Bel) Ligier-Ford
6 Jochen Mass (FRG) Arrows-Ford
Winner's speed: 187.67kph/116.62mph
Fastest lap: Gilles Villeneuve (Can) Ferrari 191.52kph/
119.00mph
Pole position: René Arnoux (Fra) Renault

1980

31 August, 306.14km/190.23 miles
1 Nelson Piquet (Bra) Brabham-Ford
2 René Arnoux (Fra) Renault
3 Jacques Laffite (Fra) Ligier-Ford
4 Carlos Reutemann (Arg) Williams-Ford
5 Jean-Pierre Jarier (Fra) Tyrrell-Ford
6 Alain Prost (Fra) McLaren-Ford
Winner's speed: 186.98kph/116.19mph
Fastest lap: Arnoux 192.91kph/119.87mph
Pole position: Arnoux

1981

30 August, 306.14km/190.23 miles
1 Alain Prost (Fra) Renault
2 Nelson Piquet (Bra) Brabham-Ford
3 Alan Jones (Aus) Williams-Ford
4 Hector Rebaque (Mex) Brabham-Ford
5 Elio de Angelis (Ita) Lotus-Ford
6 Eliseo Salazar (Chi) Ensign-Ford
Winner's speed: 183.00kph/113.72mph
Fastest lap: Jones 187.06kph/116.24mph
Pole position: Prost

1982

3 July, 306.14km/190.23 miles
1 Didier Pironi (Fra) Ferrari
2 Nelson Piquet (Bra) Brabham-BMW
3 Keke Rosberg (Fin) Williams-Ford
4 Niki Lauda (Aut) McLaren-Ford
5 Derek Daly (Ire) Williams-Ford
6 Mauro Baldi (Ita) Arrows-Ford
Winner's speed: 187.33kph/116.39mph
Fastest lap: Derek Warwick (GB) Toleman-Hart 191.87kph/
119.23mph
Pole position: René Arnoux (Fra) Renault

1983

28 August, 306.14km/190.23 miles
1 René Arnoux (Fra) Ferrari
2 Patrick Tambay (Fra) Ferrari
3 John Watson (GB) McLaren-Ford
4 Derek Warwick (GB) Toleman-Hart
5 Mauro Baldi (Ita) Alfa Romeo
6 Michele Alboreto (Ita) Tyrrell-Ford
Winner's speed: 186.10kph/115.64mph
Fastest lap: Arnoux 191.67kph/119.10mph
Pole position: Nelson Piquet (Bra) Brabham-BMW

1984

26 August, 301.89km/187.59 miles
1 Alain Prost (FRa) McLaren-Porsche
2 Niki Lauda (Aut) McLaren-Porsche
3 Nigel Mansell (GB) Lotus-Renault
4 Elio de Angelis (Ita) Lotus-Renault
5 Teo Fabi (Ita) Brabham-BMW
6 Patrick Tambay (Fra) Renault
Winner's speed: 186.05kph/115.61mph
Fastest lap: René Arnoux (Fra) Ferrari 192.63kph/
119.70mph
Pole position: Prost

1985

25 August, 297.64km/184.95 miles
1 Niki Lauda (Aut) McLaren-TAG
2 Alain Prost (Fra) McLaren-TAG
3 Ayrton Senna (Bra) Lotus-Renault
4 Michele Alboreto (Ita) Ferrari
5 Elio de Angelis (Ita) Lotus-Renault
6 Nigel Mansell (GB) Williams-Honda
Winner's speed: 193.09kph/119.99mph
Fastest lap: Prost 199.99kph/124.27mph
Pole position: Nelson Piquet (Bra) Brabham-BMW

*Niki Lauda (1) and Alain Prost made it a second
consecutive 1–2 for McLaren at Zandvoort in 1985 –
the last Dutch Grand Prix.*

EUROPEAN GP

In the early days of the World Championship, one race was annually designated as that year's *Grand Prix d'Europe*. It carried no extra points or status and was merely a title. The first such race to be called the European Grand Prix was the World Championship's inaugural race, the 1950 British Grand Prix.

However, a separate European Grand Prix was launched in 1983 with Brands Hatch being its first home. Britain thus staged two championship races that season, the British Grand Prix being held at Silverstone.

After the 1985 race the European Grand Prix disappeared but plans are afoot to relaunch it. The 1985 race was a significant milestone in the career of Nigel Mansell because it was his first Formula One Grand Prix victory.

The 1985 European Grand Prix gave Nigel Mansell his first Formula One success.

1983 Brands Hatch

25 September, 319.22km/198.66 miles
1 Nelson Piquet (Bra) Brabham-BMW
2 Alain Prost (Fra) Renault
3 Nigel Mansell (GB) Lotus-Renault
4 Andrea de Cesaris (Ita) Alfa Romeo
5 Derek Warwick (GB) Toleman-Hart
6 Bruno Giacomelli (Ita) Toleman-Hart
Winner's speed: 198.25kph/123.17mph
Fastest lap: Mansell 203.72kph/126.57mph
Pole position: Elio de Angelis (Ita) Lotus-Renault

1984 Nürburgring

7 October, 304km/189 miles
1 Alain Prost (Fra) McLaren-Porsche
2 Michele Alboreto (Ita) Ferrari
3 Nelson Piquet (Bra) Brabham-BMW
4 Niki Lauda (Aut) McLaren-Porsche
5 René Arnoux (Fra) Ferrari
6 Riccardo Patrese (Ita) Alfa Romeo

Winner's speed: 191.75kph/119.15mph
Fastest lap: Alboreto & Piquet 196.66kph/122.20mph
Pole position: Piquet

1985 Brands Hatch

6 October, 315.51km/196.05 miles
1 Nigel Mansell (GB) Williams-Honda
2 Ayrton Senna (Bra) Lotus-Renault
3 Keke Rosberg (Fin) Williams-Honda
4 Alain Prost (Fra) McLaren-TAG
5 Elio de Angelis (Ita) Lotus-Renault
6 Thierry Boutsen (Bel) Arrows-BMW
Winner's speed: 203.63kph/126.54mph
Fastest lap: Jacques Laffite (Fra) Ligier-Renault
211.73kph/131.57mph
Pole position: Senna

Race facts

Only Lotus's two appearances in pole position are worthy of note.

FRENCH GP

The French Grand Prix is the oldest in the world, dating back to 1906. That first race was won at Le Mans by F Szist in a Renault at an average speed on 101.37kph/63.00 mph . . . a far cry from Nigel Mansell's winning speed of 188.27kph/116.99mph in 1991.

Because of the race's long history, and France's close connections with the development of motor racing, it was inevitable that the French Grand Prix would form a round of the inaugural World Championship, and at Reims on 2 July 1950 Juan Manuel Fangio took the chequered flag in his Alfa Romeo.

The race has been part of the World Championship continuously with the exception of 1955 when it was cancelled in the wake of the disaster at Le Mans a month before the Grand Prix was scheduled to take place.

The 1953 French Grand Prix at Reims was one of the closest World Championship races: on the 60th and final lap any one of Juan Manuel Fangio, Mike Hawthorn, Alberto Ascari and Nino Farina could have won. But going into the final hairpin, Fangio made a slight mistake and Hawthorn used the power of his Ferrari to go on and win by 45 yards from the Argentinian and thus become the first Englishman to win a World Championship Grand Prix. He won just three races in his career; two of them were at Reims.

France's favourite son Alain Prost captured the first of his record-breaking number of race wins at Dijon-Prenois in the turbo-powered Renault in 1981.

1950 Reims

2 July, 500.22km/310.82 miles
1 Juan Manuel Fangio (Arg) Alfa Romeo
2 Luigi Fagioli (Ita) Alfa Romeo
3 Peter Whitehead (GB) Ferrari
4 Robert Manzon (Fra) Simca-Gordini
5 Philippe Etancelin (Fra)/Eugene Chaboud (Fra) Lago-Talbot
6 Charles Pozzi (Fra)/Louis Rosier (Fra) Lago-Talbot
Winner's speed: 168.73kph/104.84mph
Fastest lap: Fangio 180.83kph/112.36mph
Pole position: Fangio

1951 Reims

1 July, 601.83km/373.96 miles
1 Juan Manuel Fangio (Arg)/Luigi Fagioli (Ita) Alfa Romeo
2 Alberto Ascari (Ita)/José Froilán González(Arg) Ferrari
3 Luigi Villoresi (Ita) Ferrari
4 Reg Parnell (GB) Ferrari
5 Giuseppe Farina (Ita) Alfa Romeo
6 Louis Chiron (Mon) Lago-Talbot
Winner's speed: 178.59kph/110.97mph
Fastest lap: Fangio 190.37kph/118.29mph
Pole position: Fangio

1952 Rouen-les-Essarts

6 July, 386.87km/240.39 miles
1 Alberto Ascari (Ita) Ferrari
2 Giuseppe Farina (Ita) Ferrari
3 Piero Taruffi (Ita) Ferrari
4 Robert Manzon (Fra) Gordini
5 Maurice Trintignant (Fra) Gordini
6 Peter Collins (GB) HWM
Winner's speed: 128.94kph/80.14mph
Fastest lap: Ascari 133.72kph/83.09mph
Pole position: Ascari

1953 Reims

5 July, 500.82km/311.20 miles
1 Mike Hawthorn (GB) Ferrari
2 Juan Manuel Fangio (Arg) Maserati
3 José Froilán González(Arg) Maserati
4 Alberto Ascari (Ita) Ferrari
5 Giuseppe Farina (Ita) Ferrari
6 Luigi Villoresi (Ita) Ferrari
Winner's speed: 182.86kph/113.65mph
Fastest lap: Ascari 186.53kph/115.91mph
Pole position: Ascari

1954 Reims

4 July, 506.42km/314.68 miles
1 Juan Manuel Fangio (Arg) Mercedes-Benz
2 Karl Kling (FRG) Mercedes-Benz
3 Robert Manzon (Fra) Ferrari
4 'B Bira' (Siam) Maserati
5 Luigi Villoresi (Ita) Maserati
6 Jean Behra (Fra) Gordini
Winner's speed: 186.64kph/115.97mph
Fastest lap: Hans Herrmann (FRG) Mercedes-Benz 195.47kph/121.46mph
Pole position: Fangio

1956 Reims

1 July, 506.42km/314.68 miles
1 Peter Collins (GB) Lancia-Ferrari
2 Eugenio Castellotti (Ita) Lancia-Ferrari
3 Jean Behra (Fra) Maserati
4 Juan Manuel Fangio (Arg) Lancia-Ferrari
5 Cesare Perdisa (Ita)/Stirling Moss (GB) Maserati
6 Louis Rosier (Fra) Maserati
Winner's speed: 196.80kph/122.29mph
Fastest lap: Fangio 204.98kph/127.37mph
Pole position: Fangio

1957 Rouen-les-Essarts

7 July, 503.73km/313.01 miles
1 Juan Manuel Fangio (Arg) Maserati
2 Luigi Musso (Ita) Lancia-Ferrari
3 Peter Collins (GB) Lancia-Ferrari
4 Mike Hawthorn (GB) Lancia-Ferrari
5 Jean Behra (Fra) Maserati
6 Harry Schell (USA) Maserati
Winner's speed: 160.96kph/100.02mph
Fastest lap: Musso 165.39kph/102.77mph
Pole position: Fangio

1958 Reims

6 July, 415.10km/257.93 miles
1 Mike Hawthorn (GB) Ferrari
2 Stirling Moss (GB) Vanwall
3 Wolfgang von Trips (FRG) Ferrari
4 Juan Manuel Fangio (Arg) Maserati
5 Peter Collins (GB) Ferrari
6 Jack Brabham (Aus) Cooper-Climax
Winner's speed: 201.90kph/125.45mph
Fastest lap: Hawthorn 206.25kph/128.16mph
Pole position: Hawthorn

1959 Reims

5 July,.415.10km/257.93 miles
1 Tony Brooks (GB) Ferrari
2 Phil Hill (USA) Ferrari
3 Jack Brabham (Aus) Cooper-Climax
4 Olivier Gendebien (Bel) Ferrari
5 Bruce McLaren (NZ) Cooper-Climax
6 Ron Flockhart (GB) BRM
Winner's speed: 205.08kph/127.43mph
Fastest lap: Stirling Moss (GB) BRM 209.29kph/130.05mph
Pole position: Brooks

1960 Reims

3 July, 415.10km/257.93 miles
1 Jack Brabham (Aus) Cooper-Climax
2 Olivier Gendebien (Bel) Cooper-Climax
3 Bruce McLaren (NZ) Cooper-Climax
4 Henry Taylor (GB) Cooper-Climax
5 Jim Clark (GB) Lotus-Climax
6 Ron Flockhart (GB) Lotus-Climax
Winner's speed: 212.11kph/131.80mph
Fastest lap: Brabham 217.36kph/135.06mph
Pole position: Brabham

1961 Reims

2 July, 431.70km/268.25 miles
1 Giancarlo Baghetti (Ita) Ferrari
2 Dan Gurney (USA) Porsche
3 Jim Clark (GB) Lotus-Climax
4 Innes Ireland (GB) Lotus-Climax
5 Bruce McLaren (NZ) Cooper-Climax
6 Graham Hill (GB) BRM-Climax
Winner's speed: 192.86kph/119.85mph
Fastest lap: Phil Hill (USA) Ferrari 203.18kph/126.25mph
Pole position: Phil Hill

1962 Rouen-les-Essarts

8 July, 353.27km/219.51 miles
1 Dan Gurney (USA) Porsche
2 Tony Maggs (SAf) Cooper-Climax
3 Richie Ginther (USA) BRM
4 Bruce McLaren (NZ) Cooper-Climax
5 John Surtees (GB) Lola-Climax
6 Carel Godin de Beaufort (Hol) Porsche
Winner's speed: 166.12kph/103.23mph
Fastest lap: Graham Hill (GB) BRM 172.03kph/106.90mph
Pole position: Jim Clark (GB) Lotus-Climax

1963 Reims

30 June, 440.01km/273.41 miles
1 Jim Clark (GB) Lotus-Climax
2 Tony Maggs (SAf) Cooper-Climax
3 Graham Hill (GB) BRM
4 Jack Brabham (Aus) Brabham-Climax
5 Dan Gurney (USA) Brabham-Climax
6 Jo Siffert (Swi) Lotus-BRM
Hill received no points because he was push-started.
Winner's speed: 210.67kph/125.31mph
Fastest lap: Clark 211.06kph/131.15mph
Pole position: Clark

1964 Rouen-les-Essarts

28 June, 372.89km/231.71 miles
1 Dan Gurney (USA) Brabham-Climax
2 Graham Hill (GB) BRM
3 Jack Brabham (Aus) Brabham-Climax
4 Peter Arundell (GB) Lotus-Climax
5 Richie Ginther (USA) BRM
6 Bruce McLaren (NZ) Cooper-Climax
Winner's speed: 175.04kph/108.77mph
Fastest lap: Brabham 179.23kph/111.37mph
Pole position: Jim Clark (GB) Lotus-Climax

1965 Clermont-Ferrand

27 June, 322.20km/200.21 miles
1 Jim Clark (GB) Lotus-Climax
2 Jackie Stewart (GB) BRM
3 John Surtees (GB) Ferrari
4 Denny Hulme (NZ) Brabham-Climax
5 Graham Hill (GB) BRM
6 Jo Siffert (Swi) Brabham-BRM
Winner's speed: 143.58kph/89.22mph
Fastest lap: Clark 145.79kph/90.59mph
Pole position: Clark

1966 Reims

3 July, 398.50km/247.61 miles
1 Jack Brabham (Aus) Brabham-Repco
2 Mike Parkes (GB) Ferrari
3 Denny Hulme (NZ) Brabham-Repco
4 Jochen Rindt (Aut) Cooper-Maserati
5 Dan Gurney (USA) Eagle-Climax
6 John Taylor (GB) Brabham-BRM
Winner's speed: 220.32kph/136.90mph
Fastest lap: Lorenzo Bandini (Ita) Ferrari 227.62kph/

141.44mph
Pole position: Bandini

1967 Le Mans (Bugatti circuit)

2 July, 353.76km/219.82 miles
1 Jack Brabham (Aus) Brabham-Repco
2 Denny Hulme (NZ) Brabham-Repco
3 Jackie Stewart (GB) BRM
4 Jo Siffert (Swi) Cooper-Maserati
5 Chris Irwin (GB) BRM
6 Pedro Rodriguez (Mex) Cooper-Maserati
Winner's speed: 159.17kph/98.90mph
Fastest lap: Graham Hill (GB) Lotus-Ford 164.64kph/
102.29mph
Pole position: Hill

1968 Rouen-les-Essarts

7 July, 392.52km/243.90 miles
1 Jacky Ickx (Bel) Ferrari
2 John Surtees (GB) Honda
3 Jackie Stewart (GB) Matra-Ford
4 Vic Elford (GB) Cooper-BRM
5 Denny Hulme (NZ) McLaren-Ford
6 Piers Courage (GB) BRM
Winner's speed: 161.66kph/100.45mph
Fastest lap: Pedro Rodriguez (Mex) BRM 179.10kph/
111.29mph
Pole position: Jochen Rindt (Aut) Brabham-Repco

1969 Clermont-Ferrand

6 July, 306.09km/190.20 miles
1 Jackie Stewart (GB) Matra-Ford
2 Jean-Pierre Beltoise (Fra) Matra-Ford
3 Jacky Ickx (Bel) Brabham-Ford
4 Bruce McLaren (NZ) McLaren-Ford
5 Vic Elford (GB) McLaren-Ford
6 Graham Hill (GB) Lotus-Ford
Winner's speed: 157.25kph/97.71mph
Fastest lap: Stewart 158.72kph/98.62mph
Pole position: Stewart

1970 Clermont-Ferrand

5 July, 306.09km/190.20 miles
1 Jochen Rindt (Aut) Lotus-Ford
2 Chris Amon (NZ) March-Ford
3 Jack Brabham (Aus) Brabham-Ford
4 Denny Hulme (NZ) McLaren-Ford
5 Henri Pescarolo (Fra) Matra-Simca
6 Dan Gurney (USA) McLaren-Ford
Winner's speed: 158.39kph/98.42mph
Fastest lap: Brabham 160.43kph/99.69mph
Pole position: Jacky Ickx (Bel) Ferrari

1971 Paul Ricard

4 July, 319.55km/198.56 miles
1 Jackie Stewart (GB) Tyrrell-Ford
2 François Cevert (Fra) Tyrrell-Ford
3 Emerson Fittipaldi (Bra) Lotus-Ford
4 Jo Siffert (Swi) BRM

5 Chris Amon (NZ) Matra-Simca
6 Reine Wisell (Swe) Lotus-Ford
Winner's speed: 179.70kph/111.66mph
Fastest lap: Stewart 183.33kph/113.92mph
Pole position: Stewart

1972 Clermont-Ferrand

2 July, 306.09km/190.20 miles
1 Jackie Stewart (GB) Tyrrell-Ford
2 Emerson Fittipaldi (Bra) Lotus-Ford
3 Chris Amon (NZ) Matra-Simca
4 François Cevert (Fra) Tyrrell-Ford
5 Ronnie Peterson (Swe) March-Ford
6 Mike Hailwood (GB) Surtees-Ford
Winner's speed: 163.45kph/101.57mph
Fastest lap: Amon 166.75kph/103.61mph
Pole position: Amon

1973 Paul Ricard

1 July, 313.74km/194.95 miles
1 Ronnie Peterson (Swe) Lotus-Ford
2 François Cevert (Fra) Tyrrell-Ford
3 Carlos Reutemann (Arg) Brabham-Ford
4 Jackie Stewart (GB) Tyrrell-Ford
5 Jacky Ickx (Bel) Ferrari
6 James Hunt (GB) March-Ford
Winner's speed: 185.26kph/115.12mph
Fastest lap: Denny Hulme (NZ) McLaren-Ford 188.45kph/
117.10mph
Pole position: Stewart

1974 Dijon-Prenois

7 July, 263.12km/163.50 miles
1 Ronnie Peterson (Swe) Lotus-Ford
2 Niki Lauda (Aut) Ferrari
3 Clay Regazzoni (Swi) Ferrari
4 Jody Scheckter (SAf) Tyrrell-Ford
5 Jacky Ickx (Bel) Lotus-Ford
6 Denny Hulme (NZ) McLaren-Ford
Winner's speed: 192.72kph/119.75mph
Fastest lap: Scheckter 197.34kph/122.62mph
Pole position: Lauda

1975 Paul Ricard

6 July, 313.74km/194.95 miles
1 Niki Lauda (Aut) Ferrari
2 James Hunt (GB) Hesketh-Ford
3 Jochen Mass (FRG) McLaren-Ford
4 Emerson Fittipaldi (Bra) McLaren-Ford
5 Mario Andretti (USA) Parnelli-Ford
6 Patrick Depailler (Fra) Tyrrell-Ford
Winner's speed: 187.65kph/116.60mph
Fastest lap: Mass 189.11kph/117.51mph
Pole position: Lauda

1976 Paul Ricard

4 July, 313.74km/194.95 miles
1 James Hunt (GB) McLaren-Ford
2 Patrick Depailler (Fra) Tyrrell-Ford
3 John Watson (GB) Penske-Ford

4 Carlos Pace (Bra) Brabham-Alfa Romeo
5 Mario Andretti (USA) Lotus-Ford
6 Jody Scheckter (SAf) Tyrrell-Ford
Winner's speed: 186.42kph/115.84mph
Fastest lap: Niki Lauda (Aut) Ferrari 188.43kph/117.09mph
Pole position: Hunt

1977 Dijon-Prenois

3 July, 304.00km/188.90 miles
1 Mario Andretti (USA) Lotus-Ford
2 John Watson (GB) Brabham-Alfa Romeo
3 James Hunt (GB) McLaren-Ford
4 Gunnar Nilsson (Swe) Lotus-Ford
5 Niki Lauda (Aut) Ferrari
6 Carlos Reutemann (Arg) Ferrari
Winner's speed: 183.01kph/113.71mph
Fastest lap: Andretti 185.49kph/115.26mph
Pole position: Andretti

1978 Paul Ricard

2 July, 313.74km/194.95 miles
1 Mario Andretti (USA) Lotus-Ford
2 Ronnie Peterson (Swe) Lotus-Ford
3 James Hunt (GB) McLaren-Ford
4 John Watson (GB) Brabham-Alfa Romeo
5 Alan Jones (Aus) Williams-Ford
6 Jody Scheckter (SAf) Wolf-Ford
Winner's speed: 190.41kph/118.31mph
Fastest lap: Carlos Reutemann (Arg) Ferrari 192.67kph/
119.72mph
Pole position: Watson

1979 Dijon-Prenois

1 July, 304.00km/188.90 miles
1 Jean-Pierre Jabouille (Fra) Renault
2 Gilles Villeneuve (Can) Ferrari
3 René Arnoux (Fra) Renault
4 Alan Jones (Aus) Williams-Ford
5 Jean-Pierre Jarier (Fra) Tyrrell-Ford
6 Clay Regazzoni (Swi) Williams-Ford
Winner's speed: 191.32kph/118.88mph
Fastest lap: Arnoux 197.80kph/122.91mph
Pole position: Jabouille

1980 Paul Ricard

29 June, 313.74km/194.95 miles
1 Alan Jones (Aus) Williams-Ford
2 Didier Pironi (Fra) Ligier-Ford
3 Jacques Laffite (Fra) Ligier-Ford
4 Nelson Piquet (Bra) Brabham-Ford
5 René Arnoux (Fra) Renault
6 Carlos Reutemann (Arg) Williams-Ford
Winner's speed: 203.02kph/126.15mph
Fastest lap: Jones 206.17kph/128.11mph
Pole position: Laffite

1981 Dijon-Prenois

5 July, 304.00km/188.90 miles
1 Alain Prost (Fra) Renault
2 John Watson (GB) McLaren-Ford

3 Nelson Piquet (Bra) Brabham-Ford
4 René Arnoux (Fra) Renault
5 Didier Pironi (Fra) Ferrari
6 Elio de Angelis (Ita) Lotus-Ford
Winner's speed: 190.39kph/118.31mph
Fastest lap: Prost 197.86kph/122.95mph
Pole position: Arnoux

1982 Paul Ricard

25 July, 313.74km/194.95 miles
1 René Arnoux (Fra) Renault
2 Alain Prost (Fra) Renault
3 Didier Pironi (Fra) Ferrari
4 Patrick Tambay (Fra) Ferrari
5 Keke Rosberg (Fin) Williams-Ford
6 Michele Alboreto (Ita) Tyrrell-Ford
Winner's speed: 201.20kph/125.03mph
Fastest lap: Riccardo Patrese (Ita) Brabham-BMW
209.01kph/129.88mph
Pole position: Arnoux

1983 Paul Ricard

17 April, 313.74km/194.95 miles
1 Alain Prost (Fra) Renault
2 Nelson Piquet (Bra) Brabham-BMW
3 Eddie Cheever (USA) Renault
4 Patrick Tambay (Fra) Ferrari
5 Keke Rosberg (Fin) Williams-Ford
6 Jacques Laffite (Fra) Williams-Ford
Winner's speed: 199.87kph/124.20mph
Fastest lap: Prost 203.67kph/126.57mph
Pole position: Prost

1984 Dijon-Prenois

20 May, 307.07km/190.81 miles
1 Niki Lauda (Aut) McLaren-Porsche
2 Partick Tambay (Fra) Renault
3 Nigel Mansell (GB) Lotus-Renault
4 René Arnoux (Fra) Ferrari
5 Elio de Angelis (Ita) Lotus-Renault
6 Keke Rosberg (Fin) Williams-Honda
Winner's speed: 202.02kph/125.54mph
Fastest lap: Alain Prost (Fra) McLaren-Porsche 214.43kph/
133.25mph
Pole position: Tambay

1985 Paul Ricard

7 July, 307.93km/191.34 miles
1 Nelson Piquet (Bra) Brabham-BMW
2 Keke Rosberg (Fin) Williams-Honda
3 Alain Prost (Fra) McLaren-TAG
4 Stefan Johansson (Swe) Ferrari
5 Elio de Angelis (Ita) Lotus Renault
6 Patrick Tambay (Fra) Renault
Winner's speed: 201.32kph/125.10mph
Fastest lap: Rosberg 209.34kph/130.08mph
Pole position: Rosberg

1986 Paul Ricard

6 July, 305.04km/189.54 miles
1 Nigel Mansell (GB) Williams-Honda
2 Alain Prost (Fra) McLaren-TAG
3 Nelson Piquet (Bra) Williams-Honda
4 Keke Rosberg (Fin) McLaren-TAG
5 René Arnoux (Fra) Ligier-Renault
6 Jacques Laffite (Fra) Ligier-Renault
Winner's speed: 189.15kph/117.54mph
Fastest lap: Mansell 197.25kph/122.57mph
Pole position: Ayrton Senna (Bra) Lotus-Renault

1987 Paul Ricard

5 July, 305.04km/189.54 miles
1 Nigel Mansell (GB) Williams-Honda
2 Nelson Piquet (Bra) Williams-Honda
3 Alain Prost (Fra) McLaren-TAG
4 Ayrton Senna (Bra) Lotus-Honda
5 Teo Fabi (Ita) Benetton-Ford
6 Philippe Streiff (Fra) Tyrrell-Ford
Winner's speed: 188.56kph/117.19mph
Fastest lap: Piquet 197.37kph/122.64mph
Pole position: Mansell

1988 Paul Ricard

3 July, 305.04km/189.54 miles
1 Alain Prost (Fra) McLaren-Honda
2 Ayrton Senna (Bra) McLaren-Honda
3 Michele Alboreto (Ita) Ferrari
4 Gerhard Berger (Aut) Ferrari
5 Nelson Piquet (Bra) Lotus-Honda
6 Alessandro Nannini (Ita) Benetton-Ford
Winner's speed: 187.44kph/116.50mph
Fastest lap: Prost 191.31kph/118.90mph
Pole position: Prost

1989 Paul Ricard

9 July, 305.04km/189.54 miles
1 Alain Prost (Fra) McLaren-Honda
2 Nigel Mansell (GB) Ferrari
3 Riccardo Patrese (Ita) Williams-Renault
4 Jean Alesi (Fra) Tyrrell-Ford
5 Stefan Johannsson (Swe) Onyx-Ford
6 Olivier Grouillard (Fra) Ligier-Ford
Winner's speed: 186.91kph/116.14mph
Fastest lap: Mauricio Gugelmin (Bra) March-Judd
191.52kph/119.01mph
Pole position: Prost

1990 Paul Ricard

8 July, 305.04km/189.54 miles
1 Alain Prost (Fra) Ferrari
2 Ivan Capelli (Ita) Leyton House-Judd
3 Ayrton Senna (Bra) McLaren-Honda
4 Nelson Piquet (Bra) Benetton-Ford
5 Gerhard Berger (Aut) McLaren-Honda
6 Riccardo Patrese (Ita) Williams-Renault
Winner's speed: 195.76kph/121.67mph
Fastest lap: Nigel Mansell (GB) Ferrari 201.83kph/
125.41mph
Pole position: Mansell

1991 Nevers-Magny Cours

7 July, 307.51km/ 190.08miles
1 Nigel Mansell (GB) Williams-Renault
2 Alain Prost (Fra) Ferrari
3 Ayrton Senna (Bra) McLaren-Honda
4 Jean Alesi (Fra) Ferrari
5 Riccardo Patrese (Ita) Williams-Renault
6 Andrea de Cesaris (Ita) Jordan-Ford
Winner's speed: 188.27kph/116.99mph
Fastest lap: Mansell 194.22kph/120.68mph
Pole position: Patrese

MOST WINS

Drivers
5 Alain Prost
4 Juan Manuel Fangio
3 Jack Brabham, Nigel Mansell,
   Jackie Stewart
2 Mario Andretti, Jim Clark, Dan
   Gurney, Mike Hawthorn, Niki Lauda,
   Ronnie Peterson
Manufacturers
8 Ferrari
7 Lotus
4 Brabham, McLaren, Renault,
   Williams
2 Alfa Romeo, Tyrrell

MOST FASTEST LAPS

Drivers
4 Juan Manuel Fangio, Alain Prost
3 Jack Brabham, Nigel Mansell
2 Jim Clark, Graham Hill, Jackie
   Stewart
Manufacturers
7 Ferrari
5 Williams
4 Lotus, McLaren
3 Brabham, BRM, Renault
2 Alfa Romeo, Lancia, Matra, Tyrrell

MOST POLE POSITIONS

Drivers
5 Juan Manuel Fangio
4 Jim Clark
3 Niki Lauda, Alain Prost, Jackie
   Stewart
2 René Arnoux, Alberto Ascari, Nigel
   Mansell
Manufacturers
10 Ferrari
7 Lotus
5 Renault
3 McLaren, Williams
2 Alfa Romeo, Brabham, Tyrrell

GERMAN GP

Although a German Grand Prix has been in existence since 1926, when Rudy Caracciola won in a Mercedes at Avus, Formula One racing had not yet returned to Germany by the time the World Championship was born. The first Formula One race in post-war Germany took place on 29 July 1951 at the Nürburgring, the German Grand Prix forming the sixth round of that year's World Championship. The race was won by Italy's Alberto Ascari, his debut win in the championship.

Ascari was one of the few drivers who mastered the Nürburgring and he won the race again in 1952. Fangio also had the better of the demanding circuit and won the race three years in succession, also in the 1950s. Like the French Grand Prix, and others, the race was cancelled in 1955 following the Le Mans tragedy. The only other time it did not appear on the World Championship calendar was in 1960.

The Nürburgring became unpopular with the German crowds so the 1959 race was moved to the dangerous (and rather boring) Avus circuit. Frenchman Jean Behra was killed during a sports car race which supported the Grand Prix, won that year by Britain's Tony Brooks. But that was to be the last German Grand Prix for two years. It has, however, been a regular World Championship fixture ever since, and it returned to the 'Ring' in 1962.

But the Nürburgring has itself had more than its share of fatalities over the years with such notable drivers as Onofre Marimon, Peter Collins, John Taylor and Carel Godin de Beaufort all losing their lives on one of the longest World Championship circuits. It has since been reduced drastically in size and no longer holds the dangers of the old 'Ring'. The last race over the old circuit was the 1976 race in which Niki Lauda nearly lost his life in an horrific accident.

In addition to Avus and the Nürburgring, the German Grand Prix has also been held at Hockenheim, near Mannheim, in southern Germany.

Jackie Stewart had the last of his then record-breaking 27 Grand Prix wins at the Nürburgring in 1973, and in 1968 he won the race with one of the greatest drives ever seen. He conquered the monster course in dreadful conditions and led from start to finish, taking the chequered flag in his Matra by more than four minutes from second placed Graham Hill. It was a truly memorable drive.

1951 Nürburgring

29 July, 456.20km/283.47 miles
1 Alberto Ascari (Ita) Ferrari
2 Juan Manuel Fangio (Arg) Alfa Romeo
3 José Froilán González (Arg) Ferrari
4 Luigi Villoresi (Ita) Ferrari
5 Piero Taruffi (Ita) Ferrari
6 Rudi Fischer (Swi) Ferrari
Winner's speed: 134.80kph/83.76mph
Fastest lap: Fangio 137.83kph/85.64mph
Pole position: Ascari

1952 Nürburgring

3 August, 410.58km/255.12 miles
1 Alberto Ascari (Ita) Ferrari
2 Giuseppe Farina (Ita) Ferrari
3 Rudi Fischer (Swi) Ferrari
4 Piero Taruffi (Ita) Ferrari
5 Jean Behra (Fra) Gordini
6 Roger Laurent (Bel) Ferrari
Winner's speed: 132.29kph/82.20mph
Fastest lap: Ascari 135.71kph/84.33mph
Pole position: Ascari

1953 Nürburgring

2 August, 410.58km/255.12 miles
1 Giuseppe Farina (Ita) Ferrari
2 Juan Manuel Fangio (Arg) Maserati

3 Mike Hawthorn (GB) Ferrari
4 Felice Bonetto (Ita) Maserati
5 Emmanuel de Graffenried (Swi) Maserati
6 Stirling Moss (GB) Cooper-Alta
Winner's speed: 135.05kph/83.91mph
Fastest lap: Alberto Ascari (Ita) Ferrari 137.78kph/85.62mph
Pole position: Ascari

1954 Nürburgring

1 August, 501.82km/311.82 miles
1 Juan Manuel Fangio (Arg) Mercedes-Benz
2 José Froilán González (Arg)/Mike Hawthorn (GB) Ferrari
3 Maurice Trintignant (Fra) Ferrari
4 Karl Kling (FRG) Mercedes-Benz
5 Sergio Mantovani (Ita) Maserati
6 Piero Taruffi (Ita) Ferrari
Winner's speed: 133.37kph/82.87mph
Fastest lap: Kling 137.99kph/85.75mph
Pole position: Fangio

1956 Nürburgring

5 August, 501.82km/311.82 miles
1 Juan Manuel Fangio (Arg) Lancia-Ferrari
2 Stirling Moss (GB) Maserati
3 Jean Behra (Fra) Maserati
4 Francisco Godia (Spa) Maserati
5 Louis Rosier (Fra) Maserati

Only five finished.
Winner's speed: 137.66kph/85.54mph
Fastest lap: Fangio 141.19kph/87.73mph
Pole position: Fangio

1957 Nürburgring

4 August, 501.82km/311.82 miles
1 Juan Manuel Fangio (Arg) Maserati
2 Mike Hawthorn (GB) Lancia-Ferrari
3 Peter Collins (GB) Lancia-Ferrari
4 Luigi Musso (Ita) Lancia-Ferrari
5 Stirling Moss (GB) Vanwall
6 Jean Behra (Fra) Maserati
Winner's speed: 142.95kph/88.82mph
Fastest lap: Fangio 147.32kph/91.54mph
Pole position: Fangio

1958 Nürburgring

3 August, 342.15km/212.60 miles
1 Tony Brooks (GB) Vanwall
2 Roy Salvadori (GB) Cooper-Climax
3 Maurice Trintignant (Fra) Cooper-Climax
4 Wolfgang von Trips (FRG) Ferrari
5 Bruce McLaren (NZ) Cooper-Climax

6 Edgar Barth (GDR) Porsche
*McLaren and Barth did not receive championship points
as they were in the Formula Two race that ran concurrent
with the Formula One Grand Prix.*
Winner's speed: 145.34kph/90.31mph
Fastest lap: Stirling Moss (GB) Vanwall 149.52kph/
92.91mph
Pole position: Mike Hawthorn (GB) Ferrari

1959 Avus

2 August, 498.00km/309.44 miles
1 Tony Brooks (GB) Ferrari
2 Dan Gurney (USA) Ferrari
3 Phil Hill (USA) Ferrari
4 Maurice Trintignant (Fra) Cooper-Climax
5 Jo Bonnier (Swe) BRM
6 Ian Burgess (GB) Cooper-Maserati
Winner's speed: 230.68kph/143.34mph
Fastest lap: Brooks 239.97kph/149.14mph
Pole position: Brooks

1961 Nürburgring

6 August, 342.15km/212.60 miles
1 Stirling Moss (GB) Lotus-Climax

THE GREAT RACES

1957 German GP

It was typical of Juan Manuel Fangio that he should save what is regarded as one of his best ever drives for the the 24th and last win of his career. The great Argentinian's final triumph came over the gruelling Nürburgring circuit on a hot August day in 1957. He knew that victory would give him his fourth successive world title, but at one stage that outcome looked a near impossibility.

There was an air of expectancy about the outcome of the race and, indeed, the championship, when Fangio, driving the powerful and successful Maserati 250F, took pole position. But the early leaders were the Lancia-Ferrari pair of Mike Hawthorn and Peter Collins whose team decided to run the

312-mile race without coming in for fuel or tyre changes. The Maserati team decided otherwise.

Fangio hit the front on the third lap, with 19 laps of the monster German circuit still to cover and by the halfway stage he had gradually pulled away from the two Lancia men but he was then called in for a fuel refill and tyre change. At the time he held a 30 second lead but it took nearly one and a half minutes for his pitmen to carry out their duties and he resumed the race 50 seconds off the lead. He was now poised to engage in one of the greatest pursuits the sport has seen.

Once his tyres had bedded in and his fuel load had started to lighten, he made inroads into the lead held by the two Britons.

With 16 laps completed Fangio had cut the lead to 30 seconds but there was still a lot to do. But he set one lap record after another, and on lap 20 he cut the lap record by a staggering 11 seconds to go into the penultimate lap just two seconds in arrears. There was now a sense of optimism amongst his team and vast army of fans and Fangio had that sweet scent of victory.

He overtook Collins at the Nordkurve on the 21st lap and now had Hawthorn in his sights. Before the lap was out Fangio had regained the lead he lost 10 laps earlier. The near quarter of a million fans went wild as Fangio continued to pull away and won by more than three seconds from Hawthorn to capture his record fifth world title.

2 Wolfgang von Trips (FRG) Ferrari
3 Phil Hill (USA) Ferrari
4 Jim Clark (GB) Lotus-Climax
5 John Surtees (GB) Cooper-Climax
6 Bruce McLaren (NZ) Cooper-Climax
Winner's speed: 148.54kph/92.30mph
Fastest lap: P Hill 152.69kph/94.88mph
Pole position: P Hill

1962 Nürburgring

5 August, 3342.15km/212.60 miles
1 Graham Hill (GB) BRM
2 John Surtees (GB) Lola-Climax
3 Dan Gurney (USA) Porsche
4 Jim Clark (GB) Lotus-Climax
5 Bruce McLaren (NZ) Cooper-Climax
6 Ricardo Rodriguez (Mex) Ferrari
Winner's speed: 129.30kph/80.35mph
Fastest lap: G Hill 134.13kph/83.35mph
Pole position: Gurney

1963 Nürburgring

4 August, 342.15km/212.60 miles
1 John Surtees (GB) Ferrari
2 Jim Clark (GB) Lotus-Climax

3 Richie Ginther (USA) BRM
4 Gerhard Mitter (FRG) Porsche
5 Jim Hall (USA) Lotus-BRM
6 Jo Bonnier (Swe) Cooper-Climax
Winner's speed: 154.22kph/95.83mph
Fastest lap: Surtees 155.82kph/96.82mph
Pole position: Clark

1964 Nürburgring

2 August, 342.15km/212.60 miles
1 John Surtees (GB) Ferrari
2 Graham Hill (GB) BRM
3 Lorenzo Bandini (Ita) Ferrari
4 Jo Siffert (Swi) Brabham-BRM
5 Maurice Trintignant (Fra) BRM
6 Tony Maggs (SAf) BRM
Winner's speed: 155.43kph/96.58mph
Fastest lap: Surtees 158.22kph/98.31mph
Pole position: Surtees

1965 Nürburgring

1 August, 342.15km/212.60 miles
1 Jim Clark (GB) Lotus-Climax
2 Graham Hill (GB) BRM
3 Dan Gurney (USA) Brabham-Climax

THE GREAT RACES

1968
German GP

In 1957 Argentina's Juan Manuel Fangio drove the greatest race of his life to haul back driver after driver and win the German Grand Prix at the Nürburgring. Eleven years later Britain's Jackie Stewart also had one of the greatest races of his life to win at the infamous German circuit. But on this occasion Stewart's race was a personal one beween him and the circuit. Stewart won, and in a style not seen before or since at the 'Ring'.

The old Nürburgring was notorious even in good weather but conditions were atrocious for the 1968 German Grand Prix. Heavy rain caused a one hour delay to the start and even cast doubts as to whether it would be staged at all.

Jackie Stewart started from sixth place on the grid but the rain had posed problems in practice and the grid positions were not a true reflection of that season's championship contenders. Stewart, always an advocate of safety precautions, did not want to race because the 14-mile circuit had rivers of water around it and these were potentially lethal hazards to the drivers. But for the first time in his life Ken Tyrrell made a driver go out and drive. That decision was to be vindicated as Stewart gave the bravest performance of his career.

Stewart's Matra was fitted with Dunlop super-wet tyres and they had the desired effect; the Scot led by nine seconds after the first lap. Not that the spectators knew much about it.

Such was the spray from the cars they had little opportunity to identify the drivers.

With two laps of the 14-lap race gone Stewart was in front by 25 seconds as his rivals failed to get to grips with the conditions. His lead was stretched to a minute after four laps and by the halfway stage it was a clear one and a half minutes. Stewart was showing the rest of the field how the Nürburgring should be treated in such conditions.

Stewart had no other drivers to worry about. All he had to battle with were the elements and his own concentration. But neither proved a problem to him as he went on to win by a massive four minutes. It was surely the finest drive of his 99-race career.

4 Jochen Rindt (Aut) Cooper-Climax
5 Jack Brabham (Aus) Brabham-Climax
6 Lorenzo Bandini (Ita) Ferrari
Winner's speed: 160.54kph/99.76mph
Fastest lap: Clark 162.90kph/101.22mph
Pole position: Clark

1966 Nürburgring

7 August, 342.15km/212.60 miles
1 Jack Brabham (Aus) Brabham-Repco
2 John Surtees (GB) Cooper-Maserati
3 Jochen Rindt (Aut) Cooper-Maserati
4 Graham Hill (GB) BRM
5 Jackie Stewart (GB) BRM
6 Lorenzo Bandini (Ita) Ferrari
Winner's speed: 139.61kph/86.75mph
Fastest lap: Surtees 155.23kph/96.46mph
Pole position: Clark

1967 Nürburgring

6 August, 342.53km/212.84 miles
1 Denny Hulme (NZ) Brabham-Repco
2 Jack Brabham (Aus) Brabham-Repco
3 Chris Amon (NZ) Ferrari
4 John Surtees (GB) Honda
5 Jo Bonnier (Swe) Cooper-Maserati
6 Guy Ligier (Fra) Brabham-Repco
Winner's speed: 163.20kph/101.41mph
Fastest lap: Dan Gurney (USA) Eagle-Weslake 166.04kph/
103.17mph
Pole position: Jim Clark (GB) Lotus-Ford

1968 Nürburgring

4 August, 319.69km/198.65 miles
1 Jackie Stewart (GB) Matra-Ford
2 Graham Hill (GB) Lotus-Ford
3 Jochen Rindt (Aut) Brabham-Repco
4 Jacky Ickx (Bel) Ferrari
5 Jack Brabham (Aus) Brabham-Repco
6 Pedro Rodriguez (Mex) BRM
Winner's speed: 137.94kph/85.71mph
Fastest lap: Stewart 142.72kph/88.68mph
Pole position: Ickx

1969 Nürburgring

3 August, 319.69km/198.65 miles
1 Jacky Ickx (Bel) Brabham-Ford
2 Jackie Stewart (GB) Matra-Ford
3 Bruce McLaren (NZ) McLaren-Ford
4 Graham Hill (GB) Lotus-Ford
5 Jo Siffert (Swi) Lotus-Ford
6 Jean-Pierre Beltoise (Fra) Matra-Ford
Winner's speed: 174.50kph/108.43mph
Fastest lap: Ickx 177.24kph/110.13mph
Pole position: Ickx

1970 Hockenheim

2 August, 339.45km/210.92 miles
1 Jochen Rindt (Aut) Lotus-Ford
2 Jacky Ickx (Bel) Ferrari

3 Denny Hulme (NZ) McLaren-Ford
4 Emerson Fittipaldi (Bra) Lotus-Ford
5 Rolf Stommelen (FRG) Brabham-Ford
6 Henri Pescarolo (Fra) Matra-Simca
Winner's speed: 199.67kph/124.07mph
Fastest lap: Ickx 202.83kph/126.03mph
Pole position: Ickx

1971 Nürburgring

1 August, 274.02km/170.27 miles
1 Jackie Stewart (GB) Tyrrell-Ford
2 François Cevert (Fra) Tyrrell-Ford
3 Clay Regazzoni (Swi) Ferrari
4 Mario Andretti (USA) Ferrari
5 Ronnie Peterson (Swe) March-Ford
6 Tim Schenken (Aus) Brabham-Ford
Winner's speed: 184.19kph/114.45mph
Fastest lap: Cevert 186.79kph/116.07mph
Pole position: Stewart

1972 Nürburgring

30 July, 319.69km/198.65 miles
1 Jacky Ickx (Bel) Ferrari
2 Clay Regazzoni (Swi) Ferrari
3 Ronnie Peterson (Swe) March-Ford
4 Howden Ganley (NZ) BRM
5 Brian Redman (GB) McLaren-Ford
6 Graham Hill (GB) Brabham-Ford
Winner's speed: 187.68kph/116.62mph
Fastest lap: Ickx 189.59kph/117.81mph
Pole position: Ickx

1973 Nürburgring

5 August, 319.69km/198.65 miles
1 Jackie Stewart (GB) Tyrrell-Ford
2 François Cevert (Fra) Tyrrell-Ford
3 Jacky Ickx (Bel) McLaren-Ford
4 Carlos Pace (Bra) Surtees-Ford
5 Wilson Fittipaldi (Bra) Brabham-Ford
6 Emerson Fittipaldi (Bra) Lotus-Ford
Winner's speed: 187.96kph/116.79mph
Fastest lap: Pace 190.56kph/118.41mph
Pole position: Stewart

1974 Nürburgring

4 August, 319.69km/198.65 miles
1 Clay Regazzoni (Swi) Ferrari
2 Jody Scheckter (SAf) Tyrrell-Ford
3 Carlos Reutemann (Arg) Brabham-Ford
4 Ronnie Peterson (Swe) Lotus-Ford
5 Jacky Ickx (Bel) Lotus-Ford
6 Tom Pryce (GB) Shadow-Ford
Winner's speed: 188.83kph/117.33mph
Fastest lap: Scheckter 190.69kph/118.49mph
Pole position: Niki Lauda (Aut) Ferrari

1975 Nürburgring

3 August, 319.69km/198.65 miles
1 Carlos Reutemann (Arg) Brabham-Ford
2 Jacques Laffite (Fra) Williams-Ford

Clay Regazzoni, winner of the 1974 race at the Nürburgring in his Ferrari.

3 Niki Lauda (Aut) Ferrari
4 Tom Pryce (GB) Shadow-Ford
5 Alan Jones (Aus) Hill-Ford
6 Gijs van Lennep (Hol) Ensign-Ford
Winner's speed: 189.47kph/117.73mph
Fastest lap: Clay Regazzoni (Swi) Ferrari 192.79kph/
119.80mph
Pole position: Lauda

1976 Nürburgring

1 August, 319.69km/198.65 miles
1 James Hunt (GB) McLaren-Ford
2 Jody Scheckter (SAf) Tyrrell-Ford
3 Jochen Mass (FRG) McLaren-Ford
4 Carlos Pace (Bra) Brabham-Alfa Romeo
5 Gunnar Nilsson (Swe) Lotus-Ford
6 Rolf Stommelen (FRG) Brabham-Alfa Romeo
Winner's speed: 188.59kph/117.18mph
Fastest lap: Scheckter 190.82kph/118.57mph
Pole position: Hunt

1977 Hockenheim

31 July, 319.08km/198.27 miles
1 Niki Lauda (Aut) Ferrari
2 Jody Scheckter (SAf) Wolf-Ford
3 Hans-Joachim Stuck (FRG) Brabham-Alfa Romeo
4 Carlos Reutemann (Arg) Ferrari
5 Vittorio Brambilla (Ita) Surtees-Ford
6 Patrick Tambay (Fra) Ensign-Ford
Winner's speed: 208.53kph/129.57mph
Fastest lap: Lauda 210.71kph/130.93mph
Pole position: Scheckter

1978 Hockenheim

30 July, 305.51km/189.83 miles
1 Mario Andretti (USA) Lotus-Ford
2 Jody Scheckter (SAf) Wolf-Ford

3 Jacques Laffite (Fra) Ligier-Matra
4 Emerson Fittipaldi (Bra) Fittipaldi-Ford
5 Didier Pironi (Fra) Tyrrell-Ford
6 Hector Rebaque (Mex) Lotus-Ford
Winner's speed: 208.26kph/129.41mph
Fastest lap: Ronnie Peterson (Swe) Lotus-Ford 211.39kph/
131.35mph
Pole position: Andretti

1979 Hockenheim

29 July, 305.51km/189.83 miles
1 Alan Jones (Aus) Williams-Ford
2 Clay Regazzoni (Swi) Williams-Ford
3 Jacques Laffite (Fra) Ligier-Ford
4 Jody Scheckter (SAf) Ferrari
5 John Watson (GB) McLaren-Ford
6 Jochen Mass (FRG) Arrows-Ford
Winner's speed: 216.09kph/134.27mph
Fastest lap: Gilles Villeneuve (Can) Ferrari 218.40kph/
135.71mph
Pole position: Jean-Pierre Jabouille (Fra) Renault

1980 Hockenheim

10 August, 305.51km/189.83 miles
1 Jacques Laffite (Fra) Ligier-Ford
2 Carlos Reutemann (Arg) Williams-Ford
3 Alan Jones (Aus) Williams-Ford
4 Nelson Piquet (Bra) Brabham-Ford
5 Bruno Giacomelli (Ita) Alfa Romeo
6 Gilles Villeneuve (Can) Ferrari
Winner's speed: 220.83kph/137.22mph
Fastest lap: Jones 225.28kph/139.98mph
Pole position: Jones

1981 Hockenheim

2 August, 305.51km/189.83 miles
1 Nelson Piquet (Bra) Brabham-Ford

2 Alain Prost (Fra) Renault
3 Jacques Laffite (Fra) Talbot-Matra
4 Hector Rebaque (Mex) Brabham-Ford
5 Eddie Cheever (USA) Tyrrell-Ford
6 John Watson (GB) McLaren-Ford
Winner's speed: 213.29kph/132.54mph
Fastest lap: Alan Jones (Aus) Williams-Ford 217.37kph/
135.07mph
Pole position: Prost

1982 Hockenheim

8 August, 305.87km/190.06 miles
1 Patrick Tambay (Fra) Ferrari
2 René Arnoux (Fra) Renault
3 Keke Rosberg (Fin) Williams-Ford
4 Michele Alboreto (Ita) Tyrrell-Ford
5 Bruno Giacomelli (Ita) Alfa Romeo
6 Marc Surer (Swi) Arrows-Ford
Winner's speed: 209.93kph/130.43mph
Fastest lap: Nelson Piquet (Bra) Brabham-BMW
214.58kph/133.34mph
Pole position: Didier Pironi (Fra) Ferrari *(did not start)*

1983 Hockenheim

7 August, 305.87km/190.06 miles
1 René Arnoux (Fra) Ferrari
2 Andrea de Cesaris (Ita) Alfa Romeo
3 Riccardo Patrese (Ita) Brabham-BMW
4 Alain Prost (Fra) Renault
5 John Watson (GB) McLaren-Ford
6 Jacques Laffite (Fra) Williams-Ford
*Niki Lauda (Aut) McLaren-Ford finished 5th but was
subsequently disqualified for reversing in the pit lane.*
Winner's speed: 210.52kph/130.82mph
Fastest lap: Arnoux 214.76kph/133.45mph
Pole position: Patrick Tambay (Fra) Ferrari

1984 Hockenheim

5 August, 299.07km/185.83 miles
1 Alain Prost (Fra) McLaren-Porsche
2 Niki Lauda (Aut) McLaren-Porsche
3 Derek Warwick (GB) Renault
4 Nigel Mansell (GB) Lotus-Renault
5 Patrick Tambay (Fra) Renault
6 René Arnoux (Fra) Ferrari
Winner's speed: 211.80kph/131.61mph
Fastest lap: Prost 215.52kph/133.92mph
Pole position: Prost

1985 Nürburgring

4 August, 304.31km/189.09 miles
1 Michele Alboreto (Ita) Ferrari
2 Alain Prost (Fra) McLaren-TAG
3 Jacques Laffite (Fra) Ligier-Renault
4 Thierry Boutsen (Bel) Arrows-BMW
5 Niki Lauda (Aut) McLaren-TAG
6 Nigel Mansell (GB) Williams-Honda
Winner's speed: 191.15kph/118.78mph
Fastest lap: Lauda 197.46kph/122.70mph
Pole position: Teo Fabi (Ita) Toleman-Hart

1986 Hockenheim

27 July, 299.07km/185.83 miles
1 Nelson Piquet (Bra) Williams-Honda
2 Ayrton Senna (Bra) Lotus-Renault
3 Nigel Mansell (GB) Williams-Honda
4 René Arnoux (Fra) Ligier-Renault
5 Keke Rosberg (Fin) McLaren-TAG
6 Alain Prost (Fra) McLaren-TAG
Winner's speed: 218.46kph/135.75mph
Fastest lap: Gerhard Berger (Aut) Benetton-BMW
229.53kph/142.63mph
Pole position: Rosberg

1987 Hockenheim

26 July, 299.07km/185.83 miles
1 Nelson Piquet (Bra) Williams-Honda
2 Stefan Johansson (Swe) McLaren-TAG
3 Ayrton Senna (Bra) Lotus-Honda
4 Philippe Streiff (Fra) Tyrrell-Ford
5 Jonathan Palmer (GB) Tyrrell-Ford
6 Philippe Alliot (Fra) Lola-Ford
Winner's speed: 220.39kph/136.95mph
Fastest lap: Nigel Mansell (GB) Williams-Honda
231.46kph/143.83mph
Pole position: Mansell

1988 Hockenheim

24 July, 299.07km/185.83 miles
1 Ayrton Senna (Bra) McLaren-Honda
2 Alain Prost (Fra) McLaren-Honda
3 Gerhard Berger (Aut) Ferrari
4 Michele Alboreto (Ita) Ferrari
5 Ivan Capelli (Ita) March-Judd
6 Thierry Boutsen (Bel) Benetton-Ford
Winner's speed: 193.15kph/120.02mph
Fastest lap: Alessandro Nannini (Ita) Benetton-Ford
198.89kph/123.58mph
Pole position: Senna

1989 Hockenheim

30 July, 305.87km/190.06 miles
1 Ayrton Senna (Bra) McLaren-Honda
2 Alain Prost (Fra) McLaren-Honda
3 Nigel Mansell (GB) Ferrari
4 Riccardo Patrese (Ita) Williams-Renault
5 Nelson Piquet (Bra) Lotus-Judd
6 Derek Warwick (GB) Arrows-Ford
Winner's speed: 225.87kph/140.35mph
Fastest lap: Senna 232.44kph/144.43mph
Pole position: Senna

1990 Hockenheim

29 July, 306.09km/190.19 miles
1 Ayrton Senna (Bra) McLaren-Honda
2 Alessandro Nannini (Ita) Benetton-Ford
3 Gerhard Berger (Aut) McLaren-Honda
4 Alain Prost (Fra) Ferrari
5 Riccardo Patrese (Ita) Williams-Renault
6 Thierry Boutsen (Bel) Williams-Renault

Winner's speed: 227.33kph/141.26mph
Fastest lap: Boutsen 231.88kph/144.08mph
Pole position: Senna

1991 Hockenheim

28 July, 306.09km/190.19 miles
1 Nigel Mansell (GB) Williams-Renault

2 Riccardo Patrese (Ita) Williams-Renault
3 Jean Alesi (Fra) Ferrari
4 Gerhard Berger (Aut) McLaren-Honda
5 Andrea de Cesaris (Ita) Jordan-Ford
6 Bertrand Gachot (Bel) Jordan-Ford
Winner's speed: 231.03kph/143.55mph
Fastest lap: Patrese 236.43kph/146.91mph
Pole position: Mansell

MOST WINS

Drivers
3 Juan Manuel Fangio, Nelson Piquet,
  Ayrton Senna, Jackie Stewart
2 Alberto Ascari, Tony Brooks, Jacky
  Ickx, John Surtees
Manufacturers
12 Ferrari
 5 Brabham, McLaren
 4 Lotus, Williams
 2 Tyrrell

MOST FASTEST LAPS

Drivers
3 Juan Manuel Fangio, Jacky Ickx
2 Alberto Ascari, Alan Jones, Niki
  Lauda, Nigel Mansell, Jody
  Scheckter, John Surtees
Manufacturers
12 Ferrari
 5 Williams
 3 Brabham, McLaren, Tyrrell
 2 Benetton, Lotus

MOST POLE POSITIONS

Drivers
4 Jacky Ickx
3 Alberto Ascari, Jim Clark, Juan
  Manuel Fangio, Ayrton Senna
2 Jack Brabham, Niki Lauda, Nigel
  Mansell, Alain Prost, Jackie Stewart
Manufacturers
14 Ferrari
 6 McLaren
 4 Lotus
 3 Williams
 2 Brabham, Renault, Tyrrell

HUNGARIAN GP

All races at the Hungaroring, Budapest

When the Grand Prix circus came to Budapest in 1986 it was the first time it had gone to an Iron Curtain country. The Hungaroring is a purpose built track north-east of Budapest and its many corners provide a demanding test for the drivers. They were full of praise for the new circuit and it was voted Course of the Year after its debut season.

1986

10 August, 305.06km/189.56 miles
1 Nelson Piquet (Bra) Williams-Honda
2 Ayrton Senna (Bra) Lotus-Renault
3 Nigel Mansell (GB) Williams-Honda
4 Stefan Johansson (Swe) Ferrari
5 Johnny Dumfries (GB) Lotus-Renault
6 Martin Brundle (GB) Tyrrell-Renault
Winner's speed: 151.81kph/94.33mph
Fastest lap: Piquet 158.79kph/98.67mph
Pole position: Senna

1987

9 August, 305.06km/189.56 miles
1 Nelson Piquet (Bra) Williams-Honda
2 Ayrton Senna (Bra) Lotus-Honda
3 Alain Prost (Fra) Mclaren-TAG
4 Thierry Boutsen (Bel) Benetton-Ford
5 Riccardo Patrese (Ita) Brabham-BMW
6 Derek Warwick (GB) Arrows-Megatron
Winner's speed: 153.24kph/95.22mph
Fastest lap: Piquet 160.30kph/99.60mph
Pole position: Nigel Mansell (GB) Williams-Honda

1988

7 August, 305.06km/189.56 miles
1 Ayrton Senna (Bra) McLaren-Honda
2 Alain Prost (Fra) McLaren-Honda
3 Thierry Boutsen (Bel) Benetton-Ford
4 Gerhard Berger (Aut) Ferrari
5 Mauricio Gugelmin (Bra) March-Judd
6 Riccardo Patrese (Ita) Williams-Judd
Winner's speed: 155.40kph/96.56mph
Fastest lap: Prost 159.43kph/99.06mph
Pole position: Senna

1989

13 August, 305/54km/189.85 miles
1 Nigel Mansell (GB) Ferrari
2 Ayrton Senna (Bra) McLaren-Honda
3 Thierry Boutsen (Bel) Williams-Renault
4 Alain Prost (Fra) McLaren-Honda
5 Eddie Cheever (USA) Arrows-Ford
6 Nelson Piquet (Bra) Lotus-Judd
Winner's speed: 167.20kph/104.50mph
Fastest lap: Mansell 108.04mph/172.86kph
Pole position: Riccardo Patrese (Ita) Williams-Renault

1990

12 August, 305.54km/189.85 miles
1 Thierry Boutsen (Bel) Williams-Renault
2 Ayrton Senna (Bra) McLaren-Honda
3 Nelson Piquet (Bra) Benetton-Ford
4 Riccardo Patrese (Ita) Williams-Renault
5 Derek Warwick (GB) Lotus-Lamborghini
6 Eric Bernard (Fra) Lola-Lamborghini
Winner's speed: 167.40kph/104.02mph
Fastest lap: Patrese 174.08kph/108.17mph
Pole position: Boutsen

1991

11 August, 305.54km/189.85 miles
1 Ayrton Senna (Bra) McLaren-Honda
2 Nigel Mansell (GB) Williams-Renault
3 Riccardo Patrese (Ita) Williams-Renault
4 Gerhard Berger (Aut) McLaren-Honda
5 Jean Alesi (Fra) Ferrari
6 Ivan Capelli (Ita) Leyton House-Ilmor
Winner's speed: 168.84kph/104.91mph
Fastest lap: Bertrand Gachot (Bel) Jordan-Ford
176.20kph/109.48mph
Pole position: Senna

MOST WINS

Drivers
2 Nelson Piquet, Ayrton Senna
Manufacturers
3 Williams
2 McLaren

MOST FASTEST LAPS

Drivers
2 Nelson Piquet
Manufacturers
3 Williams

MOST POLE POSITIONS

Drivers
3 Ayrton Senna
Manufacturers
3 Williams
2 McLaren

INDIANAPOLIS 500

All drivers listed are from the US. All races at the Indianapolis Raceway on 30 May over 500 miles/804.67km, except the 1950 race which was over the reduced distance of 345 miles/555.22km.

The Indianapolis 500 has a long history, dating back to 1911 when Ray Harroun won the inaugural 500-mile race over 'The Brickyard' in a Marmon Wasp at 120.02kph/74.59 mph.

The 2.5 mile oval-shaped circuit was nicknamed the Brickyard because the original circuit was made out of thousands of bricks. Held annually at the end of May as part of the Memorial Day celebrations, it formed part of the Formula One World Championship from 1950 to 1960 but its presence rarely attracted European drivers, Alberto Ascari being the odd exception. The race clashed with European races and the drivers were happier to stay on 'home' soil.

The race was therefore dominated during its time as a World Championship race by Americans, who not only won every race but claimed every World Championship point that was available.

1950

1 Johnnie Parsons, Kurtis Kraft-Offenhauser
2 Bill Holland, Deidt-Offenhauser
3 Mauri Rose, Deidt-Offenhauser
4 Cecil Green, KK-Offenhauser
5 Joie Chitwood/Tony Bettenhausen, KK-Offenhauser
6 Lee Wallard, Moore-Offenhauser
Winner's speed: 199.56kph/124.00mph
Fastest lap: Holland 207.60kph/129.00mph
Pole position: Walt Faulkner, Kurtis Kraft-Offenhauser

1951

1 Lee Wallard, Kurtis Kraft-Offenhauser
2 Mike Nazaruk, Kurtis Kraft-Offenhauser
3 Jack McGrath/Manny Ayulo, KK-Offenhauser
4 Andy Linden, Sherman-Offenhauser
5 Bobby Ball, Schroeder-Offenhauser

6 Henry Banks, Moore-Offenhauser
Winner's speed: 203.16kph/126.24mph
Fastest lap: Wallard 215.34kph/133.81mph
Pole position: Duke Nalon, Kurtis Kraft-Novi

1952

1 Troy Ruttman, Kuzma-Offenhauser
2 Jim Rathmann, KK-Offenhauser
3 Sam Hanks, KK-Offenhauser
4 Duane Carter, Lesovsky-Offenhauser
5 Art Cross, KK-Offenhauser
6 Jimmy Bryan, KK-Offenhauser
Winner's speed: 207.43kph/128.92mph
Fastest lap: Bill Vukovich, KK-Offenhauser 217.48kph/135.14mph
Pole position: Freddie Agabashian, Kurtis Kraft-Cummins

1953

1 Bill Vukovich, KK-Offenhauser
2 Art Cross, KK-Offenhauser
3 Sam Hanks/Duane Carter, KK-Offenhauser
4 Freddie Agabashian/Paul Russo, KK-Offenhauser
5 Jack McGrath, KK-Offenhauser
6 Jimmy Daywalt, KK-Offenhauser
Winner's speed: 207.18kph/128.92mph
Fastest lap: Vukovich 218.65kph/135.87mph
Pole position: Vukovich

1954

1 Bill Vukovich, KK-Offenhauser
2 Jimmy Bryan, Kuzma-Offenhauser
3 Jack McGrath, KK-Offenhauser
4 Troy Ruttman/Duane Carter, KK-Offenhauser
5 Mike Nazaruk, KK-Offenhauser
6 Freddie Agabashian, KK-Offenhauser
Winner's speed: 210.56kph/130.84mph
Fastest lap: McGrath 226.16kph/140.54mph
Pole position: McGrath

1955

1 Bob Sweikert, KK-Offenhauser
2 Tony Bettenhausen/Paul Russo, KK-Offenhauser
3 Jimmy Davies, KK-Offenhauser
4 Johnny Thomson, Kuzma-Offenhauser
5 Walt Faulkner/Bill Homeier, KK-Offenhauser
6 Andy Linden, KK-Offenhauser
Winner's speed: 206.33kph/128.21mph
Fastest lap: Bill Vukovich, KK-Offenhauser 227.48kph/
141.35mph
Pole position: Jerry Hoyt, Stevens-Offenhauser

1956

1 Pat Flaherty, Watson-Offenhauser
2 Sam Hanks, KK-Offenhauser
3 Don Freeland, Phillips-Offenhauser
4 Johnnie Parsons, Kuzma-Offenhauser
5 Dick Rathmann, KK-Offenhauser
6 Bob Sweikert, Kuzma-Offenhauser
Winner's speed: 206.78kph/128.49mph
Fastest lap: Paul Russo, Kurtis Kraft-Novi 232.41kph/
144.42mph
Pole position: Flaherty

1957

1 Sam Hanks, Epperly-Offenhauser
2 Jim Rathmann, Epperly-Offenhauser
3 Jimmy Bryan, Kuzma-Offenhauser
4 Paul Russo, Kurtis Kraft-Novi
5 Andy Linden, KK-Offenhauser
6 Johnny Boyd, KK-Offenhauser
Winner's speed: 218.22kph/135.60mph
Fastest lap: Rathmann 230.81kph/143.43mph
Pole position: Pat O'Connor, KK-Offenhauser

1958

1 Jimmy Bryan, Epperly-Offenhauser
2 George Amick, Epperly-Offenhauser
3 Johnny Boyd, KK-Offenhauser
4 Tony Bettenhausen, Epperly-Offenhauser
5 Jim Rathmann, Epperly-Offenhauser
6 Jimmy Reece, Watson-Offenhauser
Winner's speed: 215.31kph/133.79mph
Fastest lap: Bettenhausen 232.22kph/144.30mph
Pole position: Dick Rathmann, Watson-Offenhauser

1959

1 Rodger Ward, Watson-Offenhauser
2 Jim Rathmann, Watson-Offenhauser
3 Johnny Thomson, Lesovsky-Offenhauser
4 Tony Bettenhausen, Epperly-Offenhauser
5 Paul Goldsmith, Epperly-Offenhauser
6 Johnny Boyd, Epperly-Offenhauser
Winner's speed: 218.64kph/135.86mph
Fastest lap: Thomson 234.02kph/145.42mph
Pole position: Thomson

1960

1 Jim Rathmann, Watson-Offenhauser
2 Rodger Ward, Watson-Offenhauser
3 Paul Goldsmith, Epperly-Offenhauser
4 Don Branson, Phillips-Offenhauser
5 Johnny Thomson, Lesovsky-Offenhauser
6 Eddie Johnson, Trevis-Offenhauser
Winner's speed: 223.32kph/138.77mph
Fastest lap: Rathmann 235.16kph/146.13mph
Pole position: Eddie Sachs, Ewing-Offenhauser

MOST WINS

Drivers
2 Bill Vukovich
Manufacturers
3 KK, Watson
2 Epperly, Kurtis Kraft

MOST FASTEST LAPS

Drivers
3 Bill Vukovich
2 Jim Rathmann
Manufacturers
4 KK
2 Epperly, Kurtis Kraft

MOST POLE POSITIONS

Drivers
No driver was in pole position more
than once
Manufacturers
4 KK
2 Kurtis Kraft, Watson

ITALIAN GP

All races at Monza except 1980

The Monza circuit, home of the Italian Grand Prix, has witnessed some of the fastest ever Formula One races; indeed, the 1971 Grand Prix, won by Peter Gethin in a BRM at 242.62kph/150.75mph, is *the* fastest ever World Championship race.

Along with the British Grand Prix it is the only race to have formed a World Championship round every year since the launch of the championship in 1950. Every Italian Grand Prix bar one has been held at the Monza circuit on the outskirts of Milan which can boast more World Championship Grands Prix than any other. A purpose-built track, also utilising adjacent roads, the Monza autodrome was built in 1922 and staged the second Italian Grand Prix that year (Brescia, a year earlier, was the venue for the first race).

Being the fastest Grand Prix circuit inevitably means that Monza has claimed more than its share of lives over the years and in 1933 three drivers, including Giuseppe Campari, lost their lives on one day. The Italian hero Alberto Ascari was killed at Monza while practising in a Ferrari sports car. Wolfgang von Trips was deprived of World Championship glory in 1961 when he died at Monza. His accident also resulted in the death of 15 spectators. The 1970 posthumous world champion Jochen Rindt died at Monza as did Ronnie Peterson, the popular Swedish driver.

But the vast army of race fans who pack into the Monza circuit each year have been treated to some memorable moments, not just those of disaster and tragedy. In 1967 they saw John Surtees snatch victory from Jack Brabham by a mere two tenths of a second. For Surtees it was his sixth and last Grand Prix success. For Honda, it was their first. But for sheer excitement the 1971 Italian Grand Prix must go down as the best race ever, with six tenths of a second separating the winner Peter Gethin and the fifth placed Howden Ganley of New Zealand! It was Gethin's only Grand Prix success, but what a race to claim it in.

The only other circuit to stage the Italian Grand Prix is the Imola circuit near Bologna. However, it is still used for Formula One racing because it is the home of the San Marino Grand Prix.

1950

3 September, 504.00km/313.17 miles
1 Giuseppe Farina (Ita) Alfa Romeo
2 Dorino Serafini (Ita)/Alberto Ascari (Ita) Ferrari
3 Luigi Fagioli (Ita) Alfa Romeo
4 Louis Rosier (Fra) Lago-Talbot
5 Philippe Etancelin (Fra) Lago-Talbot
6 Emmanuel de Graffenried (Swi) Maserati
Winner's speed: 176.43kph/109.63mph
Fastest lap: Juan Manuel Fangio (Arg) Alfa Romeo 189.00kph/117.44mph
Pole position: Fangio

1951

16 September, 504.00km/313.17 miles
1 Alberto Ascari (Ita) Ferrari
2 José Froilán González (Arg) Ferrari
3 Giuseppe Farina (Ita) /Felice Bonetto (Ita)Alfa Romeo
4 Luigi Villoresi (Ita) Ferrari
5 Piero Taruffi (Ita) Ferrari
6 André Simon (Fra) Simca-Gordini
Winner's speed: 185.92kph/115.53mph
Fastest lap: Farina 195.52kph/121.49mph
Pole position: Juan Manuel Fangio (Arg) Alfa Romeo

1952

7 September, 504.00km/313.17 miles
1 Alberto Ascari (Ita) Ferrari
2 José Froilán González (Arg) Maserati
3 Luigi Villoresi (Ita) Ferrari
4 Giuseppe Farina (Ita) Ferrari
5 Felice Bonetto (Ita) Maserati
6 André Simon (Fra) Ferrari
Winner's speed: 176.67kph/109.80mph
Fastest lap: Ascari & González 179.86kph/111.76mph
Pole position: Ascari

1953

13 September, 504.00km/313.17 miles
1 Juan Manuel Fangio (Arg) Maserati
2 Giuseppe Farina (Ita) Ferrari
3 Luigi Villoresi (Ita) Ferrari
4 Mike Hawthorn (GB) Ferrari
5 Maurice Trintignant (Fra) Gordini
6 Roberto Mieres (Arg) Gordini
Winner's speed: 178.13kph/110.69mph
Fastest lap: Fangio 182.17kph/113.20mph
Pole position: Alberto Ascari (Ita) Ferrari

1954

5 September, 504.00km/313.17 miles
1 Juan Manuel Fangio (Arg) Mercedes-Benz
2 Mike Hawthorn (GB) Ferrari
3 José Froilán González (Arg)/Umberto Maglioli (Ita) Ferrari
4 Hans Herrmann (FRG) Mercedes-Benz
5 Maurice Trintignant (Fra) Ferrari

6 Fred Wacker (USA) Gordini
Winner's speed: 180.21kph/111.98mph
Fastest lap: Gonzalez 187.75kph/116.66mph
Pole position: Fangio

1955

11 September, 500.00km/310.69 miles
1 Juan Manuel Fangio (Arg) Mercedes-Benz
2 Piero Taruffi (Ita) Mercedes-Benz
3 Eugenio Castellotti (Ita) Ferrari
4 Jean Behra (Fra) Maserati
5 Carlos Menditeguy (Arg) Maserati
6 Umberto Maglioli (Ita) Ferrari
Winner's speed: 206.79kph/128.49mph
Fastest lap: Stirling Moss (GB) Mercedes-Benz 215.70kph/
134.03mph
Pole position: Fangio

1956

2 September, 500.00km/310.69 miles
1 Stirling Moss (GB) Maserati
2 Peter Collins (GB)/Juan Manuel Fangio (Arg) Lancia-
Ferrari
3 Ron Flockhart (GB) Connaught
4 Francisco Godia (Spa) Maserati
5 Jack Fairman (GB) Connaught
6 Luigi Piotti (Ita) Maserati
Winner's speed: 208.79kph/129.73mph
Fastest lap: Moss 217.92kph/135.41mph
Pole position: Fangio

1957

8 September, 500.25km/310.84 miles
1 Stirling Moss (GB) Vanwall
2 Juan Manuel Fangio (Arg) Maserati
3 Wolfgang von Trips (FRG) Lancia-Ferrari
4 Masten Gregory (USA) Maserati
5 Giorgio Scarlatti (Ita)/Harry Schell (USA) Maserati
6 Mike Hawthorn (GB) Lancia-Ferrari
Winner's speed: 193.56kph/120.27mph
Fastest lap: Tony Brooks (GB) Vanwall 199.61kph/
124.03mph
Pole position: Stuart Lewis-Evans (GB) Vanwall

1958

7 September, 402.50km/250.10 miles
1 Tony Brooks (GB) Vanwall
2 Mike Hawthorn (GB) Ferrari
3 Phil Hill (USA) Ferrari
4 Masten Gregory (USA)/Carroll Shelby (USA) Maserati
5 Roy Salvadori (GB) Cooper-Climax
6 Graham Hill (GB) Lotus-Climax
*Gregory and Shelby received no points because of a
shared drive.*
Winner's speed: 195.08kph/121.22mph
Fastest lap: P Hill 201.17kph/125.00mph
Pole position: Stirling Moss (GB) Vanwall

1959

13 September, 414.00km/257.25 miles

1 Stirling Moss (GB) Cooper-Climax
2 Phil Hill (USA) Ferrari
3 Jack Brabham (Aus) Cooper-Climax
4 Dan Gurney (USA) Ferrari
5 Cliff Allison (GB) Ferrari
6 Olivier Gendebien (Bel) Ferrari
Winner's speed: 200.18kph/124.38mph
Fastest lap: P Hill 206.18kph/128.11mph
Pole position: Moss

1960

4 September, 500.00km/310.69 miles
1 Phil Hill (USA) Ferrari
2 Richie Ginther (USA) Ferrari
3 Willy Mairesse (Bel) Ferrari
4 Giulio Cabianca (Ita) Cooper-Castellotti
5 Wolfgang von Trips (FRG) Ferrari
6 Hans Herrmann (FRG) Porsche
*Due to a boycott of the race by British teams, Formula
Two cars were allowed to compete to make up the
numbers. Consequently, the Porsche driven by Herrmann
was not eligible for the constructors' championship.*
Winner's speed: 212.51kph/132.06mph
Fastest lap: P Hill 220.05kph/136.73mph
Pole position: P Hill

1961

10 September, 430.00km/267.19 miles
1 Phil Hill (USA) Ferrari
2 Dan Gurney (USA) Porsche
3 Bruce McLaren (NZ) Cooper-Climax
4 Jack Lewis (GB) Cooper-Climax
5 Tony Brooks (GB) BRM-Climax
6 Roy Salvadori (GB) Cooper-Climax
Winner's speed: 209.39kph/130.11mph
Fastest lap: Giancarlo Baghetti (Ita) Ferrari 213.78kph/
132.83mph
Pole position: Wolfgang von Trips (FRG) Ferrari

1962

16 September, 494.50km/307.27 miles
1 Graham Hill (GB) BRM
2 Richie Ginther (USA) BRM
3 Bruce McLaren (NZ) Cooper-Climax
4 Willy Mairesse (Bel) Ferrari
5 Giancarlo Baghetti (Ita) Ferrari
6 Jo Bonnier (Swe) Porsche
Winner's speed: 198.94kph/123.62mph
Fastest lap: G Hill 202.32kph/125.73mph
Pole position: Jim Clark (GB) Lotus-Climax

1963

8 September, 494.50km/307.27 miles
1 Jim Clark (GB) Lotus-Climax
2 Richie Ginther (USA) BRM
3 Bruce McLaren (NZ) Cooper-Climax
4 Innes Ireland (GB) BRP-BRM
5 Jack Brabham (Aus) Brabham-Climax
6 Tony Maggs (SAf) Cooper-Climax
Winner's speed: 205.58kph/127.74mph
Fastest lap: Clark 209.30kph/130.05mph
Pole position: John Surtees (GB) Ferrari

1964

6 September, 448.50km/278.69 miles
1 John Surtees (GB) Ferrari
2 Bruce McLaren (NZ) Cooper-Climax
3 Lorenzo Bandini (Ita) Ferrari
4 Richie Ginther (USA) BRM
5 Innes Ireland (GB) BRP-BRM
6 Mike Spence (GB) Lotus-Climax
Winner's speed: 205.63kph/127.78mph
Fastest lap: Surtees 209.51kph/130.19mph
Pole position: Surtees

1965

12 September, 437.00km/271.54 miles
1 Jackie Stewart (GB) BRM
2 Graham Hill (GB) BRM
3 Dan Gurney (USA) Brabham-Climax
4 Lorenzo Bandini (Ita) Ferrari

5 Bruce McLaren (NZ) Cooper-Climax
6 Dick Attwood (GB) Lotus-BRM
Winner's speed: 209.96kph/130.46mph
Fastest lap: Jim Clark (GB) Lotus-Climax 214.73kph/
133.43mph
Pole position: Clark

1966

4 September, 391.00km/242.96 miles
1 Ludovico Scarfiotti (Ita) Ferrari
2 Mike Parkes (GB) Ferrari
3 Denny Hulme (NZ) Brabham-Repco
4 Jochen Rindt (Aut) Cooper-Maserati
5 Mike Spence (GB) Lotus-BRM
6 Bob Anderson (GB) Brabham-Climax
Winner's speed: 218.75kph/135.92mph
Fastest lap: Scarfiotti 224.03kph/139.20mph
Pole position: Parkes

HE GREAT RACES

1967
Italian GP

The 1967 Italian Grand Prix at Monza is memorable not because it was about a winner, or even a runner-up. It is memorable because of the way the third-placed man drove. That man was the great Scottish driver Jim Clark, who drove the race of his life.

Clark started from pole position but in a farcical start Jack Brabham inadvertently 'jumped the gun' and took an early lead. The race was allowed to continue and Clark set off in pursuit of first the Australian and then his own Lotus teammate Graham Hill. And on lap five the Scot duly went past Hill to take the lead.

He lost the lead on lap nine to Denny Hulme, but the New Zealander's lead was short-lived as Clark soon regained it. The Scot then had to pull into the pits on lap 13 because of a tyre problem. The stop took over a minute and when he rejoined the race it was in 15th position. The only man behind him was

Jackie Stewart, who was having mechanical problems. Stewart last and Clark next to last . . . that must have been one of motor racing's rarest sights. But despite his position, Clark set about catching the front runners.

Having completed 25 of the 68 laps Clark had at last got back onto the same lap as the leaders, and at the halfway stage he was in seventh place and rapidly moving up the field. At three-quarter distance he overtook Jochen Rindt and moved into fourth place. Suddenly a remarkable victory was not being ruled out.

Clark caught John Surtees in the new Honda RA300 and took third place, and then almost immediately found himself in second place because Graham Hill was forced out of the race with engine trouble to his Lotus. Two laps later, to the delight of the large crowd, Clark slipped past Jack Brabham and into the lead, and as he had been gaining on each lap there was nothing to

suggest that Clark would not go on to register a sensational victory.

Brabham now dropped out of the chase and Surtees went back into second place but he never looked like catching the brilliant Scot. But all of a sudden Clark's Lotus started having problems; the fuel wasn't getting through properly. He was clearly in trouble.

Despite his problems Clark still led, albeit by just two seconds at the start of the last lap, but Surtees and Brabham knew they had been given a piece of saving grace and as they reached Lesmos they both went past the Lotus and its desperately unfortunate driver. Brabham and Surtees then battled it out for the finish line with the Honda taking it by just two tenths of a second but the race is not remembered for the finish; it is remembered for the way Jim Clark took on and beat the field until finally losing out to mechanical problems.

1967

10 September, 391.00km/242.96 miles
1 John Surtees (GB) Honda
2 Jack Brabham (Aus) Brabham-Repco
3 Jim Clark (GB) Lotus-Ford
4 Jochen Rindt (Aut) Cooper-Maserati
5 Mike Spence (GB) BRM
6 Jacky Ickx (Bel) Cooper-Maserati
Winner's speed: 226.12kph/140.50mph
Fastest lap: Clark 233.90kph/145.34mph
Pole position: Clark

1968

8 September, 391.00km/242.96 miles
1 Denny Hulme (NZ) McLaren-Ford
2 Johnny Servoz-Gavin (Fra) Matra-Ford
3 Jacky Ickx (Bel) Ferrari
4 Piers Courage (GB) BRM
5 Jean-Pierre Beltoise (Fra) Matra
6 Jo Bonnier (Swe) McLaren-BRM
Winner's speed: 234.02kph/145.41mph
Fastest lap: Jackie Oliver (GB) Lotus-Ford 239.31kph/
148.70mph
Pole position: John Surtees (GB) Honda

1969

7 September, 391.00km/242.96 miles
1 Jackie Stewart (GB) Matra-Ford
2 Jochen Rindt (Aut) Lotus-Ford
3 Jean-Pierre Beltoise (Fra) Matra-Ford
4 Bruce McLaren (NZ) McLaren-Ford
5 Piers Courage (GB) Brabham-Ford
6 Pedro Rodriguez (Mex) Ferrari
Winner's speed: 236.52kph/146.97mph
Fastest lap: Beltoise 242.96kph/150.97mph
Pole position: Rindt

1970

6 September, 391.00km/242.96 miles
1 Clay Regazzoni (Swi) Ferrari
2 Jackie Stewart (GB) March-Ford
3 Jean-Pierre Beltoise (Fra) Matra-Simca
4 Denny Hulme (NZ) McLaren-Ford
5 Rolf Stommelen (FRG) Brabham-Ford
6 François Cevert (Fra) March-Ford
Winner's speed: 236.70kph/147.08mph
Fastest lap: Regazzoni 242.96kph/150.97mph
Pole position: Jacky Ickx (Bel) Ferrari

1971

5 September, 316.25km/196.51 miles
1 Peter Gethin (GB) BRM
2 Ronnie Peterson (Swe) March-Ford
3 François Cevert (Fra) Tyrrell-Ford
4 Mike Hailwood (GB) Surtees-Ford
5 Howden Ganley (NZ) BRM
6 Chris Amon (NZ) Matra-Simca
Winner's speed: 242.62kph/150.75mph
Fastest lap: Henri Pescarolo (Fra) March-Ford 247.02kph/
153.49mph
Pole position: Amon

1972

10 September, 317.63km/197.36 miles
1 Emerson Fittipaldi (Bra) Lotus-Ford
2 Mike Hailwood (GB) Surtees-Ford
3 Denny Hulme (NZ) McLaren-Ford
4 Peter Revson (USA) McLaren-Ford
5 Graham Hill (GB) Brabham-Ford
6 Peter Gethin (GB) BRM
Winner's speed: 211.81kph/131.61mph
Fastest lap: Jacky Ickx (Bel) Ferrari 215.89kph/134.15mph
Pole position: Ickx

1973

9 September, 317.63km/197.36 miles
1 Ronnie Peterson (Swe) Lotus-Ford
2 Emerson Fittipaldi (Bra) Lotus-Ford
3 Peter Revson (USA) McLaren-Ford
4 Jackie Stewart (GB) Tyrrell-Ford
5 François Cevert (Fra) Tyrrell-Ford
6 Carlos Reutemann (Arg) Brabham-Ford
Winner's speed: 213.45kph/132.63mph
Fastest lap: Stewart 218.15kph/135.55mph
Pole position: Peterson

1974

8 September, 300.56km/186.76 miles
1 Ronnie Peterson (Swe) Lotus-Ford
2 Emerson Fittipaldi (Bra) McLaren-Ford
3 Jody Scheckter (SAf) Tyrrell-Ford
4 Arturo Merzario (Ita) Williams-Ford
5 Carlos Pace (Bra) Brabham-Ford
6 Denny Hulme (NZ) McLaren-Ford
Winner's speed: 217.42kph/135.10mph
Fastest lap: Pace 220.89kph/137.26mph
Pole position: Niki Lauda (Aut) Ferrari

1975

7 September, 300.56km/186.76 miles
1 Clay Regazzoni (Swi) Ferrari
2 Emerson Fittipaldi (Bra) McLaren-Ford
3 Niki Lauda (Aut) Ferrari
4 Carlos Reutemann (Arg) Brabham-Ford
5 James Hunt (GB) Hesketh-Ford
6 Tom Pryce (GB) Shadow-Ford
Winner's speed: 218.03kph/135.48mph
Fastest lap: Regazzoni 223.50kph/138.88mph
Pole position: Lauda

1976

12 September, 301.60km/187.41 miles
1 Ronnie Peterson (Swe) March-Ford
2 Clay Regazzoni (Swi) Ferrari
3 Jacques Laffite (Fra) Ligier-Matra
4 Niki Lauda (Aut) Ferrari
5 Jody Scheckter (SAf) Tyrrell-Ford
6 Patrick Depailler (Fra) Tyrrell-Ford
Winner's speed: 199.75kph/124.12mph
Fastest lap: Peterson 206.12kph/128.08mph
Pole position: Laffite

HE GREAT RACES

1971
Italian GP

Monza has seen some great moments during its time and has been graced with the finest drivers and machines that the world of Formula One has seen. But on 5 September 1971 not even the traditionally over-enthusiastic Italian fans could have dreamed up a race like that year's Italian Grand Prix. It was sheer storybook material.

Not only did the race become – and it still is – the fastest Grand Prix of all time, it was also the closest race ever with 61 hundredths of a second separating the first five drivers across the line.

Chris Amon in the Matra-Simca and Jacky Ickx in the Ferrari occupied the front row of the grid and they were followed by the BRM pair of Jo Siffert and Howden Ganley. But the early pace was set by Ickx's team-mate Clay Regazzoni though he soon lost his lead and it was an ever-changing situation at the top of the leaderboard with Ronnie Peterson, Peter Gethin, Jackie Stewart, François Cevert, Siffert and Ickx all sharing the spoils, but with Peterson's March at the head of the field more often than his rivals.

The race was over 55 laps and after 16 of them two of the contenders, Ickx and Stewart, were out of the race with mechanical problems. Another one-time leader, Regazzoni, was also forced out with engine trouble. But at the front of the field, Cevert and Peterson had been joined by Mike Hailwood as the lead, again, kept changing hands.

Siffert led at the halfway mark but then had problems with his gearbox and dropped down the field. It was as close as ever at the front with Peterson, Cevert and Hailwood still setting the pace. But now Chris Amon entered the fray and on lap 37 he took the lead and held it for ten laps. For the first time this amazing race seemed to have a likely winner.

But Amon, in attempting to remove one of his visors, had problems when it all came away. This lapse cost him dear and in no time he went from first to

sixth. In front of Amon at that stage were Peterson, Hailwood, Cevert, Gethin and Ganley. Just two seconds separated them, and they soon left Amon trailing. The race for the chequered flag was now between these five.

Gethin went into the lead three laps from home but the outcome was far from decided. Cevert led the other four through the Parabolica for the last time. But he then braked late and Peterson took the lead. *He* then went too wide and allowed Cevert and Gethin to pass on the inside, and with a slight burst of power Gethin managed to get the nose of his BRM over the finish-line first for the one and only Grand Prix win of his career. His winning speed of 242.62kph/150.75mph is the fastest ever recorded in a World Championship Grand Prix, but the next four men across the line must also take credit for making the 1971 Italian Grand Prix the closest ever.

This is how far the other four finished behind the winner, Peter Gethin:

Pos.	Driver (Car)	Time
2nd	Ronnie Peterson (March-Ford)	0.01 sec
3rd	François Cevert (Tyrrell-Ford)	0.09 sec
4th	Mike Hailwood (Surtees-Ford)	0.18 sec
5th	Howden Ganley (BRM)	0.61 sec

1977

11 September, 301.60km/187.41 miles
1 Mario Andretti (USA) Lotus-Ford
2 Niki Lauda (Aut) Ferrari
3 Alan Jones (Aus) Shadow-Ford
4 Jochen Mass (FRG) McLaren-Ford
5 Clay Regazzoni (Swi) Ensign-Ford
6 Ronnie Peterson (Swe) Tyrrell-Ford
Winner's speed: 206.02kph/128.01mph
Fastest lap: Andretti 210.70kph/130.92mph
Pole position: James Hunt (GB) McLaren-Ford

1978

10 September, 232.00km/144.16 miles
1 Niki Lauda (Aut) Brabham-Alfa Romeo
2 John Watson (GB) Brabham-Alfa Romeo
3 Carlos Reutemann (Arg) Ferrari
4 Jacques Laffite (Fra) Ligier-Matra
5 Patrick Tambay (Fra) McLaren-Ford
6 Mario Andretti (USA) Lotus-Ford
Mario Andretti finished 1st but was penalised one minute
for jumping the start and placed 6th. Gilles Villeneuve was
also penalised one minute for jumping the start. He

finished 2nd but was classified 7th.
Winner's speed: 207.52kph/128.95mph
Fastest lap: Andretti 212.56kph/132.08mph
Pole position: Andretti

1979

9 September, 290.00km/180.20 miles
1 Jody Scheckter (SAf) Ferrari
2 Gilles Villeneuve (Can) Ferrari
3 Clay Regazzoni (Swi) Williams-Ford
4 Niki Lauda (Aut) Brabham-Alfa Romeo
5 Mario Andretti (USA) Lotus-Ford
6 Jean-Pierre Jarier (Fra) Tyrrell-Ford
Winner's speed: 212.19kph/131.85mph
Fastest lap: Regazzoni 218.41kph/135.71mph
Pole position: Jean-Pierre Jabouille (Fra) Renault

1980 Imola

14 September, 300.00km/186.41 miles
1 Nelson Piquet (Bra) Brabham-Ford
2 Alan Jones (Aus) Williams-Ford
3 Carlos Reutemann (Arg) Williams-Ford
4 Elio de Angelis (Ita) Lotus-Ford
5 Keke Rosberg (Fin) Fittipaldi-Ford
6 Didier Pironi (Fra) Ligier-Ford
Winner's speed: 183.44kph/113.98mph
Fastest lap: Jones 187.33kph/116.40mph
Pole position: René Arnoux (Fra) Renault

1981

13 September, 301.60km/187.41 miles
1 Alain Prost (Fra) Renault
2 Alan Jones (Aus) Williams-Ford
3 Carlos Reutemann (Arg) Williams-Ford
4 Elio de Angelis (Ita) Lotus-Ford
5 Didier Pironi (Fra) Ferrari
6 Nelson Piquet (Bra) Brabham-Ford
Winner's speed: 209.05kph/129.90mph
Fastest lap: Reutemann 214.09kph/133.04mph
Pole position: René Arnoux (Fra) Renault

1982

12 September, 301.60km/187.41 miles
1 René Arnoux (Fra) Renault
2 Patrick Tambay (Fra) Ferrari
3 Mario Andretti (USA) Ferrari
4 John Watson (GB) McLaren-Ford
5 Michele Alboreto (Ita) Tyrrell-Ford
6 Eddie Cheever (USA) Talbot-Matra
Winner's speed: 219.50kph/136.40mph
Fastest lap: Arnoux 223.03kph/138.59mph
Pole position: Andretti

1983

11 September, 301.60km/187.41 miles
1 Nelson Piquet (Bra) Brabham-BMW
2 René Arnoux (Fra) Ferrari
3 Eddie Cheever (USA) Renault
4 Patrick Tambay (Fra) Ferrari

5 Elio de Angelis (Ita) Lotus-Renault
6 Derek Warwick (GB) Toleman-Hart
Winner's speed: 217.55kph/135.19mph
Fastest lap: Piquet 221.11kph/137.40mph
Pole position: Riccardo Patrese (Ita) Brabham-BMW

1984

9 September, 295.80km/183.80 miles
1 Niki Lauda (Aut) McLaren-Porsche
2 Michele Alboreto (Ita) Ferrari
3 Riccardo Patrese (Ita) Alfa Romeo
4 Stefan Johansson (Swe) Toleman-Hart
5 Jo Gartner (Aut) Osella-Alfa
6 Gerhard Berger (Aut) ATS-BMW
Gartner and Berger were ineligible for points because they were not regular competitors.
Winner's speed: 220.51kph/137.02mph
Fastest lap: Lauda 227.17kph/141.16mph
Pole position: Nelson Piquet (Bra) Brabham-BMW

1985

8 September, 295.80km/183.80 miles
1 Alain Prost (Fra) McLaren-TAG
2 Nelson Piquet (Bra) Brabham-BMW
3 Ayrton Senna (Bra) Lotus-Renault
4 Marc Surer (Swi) Brabham-BMW
5 Stefan Johansson (Swe) Ferrari
6 Elio de Angelis (Ita) Lotus-Renault
Winner's speed: 227.57kph/141.41mph
Fastest lap: Nigel Mansell (GB) Williams-Honda
236.51kph/146.97mph
Pole position: Senna

1986

7 September, 295.80km/183.80 miles
1 Nelson Piquet (Bra) Williams-Honda
2 Nigel Mansell (GB) Williams-Honda
3 Stefan Johansson (Swe) Ferrari
4 Keke Rosberg (Fin) McLaren-TAG
5 Gerhard Berger (Aut) Benetton-BMW
6 Alan Jones (Aus) Lola-Ford
Winner's speed: 228.35kph/141.90mph
Fastest lap: Teo Fabi (Ita) Benetton-BMW 236.99kph/
147.27mph
Pole position: Fabi

1987

6 September, 290.00km/180.20 miles
1 Nelson Piquet (Bra) Williams-Honda
2 Ayrton Senna (Bra) Lotus-Honda
3 Nigel Mansell (GB) Williams-Honda
4 Gerhard Berger (Aut) Ferrari
5 Thierry Boutsen (Bel) Benetton-Ford
6 Stefan Johansson (Swe) McLaren-TAG
Winner's speed: 232.64kph/144.55mph
Fastest lap: Senna 240.56kph/149.48kph
Pole position: Piquet

1988

11 September, 295.80km/183.80 miles
1 Gerhard Berger (Aut) Ferrari
2 Michele Alboreto (Ita) Ferrari
3 Eddie Cheever (USA) Arrows-Megatron
4 Derek Warwick (GB) Arrows-Megatron
5 Ivan Capelli (Ita) March-Judd
6 Thierry Boutsen (Bel) Benetton-Ford
Winner's speed: 228.53kph/142.00mph
Fastest lap: Alboreto 234.42kph/145.66mph
Pole position: Ayrton Senna (Bra) McLaren-Honda

1989

10 September, 307.40km/191.01 miles
1 Alain Prost (Fra) McLaren-Honda
2 Gerhard Berger (Aut) Ferrari
3 Thierry Boutsen (Bel) Williams-Renault
4 Riccardo Patrese (Ita) Williams-Renault
5 Jean Alesi (Fra) Tyrrell-Ford
6 Martin Brundle (GB) Brabham-Judd
Winner's speed: 232.12kph/144.23mph
Fastest lap: Prost 236.99kph/146.72mph
Pole position: Ayrton Senna (Bra) McLaren-Honda

1990

9 September, 307.40km/191.01 miles
1 Ayrton Senna (Bra) McLaren-Honda
2 Alain Prost (Fra) Ferrari
3 Gerhard Berger (Aut) McLaren-Honda
4 Nigel Mansell (GB) Ferrari
5 Riccardo Patrese (Ita) Williams-Renault
6 Satoru Nakajima (Jap) Tyrrell-Ford
Winner's speed: 236.57kph/147.00mph
Fastest lap: Senna 242.08kph/150.42mph
Pole position: Senna

1991

8 September, 307.340km/191.01 miles
1 Nigel Mansell (GB) Williams-Renault
2 Ayrton Senna (Bra) McLaren-Honda
3 Alain Prost (Fra) Ferrari
4 Gerhard Berger (Aut) McLaren-Honda
5 Michael Schumacher (Ger) Benetton-Ford
6 Nelson Piquet (Bra) Benetton-Ford
Winner's speed: 236.75kph/147.11mph
Fastest lap: Senna 242.62kph/150.76mph
Pole position: Senna

MOST WINS

Drivers
4 Nelson Piquet
3 Juan Manuel Fangio, Stirling Moss,
  Ronnie Peterson, Alain Prost
2 Alberto Ascari, Phil Hill, Niki Lauda,
  Clay Regazzoni, Jackie Stewart,
  John Surtees
Manufacturers
10 Ferrari
5 Lotus, McLaren
3 Brabham, BRM, Williams
2 Maserati, Mercedes-Benz, Renault,
  Vanwall

MOST FASTEST LAPS

Drivers
3 Jim Clark, Phil Hill, Clay Regazzoni,
  Ayrton Senna
2 Mario Andretti, Juan Manuel Fangio,
  José Froilán González, Stirling Moss
Manufacturers
12 Ferrari
7 Lotus
4 McLaren, Williams
3 Maserati
2 Alfa Romeo, Brabham, March

MOST POLE POSITIONS

Drivers
5 Juan Manuel Fangio, Ayrton Senna
3 Jim Clark, John Surtees
2 Alberto Ascari, Mario Andretti, René
  Arnoux, Jackie Ickx, Niki Lauda,
  Stirling Moss, Nelson Piquet
Manufacturers
12 Ferrari
7 Lotus
5 McLaren
3 Renault
2 Alfa Romeo, Brabham, Mercedes-
  Benz, Vanwall

JAPANESE GP

Being an end-of-season race, it is hardly surprising that several world titles have been clinched at the Japanese Grand Prix. And the first race in 1976 was no exception.

It saw Niki Lauda and James Hunt continue their season-long battle right into the final race with the championship still undecided. The Austrian was favourite but pulled out after two laps, claiming his life was more important than the world title. Hunt kept going in the rain, needing to finish in fourth place or better to win the title. He finished third.

In recent years, at the race's new home at Suzuka, the Japanese Grand Prix has developed into a personal battle between Ayrton Senna and Alain Prost. It was at Suzuka that Senna pushed Prost off the track at the first bend in 1990 and won the world title. A year later the Brazilian retained his title at Suzuka, pipping Britain's Nigel Mansell.

Many teams did not attend the second Japanese Grand Prix in 1977 and it was taken off the calendar until reappearing at Suzuka ten years later.

MOST WINS

Drivers
2 Gerhard Berger
Manufacturers
3 McLaren
2 Benetton

1976 Fuji

24 October, 318.21km/197.73 miles
1 Mario Andretti (USA) Lotus-Ford
2 Patrick Depailler (Fra) Tyrrell-Ford
3 James Hunt (GB) McLaren-Ford
4 Alan Jones (Aus) Surtees-Ford
5 Clay Regazzoni (Swi) Ferrari
6 Gunnar Nilsson (Swe) Lotus-Ford
Winner's speed: 183.62kph/114.09mph
Fastest lap: Masahiro Hasemi (Jap) Kojima-Ford
200.59kph/124.64mph
Pole position: Andretti

1977 Fuji

23 October, 318.21km/197.73 miles
1 James Hunt (GB) McLaren-Ford
2 Carlos Reutemann (Arg) Ferrari
3 Patrick Depailler (Fra) Tyrrell-Ford
4 Alan Jones (Aus) Shadow-Ford
5 Jacques Laffite (Fra) Ligier-Matra
6 Riccardo Patrese (Ita) Shadow-Ford
Winner's speed: 207.84kph/129.15mph
Fastest lap: Jody Scheckter (SAf) Wolf-Ford 211.20kph/
131.24mph
Pole position: Mario Andretti (USA) Lotus-Ford

1987 Suzuka

1 November, 298.81km/185.67 miles
1 Gerhard Berger (Aut) Ferrari
2 Ayrton Senna (Bra) Lotus-Honda
3 Stefan Johansson (Swe) McLaren-TAG
4 Michele Alboreto (Ita) Ferrari
5 Thierry Boutsen (Bel) Benetton-Ford
6 Satoru Nakajima (Jap) Lotus-Honda
Winner's speed: 192.85kph/119.83mph
Fastest lap: Alain Prost (Fra) McLaren-TAG 203.12kph/
126.21mph
Pole position: Berger

1988 Suzuka

30 October, 298.81km/185.67 miles
1 Ayrton Senna (Bra) McLaren-Honda
2 Alain Prost (Fra) McLaren-Honda
3 Thierry Boutsen (Bel) Benetton-Ford
4 Gerhard Berger (Aut) Ferrari

5 Alessandro Nannini (Ita) Benetton-Ford
6 Riccardo Patrese (Ita) Williams-Judd
Winner's speed: 191.72kph/119.16mph
Fastest lap: Senna 198.21kph/123.19mph
Pole position: Senna

1989 Suzuka

22 October, 310.53km/192.97 miles
1 Alessandro Nannini (Ita) Benetton-Ford
2 Riccardo Patrese (Ita) Williams-Renault
3 Thierry Boutsen (Bel) Williams-Renault
4 Nelson Piquet (Bra) Lotus-Judd
5 Martin Brundle (GB) Brabham-Judd
6 Derek Warwick (GB) Arrows-Ford
*Ayrton Senna (Bra) McLaren-Honda finished 1st but was
subsequently disqualified for taking an illegal track in
colliding with Alain Prost.*
Winner's speed: 197.14kph/122.50mph
Fastest lap: Alain Prost (Fra) McLaren-Honda 205.03kph/
127.4mph
Pole position: Senna

1990 Suzuka

21 October, 310.53km/192.97 miles
1 Nelson Piquet (Bra) Benetton-Ford
2 Roberto Moreno (Bra) Benetton-Ford
3 Aguri Suzuki (Jap) Lola-Lamborghini
4 Riccardo Patrese (Ita) Williams-Renault
5 Thierry Boutsen (Bel) Williams-Renault
6 Satoru Nakajima (Jap) Tyrrell-Ford
Winner's speed: 198.08kph/123.08mph
Fastest lap: Patrese 203.79kph/126.63mph
Pole position: Ayrton Senna (Bra) McLaren-Honda

1991 Suzuka

20 October, 310.53km/192.97 miles
1 Gerhard Berger (Aut) McLaren-Honda
2 Ayrton Senna (Bra) McLaren-Honda
3 Riccardo Patrese (Ita) Williams-Renault
4 Alain Prost (Fra) Ferrari
5 Martin Brundle (GB) Brabham-Yamaha
6 Stefano Modena (Ita) Tyrrell-Honda
Winner's speed: 202.30kph/125.70mph
Fastest lap: Senna 207.92kph/129.20mph
Pole position: Berger

MOST FASTEST LAPS

Drivers
2 Alain Prost, Ayrton Senna
Manufacturers
4 McLaren

MOST POLE POSITIONS

Drivers
3 Ayrton Senna
2 Mario Andretti, Gerhard Berger

Manufacturers
4 McLaren
2 Lotus

HE GREAT RACES
1976
Japanese GP

The 1976 Japanese Grand Prix, held in the shadow of Mount Fuji, was memorable because it brought an end to a dramatic, tense and controversial season which eventually saw a British success, James Hunt capturing the world title in the final race of the season in the Japanese rain.

Hunt seemed destined not to get his hands on the title; points had been taken off him, reinstated, and so on in a season of controversy. He was nearly handed the title when his nearest rival, Niki Lauda, was involved in an horrific accident at the Nürburgring. But the Austrian made a remarkable recovery and came back determined to hold on to his title.

When they arrived in Japan for the final leg, Lauda led Hunt in the race for the championship by three points and very little separated the two men in practice with Hunt having the slight edge and sharing the front row of the grid with Mario Andretti, who was in pole position.

Weather conditions on race day were appalling with the rain reducing visibility to little more than 100 yards, and after just two laps of the 73-lap race Niki Lauda came into the pits and announced he was out of the race. Having survived with his life at the Nürburgring he was not prepared to risk it in the rain at Fuji; his life was more important than the World Championship.

Hunt kept going, and with Lauda out of the race he now knew what he had to do: finish fourth or better to capture the title. He had been in the lead for much of the race but as the rain subsided and the track dried out it caused problems for his wet weather tyres. With 20 laps remaining one was badly worn as a result of overheating but Hunt resisted the temptation to pull into the pits. With six laps to go the tyre ended up in shreds

but, fortunately, it happened outside the pits and he pulled in for a complete tyre-change which took a seemingly never-ending 30 seconds.

With four laps to go Hunt was in fifth place and out of the World Championship title race. However, Alan Jones and Clay Regazzoni, both in front of Hunt, were also having tyre problems and were clearly slowing down, thus giving the Briton a chance. He overtook them both on the penultimate lap to move into third place and that is where he stayed behind the race leaders Mario Andretti and Patrick Depailler.

Hunt's third place was good enough to give him the title. But so confusing were the signals sent out to Hunt by his McLaren team in the closing laps that he wasn't sure where he was positioned, and it was not until a while after the end of the race that he realised he was the world champion.

James Hunt keeps going in the rain to clinch the 1976 drivers' title.

LAS VEGAS GP

All races at Las Vegas

Another of America's short-lived Grands Prix, the Las Vegas race lasted just two years and was held on the car park of the Caesar's Palace Hotel complex. The gambling machines and crap tables were little more than 100 yards from the pits area. The circuit was rather boring, with 14 tough bends and just one major straight. Michele Alboreto wasn't complaining: he won his first Grand Prix there in 1982.

1981

17 October, 273.75km/170.10 miles
1 Alan Jones (Aus) Williams-Ford
2 Alain Prost (Fra) Renault
3 Bruno Giacomelli (Ita) Alfa-Romeo
4 Nigel Mansell (GB) Lotus-Ford
5 Nelson Piquet (Bra) Brabham-Ford
6 Jacques Laffite (Fra) Talbot-Matra
Winner's speed: 157.55kph/97.90mph
Fastest lap: Didier Pironi (Fra) Ferrari 163.93kph/101.87mph
Pole position: Carlos Reutemann (Arg) Williams-Ford

1982

25 September, 273.75km/170.10 miles
1 Michele Alboreto (Ita) Tyrrell-Ford
2 John Watson (GB) McLaren-Ford
3 Eddie Cheever (USA) Talbot-Matra
4 Alain Prost (Fra) Renault
5 Keke Rosberg (Fin) Williams-Ford
6 Derek Daly (Ire) Williams-Ford
Winner's speed: 161.09kph/100.10mph
Fastest lap: Alboreto 164.99kph/102.52mph
Pole position: Prost

MEXICAN GP

All races at Mexico City

The first Mexican Grand Prix was in 1962 and the following year it was granted World Championship status and was won by that year's world champion, Jim Clark. All races have been at an altitude of 7000ft/2133m at Mexico City's *Autodromo Hermanos Rodriguez,* named after the country's two leading drivers, the brothers Pedro and Ricardo Rodriguez. The race remained on the calendar until 1970 but did not return again until 1986 when Gerhard Berger enjoyed the first Grand Prix success of his career.

The most exciting Mexican Grand Prix was in 1964 when it was the last race of the season. On the starting grid Graham Hill, Jim Clark and John Surtees all had a chance to capture the title. Hill at one stage looked like winning the race but was taken out of contention after a shunt with Lorenzo Bandini, Surtees' team-mate. Jim Clark then took the lead and he looked like being world champion only for his engine to blow up on the penultimate lap. Surtees was still running; he finished second and gained enough points to snatch the title.

1963

27 October, 325.00km/201.95 miles
1 Jim Clark (GB) Lotus-Climax
2 Jack Brabham (Aus) Brabham-Climax
3 Richie Ginther (USA) BRM
4 Graham Hill (GB) BRM
5 Jo Bonnier (Swe) Cooper-Climax
6 Dan Gurney (USA) Brabham-Climax
Winner's speed: 150.15kph/93.30mph
Fastest lap: Clark 152.42kph/94.71mph
Pole position: Clark

1964

25 October, 325.00km/201.95 miles
1 Dan Gurney (USA) Brabham-Climax
2 John Surtees (GB) Ferrari
3 Lorenzo Bandini (Ita) Ferrari
4 Mike Spence (GB) Lotus-Climax
5 Jim Clark (GB) Lotus-Climax
6 Pedro Rodriguez (Mex) Ferrari
Winner's speed: 150.16kph/93.32mph
Fastest lap: Clark 152.07kph/94.49 mph
Pole position: Clark

1965

24 October, 325.00km/201.95 miles
1 Richie Ginther (USA) Honda
2 Dan Gurney (USA) Brabham-Climax
3 Mike Spence (GB) Lotus-Climax
4 Jo Siffert (Swi) Brabham-BRM
5 Ron Bucknum (USA) Honda
6 Dick Attwood (GB) Lotus-BRM
Winner's speed: 151.70kph/94.26mph
Fastest lap: Gurney 155.39kph/96.55mph
Pole position: Jim Clark (GB) Lotus-Climax

1966

23 October, 325.00km/201.95 miles
1 John Surtees (GB) Cooper-Maserati
2 Jack Brabham (Aus) Brabham-Repco
3 Denny Hulme (NZ) Brabham-Repco
4 Richie Ginther (USA) Honda
5 Dan Gurney (USA) Eagle-Climax
6 Jo Bonnier (Swe) Cooper-Maserati
Winner's speed: 154.04kph/95.72mph
Fastest lap: Ginther 158.24kph/98.33mph
Pole position: Surtees

1967

22 October, 325.00km/201.95 miles
1 Jim Clark (GB) Lotus-Ford
2 Jack Brabham (Aus) Brabham-Repco
3 Denny Hulme (NZ) Brabham-Repco
4 John Surtees (GB) Honda
5 Mike Spence (GB) BRM
6 Pedro Rodriguez (Mex) Cooper-Maserati
Winner's speed: 163.22kph/101.42mph
Fastest lap: Clark 166.47kph/103.44mph
Pole position: Clark

1968

3 November, 325.00km/201.95 miles
1 Graham Hill (GB) Lotus-Ford
2 Bruce McLaren (NZ) McLaren-Ford
3 Jackie Oliver (GB) Lotus-Ford
4 Pedro Rodriguez (Mex) BRM
5 Jo Bonnier (Swe) Honda
6 Jo Siffert (Swi) Lotus-Ford
Winner's speed: 167.05kph/103.80mph
Fastest lap: Siffert 172.70kph/107.31mph
Pole position: Siffert

1969

9 October, 325.00km/201.95 miles
1 Denny Hulme (NZ) McLaren-Ford
2 Jacky Ickx (Bel) Brabham-Ford
3 Jack Brabham (Aus) Brabham-Ford
4 Jackie Stewart (GB) Matra-Ford
5 Jean-Pierre Beltoise (Fra) Matra-Ford
6 Jackie Oliver (GB) BRM
Winner's speed: 170.83kph/106.15mph
Fastest lap: Ickx 174.67kph/108.54mph
Pole position: Brabham

1970

25 October, 325.00km/201.95 miles
1 Jacky Ickx (Bel) Ferrari
2 Clay Regazzoni (Swi) Ferrari
3 Denny Hulme (NZ) McLaren-Ford
4 Chris Amon (NZ) March-Ford
5 Jean-Pierre Beltoise (Fra) Matra-Simca
6 Pedro Rodriguez (Mex) BRM
Winner's speed: 171.85kph/106.78mph
Fastest lap: Ickx 174.57kph/108.47mph
Pole position: Regazzoni

1986

2 October, 300.63km/186.80 miles
1 Gerhard Berger (Aut) Benetton-BMW
2 Alain Prost (Fra) McLaren-TAG
3 Ayrton Senna (Bra) Lotus-Renault
4 Nelson Piquet (Bra) Williams-Honda
5 Nigel Mansell (GB) Williams-Honda
6 Philippe Alliot (Fra) Ligier-Renault
Winner's speed: 193.34kph/120.14mph
Fastest lap: Piquet 200.50kph/124.60mph
Pole position: Senna

*Gerhard Berger celebrates as he wins the 1986
Mexican Grand Prix for Benetton. It was the
Austrian's first ever Formula One success.*

1987

18 October, 278.52km/173.07 miles
1 Nigel Mansell (GB) Williams-Honda
2 Nelson Piquet (Bra) Williams-Honda
3 Riccardo Patrese (Ita) Brabham-BMW
4 Eddie Cheever (USA) Arrows-Megatron
5 Teo Fabi (Ita) Benetton-Ford
6 Philippe Alliot (Fra) Lola-Ford
Winner's speed: 193.41kph/120.18mph
Fastest lap: Piquet 201.13kph/124.97mph
Pole position: Mansell

1988

29 May, 296.21km/184.05 miles
1 Alain Prost (Fra) McLaren-Honda
2 Ayrton Senna (Bra) McLaren-Honda
3 Gerhard Berger (Aut) Ferrari
4 Michele Alboreto (Ita) Ferrari
5 Derek Warwick (GB) Arrows-Megatron
6 Eddie Cheever (USA) Arrows-Megatron
Winner's speed: 196.90kph/122.35mph
Fastest lap: Prost 202.47kph/125.80mph
Pole position: Senna

1989

28 May, 305.05km/189.54 miles
1 Ayrton Senna (Bra) McLaren-Honda
2 Riccardo Patrese (Ita) Williams-Renault
3 Michele Alboreto (Ita) Tyrrell-Ford
4 Alessandro Nannini (Ita) Benetton-Ford
5 Alain Prost (Fra) McLaren-Honda
6 Gabriele Tarquini (Ita) AGS-Ford
Winner's speed: 193.06kph/119.96mph
Fastest lap: Mansell (GB) Ferrari 197.91kph/122.97mph
Pole position: Senna

1990

24 June, 305.05km/189.54 miles
1 Alain Prost (Fra) Ferrari
2 Nigel Mansell (GB) Ferrari
3 Gerhard Berger (Aut) McLaren-Honda
4 Alessandro Nannini (Ita) Benetton-Ford
5 Thierry Boutsen (Bel) Williams-Renault
6 Nelson Piquet (Bra) Benetton-Ford
Winner's speed: 197.66kph123.54mph
Fastest lap: Prost 204.16kph/126.86mph
Pole position: Berger

1991

16 June, 296.21km/184.05miles
1 Riccardo Patrese (Ita) Williams-Renault
2 Nigel Mansell (GB) Williams-Renault
3 Ayrton Senna (Bra) McLaren-Honda
4 Andrea de Cesaris (Ita) Jordan-Ford
5 Roberto Moreno (Bra) Benetton-Ford
6 Eric Bernard (Fra) Lola-Ford
Winner's speed: 197.76kph/122.88mph
Fastest lap: Mansell 207.27kph/128.79mph
Pole position: Patrese

MOST WINS

Drivers
2 Jim Clark, Alain Prost
Manufacturers
3 Lotus, McLaren
2 Ferrari, Williams

MOST FASTEST LAPS

Drivers
2 Jim Clark, Jacky Ickx, Nigel Mansell,
  Nelson Piquet, Alain Prost
Manufacturers
3 Ferrari, Lotus, Williams
2 Brabham

MOST POLE POSITIONS

Drivers
3 Jim Clark, Ayrton Senna
Manufacturers
5 Lotus
3 McLaren
2 Williams

MONACO GP

All races at Monte Carlo

The Monaco Grand Prix through the streets of Monte Carlo is the best known round-the-houses race in motor racing. Other venues over the years have tried to emulate the great race but none has successfully captured the atmosphere of the Monaco Grand Prix.

The race was inaugurated in 1929 after the Automobile Club of Monaco was denied international status. Being an independent state they felt they should be granted international recognition and after Anthony Noghès, the man behind the Monte Carlo Rally, conceived the idea, the Monaco Grand

Graham Hill in the Brabham BT34 at Monaco. He won the race five times in the 1960s.

Prix was duly accepted as one of the leading Grands Prix and became one of the rounds of the inaugural World Championship.

During the first championship race a giant wave blew over the sea wall and left a large puddle on the track. It caused problems for the drivers who, one after the other, skidded out of the race. It was left off the calendar in 1951 and did not return until 1955 but has been a regular fixture ever since. There was

a 1952 Monaco Grand Prix, but it was for sports cars. The 1955 race was as dramatic as any seen around the Monte Carlo streets. Alberto Ascari's Lancia went out of control as he came out of the tunnel and shot into the harbour. Miraculously the Italian driver got out of his car and swam to safety.

Graham Hill had an affection for the demanding circuit because he won the race five times in seven years, 1963–69. Hill finished fifth in 1970 in a

race won in dramatic style by Jochen Rindt, that year's world champion. The Austrian trailed Jack Brabham but was on his tail as they went into the tunnel for the last time. Brabham had the race won, provided he made no mistakes. But he did. Coming out of the tunnel he was late in breaking and slid into a straw bale. Rindt went past him and took the chequered flag for the first of his six victories in his posthumous World Championship season.

1950

21 May, 318.00km/197.60 miles
1 Juan Manuel Fangio (Arg) Alfa Romeo
2 Alberto Ascari (Ita) Ferrari
3 Louis Chiron (Mon) Maserati
4 Raymond Sommer (Fra) Ferrari
5 'B Bira' (Siam) Maserati
6 Bob Gerard (GB) ERA
Winner's speed: 98.70kph/61.33mph
Fastest lap: Fangio 103.14kph/64.09mph
Pole position: Fangio

1955

22 May, 314.50km/195.42 miles
1 Maurice Trintignant (Fra) Ferrari
2 Eugenio Castellotti (Ita) Lancia
3 Jean Behra (Fra)/Cesare Perdisa (Ita) Maserati
4 Giuseppe Farina (Ita) Ferrari
5 Luigi Villoresi (Ita) Lancia
6 Louis Chiron (Mon) Lancia
Winner's speed: 105.91kph/65.81mph
Fastest lap: Juan Manuel Fangio (Arg) Mercedes-Benz 110.57kph/68.70mph
Pole position: Fangio

1956

3 May, 314.50km/195.42 miles
1 Stirling Moss (GB) Maserati
2 Peter Collins (GB)/Juan Manuel Fangio (Arg) Lancia-Ferrari
3 Jean Behra (Fra) Maserati
4 Juan Manuel Fangio (Arg)/Eugenio Castellotti (Ita) Lancia-Ferrari
5 Nano de Silva Ramos (Bra) Gordini
6 Elie Bayol (Fra)/André Pilette (Bel) Gordini
Despite sharing drives and being classified in 2nd and 4th places, Fangio received points only for his shared drive with Collins.
Winner's speed: 104.51kph/64.94mph
Fastest lap: Fangio 108.49kph/67.39mph
Pole position: Fangio

1957

19 May, 330.23km/205.19 miles
1 Juan Manuel Fangio (Arg) Maserati
2 Tony Brooks (GB) Vanwall
3 Masten Gregory (USA) Maserati
4 Stuart Lewis-Evans (GB) Connaught
5 Maurice Trintignant (Fra) Lancia-Ferrari
6 Jack Brabham (Aus) Cooper-Climax
Winner's speed: 104.16kph/64.72mph
Fastest lap: Fangio 107.22kph/66.62mph
Pole position: Fangio

1958

18 May, 314.50km/195.42 miles
1 Maurice Trintignant (Fra) Cooper-Climax
2 Luigi Musso (Ita) Ferrari
3 Peter Collins (GB) Ferrari
4 Jack Brabham (Aus) Cooper-Climax
5 Harry Schell (USA) BRM
6 Cliff Allison (GB) Lotus-Climax
Winner's speed: 109.41kph/67.99mph
Fastest lap: Mike Hawthorn (GB) Ferrari 112.55kph/69.93mph
Pole position: Tony Brooks (GB) Vanwall

1959

10 May, 314.50km/195.42 miles
1 Jack Brabham (Aus) Cooper-Climax
2 Tony Brooks (GB) Ferrari
3 Maurice Trintignant (Fra) Cooper-Climax
4 Phil Hill (USA) Ferrari
5 Bruce McLaren (NZ) Cooper-Climax
6 Roy Salvadori (GB) Cooper-Maserati
Winner's speed: 107.36kph/66.71mph
Fastest lap: Brabham 112.77kph/70.07mph
Pole position: Stirling Moss (GB) Cooper-Climax

1960

29 May, 3314.50km/195.42 miles
1 Stirling Moss (GB) Lotus-Climax
2 Bruce McLaren (NZ) Cooper-Climax
3 Phil Hill (USA) Ferrari

4 Tony Brooks (GB) Cooper-Climax
5 Jo Bonnier (Swe) BRM
6 Richie Ginther (USA) Ferrari
Winner's speed: 108.60kph/67.48mph
Fastest lap: McLaren 117.69kph/73.13mph
Pole position: Moss

1961

14 May, 3314.50km/195.42 miles
1 Stirling Moss (GB) Lotus-Climax
2 Richie Ginther (USA) Ferrari
3 Phil Hill (USA) Ferrari
4 Wolfgang von Trips (FRG) Ferrari
5 Dan Gurney (USA) Porsche
6 Bruce McLaren (NZ) Cooper-Climax
Winner's speed: 113.79kph/70.70
Fastest lap: Ginther/Moss 117.57kph/73.05mph
Pole position: Moss

1962

3 June, 314.50km/195.42 miles
1 Bruce McLaren (NZ) Cooper-Climax
2 Phil Hill (USA) Ferrari
3 Lorenzo Bandini (Ita) Ferrari
4 John Surtees (GB) Lola-Climax
5 Jo Bonnier (Swe) Porsche
6 Graham Hill (GB) BRM
Winner's speed: 113.37kph/70.46mph
Fastest lap: Jim Clark (GB) Lotus-Climax 118.56kph/73.67mph
Pole position: Clark

1963

26 May, 314.50km/195.42 miles
1 Graham Hill (GB) BRM
2 Richie Ginther (USA) BRM
3 Bruce McLaren (NZ) Cooper-Climax
4 John Surtees (GB) Ferrari
5 Tony Maggs (SAf) Cooper-Climax
6 Trevor Taylor (GB) Lotus-Climax
Winner's speed: 116.56kph/72.42mph
Fastest lap: Surtees 119.81kph/74.45mph
Pole position: Jim Clark (GB) Lotus-Climax

1964

10 May, 314.50km/195.42 miles
1 Graham Hill (GB) BRM
2 Richie Ginther (USA) BRM
3 Peter Arundell (GB) Lotus-Climax
4 Jim Clark (GB) Lotus-Climax
5 Jo Bonnier (Swe) Cooper-Climax
6 Mike Hailwood (GB) Lotus-BRM
Winner's speed: 116.88kph/72.64mph
Fastest lap: G Hill 120.58kph/74.92mph
Pole position: Clark

1965

30 May, 314.50km/195.42 miles
1 Graham Hill (GB) BRM
2 Lorenzo Bandini (Ita) Ferrari

3 Jackie Stewart (GB) BRM
4 John Surtees (GB) Ferrari
5 Bruce McLaren (NZ) Cooper-Climax
6 Jo Siffert (Swi) Brabham-BRM
Winner's speed: 119.60kph/74.34mph
Fastest lap: Hill 123.47kph/76.72mph
Pole position: Hill

1966

22 May, 314.50km/195.42 miles
1 Jackie Stewart (GB) BRM
2 Lorenzo Bandini (Ita) Ferrari
3 Graham Hill (GB) BRM
4 Bob Bondurant (USA) BRM
Only four were classified.
Winner's speed: 123.14kph/76.52mph
Fastest lap: Bandini 126.08kph/78.84mph
Pole position: Jim Clark (GB) Lotus-Climax

1967

7 May, 314.50km/195.42 miles
1 Denny Hulme (NZ) Brabham-Repco
2 Graham Hill (GB) Lotus-BRM
3 Chris Amon (NZ) Ferrari
4 Bruce McLaren (NZ) McLaren-BRM
5 Pedro Rodriguez (Mex) Cooper-Maserati
6 Mike Spence (GB) BRM
Winner's speed: 122.14kph/75.90mph
Fastest lap: Jim Clark (GB) Lotus-Climax 126.50kph/78.61mph
Pole position: Jack Brabham (Aus) Brabham-Repco

1968

26 May, 251.60km/156.34 miles
1 Graham Hill (GB) Lotus-Ford
2 Dick Attwood (GB) BRM
3 Lucien Bianchi (Bel) Cooper-BRM
4 Ludovico Scarfiotti (Ita) Cooper-BRM
5 Denny Hulme (NZ) McLaren-Ford
Only five were classified.
Winner's speed: 125.24kph/77.82mph
Fastest lap: Attwood 128.51kph/79.85mph
Pole position: Hill

1969

18 May, 251.60km/156.34 miles
1 Graham Hill (GB) Lotus-Ford
2 Piers Courage (GB) Brabham-Ford
3 Jo Siffert (Swi) Lotus-Ford
4 Dick Attwood (GB) Lotus-Ford
5 Bruce McLaren (NZ) McLaren-Ford
6 Denny Hulme (NZ) McLaren-Ford
Winner's speed: 129.04kph/80.18mph
Fastest lap: Jackie Stewart (GB) Matra-Ford 133.04kph/82.67mph
Pole position: Stewart

1970

10 May, 251.60km/156.34 miles
1 Jochen Rindt (Aut) Lotus-Ford

2 Jack Brabham (Aus) Brabham-Ford
3 Henri Pescarolo (Fra) Matra-Simca
4 Denny Hulme (NZ) McLaren-Ford
5 Graham Hill (GB) Lotus-Ford
6 Pedro Rodriguez (Mex) BRM
Winner's speed: 131.72kph/81.85mph
Fastest lap: Rindt 136.08kph/84.56mph
Pole position: Jackie Stewart (GB) March-Ford

1971

23 May, 251.60km/156.34 miles
1 Jackie Stewart (GB) Tyrrell-Ford
2 Ronnie Peterson (Swe) March-Ford
3 Jacky Ickx (Bel) Ferrari
4 Denny Hulme (NZ) McLaren-Ford
5 Emerson Fittipaldi (Bra) Lotus-Ford
6 Rolf Stommelen (FRG) Surtees-Ford
Winner's speed: 134.36kph/83.49mph
Fastest lap: Stewart 137.74kph/85.59mph
Pole position: Stewart

1972

14 May, 251.60km/156.34 miles
1 Jean-Pierre Beltoise (Fra) BRM
2 Jacky Ickx (Bel) Ferrari
3 Emerson Fittipaldi (Bra) Lotus-Ford
4 Jackie Stewart (GB) Tyrrell-Ford
5 Brian Redman (GB) McLaren-Ford
6 Chris Amon (NZ) Matra-Simca
Winner's speed: 102.76kph/63.85mph
Fastest lap: Beltoise 113.22kph/70.35mph
Pole position: Fittipaldi

1973

3 June, 255.68km/158.88 miles
1 Jackie Stewart (GB) Tyrrell-Ford
2 Emerson Fittipaldi (Bra) Lotus-Ford
3 Ronnie Peterson (Swe) Lotus-Ford
4 François Cevert (Fra) Tyrrell-Ford
5 Peter Revson (USA) McLaren-Ford
6 Denny Hulme (NZ) McLaren-Ford
Winner's speed: 130.30kph/80.96mph
Fastest lap: Fittipaldi 133.95kph/83.23mph
Pole position: Stewart

1974

26 May, 255.68km/158.88 miles
1 Ronnie Peterson (Swe) Lotus-Ford
2 Jody Scheckter (SAf) Tyrrell-Ford
3 Jean-Pierre Jarier (Fra) Shadow-Ford
4 Clay Regazzoni (Swi) Ferrari
5 Emerson Fittipaldi (Bra) McLaren-Ford
6 John Watson (GB) Brabham-Ford
Winner's speed: 129.94kph/80.74mph
Fastest lap: Peterson 134.25kph/83.42mph
Pole position: Niki Lauda (Aut) Ferrari

1975

11 May, 245.85km/152.76 miles
1 Niki Lauda (Aut) Ferrari

2 Emerson Fittipaldi (Bra) McLaren-Ford
3 Carlos Pace (Bra) Brabham-Ford
4 Ronnie Peterson (Swe) Lotus-Ford
5 Patrick Depailler (Fra) Tyrrell-Ford
6 Jochen Mass (FRG) McLaren-Ford
Winner's speed: 121.55kph/75.35mph
Fastest lap: Depailler 133.09kph/82.70mph
Pole position: Lauda

1976

30 May, 258.34km/160.52 miles
1 Niki Lauda (Aut) Ferrari
2 Jody Scheckter (SAf) Tyrrell-Ford
3 Patrick Depailler (Fra) Tyrrell-Ford
4 Hans-Joachim Stuck (FRG) March-Ford
5 Jochen Mass (FRG) McLaren-Ford
6 Emerson Fittipaldi (Bra) Fittipaldi-Ford
Winner's speed: 129.32kph/80.35mph
Fastest lap: Clay Regazzoni (Swi) Ferrari 132.07kph/
82.06mph
Pole position: Lauda

1977

22 May, 251.71km/156.41 miles
1 Jody Scheckter (SAf) Wolf-Ford
2 Niki Lauda (Aut) Ferrari
3 Carlos Reutemann (Arg) Ferrari
4 Jochen Mass (FRG) McLaren-Ford
5 Mario Andretti (USA) Lotus-Ford
6 Alan Jones (Aus) Shadow-Ford
Winner's speed: 128.12kph/79.61mph
Fastest lap: Scheckter 130.92kph/81.35mph
Pole position: John Watson (GB) Brabham-Alfa Romeo

1978

7 May, 248.40km/154.35 miles
1 Patrick Depailler (Fra) Tyrrell-Ford
2 Niki Lauda (Aut) Brabham-Alfa Romeo
3 Jody Scheckter (SAf) Wolf-Ford
4 John Watson (GB) Brabham-Alfa Romeo
5 Didier Pironi (Fra) Tyrrell-Ford
6 Riccardo Patrese (Ita) Arrows-Ford
Winner's speed: 129.33kph/80.36mph
Fastest lap: Lauda 134.50kph/83.57mph
Pole position: Carlos Reutemann (Arg) Ferrari

1979

27 May, 251.71km/156.41 miles
1 Jody Scheckter (SAf) Ferrari
2 Clay Regazzoni (Swi) Williams-Ford
3 Carlos Reutemann (Arg) Lotus-Ford
4 John Watson (GB) McLaren-Ford
5 Patrick Depailler (Fra) Ligier-Ford
6 Jochen Mass (FRG) Arrows-Ford
Winner's speed: 130.90kph/81.34mph
Fastest lap: Depailler 134.24kph/83.41mph
Pole position: Scheckter

1980

18 May, 251.71km/156.41 miles

1 Carlos Reutemann (Arg) Williams-Ford
2 Jacques Laffite (Fra) Ligier-Ford
3 Nelson Piquet (Bra) Brabham-Ford
4 Jochen Mass (FRG) Arrows-Ford
5 Gilles Villeneuve (Can) Ferrari
6 Emerson Fittipaldi (Bra) Fittipaldi-Ford
Winner's speed: 130.68kph/81.20mph
Fastest lap: Riccardo Patrese (Ita) Arrows-Ford
138.55kph/86.09mph
Pole position: Didier Pironi (Fra) Ligier-Ford

1981

31 May, 251.71km/156.41 miles
1 Gilles Villeneuve (Can) Ferrari
2 Alan Jones (Aus) Williams-Ford
3 Jacques Laffite (Fra) Talbot-Matra
4 Didier Pironi (Fra) Ferrari
5 Eddie Cheever (USA) Tyrrell-Ford
6 Marc Surer (Swi) Ensign-Ford
Winner's speed: 132.03kph/82.04mph
Fastest lap: Jones 136.31kph/84.70mph
Pole position: Nelson Piquet (Bra) Brabham-Ford

1982

23 May, 251.71km/156.41 miles
1 Riccardo Patrese (Ita) Brabham-Ford
2 Didier Pironi (Fra) Ferrari
3 Andrea de Cesaris (Ita) Alfa Romeo
4 Nigel Mansell (GB) Lotus-Ford
5 Elio de Angelis (Ita) Lotus-Ford
6 Derek Daly (Ire) Williams-Ford
Winner's speed: 132.26kph/82.18mph
Fastest lap: Patrese 138.07kph/85.79mph
Pole position: René Arnoux (Fra) Renault

1983

15 May, 251.71km/156.41 miles
1 Keke Rosberg (Fin) Williams-Ford
2 Nelson Piquet (Bra) Brabham-BMW
3 Alain Prost (Fra) Renault
4 Patrick Tambay (Fra) Ferrari
5 Danny Sullivan (USA) Tyrrell-Ford
6 Mauro Baldi (Ita) Alfa Romeo
Winner's speed: 129.49kph/80.46mph
Fastest lap: Piquet 136.61kph/84.89mph
Pole position: Prost

1984

3 June, 102.67km/63.80 miles
1 Alain Prost (Fra) McLaren-Porsche
2 Ayrton Senna (Bra) Toleman-Hart
3 René Arnoux (Fra) Ferrari
4 Keke Rosberg (Fin) Williams-Honda
5 Elio de Angelis (Ita) Lotus-Renault
6 Michele Alboreto (Ita) Ferrari
Stefan Bellof (FRG) Tyrrell-Ford finished 3rd but all Tyrrell points for drivers and manufacturer were deducted because of rule infringement.
Only half points were awarded because insufficient distance was covered.
Winner's speed: 100.78kph/62.62mph
Fastest lap: Senna 104.28kph/64.80mph

Pole position: Prost

1985

19 May, 258.34km/160.52 miles
1 Alain Prost (Fra) McLaren-TAG
2 Michele Alboreto (Ita) Ferrari
3 Elio de Angelis (Ita) Lotus-Renault
4 Andrea de Cesaris (Ita) Ligier-Renault
5 Derek Warwick (GB) Renault
6 Jacques Laffite (Fra) Ligier-Renault
Winner's speed: 138.43kph/86.02mph
Fastest lap: Alboreto 144.28kph/89.65mph
Pole position: Ayrton Senna (Bra) Lotus-Renault

1986

11 May, 259.58km/161.30 miles
1 Alain Prost (Fra) McLaren-TAG
2 Keke Rosberg (Fin) McLaren-TAG
3 Ayrton Senna (Bra) Lotus-Renault
4 Nigel Mansell (GB) Williams-Honda
5 René Arnoux (Fra) Ligier-Renault
6 Jacques Laffite (Fra) Ligier-Renault
Winner's speed: 134.56kph/83.66mph
Fastest lap: Prost 138.34kph/85.96mph
Pole position: Prost

1987

31 May, 259.58km/161.30 miles
1 Ayrton Senna (Bra) Lotus-Honda
2 Nelson Piquet (Bra) Williams-Honda
3 Michele Alboreto (Ita) Ferrari
4 Gerhard Berger (Aut) Ferrari
5 Jonathan Palmer (GB) Tyrrell-Ford
6 Ivan Capelli (Ita) March-Ford
Winner's speed: 132.10kph/82.08mph
Fastest lap: Senna 136.64kph/84.90mph
Pole position: Nigel Mansell (GB) Williams-Honda

1988

15 May, 259.58km/161.30 miles
1 Alain Prost (Fra) McLaren-Honda
2 Gerhard Berger (Aut) Ferrari
3 Michele Alboreto (Ita) Ferrari
4 Derek Warwick (GB) Arrows-Megatron
5 Jonathan Palmer (GB) Tyrrell-Ford
6 Riccardo Patrese (Ita) Williams-Judd
Winner's speed: 132.80kph/82.52mph
Fastest lap: Ayrton Senna (Bra) McLaren-Honda
138.79kph/86.24mph
Pole position: Senna

1989

7 May, 256.26km/159.23 miles
1 Ayrton Senna (Bra) McLaren-Honda
2 Alain Prost (Fra) McLaren-Honda
3 Stefano Modena (Ita) Brabham-Judd
4 Alex Caffi (Ita) Dallara-Ford
5 Michele Alboreto (Ita) Tyrrell-Ford
6 Martin Brundle (GB) Brabham-Judd
Winner's speed: 135.40kph/84.13mph
Fastest lap: Alain Prost 140.125kph/87.07mph

Pole position: Senna

1990

27 May, 259.58km/161.30 miles
1 Ayrton Senna (Bra) McLaren-Honda
2 Jean Alesi (Fra) Tyrrell-Ford
3 Gerhard Berger (Aut) McLaren-Honda
4 Thierry Boutsen (Bel) Williams-Renault
5 Alex Caffi (Ita) Arrows-Ford
6 Eric Bernard (Fra) Lola-Lamborghini
Winner's speed: 138.10kph/85.83mph
Fastest lap: Senna 141.84kph/88.13mph
Pole position: Senna

1991

12 May, 259.58km/161.30 miles
1 Ayrton Senna (Bra) McLaren-Honda
2 Nigel Mansell (GB) Williams-Renault
3 Jean Alesi (Fra) Ferrari
4 Roberto Moreno (Bra) Benetton-Ford
5 Alain Prost (Fra) Ferrari
6 Emanuele Pirro (Ita) Dallara-Judd
Winner's speed: 137.79kph/85.62mph
Fastest lap: Prost 142.01kph/88.24mph
Pole position: Senna

MOST WINS

Drivers
5 Graham Hill
4 Alain Prost, Ayrton Senna
3 Stirling Moss, Jackie Stewart
2 Juan Manuel Fangio, Niki Lauda,
  Jody Scheckter, Maurice Trintignant
Manufacturers
7 Lotus, McLaren, BRM, Ferrari
3 Cooper, Tyrrell
2 Brabham, Maserati, Williams

MOST FASTEST LAPS

Drivers
4 Juan Manuel Fangio, Ayrton Senna
3 Alain Prost;
2 Jim Clark, Patrick Depailler, Graham
  Hill, Riccardo Patrese, Jackie
  Stewart
Manufacturers
7 Ferrari, Lotus
4 BRM, McLaren
3 Brabham   2 Cooper, Tyrrell

MOST POLE POSITIONS

Drivers
5 Ayrton Senna
4 Jim Clark, Juan Manuel Fangio, Jim
  Stewart
3 Niki Lauda, Stirling Moss, Alain Prost
2 Graham Hill
Manufacturers
9 Lotus
6 McLaren   3 Brabham
5 Ferrari   2 Renault, Tyrrell

MOROCCAN GP

1958

19 October, 403.75km/250.88 miles
1 Stirling Moss (GB) Vanwall
2 Mike Hawthorn (GB) Ferrari
3 Phil Hill (USA) Ferrari
4 Jo Bonnier (Swe) BRM
5 Harry Schell (USA) BRM
6 Masten Gregory (USA) Maserati
Winner's speed: 187.43kph/116.46mph
Fastest lap: Moss 192.46kph/119.59mph
Pole position: Hawthorn

Morocco's, and indeed Africa's, only World Championship Grand Prix was over the near-rectangular Ain-Diab circuit. It was the seventh Moroccan Grand Prix, the race having first been held as a tourist car event in 1925, but the first to be accorded World Championship status. In finishing second, Mike Hawthorn clinched the World Championship at Casablanca. It was his final Grand Prix before his retirement and subsequent untimely death.

PESCARA GP

Pescara is one of three Italian circuits to have staged World Championship races, and its monster 25.58km/15.89 mile road circuit is the longest ever to have staged a Grand Prix.

The Pescara Grand Prix was inaugurated in 1924 when Enzo Ferrari enjoyed one of his rare successes as a driver. The circuit started outside Pescara on the Adriatic coast and made its way through the Abruzzi mountains before returning to Pescara. Granted World Championship status in 1957 only because of the cancellation of the Dutch and Belgian races, the circuit was not popular with the drivers and the race did not reappear.

1957

18 August, 460.42km/286.09 miles
1 Stirling Moss (GB) Vanwall
2 Juan Manuel Fangio (Arg) Maserati
3 Harry Schell (USA) Maserati
4 Masten Gregory (USA) Maserati
5 Stuart Lewis-Evans (GB) Vanwall
6 Giorgio Scarlatti (Ita) Maserati
Winner's speed: 154.01kph/95.70mph
Fastest lap: Moss 157.52kph/97.88mph
Pole position: Fangio

PORTUGUESE GP

Like the Moroccan Grand Prix, the Portuguese race also made its World Championship debut in 1958. But unlike its African counterpart, Portugal's Grand Prix is still in existence despite a chequered(!) career.

The first Portuguese Grand Prix in 1951 was for sports cars. The inaugural Formula One Grand Prix was through the streets of Oporto, one of three circuits to have been used for the race. Oporto was the race's home in 1958 and 1960. In 1959 it had moved to Monsanto on the outskirts of Lisbon.

Because of the unsuitability of both Oporto and Monsanto the 1960 race was the last for 24 years until it returned at its new permanent home of Estoril. And it was in the revived race that Niki Lauda, despite finishing runner-up to Alain Prost, clinched his third world title. The following year the winner of the Portuguese Grand Prix was a young man who has certainly since made his mark on Formula One racing – Ayrton Senna.

1958 Oporto

24 August, 370.35km/230.13 miles
1 Stirling Moss (GB) Vanwall
2 Mike Hawthorn (GB) Ferrari
3 Stuart Lewis-Evans (GB) Vanwall
4 Jean Behra (Fra) BRM
5 Wolfgang von Trips (FRG) Ferrari
6 Harry Schell (USA) BRM
Winner's speed: 169.03kph/105.03mph
Fastest lap: Hawthorn 175.00kph/108.74mph
Pole position: Moss

1959 Monsanto

23 August, 337.28km/209.58 miles
1 Stirling Moss (GB) Cooper-Climax
2 Masten Gregory (USA) Cooper-Climax
3 Dan Gurney (USA) Ferrari
4 Maurice Trintignant (Fra) Cooper-Climax
5 Harry Schell (USA) BRM
6 Roy Salvadori (GB) Aston Martin
Winner's speed: 153.40kph/95.32mph
Fastest lap: Moss 156.58kph/97.30mph
Pole position: Moss

1960 Oporto

14 August, 407.37km/253.14 miles
1 Jack Brabham (Aus) Cooper-Climax
2 Bruce McLaren (NZ) Cooper-Climax
3 Jim Clark (GB) Lotus-Climax
4 Wolfgang von Trips (FRG) Ferrari
5 Tony Brooks (GB) Cooper-Climax
6 Innes Ireland (GB) Lotus-Climax
Winner's speed: 175.85kph/109.27mph
Fastest lap: John Surtees (GB) Lotus-Climax 180.74kph/112.31mph
Pole position: Surtees

1984 Estoril

21 October, 304.50km/189.21 miles
1 Alain Prost (Fra) McLaren-Porsche
2 Niki Lauda (Aut) McLaren-Porsche
3 Ayrton Senna (Bra) Toleman-Hart
4 Michele Alboreto (Ita) Ferrari
5 Elio de Angelis (Ita) Lotus-Renault

6 Nelson Piquet (Bra) Brabham-BMW
Winner's speed: 180.54kph/112.19mph
Fastest lap: Lauda 188.68kph/117.25mph
Pole position: Piquet

1985 Estoril

21 April, 291.45km/181.09 miles
1 Ayrton Senna (Bra) Lotus-Renault
2 Michele Alboreto (Ita) Ferrari
3 Patrick Tambay (Fra) Renault
4 Elio de Angelis (Ita) Lotus-Renault
5 Nigel Mansell (GB) Williams-Honda
6 Stefan Bellof (FRG) Tyrrell-Ford
Winner's speed: 145.16kph/90.20mph
Fastest lap: Senna 150.40kph/93.46mph
Pole position: Senna

1986 Estoril

21 September, 304.50km/189.21 miles
1 Nigel Mansell (GB) Williams-Honda
2 Alain Prost (Fra) McLaren-TAG
3 Nelson Piquet (Bra) Williams-Honda
4 Ayrton Senna (Bra) Lotus-Renault
5 Michele Alboreto (Ita) Ferrari
6 Stefan Johansson (Swe) Ferrari
Winner's speed: 187.64kph/116.60mph
Fastest lap: Mansell 193.47kph/120.22mph
Pole position: Senna

1987 Estoril

20 September, 304.50km/189.21 miles
1 Alain Prost (Fra) McLaren-TAG
2 Gerhard Berger (Aut) Ferrari
3 Nelson Piquet (Bra) Williams-Honda
4 Teo Fabi (Ita) Benetton-Ford
5 Stefan Johansson (Swe) McLaren-TAG
6 Eddie Cheever (USA) Arrows-Megatron
Winner's speed: 188.22kph/116.96mph
Fastest lap: Berger 197.53kph/122.74mph
Pole position: Berger

1988 Estoril

25 September, 304.50km/189.21 miles
1 Alain Prost (Fra) McLaren-Honda
2 Ivan Capelli (Ita) March-Judd
3 Thierry Boutsen (Bel) Benetton-Ford
4 Derek Warwick (GB) Arrows-Megatron
5 Michele Alboreto (Ita) Ferrari
6 Ayrton Senna (Bra) McLaren-Honda
Winner's speed: 186.88kph/116.15mph
Fastest lap: Gerhard Berger (Aut) Ferrari 190.91kph/
118.65mph
Pole position: Prost

1989 Estoril

24 September, 308.85km/191.91 miles
1 Gerhard Berger (Aut) Ferrari
2 Alain Prost (Fra) McLaren-Honda
3 Stefan Johansson (Swe) Onyx-Ford
4 Alessandro Nannini (Ita) Benetton-Ford
5 Pierluigi Martini (Ita) Minardi-Ford
6 Jonathan Palmer (GB) Tyrrell-Ford
Winner's speed: 191.42kph/118.94mph
Fastest lap: Berger 198.26kph/123.19mph
Pole position: Ayrton Senna (Bra) McLaren-Honda

1990 Estoril

23 September, 265.35km/164.88 miles
1 Nigel Mansell (GB) Ferrari
2 Ayrton Senna (Bra) McLaren-Honda
3 Alain Prost (Fra) Ferrari
4 Gerhard Berger (Aut) McLaren-Honda
5 Nelson Piquet (Bra) Benetton-Ford
6 Alessandro Nannini (Ita) Benetton-Ford
Winner's speed: 199.84kph/121.07mph
Fastest lap: Riccardo Patrese (Ita) Williams-Renault
201.15kph/124.99mph
Pole position: Mansell

1991 Estoril

22 September, 308.85km/191.91 miles
1 Riccardo Patrese (Ita) Williams-Renault
2 Ayrton Senna (Bra) McLaren-Honda
3 Jean Alesi (Fra) Ferrari
4 Pierluigi Martini (Ita) Minardi-Ferrari
5 Nelson Piquet (Bra) Benetton-Ford
6 Michael Schumacher (Ger) Benetton-Ford
Winner's speed: 193.63kph/120.31mph
Fastest lap: Nigel Mansell (GB) Williams-Renault
124.47mph/200.31kph
Pole position: Patrese

MOST WINS

Drivers
3 Alain Prost
2 Nigel Mansell, Stirling Moss
Manufacturers
3 McLaren
2 Cooper, Ferrari, Williams

MOST FASTEST LAPS

Drivers
3 Gerhard Berger
2 Nigel Mansell
Manufacturers
4 Ferrari   2 Lotus
3 Williams

MOST POLE POSITIONS

Drivers
3 Ayrton Senna
2 Stirling Moss
Manufacturers
3 Lotus
2 Ferrari, McLaren

SAN MARINO GP

All races at Imola

Raced at Imola, the home of the 1980 Italian Grand Prix, the San Marino Grand Prix was inaugurated the following year and thus meant that the Italian track was retained as a Formula One circuit. Nelson Piquet won both the 1980 and 1981 races and thus won two different Grands Prix on the same circuit in successive years, a feat subsequently matched by Nigel Mansell in winning the 1985 European and 1986 British Grands Prix, both at Brands Hatch.

It was at Imola in 1985 that Elio de Angelis had the second and last of his Grand Prix wins. The following year the popular Italian lost his life while testing his Brabham at Paul Ricard.

1981

3 May, 302.40km/187.90 miles
1 Nelson Piquet (Bra) Brabham-Ford
2 Riccardo Patrese (Ita) Arrows-Ford
3 Carlos Reutemann (Arg) Williams-Ford
4 Hector Rebaque (Mex) Brabham-Ford
5 Didier Pironi (Fra) Ferrari
6 Andrea de Cesaris (Ita) McLaren-Ford
Winner's speed: 162.87kph/101.21mph
Fastest lap: Villeneuve (Can) Ferrari 167.90kph/104.33mph

Pole position: Villeneuve

1982

25 April, 302.40km/187.90 miles
1 Didier Pironi (Ita) Ferrari
2 Gilles Villeneuve (Can) Ferrari
3 Michele Alboreto (Ita) Tyrrell-Ford
4 Jean-Pierre Jarier (Fra) Osella-Ford
5 Eliseo Salazar (Chi) ATS-Ford
Only five were classified.

Manfred Winkelhock (FRG) ATS-Ford finished 6th but was subsequently disqualified for having an underweight car.
Winner's speed: 187.77kph/117.30mph
Fastest lap: Pironi 190.92kph/118.64mph
Pole position: René Arnoux (Fra) Renault

1983

1 May, 302.40km/187.90 miles
1 Patrick Tambay (Fra) Ferrari
2 Alain Prost (Fra) Renault
3 René Arnoux (Fra) Ferrari
4 Keke Rosberg (Fin) Williams-Ford
5 John Watson (GB) McLaren-Ford
6 Marc Surer (Swi) Arrows-Ford
Winner's speed: 185.48kph/115.26mph
Fastest lap: Riccardo Patrese (Ita) Brabham-BMW 192.13kph/119.39mph
Pole position: Arnoux

1984

6 May, 302.40km/187.90 miles
1 Alain Prost (Fra) McLaren-Porsche
2 René Arnoux (Fra) Ferrari
3 Elio de Angelis (Ita) Lotus-Renault
4 Derek Warwick (GB) Renault
5 Thierry Boutsen (Bel) Arrows-Ford
6 Andrea de Cesaris (Ita) Ligier-Renault
Stefan Bellof (FRG) Tyrrell-Ford finished 5th but all Tyrrell points for drivers and manufacturer were deducted because of rule infringement.
Winner's speed: 187.25kph/116.36mph
Fastest lap: Nelson Piquet (Bra) Brabham-BMW 194.52kph/120.87mph
Pole position: Piquet

1985

5 May, 5 302.40km/187.90 miles
1 Elio de Angelis (Ita) Lotus-Renault
2 Thierry Boutsen (Bel) Arrows-BMW
3 Patrick Tambay (Fra) Renault
4 Niki Lauda (Aut) McLaren-TAG
5 Nigel Mansell (GB) Williams-Honda
6 Stefan Johansson (Swe) Ferrari
Alain Prost (Fra) McLaren-Ford finished 1st but was subsequently disqualified for having an underweight car.
Winner's speed: 191.80kph/119.18mph
Fastest lap: Michele Alboreto (Ita) Ferrari 199.47kph/123.95mph
Pole position: Ayrton Senna (Bra) Lotus-Renault

1986

27 April, 302.40km/187.90 miles
1 Alain Prost (Fra) McLaren-TAG
2 Nelson Piquet (Bra) Williams-Honda
3 Gerhard Berger (Aut) Benetton-BMW
4 Stefan Johansson (Swe) Ferrari
5 Keke Rosberg (Fin) McLaren-TAG
6 Riccardo Patrese (Ita) Brabham-BMW
Winner's speed: 196.20kph/121.92mph
Fastest lap: Piquet 204.63kph/127.15mph
Pole position: Ayrton Senna (Bra) Lotus-Renault

1987

3 May, 297.36km/184.77 miles
1 Nigel Mansell (GB) Williams-Honda
2 Ayrton Senna (Bra) Lotus-Honda
3 Michele Alboreto (Ita) Ferari
4 Stefan Johansson (Swe) McLaren-TAG
5 Martin Brundle (GB) Zakspeed
6 Satoru Nakajima (Jap) Lotus-Honda
Winner's speed: 195.20kph/121.29mph
Fastest lap: Teo Fabi (Ita) Benetton-Ford 203.30kph/126.33mph
Pole position: Senna

1988

1 May, 302.40km/187.90 miles
1 Ayrton Senna (Bra) McLaren-Honda
2 Alain Prost (Fra) McLaren-Honda
3 Nelson Piquet (Bra) Lotus-Honda
4 Thierry Boutsen (Bel) Benetton-Ford
5 Gerhard Berger (Aut) Ferrari
6 Alessandro Nannini (Ita) Benetton-Ford
Winner's speed: 196.78kph/122.30mph
Fastest lap: Prost 202.31kph/125.71mph
Pole position: Senna

1989

23 April, 297.36km/184.77 miles
1 Ayrton Senna (Bra) McLaren-Honda
2 Alain Prost (Fra) McLaren-Honda
3 Alessandro Nannini (Ita) Benetton-Ford
4 Thierry Boutsen (Bel) Williams-Renault
5 Derek Warwick (GB) Arrows-Ford
6 Jonathan Palmer (GB) Tyrrell-Ford
Winner's speed: 203.12kph/126.21mph
Fastest lap: Prost 210.26kph/130.65mph
Pole position: Senna

1990

13 May, 307.44km/191.05 miles
1 Riccardo Patrese (Ita) Williams-Renault
2 Gerhard Berger (Aut) McLaren-Honda
3 Alessandro Nannini (Ita) Benetton-Ford
4 Alain Prost (Fra) Ferrari
5 Nelson Piquet (Bra) Benetton-Ford
6 Jean Alesi (Fra) Tyrrell-Ford
Winner's speed: 202.88kph/126.06mph
Fastest lap: Nannini 208.18kph/129.36mph
Pole position: Ayrton Senna (Bra) McLaren-Honda

1991

28 April, 307.44km/ 191.05miles
1 Ayrton Senna (Bra) McLaren-Honda
2 Gerhard Berger (Aut) McLaren-Honda
3 J J Lehto (Fin) Dallara-Judd
4 Pierluigi Martini (Ita) Minardi-Ferrari
5 Miki Hakkinen (Fin) Lotus-Judd
6 Julian Bailey (GB) Lotus-Judd
Winner's speed: 193.67kph/120.34mph
Fastest lap: Berger 209.68kph/130.29mph
Pole position: Senna

MOST WINS

Drivers
3 Ayrton Senna
2 Alain Prost
Manufacturers
5 McLaren
2 Ferrari, Williams

MOST FASTEST LAPS

Drivers
2 Nelson Piquet, Alain Prost
Manufacturers
3 Ferrari, McLaren
2 Benetton, Brabham

MOST POLE POSITIONS

Drivers
7 Ayrton Senna
2 René Arnoux
Manufacturers
4 McLaren   2 Ferrari
3 Lotus

SOUTH AFRICAN GP

The first South African Grand Prix took place in 1934 over the East London circuit. It was a handicap race with a £250 first prize which went to Whitney Straight in his Maserati. The race was discontinued at the outbreak of war and did not return until 1960 when it was a *Formula Libre* event. Two years later the first World Championship Grand Prix was held at the Prince George Circuit at East London.

Practice started on Boxing Day and three days later the drivers lined up for what was to be a championship decider between the two Britons, Graham Hill and Jim Clark. The two men occupied the front row of the grid and with Hill holding a three point lead over Clark it was an exciting climax to the season and a great baptism for the South African Grand Prix.

Clark had built up a half-minute lead at the halfway stage but 20 laps from home an oil leak forced his retirement. Hill went on to take the chequered flag and the championship. Clark, however, won at East London in 1963 by which time he had already clinched the championship. Clark won again

in 1965 when the race moved from the end of the season to the beginning.

The 1966 race was the first of the new 3-litre formula and was held at the new Kyalami circuit on the outskirts of Johannesburg, but it did not receive championship status. This returned in 1967 and the Mexican Pedro Rodriguez enjoyed the first Grand Prix success of his career in the somewhat ill-fated Cooper-Maserati.

With the exception of 1981 the South African Grand Prix was held every year from 1967 to 1985 when it was removed from the championship rota. The improved political climate allowed it to return in 1992. It was at Kyalami in 1968 that Jim Clark had his 25th and last Grand Prix win.

1962 East London

29 December, 321.47km199.75 miles
1 Graham Hill (GB) BRM
2 Bruce McLaren (NZ) Cooper-Climax
3 Tony Maggs (SAf) Cooper-Climax
4 Jack Brabham (Aus) Brabham-Climax
5 Innes Ireland (GB) Lotus-Climax
6 Neville Lederle (SAf) Lotus-Climax
Winner's speed: 150.55kph/93.57mph
Fastest lap: Jim Clark (GB) Lotus-Climax 155.03kph/96.35mph
Pole position: Clark

1963 East London

28 December, 333.23km/207.06 miles
1 Jim Clark (GB) Lotus-Climax
2 Dan Gurney (USA) Brabham-Climax
3 Graham Hill (GB) BRM
4 Bruce McLaren (NZ) Cooper-Climax
5 Lorenzo Bandini (Ita) Ferrari
6 Jo Bonnier (Swe) Cooper-Climax
Winner's speed: 153.05kph/95.10mph
Fastest lap: Gurney 158.42kph/98.41mph
Pole position: Clark

1965 East London

1 January, 333.23km/207.06 miles
1 Jim Clark (GB) Lotus-Climax
2 John Surtees (GB) Ferrari
3 Graham Hill (GB) BRM
4 Mike Spence (GB) Lotus-Climax
5 Bruce McLaren (NZ) Cooper-Climax
6 Jackie Stewart (GB) BRM
Winner's speed: 157.63kph/97.97mph
Fastest lap: Clark 161.11kph/100.11mph
Pole position: Clark

1967 Kyalami

2 January, 327.53km/203.52 miles
1 Pedro Rodriguez (Mex) Cooper-Maserati
2 John Love (SAf) Cooper-Climax
3 John Surtees (GB) Honda
4 Denny Hulme (NZ) Brabham-Repco
5 Bob Anderson (GB) Brabham-Climax
6 Jack Brabham (Aus) Brabham-Repco
Winner's speed: 156.26kph/97.09mph
Fastest lap: Hulme 163.95kph/101.87mph
Pole position: Brabham

1968 Kyalami

1 January, 328.32km/204.01 miles
1 Jim Clark (GB) Lotus-Ford
2 Graham Hill (GB) Lotus-Ford
3 Jochen Rindt (Aut) Brabham-Repco
4 Chris Amon (NZ) Ferrari
5 Denny Hulme (NZ) McLaren-BRM
6 Jean-Pierre Beltoise (Fra) Matra-Ford
Winner's speed: 172.89kph/107.42mph
Fastest lap: Clark 176.51kph/109.68mph
Pole position: Clark

1969 Kyalami

1 March, 328.32km/204.01 miles
1 Jackie Stewart (GB) Matra-Ford
2 Graham Hill (GB) Lotus-Ford
3 Denny Hulme (NZ) McLaren-Ford
4 Jo Siffert (Swi) Lotus-Ford
5 Bruce McLaren (NZ) McLaren-Ford
6 Jean-Pierre Beltoise (Fra) Matra-Ford
Winner's speed: 178.03kph/110.62mph
Fastest lap: Stewart 181.05kph/112.50mph
Pole position: Jack Brabham (Aus) Brabham-Ford

1970 Kyalami

7 March, 328.32km/204.01 miles
1 Jack Brabham (Aus) Brabham-Ford
2 Denny Hulme (NZ) McLaren-Ford
3 Jackie Stewart (GB) March-Ford
4 Jean-Pierre Beltoise (Fra) Matra-Simca
5 John Miles (GB) Lotus-Ford
6 Graham Hill (GB) Lotus-Ford
Winner's speed: 179.76kph/111.70mph
Fastest lap: Brabham & John Surtees (GB) McLaren-Ford
182.84kph/113.61mph
Pole position: Stewart

1971 Kyalami

6 March, 324.22km/201.46 miles
1 Mario Andretti (USA) Ferrari
2 Jackie Stewart (GB) Tyrrell-Ford
3 Clay Regazzoni (Swi) Ferrari
4 Reine Wisell (Swe) Lotus-Ford
5 Chris Amon (NZ) Matra-Simca
6 Denny Hulme (NZ) McLaren-Ford
Winner's speed: 180.80kph/112.35mph
Fastest lap: Andretti 183.99kph/114.33mph
Pole position: Stewart

1972 Kyalami

4 March, 324.22km/201.46 miles
1 Denny Hulme (NZ) McLaren-Ford
2 Emerson Fittipaldi (Bra) Lotus-Ford
3 Peter Revson (USA) McLaren-Ford
4 Mario Andretti (USA) Ferrari
5 Ronnie Peterson (Swe) March-Ford
6 Graham Hill (GB) Brabham-Ford
Winner's speed: 183.83kph/114.23mph
Fastest lap: Mike Hailwood (GB) Surtees-Ford 187.25kph/

116.35mph
Pole position: Jackie Stewart (GB) Tyrrell-Ford

1973 Kyalami

3 March, 324.22km/201.46 miles
1 Jackie Stewart (GB) Tyrrell-Ford
2 Peter Revson (USA) McLaren-Ford
3 Emerson Fittipaldi (Bra) Lotus-Ford
4 Arturo Merzario (Ita) Ferrari
5 Denny Hulme (NZ) McLaren-Ford
6 George Follmer (USA) Shadow-Ford
Winner's speed: 188.53kph/117.14mph
Fastest lap: Fittipaldi 191.63kph/119.07mph
Pole position: Hulme

1974 Kyalami

30 March, 320.11km/198.91 miles
1 Carlos Reutemann (Arg) Brabham-Ford
2 Jean-Pierre Beltoise (Fra) BRM
3 Mike Hailwood (GB) McLaren-Ford
4 Patrick Depailler (Fra) Tyrrell-Ford
5 Hans-Joachim Stuck (FRG) March-Ford
6 Arturo Merzario (Ita) Williams-Ford
Winner's speed: 187.05kph/116.23mph
Fastest lap: Reutemann 189.03kph/117.46mph
Pole position: Niki Lauda (Aut) Ferrari

1975 Kyalami

1 March, 320.11km/198.91 miles
1 Jody Scheckter (SAf) Tyrrell-Ford
2 Carlos Reutemann (Arg) Brabham-Ford
3 Patrick Depailler (Fra) Tyrrell-Ford
4 Carlos Pace (Bra) Brabham-Ford
5 Niki Lauda (Aut) Ferrari
6 Jochen Mass (FRG) McLaren-Ford
Winner's speed: 185.96kph/115.55mph
Fastest lap: Pace 191.38kph/118.92mph
Pole position: Pace

1976 Kyalami

6 March, 320.11km/198.91 miles
1 Niki Lauda (Aut) Ferrari
2 James Hunt (GB) McLaren-Ford
3 Jochen Mass (FRG) McLaren-Ford
4 Jody Scheckter (SAf) Tyrrell-Ford
5 John Watson (GB) Penske-Ford
6 Mario Andretti (USA) Parnelli-Ford
Winner's speed: 187.74kph/116.65mph
Fastest lap: Lauda 189.49kph/117.74mph
Pole position: Hunt

1977 Kyalami

5 March, 320.11km/198.91 miles
1 Niki Lauda (Aut) Ferrari
2 Jody Scheckter (SAf) Wolf-Ford
3 Patrick Depailler (Fra) Tyrrell-Ford
4 James Hunt (GB) McLaren-Ford
5 Jochen Mass (FRG) McLaren-Ford
6 John Watson (GB) Brabham-Alfa Romeo
Winner's speed: 187.64kph/116.59mph

Fastest lap: Watson 190.32kph/118.26mph
Pole position: Hunt

1978 Kyalami

4 March, 320.11km/198.91 miles
1 Ronnie Peterson (Swe) Lotus-Ford
2 Patrick Depailler (Fra) Tyrrell-Ford
3 John Watson (GB) Brabham-Alfa Romeo
4 Alan Jones (Aus) Williams-Ford
5 Jacques Laffite (Fra) Ligier-Matra
6 Didier Pironi (Fra) Tyrrell-Ford
Winner's speed: 187.81kph/116.70mph
Fastest lap: Mario Andretti (USA) Lotus-Ford 191.64kph/
119.08mph
Pole position: Niki Lauda (Aut) Brabham-Alfa Romeo

1979 Kyalami

3 March, 320.11km/198.91 miles
1 Gilles Villeneuve (Can) Ferrari
2 Jody Scheckter (SAf) Ferrari
3 Jean-Pierre Jarier (Fra) Tyrrell-Ford
4 Mario Andretti (USA) Lotus-Ford
5 Carlos Reutemann (Bra) Lotus-Ford
6 Niki Lauda (Aut) Brabham-Alfa Romeo
Winner's speed: 188.60kph/117.19mph
Fastest lap: Villeneuve 198.54kph/123.38mph
Pole position: Jean-Pierre Jabouille (Fra) Renault

1980 Kyalami

1 March, 320.11km/198.91 miles
1 René Arnoux (Fra) Renault
2 Jacques Laffite (Fra) Ligier-Ford
3 Didier Pironi (Fra) Ligier-Ford
4 Nelson Piquet (Bra) Brabham-Ford
5 Carlos Reutemann (Arg) Williams-Ford
6 Jochen Mass (FRG) Arrows-Ford
Winner's speed: 198.25kph/123.19mph
Fastest lap: Arnoux 201.97kph/125.50mph
Pole position: Jean-Pierre Jabouille (Fra) Renault

1982 Kyalami

23 January, 316.01km/196.36 miles
1 Alain Prost (Fra) Renault
2 Carlos Reutemann (Arg) Williams-Ford

3 René Arnoux (Fra) Renault
4 Niki Lauda (Aut) McLaren-Ford
5 Keke Rosberg (Fin) Williams-Ford
6 John Watson (GB) McLaren-Ford
Winner's speed: 205.70kph/127.82mph
Fastest lap: Prost 216.39kph/134.46mph
Pole position: Arnoux

1983 Kyalami

16 October, 316.01km/196.36 miles
1 Riccardo Patrese (Ita) Brabham-BMW
2 Andrea de Cesaris (Ita) Alfa Romeo
3 Nelson Piquet (Bra) Brabham-BMW
4 Derek Warwick (GB) Toleman-Hart
5 Keke Rosberg (Fin) Williams-Honda
6 Eddie Cheever (USA) Renault
Winner's speed: 202.94kph/126.11mph
Fastest lap: Piquet 211.22kph/131.25mph
Pole position: Patrick Tambay (Fra) Ferrari

1984 Kyalami

7 April, 307.80km/191.26 miles
1 Niki Lauda (Aut) McLaren-Porsche
2 Alain Prost (Fra) McLaren-Porsche
3 Derek Warwick (GB) Renault
4 Riccardo Patrese (Ita) Alfa Romeo
5 Andrea de Cesaris (Ita) Ligier-Renault
6 Ayrton Senna (Bra) Toleman-Hart
Winner's speed: 206.59kph/128.38mph
Fastest lap: Patrick Tambay (Fra) Renault 214.49kph/
133.28mph
Pole position: Nelson Piquet (Bra) Brabham-BMW

1985 Kyalami

19 October, 307.80km/191.26 miles
1 Nigel Mansell (GB) Williams-Honda
2 Keke Rosberg (Fin) Williams-Honda
3 Alain Prost (Fra) McLaren-TAG
4 Stefan Johansson (Swe) Ferrari
5 Gerhard Berger (Aut) Arrows-BMW
6 Thierry Boutsen (Bel) Arrows-BMW
Winner's speed: 208.96kph/129.85mph
Fastest lap: Rosberg 216.80kph/134.71mph
Pole position: Mansell

MOST WINS

Drivers
3 Jim Clark, Niki Lauda
2 Jackie Stewart
Manufacturers
4 Ferrari, Lotus
3 Brabham
2 McLaren, Renault, Tyrrell

MOST FASTEST LAPS

Drivers
3 Jim Clark
Manufacturers
7 Brabham
5 Lotus
3 Ferrari, Renault

MOST POLE POSITIONS

Drivers
4 Jim Clark
3 Jackie Stewart
2 Jack Brabham, James Hunt,
   Jean-Pierre Jabouille
Manufacturers
4 Brabham, Lotus, McLaren
3 Renault
2 Ferrari, Tyrrell

SPANISH GP

The history of the Spanish Grand Prix as a World Championship race has been more chequered than most. It has come and gone from the championship list no fewer than five times. However, it now seems to be firmly established as a championship race.

The first race to carry the title of Spanish Grand Prix was at Guadarrama in 1913. The race was held in the grounds of one of King Alfonso's palaces. In the 1920s the Spanish Grands Prix became as popular as any across Europe and the Bugatti of Louis Chiron twice won in that decade. The race ceased in 1935 and was not revived until 1951 when it formed a round of the World Championship. Juan Manuel Fangio won, with his fellow Argentinian José Froilán González in second place, and this success assured Fangio of his first world title.

Mike Hawthorn won in 1954 but the 1955 Le Mans disaster and Spain's subsequent ban on motor racing meant that this was to be the last Spanish Grand Prix until 1967 when Jim Clark won. But there were too few entries that year and the race was not granted championship status. Graham Hill kept the Lotus flag flying when he won the following year in what was the first championship race in Spain for 14 years.

In 1980 the race, although held, was not classified for World Championship purposes. It was held again in 1981 but disappeared between 1982 and 1985. However, it has been a regular fixture since 1986 with Jerez as its home until 1991 when the new Catalunya Circuit near Barcelona was used for the first time. Niki Lauda won his first Grand Prix at Jarama in 1974.

The finishing straight at Jerez, home of the Spanish Grand Prix for five years.

1951 Pedralbes

28 October, 442.12km/274.72 miles
1 Juan Manuel Fangio (Arg) Alfa Romeo
2 José Froilán González (Arg) Ferrari
3 Giuseppe Farina (Ita) Alfa Romeo
4 Alberto Ascari (Ita) Ferrari
5 Felice Bonetto (Ita) Alfa Romeo
6 Emmanuel de Graffenried (Swi) Alfa Romeo
Winner's speed: 158.94kph/98.76mph
Fastest lap: Fangio 166.05kph/103.18mph
Pole position: Ascari

1954 Pedralbes

24 October, 505.28km/313.97 miles
1 Mike Hawthorn (GB) Ferrari
2 Luigi Musso (Ita) Maserati
3 Juan Manuel Fangio (Arg) Mercedes-Benz
4 Roberto Mieres (Arg) Maserati
5 Karl Kling (FRG) Mercedes-Benz
6 Francisco Godia (Spa) Maserati
Winner's speed: 156.38kph/97.16mph
Fastest lap: Alberto Ascari (Ita) Lancia 161.97kph/
100.64mph
Pole position: Ascari

1968 Jarama

12 May, 306.36km/190.36 miles
1 Graham Hill (GB) Lotus-Ford
2 Denny Hulme (NZ) McLaren-Ford
3 Brian Redman (GB) Cooper-BRM
4 Ludovico Scarfiotti (Ita) Cooper-BRM
5 Jean-Pierre Beltoise (Fra) Matra-Ford
Only five were classified.
Winner's speed: 135.84kph/84.40mph
Fastest lap: Beltoise 138.80kph/86.24mph
Pole position: Chris Amon (NZ) Ferrari

1969 Montjuich

4 May, 341.19km/212.01 miles
1 Jackie Stewart (GB) Matra-Ford
2 Bruce McLaren (NZ) McLaren-Ford
3 Jean-Pierre Beltoise (Fra) Matra-Ford
4 Denny Hulme (NZ) McLaren-Ford
5 John Surtees (GB) BRM
6 Jacky Ickx (Bel) Brabham-Ford
Winner's speed: 149.52kph/92.91mph
Fastest lap: Jochen Rindt (Aut) Lotus-Ford 154.54kph/
96.02mph
Pole position: Rindt

1970 Jarama

19 April, 306.36km/190.36 miles
1 Jackie Stewart (GB) March-Ford
2 Bruce McLaren (NZ) McLaren-Ford
3 Mario Andretti (USA) March-Ford
4 Graham Hill (GB) Lotus-Ford
5 Johnny Servoz-Gavin (Fra) March-Ford
Only five were classified.
Winner's speed: 140.36kph/87.22mph
Fastest lap: Jack Brabham (Aus) Brabham-Ford
145.38kph/90.33mph
Pole position: Brabham

1971 Montjuich

18 April, 284.33km/176.67 miles
1 Jackie Stewart (GB) Tyrrell-Ford
2 Jacky Ickx (Bel) Ferrari
3 Chris Amon (NZ) Matra-Simca
4 Pedro Rodriguez (Mex) BRM
5 Denny Hulme (NZ) McLaren-Ford
6 Jean-Pierre Beltoise (Fra) Matra-Simca
Winner's speed: 156.41kph/97.19mph
Fastest lap: Ickx 160.36kph/99.64mph
Pole position: Ickx

1972 Jarama

1 May, 306.36km/190.36 miles
1 Emerson Fittipaldi (Bra) Lotus-Ford
2 Jacky Ickx (Bel) Ferrari
3 Clay Regazzoni (Swi) Ferrari
4 Andrea de Adamich (Ita) Surtees-Ford
5 Peter Revson (USA) McLaren-Ford
6 Carlos Pace (Bra) March-Ford
Winner's speed: 148.63kph/92.35mph

Fastest lap: Ickx 151.28kph/94.00mph
Pole position: Ickx

1973 Montjuich

29 April, 284.33km/176.67 miles
1 Emerson Fittipaldi (Bra) Lotus-Ford
2 François Cevert (Fra) Tyrrell-Ford
3 George Follmer (USA) Shadow-Ford
4 Peter Revson (USA) McLaren-Ford
5 Jean-Pierre Beltoise (Fra) BRM
6 Denny Hulme (NZ) McLaren-Ford
Winner's speed: 157.49kph/97.86mph
Fastest lap: Ronnie Peterson (Swe) Lotus-Ford 162.86kph/
101.20mph
Pole position: Peterson

1974 Jarama

28 April, 285.94km/177.67 miles
1 Niki Lauda (Aut) Ferrari
2 Clay Regazzoni (Swi) Ferrari
3 Emerson Fittipaldi (Bra) McLaren-Ford
4 Hans-Joachim Stuck (FRG) March-Ford
5 Jody Scheckter (SAf) Tyrrell-Ford
6 Denny Hulme (NZ) McLaren-Ford
Winner's speed: 142.40kph/88.48mph
Fastest lap: Lauda 151.62kph/94.21mph
Pole position: Lauda

1975 Montjuich

27 April, 109.94km/68.31 miles
1 Jochen Mass (FRG) McLaren-Ford
2 Jacky Ickx (Bel) Lotus-Ford
3 Carlos Reutemann (Arg) Brabham-Ford
4 Jean-Pierre Jarier (Fra) Shadow-Ford
5 Vittorio Brambilla (Ita) March-Ford
6 Lella Lombardi (Ita) March-Ford
*Half points only awarded because insufficient distance
covered.*
Winner's speed: 153.76kph/95.54mph
Fastest lap: Mario Andretti (USA) Parnelli-Ford 160.36kph/
99.64mph
Pole position: Niki Lauda (Aut) Ferrari

1976 Jarama

2 May, 255.30km/158.64 miles
1 James Hunt (GB) McLaren-Ford
2 Niki Lauda (Aut) Ferrari
3 Gunnar Nilsson (Swe) Lotus-Ford
4 Carlos Reutemann (Arg) Brabham-Alfa Romeo
5 Chris Amon (NZ) Ensign-Ford
6 Carlos Pace (Bra) Brabham-Alfa Romeo
Winner's speed: 149.69kph/93.01mph
Fastest lap: Jochen Mass (FRG) McLaren-Ford
151.43kph/94.10mph
Pole position: Hunt

1977 Jarama

8 May, 255.30km/158.64 miles
1 Mario Andretti (USA) Lotus-Ford
2 Carlos Reutemann (Arg) Ferrari
3 Jody Scheckter (SAf) Wolf-Ford
4 Jochen Mass (FRG) McLaren-Ford
5 Gunnar Nilsson (Swe) Lotus-Ford
6 Hans-Joachim Stuck (FRG) Brabham-Alfa Romeo
Winner's speed: 148.92kph/92.53mph
Fastest lap: Jacques Laffite (Fra) Ligier-Matra 151.66kph/
94.24mph
Pole position: Andretti

1978 Jarama

4 June, 255.30km/158.64 miles
1 Mario Andretti (USA) Lotus-Ford
2 Ronnie Peterson (Swe) Lotus-Ford
3 Jacques Laffite (Fra) Ligier-Matra
4 Jody Scheckter (SAf) Wolf-Ford
5 John Watson (GB) Brabham-Alfa Romeo
6 James Hunt (GB) McLaren-Ford
Winner's speed: 150.51kph/93.52mph
Fastest lap: Andretti 153.08kph/95.12mph
Pole position: Andretti

THE GREAT RACES

1981
Spanish GP

Canadian Gilles Villeneuve took the race by a mere 22 *thousandths* of a second from Jacques Laffite. It was the sixth and last win of Villeneuve's career before he lost his life at Zolder the following year. But what an exciting race it was with just over one second separating the first four drivers. Villeneuve started from the fourth row of the grid, took the lead on the 14th lap when Alan Jones spun off, and kept his nose in front before taking the chequered flag with three other drivers hotly in pursuit.

The race was held in glorious sunshine with temperatures in excess of 100 degrees. Laffite was in pole position but was soon left at the line after making a mess of the getaway. Alan Jones shot to the front of the pack and after the first lap he started to pull away. He was driving superbly. Behind him came Villeneuve and Reutemann who, in turn, were pulling away from the rest of the field, but they kept slipping behind the Australian with each lap.

Jones was driving so steadily that a victory was already being talked about with less than a fifth of the race gone but then, on the 14th lap, he understeered his Williams after taking a corner too quickly and off he went. Villeneuve in the Ferrari, and 14 other drivers, went past him before he could get going again.

Having thus taken the lead, Villeneuve was aware that while his Ferrari was better and faster on the straights than the likes of the Lotus and Williams, they had the better of his car on the bends and it would be here that the Canadian would lose the race, if he was going to.

Reutemann kept the pressure on the leader from second place while there was a lot of jockeying for third and fourth place behind him. Alain Prost held third place for a while, but made a mistake and let in John Watson. At the halfway stage, Villeneuve led, Reutemann was second with Watson just holding off Laffite in third place. But the Argentinian was getting frustrated at not being able to keep up with Villeneuve on the straight after closing the gap at each bend.

Once Laffite, in the Talbot-Matra, got past Watson he started chasing the leaders but Villeneuve dominated the race and ran it at his own pace, even if it did not suit the drivers behind him. Laffite was putting pressure on Reutemann all the time and by the 60th lap, with the three leaders close to each other at the bends but with Villeneuve's Ferrari gaining on each straight, Laffite went past Reutemann's Williams and into second place. So astounded was the Argentinian that he allowed Watson to go past and the South American was relegated to fourth place.

Laffite was now in hot pursuit of the Ferrari with 20 laps remaining and with 15 to go there were five men in the hunt because Elio de Angelis had joined the pursuers in his Lotus. But Villeneuve was totally in control and at the corners he gave a fine display of precision driving without baulking any of his rivals. He maintained his great tactical advantage and then utilised the Ferrari's great power on the straight to take the chequered flag. Just one second split the first four drivers.

1979 Jarama

29 April, 255.30km/158.64 miles
1 Patrick Depailler (Fra) Ligier-Ford
2 Carlos Reutemann (Arg) Lotus-Ford
3 Mario Andretti (USA) Lotus-Ford
4 Jody Scheckter (SAf) Ferrari
5 Jean-Pierre Jarier (Fra) Tyrrell-Ford
6 Didier Pironi (Fra) Tyrrell-Ford
Winner's speed: 154.45kph/95.97mph
Fastest lap: Gilles Villeneuve (Can) Ferrari 160.31kph/
99.61mph
Pole position: Jacques Laffite (Fra) Ligier-Ford

1981 Jarama

21 June, 264.96km/164.64 miles
1 Gilles Villeneuve (Can) Ferrari
2 Jacques Laffite (Fra) Talbot-Matra
3 John Watson (GB) McLaren-Ford
4 Carlos Reutemann (Arg) Williams-Ford
5 Elio de Angelis (Ita) Lotus-Ford
6 Nigel Mansell (GB) Lotus-Ford
Winner's speed: 149.10kph/92.65mph
Fastest lap: Alan Jones (Aus) Williams-Ford 153.22kph/
95.21mph
Pole position: Laffite

1986 Jerez

13 April, 303.70km/188.71 miles
1 Ayrton Senna (Bra) Lotus-Renault
2 Nigel Mansell (GB) Williams-Honda
3 Alain Prost (Fra) McLaren-TAG
4 Keke Rosberg (Fin) McLaren-TAG
5 Teo Fabi (Ita) Benetton-BMW
6 Gerhard Berger (Aut) Benetton-BMW
Winner's speed: 167.48kph/104.07mph
Fastest lap: Mansell 174.17kph/108.23mph
Pole position: Senna

1987 Jerez

27 September, 303.70km/188.71 miles
1 Nigel Mansell (GB) Williams-Honda
2 Alain Prost (Fra) McLaren-TAG
3 Stefan Johansson (Swe) McLaren-TAG
4 Nelson Piquet (Bra) Williams-Honda
5 Ayrton Senna (Bra) Lotus-Honda
6 Philippe Alliot (Fra) Lola-Ford
Winner's speed: 166.85kph/103.67mph
Fastest lap: Gerhard Berger (Aut) Ferrari 174.57kph/
108.47mph

Pole position: Piquet

1988 Jerez

2 October, 303.70km/188.71 miles
1 Alain Prost (Fra) McLaren-Honda
2 Nigel Mansell (GB) Williams-Judd
3 Alessandro Nannini (Ita) Benetton-Ford
4 Ayrton Senna (Bra) McLaren-Honda
5 Riccardo Patrese (Ita) Williams-Judd
6 Gerhard Berger (Aut) Ferrari
Winner's speed: 167.59kph/104.13mph
Fastest lap: Prost 172.86kph/107.41mph
Pole position: Senna

1989 Jerez

1 October, 307.94km/191.32 miles
1 Ayrton Senna (Bra) McLaren-Honda
2 Gerhard Berger (Aut) Ferrari
3 Alain Prost (Fra) McLaren-Honda
4 Jean Alesi (Fra) Tyrrell-Ford
5 Riccardo Patrese (Ita) Williams-Renault
6 Philippe Alliot (Fra) Lola-Lamborghini
Winner's speed: 172.37kph/107.11mph
Fastest lap: Senna 177.02kph/109.10mph
Pole position: Senna

1990 Jerez

30 September, 307.91km/191.32 miles
1 Alain Prost (Fra) Ferrari
2 Nigel Mansell (GB) Ferrari
3 Alessandro Nannini (Ita) Benetton-Ford
4 Thierry Boutsen (Bel) Williams-Renault
5 Riccardo Patrese (Ita) Williams-Renault
6 Aguru Suzuki (Jap) Lola-Lamborghini
Winner's speed: 171.02kph/106.27mph
Fastest lap: Patrese 179.67kph/111.64mph
Pole position: Ayrton Senna (Bra) McLaren-Honda

1991 Catalunya, Barcelona

29 September, 308.49km/191.69 miles
1 Nigel Mansell (GB) Williams-Renault
2 Alain Prost (Fra) Ferrari
3 Riccardo Patrese (Ita) Williams-Renault
4 Jean Alesi (Fra) Ferrari
5 Ayrton Senna (Bra) McLaren-Honda
6 Michael Schumacher (Ger) Benetton-Ford
Winner's speed: 187.59kph/116.56mph
Fastest Lap: Patrese 128.19mph/206.30kph
Pole position: Gerhard Berger (Aut) McLaren-Honda

MOST WINS

Drivers
3 Jackie Stewart
2 Mario Andretti, Emerson Fittipaldi,
  Nigel Mansell, Alain Prost, Ayrton
  Senna
Manufacturers
6 Lotus
4 Ferrari, McLaren   2 Williams

MOST FASTEST LAPS

Drivers
2 Mario Andretti, Jacky Ickx, Riccardo
  Patrese
Manufacturers
5 Ferrari
4 Williams
3 Lotus, McLaren

MOST POLE POSITIONS

Drivers
4 Ayrton Senna
2 Mario Andretti, Alberto Ascari, Jacky
  Ickx, Jacques Laffite, Niki Lauda
Manufacturers
6 Ferrari
5 Lotus, McLaren

SWEDISH GP

All races at Anderstorp

Jacques Laffite's first ever Grand Prix win was in Sweden in 1977. He finished ahead of Jochen Mass (left) and Carlos Reutemann.

The rather uninteresting Scandinavian Raceway just outside Anderstorp was the venue for the six runnings of the Swedish Grand Prix to carry World Championship status. There had previously been three races carrying the same title between 1955 and 1957 but they were for sports cars. Jody Scheckter (1974) and Jacques Laffite (1977) both had their debut Grand Prix wins at Anderstorp.

MOST WINS

Drivers
2 Niki Lauda, Jody Scheckter
Manufacturers
2 Tyrrell

MOST FASTEST LAPS

Drivers
2 Mario Andretti, Niki Lauda
Manufacturers
2 Lotus

MOST POLE POSITIONS

Drivers
2 Mario Andretti
Manufacturers
3 Lotus
2 Tyrrell

1973

17 June, 321.44km/199.73 miles
1 Denny Hulme (NZ) McLaren-Ford
2 Ronnie Peterson (Swe) Lotus-Ford
3 François Cevert (Fra) Tyrrell-Ford
4 Carlos Reutemann (Arg) Brabham-Ford
5 Jackie Stewart (GB) Tyrrell-Ford
6 Jacky Ickx (Bel) Ferrari
Winner's speed: 165.17kph/102.63mph
Fastest lap: Hulme 167.91kph/104.33mph
Pole position: Peterson

1974

9 June, 321.44km/199.73 miles
1 Jody Scheckter (SAf) Tyrrell-Ford
2 Patrick Depailler (Fra) Tyrrell-Ford
3 James Hunt (GB) Hesketh-Ford
4 Emerson Fittipaldi (Bra) McLaren-Ford
5 Jean-Pierre Jarier (Fra) Shadow-Ford
6 Graham Hill (GB) Lola-Ford
Winner's speed: 162.72kph/101.11mph
Fastest lap: Depailler 165.76kph/103.00mph
Pole position: Depailler

1975

8 June, 321.44km/199.73 miles
1 Niki Lauda (Aut) Ferrari
2 Carlos Reutemann (Arg) Brabham-Ford
3 Clay Regazzoni (Swi) Ferrari
4 Mario Andretti (USA) Parnelli-Ford
5 Mark Donohue (USA) Penske-Ford
6 Tony Brise (GB) Hill-Ford
Winner's speed: 161.66kph/100.45mph
Fastest lap: Lauda 163.88kph/101.83mph
Pole position: Vittorio Brambilla (Ita) March-Ford

1976

13 June, 289.30km/179.76 miles
1 Jody Scheckter (SAf) Tyrrell-Ford
2 Patrick Depailler (Fra) Tyrrell-Ford
3 Niki Lauda (Aut) Ferrari
4 Jacques Laffite (Fra) Ligier-Matra
5 James Hunt (GB) McLaren-Ford
6 Clay Regazzoni (Swi) Ferrari
Winner's speed: 162.38kph/100.90mph
Fastest lap: Mario Andretti (USA) Lotus-Ford 164.37kph/102.13mph
Pole position: Scheckter

1977

19 June, 289.30km/179.76 miles
1 Jacques Laffite (Fra) Ligier-Matra
2 Jochen Mass (FRG) McLaren-Ford
3 Carlos Reutemann (Arg) Ferrari
4 Patrick Depailler (Fra) Tyrrell-Ford
5 John Watson (GB) Brabham-Alfa Romeo
6 Mario Andretti (USA) Lotus-Ford
Winner's speed: 162.34kph/100.87mph
Fastest lap: Andretti 165.11kph/102.59mph
Pole position: Andretti

1978

17 June, 282.17km/175.33 miles
1 Niki Lauda (Aut) Brabham-Alfa Romeo
2 Riccardo Patrese (Ita) Arrows-Ford
3 Ronnie Peterson (Swe) Lotus-Ford
4 Patrick Tambay (Fra) McLaren-Ford
5 Clay Regazzoni (Swi) Shadow-Ford
6 Emerson Fittipaldi (Bra) Fittipaldi-Ford
Winner's speed: 167.61kph/104.15mph
Fastest lap: Lauda 171.06kph/106.29mph
Pole position: Mario Andretti (USA) Lotus-Ford

SWISS GP

Motor sport had been popular in Switzerland since the first running of the Swiss Grand Prix at Bremgarten near Berne in 1934. It was held annually up to the outbreak of the Second World War and three of the six runnings were won by Rudi Caracciola in a Mercedes. The event was revived shortly after the war.

The Swiss Grand Prix was one of the seven races that formed the initial drivers' championship in 1950. And it was firmly established as a World Championship round until 1955 when disaster struck at Le Mans and Switzerland immediately banned motor racing. That ban remains today. A Swiss Grand Prix did return to the Formula One calendar in 1982 but was held over the border at the Dijon-Prenois circuit in France.

MOST WINS

Drivers
2 Juan Manuel Fangio
Manufacturers
2 Alfa Romeo, Ferrari

MOST FASTEST LAPS

Drivers
2 Juan Manuel Fangio
Manufacturers
2 Alfa Romeo, Ferrari

MOST POLE POSITIONS

Drivers
3 Juan Manuel Fangio
Manufacturers
2 Alfa Romeo, Ferrari

1950 Bremgarten

4 June, 305.76km/189.99 miles
1 Giuseppe Farina (Ita) Alfa Romeo
2 Luigi Fagioli (Ita) Alfa Romeo
3 Louis Rosier (Fra) Lago-Talbot
4 'B Bira' (Siam) Maserati
5 Felice Bonetto (Ita) Maserati
6 Emmanuel de Graffenried (Swi) Maserati
Winner's speed: 149.28kph/92.76mph
Fastest lap: Farina 162.18kph/100.78mph
Pole position: Juan Manuel Fangio (Arg) Alfa Romeo

1951 Bremgarten

27 May, 305.76km/189.99 miles
1 Juan Manuel Fangio (Arg) Alfa Romeo
2 Piero Taruffi (Ita) Ferrari
3 Giuseppe Farina (Ita) Alfa Romeo
4 Consalvo Sanesi (Ita) Alfa Romeo
5 Emmanuel de Graffenried (Swi) Alfa Romeo
6 Alberto Ascari (Ita) Ferrari
Winner's speed: 143.28kph/89.05mph
Fastest lap: Fangio 153.18kph/95.18mph
Pole position: Fangio

1952 Bremgarten

18 May, 451.36km/280.46 miles
1 Piero Taruffi (Ita) Ferrari
2 Rudi Fischer (Swi) Ferrari
3 Jean Behra (Fra) Gordini
4 Ken Wharton (GB) Frazer Nash
5 Alan Brown (GB) Cooper-Bristol
6 Emmanuel de Graffenried (Swi) Maserati-Plate
Winner's speed: 149.38kph/92.78mph
Fastest lap: Taruffi 154.84kph/96.25mph
Pole position: Giuseppe Farina (Ita) Ferrari

1953 Bremgarten

23 August, 473.20km/294.03 miles
1 Alberto Ascari (Ita) Ferrari
2 Giuseppe Farina (Ita) Ferrari
3 Mike Hawthorn (GB) Ferrari
4 Felice Bonetto (Ita)/Juan Manuel Fangio (Arg) Maserati
5 Hermann Lang (FRG) Maserati
6 Luigi Villoresi (Ita) Ferrari
Winner's speed: 156.37kph/97.17mph
Fastest lap: Ascari 162.48kph/100.96mph
Pole position: Fangio

1954 Bremgarten

22 August, 480.48km/298.56 miles
1 Juan Manuel Fangio (Arg) Mercedes-Benz
2 José Froilán González (Arg) Ferrari
3 Hans Herrmann (FRG) Mercedes-Benz
4 Roberto Mieres (Arg) Maserati
5 Sergio Mantovani (Ita) Maserati
6 Ken Wharton (GB) Maserati
Winner's speed: 159.56kph/99.17mph
Fastest lap: Fangio 164.10kph/101.97mph
Pole position: González

1982 Dijon-Prenois (France)

29 August, 304.00km/188.90 miles
1 Keke Rosberg (Fin) Williams-Ford
2 Alain Prost (Fra) Renault
3 Niki Lauda (Aut) McLaren-Ford
4 Nelson Piquet (Bra) Brabham-BMW
5 Riccardo Patrese (Ita) Brabham-BMW
6 Elio de Angelis (Ita) Lotus-Ford
Winner's speed: 196.80kph/122.29mph
Fastest lap: Prost 202.74kph/125.98mph
Pole position: Prost

UNITED STATES GP

The inaugural United States Grand Prix in 1958 was a sports car race. The following year it joined the Indianapolis 500 and became the second American race to form part of the Formula One World Championship.

The 1958 race had been held at the Riverside Speedway in California but the first World Championship race was at the Sebring Circuit in Florida. Sadly, the event was poorly attended and the following year it returned to Riverside. Crowds improved but financial difficulties left the future of the race uncertain until the Watkins Glen Grand Prix Corporation stepped in with a lifeline and they offered the United States Grand Prix a new permanent home overlooking Lake Seneca in New York State. It remained the race's home for 20 years until the surface became too bumpy. It was removed from the calendar and Watkins Glen had seen the last of Formula One racing although it continued to stage NASCAR races.

With the launch of the United States Grand Prix (West) at Long Beach, California, in 1976, the Watkins Glen race became known as the United States Grand Prix (East) until its demise in 1980. However, a United States Grand Prix returned in 1987 with Detroit as its new home and since 1989 it has been held at Phoenix.

The first race in 1959 set the standard for future US Grands Prix when Jack Brabham hung onto fourth place behind Tony Brooks to beat the Briton to the title by just four points. It was the first time the drivers' championship had been won at the wheel of a British car, a Cooper. The winner of the race was New Zealander Bruce McLaren and it was his first Grand Prix win.

1959 Sebring

12 December, 351.48km/218.40 miles
1 Bruce McLaren (NZ) Cooper-Climax
2 Maurice Trintignant (Fra) Cooper-Climax
3 Tony Brooks (GB) Ferrari
4 Jack Brabham (Aus) Cooper-Climax
5 Innes Ireland (GB) Lotus-Climax
6 Wolfgang von Trips (FRG) Ferrari
Winner's speed: 159.06kph/98.83mph
Fastest lap: Trintignant 162.85kph/101.19mph
Pole position: Stirling Moss (GB) Cooper-Climax

1960 Riverside

20 November, 395.30km/245.63 miles
1 Stirling Moss (GB) Lotus-Climax
2 Innes Ireland (GB) Lotus-Climax
3 Bruce McLaren (NZ) Cooper-Climax
4 Jack Brabham (Aus) Cooper-Climax
5 Jo Bonnier (Swe) BRM
6 Phil Hill (USA) Cooper-Climax
Winner's speed: 159.31kph/99.00mph
Fastest lap: Brabham 163.15kph/101.38mph
Pole position: Moss

1961 Watkins Glen

8 October, 370.15km/230.00 miles
1 Innes Ireland (GB) Lotus-Climax
2 Dan Gurney (USA) Porsche
3 Tony Brooks (GB) BRM-Climax
4 Bruce McLaren (NZ) Cooper-Climax
5 Graham Hill (GB) BRM-Climax
6 Jo Bonnier (Swe) Porsche
Winner's speed: 166.03kph/103.17mph
Fastest lap: Jack Brabham (Aus) Cooper-Climax
170.40kph/105.88mph
Pole position: Brabham

1962 Watkins Glen

7 October, 370.15km/230.00 miles
1 Jim Clark (GB) Lotus-Climax
2 Graham Hill (GB) BRM
3 Bruce McLaren (NZ) Cooper-Climax
4 Jack Brabham (Aus) Brabham-Climax
5 Dan Gurney (USA) Porsche
6 Masten Gregory (USA) Lotus-BRM
Winner's speed: 174.58kph/108.48mph

Fastest lap: Clark 177.67kph/110.40mph
Pole position: Clark

1963 Watkins Glen

6 October, 407.16km/253.00 miles
1 Graham Hill (GB) BRM
2 Richie Ginther (USA) BRM
3 Jim Clark (GB) Lotus-Climax
4 Jack Brabham (Aus) Brabham-Climax
5 Lorenzo Bandini (Ita) Ferrari
6 Carel Godin de Beaufort (Hol) Porsche
Winner's speed: 175.29kph/108.92mph
Fastest lap: Clark 178.86kph/111.14mph
Pole position: G Hill

1964 Watkins Glen

4 October, 407.16km/253.00 miles
1 Graham Hill (GB) BRM
2 John Surtees (GB) Ferrari
3 Jo Siffert (Swi) Brabham-BRM
4 Richie Ginther (USA) BRM
5 Walter Hansgen (USA) Lotus-Climax
6 Trevor Taylor (GB) BRP-BRM
Winner's speed: 178.80kph/111.10mph
Fastest lap: Jim Clark (GB) Lotus-Climax 183.29kph/
113.89mph
Pole position: Clark

1965 Watkins Glen

3 October, 407.16km/253.00 miles
1 Graham Hill (GB) BRM
2 Dan Gurney (USA) Brabham-Climax
3 Jack Brabham (Aus) Brabham-Climax
4 Lorenzo Bandini (Ita) Ferrari
5 Pedro Rodriguez (Mex) Ferrari
6 Jochen Rindt (Aut) Cooper-Climax
Winner's speed: 173.74kph/107.98mph
Fastest lap: Hill 185.33kph/115.16mph
Pole position: Hill

1966 Watkins Glen

2 October, 399.76km/248.40 miles
1 Jim Clark (GB) Lotus-BRM
2 Jochen Rindt (Aut) Cooper-Maserati
3 John Surtees (GB) Cooper-Maserati
4 Jo Siffert (Swi) Cooper-Maserati
5 Bruce McLaren (NZ) McLaren-Ford
6 Peter Arundell (GB) Lotus-Climax
Winner's speed: 184.98kph/114.94mph
Fastest lap: Surtees 191.26kph/118.85mph
Pole position: Jack Brabham (Aus) Brabham-Repco

1967 Watkins Glen

1 October, 399.76km/248.40 miles
1 Jim Clark (GB) Lotus-Ford
2 Graham Hill (GB) Lotus-Ford
3 Denny Hulme (NZ) Brabham-Repco
4 Jo Siffert (Swi) Cooper-Maserati
5 Jack Brabham (Aus) Brabham-Repco
6 Jo Bonnier (Swe) Cooper-Maserati

Winner's speed: 194.66kph/120.95mph
Fastest lap: Hill 201.90kph/125.46mph
Pole position: Hill

1968 Watkins Glen

6 October, 399.76km/248.40 miles
1 Jackie Stewart (GB) Matra-Ford
2 Graham Hill (GB) Lotus-Ford
3 John Surtees (GB) Honda
4 Dan Gurney (USA) McLaren-Ford
5 Jo Siffert (Swi) Lotus-Ford
6 Bruce McLaren (NZ) McLaren-Ford
Winner's speed: 200.99kph/124.90mph
Fastest lap: Stewart 204.31kph/126.96mph
Pole position: Mario Andretti (USA) Lotus-Ford

1969 Watkins Glen

5 October, 399.76km/248.40 miles
1 Jochen Rindt (Aut) Lotus-Ford
2 Piers Courage (GB) Brabham-Ford
3 John Surtees (GB) BRM
4 Jack Brabham (Aus) Brabham-Ford
5 Pedro Rodriguez (Mex) Ferrari
6 Silvio Moser (Swi) Brabham-Ford
Winner's speed: 203.36kph/126.36mph
Fastest lap: Rindt 207.11kph/128.69mph
Pole position: Rindt

1970 Watkins Glen

4 October, 399.76km/248.40 miles
1 Emerson Fittipaldi (Bra) Lotus-Ford
2 Pedro Rodriguez (Mex) BRM
3 Reine Wisell (Swe) Lotus-Ford
4 Jacky Ickx (Bel) Ferrari
5 Chris Amon (NZ) March-Ford
6 Derek Bell (GB) Surtees-Ford
Winner's speed: 204.05kph/126.79mph
Fastest lap: Ickx 212.39kph/131.97mph
Pole position: Ickx

1971 Watkins Glen

3 October, 320.65km/199.24 miles
1 François Cevert (Fra) Tyrrell-Ford
2 Jo Siffert (Swi) BRM
3 Ronnie Peterson (Swe) March-Ford
4 Howden Ganley (NZ) BRM
5 Jackie Stewart (GB) Tyrrell-Ford
6 Clay Regazzoni (Swi) Ferrari
Winner's speed: 185.24kph/115.10mph
Fastest lap: Jacky Ickx (Bel) Ferrari 189.09kph/117.50mph
Pole position: Stewart

1972 Watkins Glen

8 October, 320.65km/199.24 miles
1 Jackie Stewart (GB) Tyrrell-Ford
2 François Cevert (Fra) Tyrrell-Ford
3 Denny Hulme (NZ) McLaren-Ford
4 Ronnie Peterson (Swe) March-Ford
5 Jacky Ickx (Bel) Ferrari
6 Mario Andretti (USA) Ferrari

Winner's speed: 189.09kph/117.49mph
Fastest lap: Stewart 192.50kph/119.61mph
Pole position: Stewart

1973 Watkins Glen

7 October, 320.65km/199.24 miles
1 Ronnie Peterson (Swe) Lotus-Ford
2 James Hunt (GB) March-Ford
3 Carlos Reutemann (Arg) Brabham-Ford
4 Denny Hulme (NZ) McLaren-Ford
5 Peter Revson (USA) McLaren-Ford
6 Emerson Fittipaldi (Bra) Lotus-Ford
Winner's speed: 189.99kph/118.06mph
Fastest lap: Hunt 192.47kph/119.60mph
Pole position: Peterson

1974 Watkins Glen

6 October, 320.65km/199.24 miles
1 Carlos Reutemann (Arg) Brabham-Ford
2 Carlos Pace (Bra) Brabham-Ford
3 James Hunt (GB) Hesketh-Ford
4 Emerson Fittipaldi (Bra) McLaren-Ford
5 John Watson (GB) Brabham-Ford
6 Patrick Depailler (Fra) Tyrrell-Ford
Winner's speed: 191.71kph/119.12mph
Fastest lap: Pace 194.47kph/120.84mph
Pole position: Reutemann

1975 Watkins Glen

5 October, 320.65km/199.24 miles
1 Niki Lauda (Aut) Ferrari
2 Emerson Fittipaldi (Bra) McLaren-Ford
3 Jochen Mass (FRG) McLaren-Ford
4 James Hunt (GB) Hesketh-Ford
5 Ronnie Peterson (Swe) Lotus-Ford
6 Jody Scheckter (SAf) Tyrrell-Ford
Winner's speed: 186.84kph/116.10mph
Fastest lap: Fittipaldi 189.27kph/117.60mph
Pole position: Lauda

1976 Watkins Glen

10 October, 320.65km/199.24 miles
1 James Hunt (GB) McLaren-Ford
2 Jody Scheckter (SAf) Tyrrell-Ford
3 Niki Lauda (Aut) Ferrari
4 Jochen Mass (FRG) McLaren-Ford
5 Hans-Joachim Stuck (FRG) March-Ford
6 John Watson (GB) Penske-Ford
Winner's speed: 187.37kph/116.43mph
Fastest lap: Hunt 190.22kph/118.20mph
Pole position: Hunt

1977 Watkins Glen

2 October, 320.65km/199.24 miles
1 James Hunt (GB) McLaren-Ford
2 Mario Andretti (USA) Lotus-Ford
3 Jody Scheckter (SAf) Wolf-Ford
4 Niki Lauda (Aut) Ferrari
5 Clay Regazzoni (Swi) Ensign-Ford
6 Carlos Reutemann (Arg) Ferrari

Winner's speed: 162.51kph/100.98mph
Fastest lap: Ronnie Peterson (Swe) Tyrrell-Ford
174.92kph/108.69mph
Pole position: Hunt

1978 Watkins Glen

1 October, 320.65km/199.24 miles
1 Carlos Reutemann (Arg) Ferrari
2 Alan Jones (Aus) Williams-Ford
3 Jody Scheckter (SAf) Wolf-Ford
4 Jean-Pierre Jabouille (Fra) Renault
5 Emerson Fittipaldi (Bra) Fittipaldi-Ford
6 Patrick Tambay (Fra) McLaren-Ford
Winner's speed: 190.85kph/118.59mph
Fastest lap: Jean-Pierre Jarier (Fra) Lotus-Ford 196.53kph/
122.12mph
Pole position: Mario Andretti (USA) Lotus-Ford

1979 Watkins Glen

7 October, 320.65km/199.24 miles
1 Gilles Villeneuve (Can) Ferrari
2 René Arnoux (Fra) Renault
3 Didier Pironi (Fra) Tyrrell-Ford
4 Elio de Angelis (Ita) Shadow-Ford
5 Hans-Joachim Stuck (FRG) ATS-Ford
6 John Watson (GB) McLaren-Ford
Winner's speed: 171.33kph/106.46mph
Fastest lap: Nelson Piquet (Bra) Brabham-Ford 195.55kph/
121.51mph
Pole position: Alan Jones (Aus) Williams-Ford

1980 Watkins Glen

5 October, 320.65km/199.24 miles
1 Alan Jones (Aus) Williams-Ford
2 Carlos Reutemann (Arg) Williams-Ford
3 Didier Pironi (Fra) Ligier-Ford
4 Elio de Angelis (Ita) Lotus-Ford
5 Jacques Laffite (Fra) Ligier-Ford
6 Mario Andretti (USA) Lotus-Ford
Winner's speed: 203.37kph/126.37mph
Fastest lap: Jones 207.99kph/129.24mph
Pole position: Bruno Giacomelli (Ita) Alfa Romeo

1987 Detroit

21 June, 253.47km/157.50 miles
1 Ayrton Senna (Bra) Lotus-Honda
2 Nelson Piquet (Bra) Williams-Honda
3 Alain Prost (Fra) McLaren-TAG
4 Gerhard Berger (Aut) Ferrari
5 Nigel Mansell (GB) Williams-Honda
6 Eddie Cheever (USA) Arrows-Megatron
Winner's speed: 137.92kph/85.70mph
Fastest lap: Senna 144.17kph/89.58mph
Pole position: Mansell

1988 Detroit

19 June, 253.47km/157.50 miles
1 Ayrton Senna (Bra) McLaren-Honda
2 Alain Prost (Fra) McLaren-Honda
3 Thierry Boutsen (Bel) Benetton-Ford

4 Andrea de Cesaris (Ita) Rial-Ford
5 Jonathan Palmer (GB) Tyrrell-Ford
6 Pierluigi Martini (Ita) Minardi-Ford
Winner's speed: 132.32kph/82.22mph
Fastest lap: Prost 138.16kph/85.84mph
Pole position: Senna

1989 Phoenix

4 June, 284.85km/177.00 miles
1 Alain Prost (Fra) McLaren-Honda
2 Riccardo Patrese (Ita) Williams-Renault
3 Eddie Cheever (USA) Arrows-Ford
4 Christian Danner (FRG) Rial-Ford
5 Johnny Herbert (GB) Benetton-Ford
6 Thierry Boutsen (Bel) Williams-Renault
Winner's speed: 140.60kph/87.37mph
Fastest lap: Ayrton Senna (Bra) McLaren-Honda
145.51kph/90.41mph
Pole position: Senna

1990 Phoenix

11 March, 273.46km/169.92 miles
1 Ayrton Senna (Bra) McLaren-Honda
2 Jean Alesi (Fra) Tyrrell-Ford
3 Thierry Boutsen (Bel) Williams-Renault
4 Nelson Piquet (Bra) Benetton-Ford
5 Stefano Modena (Ita) Brabham-Judd
6 Satoru Nakajima (Jap) Tyrrell-Ford
Winner's speed: 145.65kph/90.50mph
Fastest lap: Gerhard Berger (Aut) McLaren-Honda
150.17kph/93.31mph
Pole position: Berger

1991 Phoenix

10 March, 301.40km/ 187.27 miles
1 Ayrton Senna (Bra) McLaren-Honda
2 Alain Prost (Fra) Ferrari
3 Nelson Piquet (Bra) Benetton-Ford
4 Stefano Modena (Ita) Tyrrell-Honda
5 Satoru Nakajima (Jap) Tyrrell-Honda
6 Aguri Suzuki (Jap) Lola-Ford
Winner's speed: 149.84kph/93.02mph
Fastest lap: Jean Alesi (Fra) Ferrari 154.40km/95.94mph
Pole position: Senna

MOST WINS

Drivers
4 Ayrton Senna
3 Jim Clark, Graham Hill
2 James Hunt, Carlos Reutemann,
  Jackie Stewart
Manufacturers
9 Lotus   2 Tyrrell
6 McLaren
3 BRM, Ferrari

MOST FASTEST LAPS

Drivers
3 Jim Clark
2 Graham Hill, James Hunt, Jacky
  Ickx, Ayrton Senna, Jackie Stewart
Manufacturers
8 Lotus
5 McLaren
3 Cooper, Ferrari
2 Brabham, Tyrrell

MOST POLE POSITIONS

Drivers
3 Graham Hill, Ayrton Senna
2 Mario Andretti, Jack Brabham, Jim
  Clark, James Hunt, Stirling Moss
Manufacturers
8 Lotus
7 McLaren
2 Brabham, BRM, Cooper, Ferrari,
  Williams

UNITED STATES GP (WEST)

All races at Long Beach

With the launch of the United States Grand Prix (West) in 1976 it meant the United States hosted two championship races in a season for the first time since 1960.

It was a Briton living in Long Beach, Chris Pook, who thought up the idea of turning the streets of the city into a racing circuit and in 1975 a Formula 5000 race was held there. The following year Pook's dream was fulfilled when Formula One came to Long Beach.

The course was extremely tight and despite a major overhaul in 1983 the bump at the bottom of Linden Avenue was regarded as too dangerous for the Formula One cars and the race disappeared in 1984 after nine years.

1976

28 March, 260.07km/161.60 miles
1 Clay Regazzoni (Swi) Ferrari
2 Niki Lauda (Aut) Ferrari
3 Patrick Depailler (Fra) Tyrrell-Ford
4 Jacques Laffite (Fra) Ligier-Matra
5 Jochen Mass (FRG) McLaren-Ford
6 Emerson Fittipaldi (Bra) Fittipaldi-Ford
Winner's speed: 137.72kph/85.57mph
Fastest lap: Regazzoni 140.87kph/87.53mph
Pole position: Regazzoni

1977

3 April, 260.07km/161.60 miles
1 Mario Andretti (USA) Lotus-Ford
2 Niki Lauda (Aut) Ferrari
3 Jody Scheckter (SAf) Wolf-Ford
4 Patrick Depailler (Fra) Tyrrell-Ford
5 Emerson Fittipaldi (Bra) Fittipaldi-Ford
6 Jean-Pierre Jarier (Fra) Penske-Ford
Winner's speed: 139.84kph/86.89mph
Fastest lap: Lauda 141.42kph/87.88mph
Pole position: Lauda

1978

2 April, 261.70km/162.61 miles
1 Carlos Reutemann (Arg) Ferrari
2 Mario Andretti (USA) Lotus-Ford
3 Patrick Depailler (Fra) Tyrrell-Ford
4 Ronnie Peterson (Swe) Lotus-Ford
5 Jacques Laffite (Fra) Ligier-Matra
6 Riccardo Patrese (Ita) Arrows-Ford
Winner's speed: 140.17kph/87.10mph
Fastest lap: Alan Jones (Aus) Williams-Ford 142.35kph/
88.45mph
Pole position: Reutemann

1979

8 April, 261.70km/162.61 miles
1 Gilles Villeneuve (Can) Ferrari
2 Jody Scheckter (SAf) Ferrari
3 Alan Jones (Aus) Williams-Ford
4 Mario Andretti (USA) Lotus-Ford
5 Patrick Depailler (Fra) Ligier-Ford
6 Jean-Pierre Jarier (Fra) Tyrrell-Ford
Winner's speed: 141.31kph/87.81mph
Fastest lap: Villeneuve 144.28kph/89.65mph
Pole position: Villeneuve

1980

30 March, 261.70km/162.61 miles
1 Nelson Piquet (Bra) Brabham-Ford
2 Riccardo Patrese (Ita) Arrows-Ford
3 Emerson Fittipaldi (Bra) Fittipaldi-Ford
4 John Watson (GB) McLaren-Ford
5 Jody Scheckter (SAf) Ferrari
6 Didier Pironi (Fra) Ligier-Ford
Winner's speed: 142.35kph/88.45mph
Fastest lap: Piquet 146.61kph/91.10mph
Pole position: Piquet

1981

15 March, 261.70km/162.61 miles
1 Alan Jones (Aus) Williams-Ford
2 Carlos Reutemann (Arg) Williams-Ford
3 Nelson Piquet (Bra) Brabham-Ford
4 Mario Andretti (USA) Alfa Romeo
5 Eddie Cheever (USA) Tyrrell-Ford
6 Patrick Tambay (Fra) Theodore-Ford
Winner's speed: 140.98kph/87.60mph
Fastest lap: Jones 144.66kph/89.89mph
Pole position: Riccardo Patrese (Ita) Arrows-Ford

1982

4 April, 258.81km/160.82 miles
1 Niki Lauda (Aut) McLaren-Ford
2 Keke Rosberg (Fin) Williams-Ford
3 Riccardo Patrese (Ita) Brabham-Ford
4 Michele Alboreto (Ita) Tyrrell-Ford
5 Elio de Angelis (Ita) Lotus-Ford
6 John Watson (GB) MacLaren-Ford
*Gilles Villeneuve (Can) Ferrari finished 3rd but was
subsequently disqualified for having an illegal wing on his
car.*
Winner's speed: 131.13kph/81.48mph
Fastest lap: Lauda 135.86kph/84.42mph
Pole position: Andrea de Cesaris (Ita) Alfa Romeo

1983

27 March, 245.63km/152.63 miles
1 John Watson (GB) McLaren-Ford
2 Niki Lauda (Aut) McLaren-Ford
3 René Arnoux (Fra) Ferrari
4 Jacques Laffite (Fra) Williams-Ford
5 Marc Surer (Swi) Arrows-Ford
6 Johnny Cecotto (Ven) Theodore-Ford
Winner's speed: 129.79kph/80.65mph
Fastest lap: Lauda 133.48kph/82.94mph
Pole position: Patrick Tambay (Fra) Ferrari

MOST WINS

Drivers
No driver won two races
Manufacturers
3 Ferrari
2 McLaren

MOST FASTEST LAPS

Drivers
3 Niki Lauda
2 Alan Jones
Manufacturers
3 Ferrari
2 McLaren, Williams

MOST POLE POSITIONS

Drivers
No driver was on pole position on
more than one occasion.
Manufacturers
5 Ferrari

CHAMPIONSHIP REVIEWS: SEASON-BY-SEASON

Notes on tables

Figures in brackets indicate points actually scored, as distinct from points that counted towards the championship.

Where two makes of car are shown alongside a driver's name it indicates he *obtained championship points* in those cars. (There were many instances when drivers drove for two or more manufacturers in a season, but did not gain points with all of them.)

1950

It all started on a sunny day at Silverstone on 13 May 1950 when the British Grand Prix, also designated as that year's European Grand Prix, launched the new World Championship for drivers. In front of a packed crowd, including King George VI, Giuseppe 'Nino' Farina of Italy, driving an Alfa Romeo, won the first World Championship race.

Seven races featured in the inaugural championship with the best four results counting. Among the seven races was the Indianapolis 500 which formed a round of the championship until 1960. However, it was very much an American-only domain and the European drivers preferred to keep their feet on 'home' soil instead of making the trip across the Atlantic each May.

Unlike today, only the first five drivers across the line received championship points, with the one who set the fastest lap receiving an extra point.

Farina, winner of the first ever championship race, went on to win the inaugural championship after winning three races, the same as runner-up Juan Manuel Fangio.

DRIVERS

Pts	Driver (Nationality)	Car
30	Giuseppe Farina (Ita)	Alfa Romeo
27	Juan Manuel Fangio (Arg)	Alfa Romeo
24 (28)	Luigi Fagioli (Ita)	Alfa Romeo
13	Louis Rosier (Fra)	Talbot-Lago
11	Alberto Ascari (Ita)	Ferrari
8	Johnny Parsons (USA)	Kurtis Kraft-Offenhauser
6	Bill Holland (USA)	Deidt-Offenhauser
5	'B Bira' (Siam)	Maserati
4	Louis Chiron (Mon)	Maserati
4	Reg Parnell (GB)	Alfa Romeo
4	Mauri Rose (USA)	Deidt-Offenhauser
4	Peter Whitehead (GB)	Ferrari
3	Philippe Etancelin (Fra)	Talbot-Lago
3	Yves Giraud-Cabantous (Fra)	Talbot-Lago
3	Cecil Green (USA)	Kurtis Kraft-Offenhauser
3	Robert Manzon (Fra)	Simca-Gordini
3	Dorino Serafini (Ita)	Ferrari
3	Raymond Sommer (Fra)	Ferrari
2	Felice Bonetto (Ita)	Maserati
1	Tony Bettenhausen (USA)	Kurtis Kraft-Offenhauser
1	Eugene Chaboud (Fra)	Talbot-Lago
1	Joie Chitwood (USA)	Kurtis Kraft-Offenhauser

'B Bira' was the pseudonym of Prince Birabongse

Points scoring

1st – 8 pts; 2nd – 6 pts; 3rd – 4 pts; 4th – 3 pts; 5th – 2 pts; fastest lap – 1 pt.

Best four results only to count. Shared fastest laps to receive shared points. Drivers sharing drives received half points.

1951

Eight races made up the second championship with the German and Spanish Grands Prix being added to the calendar while the Monaco Grand Prix temporarily disappeared.

The Italian manufacturers continued to dominate, winning seven of the eight rounds, but this time the Alfas were challenged by the Ferraris of Ascari, Gonzalez, Villoresi and Taruffi. But Fangio in his Alfa 149 managed to hold off their challenge and win three rounds to capture the first of his record five world titles.

DRIVERS

Pts	Driver (Nationality)	Car
31 (37)	Juan Manuel Fangio (Arg)	Alfa Romeo
25 (28)	Alberto Ascari (Ita)	Ferrari
24 (27)	José Froilán González (Arg)	Ferrari
19 (22)	Giuseppe Farina (Ita)	Alfa Romeo
15 (18)	Luigi Villoresi (Ita)	Ferrari
10	Piero Taruffi (Ita)	Ferrari
9	Lee Wallard (USA)	Kurtis Kraft-Offenhauser
7	Felice Bonetto (Ita)	Alfa Romeo
6	Mike Nazaruk (USA)	Kurtis Kraft-Offenhauser
5	Reg Parnell (GB)	BRM/Ferrari
4	Luigi Fagioli (Ita)	Alfa Romeo
3	Louis Rosier (Fra)	Talbot-Lago
3	Consalvo Sanesi (Ita)	Alfa Romeo
3	Andy Linden (USA)	Shermann-Offenhauser
2	Jack McGrath (USA)	Kurtis Kraft-Offenhauser
2	Manuel Ayulo (USA)	Kurtis Kraft-Offenhauser
2	Bobby Ball (USA)	Schroeder-Offenhauser
2	Emmanuel de Graffenried (Swi)	Alfa Romeo
2	Yves Giraud-Cabantous (Fra)	Talbot-Lago

Points scoring
1st – 8 pts; 2nd – 6 pts; 3rd – 4 pts; 4th – 3 pts; 5th – 2 pts; fastest lap – 1 pt.
  Best four results only to count. Shared fastest laps to receive shared points.
Drivers sharing drives received half points.

Juan Manuel Fangio (right) in conversation with Giuseppe Farina at the pits during practice for the 1951 Italian Grand Prix.

1952

The Ferrari challenge gained momentum in 1952 when the championship was run to the Formula Two class. The Ferrari Tipo 500 was an outstanding car and it won all seven European rounds of the championship with Alberto Ascari winning the last six of the season to herald the beginning of the best winning streak in the history of the championship.

Ferrari virtually had the championship their own way as Alfa Romeo withdrew from Grand Prix racing because of financial problems brought about by their quest to remain as competitive as Ferrari.

The points system remained unaltered and therefore the maximum points available to any one driver was 36. Ascari won the championship with the maximum score. It is the only time this has happened. Fellow Ferrari drivers helped the Italian manufacturer occupy the first four places in the championship.

DRIVERS

Pts	Driver (Nationality)	Car
36 (53½)	Alberto Ascari (Ita)	Ferrari
24 (27)	Giuseppe Farina (Ita)	Ferrari
22	Piero Taruffi (Ita)	Ferrari
10	Rudi Fischer (Swi)	Ferrari
10	Mike Hawthorn (GB)	Cooper-Bristol
9	Robert Manzon (Fra)	Gordini
8	Luigi Villoresi (Ita)	Ferrari
8	Troy Ruttman (USA)	Kurtis Kraft-Offenhauser
6½	José Froilán González (Arg)	Maserati
6	Jean Behra (Fra)	Gordini
6	Jim Rathmann (USA)	Kurtis Kraft-Offenhauser
4	Sam Hanks (USA)	Kuzma-Offenhauser
3	Ken Wharton (GB)	Frazer Nash
3	Dennis Poore (GB)	Connaught
3	Duane Carter (USA)	Lesovsky-Offenhauser
2	Alan Brown (GB)	Cooper-Bristol
2	Paul Frére (Bel)	HWM
2	Maurice Trintignant (Fra)	Gordini
2	Eric Thompson (GB)	Connaught
2	Felice Bonetto (Ita)	Maserati
2	Art Cross (USA)	Kurtis Kraft-Offenhauser
1	Bill Vukovich (USA)	Kurtis Kraft-Offenhauser

Points scoring

1st – 8 pts; 2nd – 6 pts; 3rd – 4 pts; 4th – 3 pts; 5th – 2 pts; fastest lap – 1 pt.
   Best four results only to count. Shared fastest laps to receive shared points.
Drivers sharing drives received half points.

Alberto Ascari on his way to winning the last race of the 1952 season at Monza. The victory assured him of the first of his two successive world titles.

1953

Ascari's remarkable winning streak continued with his winning the opening round of the 1953 championship at Buenos Aires, the first ever championship race outside Europe other than the Indianapolis 500. He then followed that success with further wins at Zandvoort and Spa to extend his run to nine consecutive wins, a tremendous achievement.

Ferrari and Ascari were pushed hard by the Maserati of Fangio who was back in action following a bad accident at Monza the previous year. It was Monza that witnessed the closest race of the 1953 season with Farina, Fangio and Ascari, already proclaimed champion, all in contention for the chequered flag on the last lap. At the final corner Ascari spun, Farina went on to the grass to avoid him and Fangio came through to win by 1.4 seconds from Farina. But the title was already safely in Ascari's hands as he became the first man to win it in successive years.

DRIVERS

Pts	Driver (Nationality)	Car
34½ (47)	Alberto Ascari (Ita)	Ferrari
28 (29½)	Juan Manuel Fangio (Arg)	Maserati
26 (32)	Giuseppe Farina (Ita)	Ferrari
19 (27)	Mike Hawthorn (GB)	Ferrari
17	Luigi Villoresi (Ita)	Ferrari
13½ (14½)	José Froilán González (Arg)	Maserati
9	Bill Vukovich (USA)	Kurtis Kraft-Offenhauser
7	Emmanuel de Graffenried (Swi)	Maserati
6½	Felice Bonetto (Ita)	Maserati
6	Art Cross (USA)	Kurtis Kraft-Offenhauser
4	Onofre Marimon (Arg)	Maserati
4	Maurice Trintignant (Fra)	Gordini
2	Sam Hanks (USA)	Kurtis Kraft-Offenhauser
2	Duane Carter (USA)	Kurtis Kraft-Offenhauser
2	Oscar Galvez (Arg)	Maserati
2	Hermann Lang (FRG)	Maserati
2	Jack McGrath (USA)	Kurtis Kraft-Offenhauser
1½	Fred Agabashian (USA)	Kurtis Kraft-Offenhauser
1½	Paul Russo (USA)	Kurtis Kraft-Offenhauser

Points scoring

1st – 8 pts; 2nd – 6 pts; 3rd – 4 pts; 4th – 3 pts; 5th – 2 pts; fastest lap – 1 pt.
 Best four results only to count. Shared fastest laps to receive shared points.
Drivers sharing drives received half points.

1954

Formula One class returned in 1954, a year which also saw the return of one of the sport's great names, Mercedes-Benz, to Grand Prix racing.

Alfred Neubauer, who led the team before the war, had brought the great German manufacturer back into motor sport in 1952 via sports car racing. Now he was ready to challenge the Grand Prix domination held

by the Italians, particularly with the Formula Two rules being scrapped. The new rules allowed supercharged cars up to 750cc and unsupercharged up to 2.5 litres. The Mercedes W196 was a straight-eight engine of 2496cc and capable of producing 270bhp. It was to be an outstanding car.

The driver entrusted with the new car was Fangio; he switched from Maserati when the new car was ready in time for the French Grand Prix, the third race of the season. He powered the W196 to victory in its first Grand Prix, marginally ahead of team-mate Karl Kling. It was the first of five wins for Fangio that season as he went on to win the title with three Ferrari drivers in his wake.

Fangio powering the Mercedes W196 to victory in Italy. It was one of six wins for the Argentinian that season, all but one of them in the famous W196.

DRIVERS

Pts	Driver (Nationality)	Car
42 (57½)	Juan Manuel Fangio (Arg)	Maserati/Mercedes-Benz
25½ (26⁹⁄₁₄)	José Froilán González (Arg)	Ferrari
24⁹⁄₁₄	Mike Hawthorn (GB)	Ferrari
17	Maurice Trintignant (Fra)	Ferrari
12	Karl Kling (FRG)	Mercedes-Benz
8	Hans Herrmann (FRG)	Mercedes-Benz
8	Bill Vukovich (USA)	Kurtis Kraft-Offenhauser
6	Roberto Mieres (Arg)	Maserati
6	Luigi Musso (Ita)	Maserati
6	Giuseppe Farina (Ita)	Ferrari
6	Jimmy Bryan (USA)	Kuzma-Offenhauser
5	Jack McGrath (USA)	Kurtis Kraft-Offenhauser
4½	Stirling Moss (GB)	Maserati
4½	Onofre Marimon (Arg)	Maserati
4	Robert Manzon (Fra)	Ferrari
4	Sergio Mantovani (Ita)	Maserati
3	'B Bira' (Siam)	Maserati
2	Luigi Villoresi (Ita)	Maserati
2	Umberto Maglioli (Ita)	Ferrari
2	André Pilette (Bel)	Gordini
2	Elie Bayol (Fra)	Gordini
2	Mike Nazaruk (USA)	Kurtis Kraft-Offenhauser
1½	Troy Ruttman (USA)	Kurtis Kraft-Offenhauser
1½	Duane Carter (USA)	Kurtis Kraft-Offenhauser
1½	Alberto Ascari (Ita)	Maserati/Lancia
0½	Jean Behra (Fra)	Gordini

The sevenths of a point came about because seven men shared the fastest lap at the British Grand Prix. One of them was Mike Hawthorn, who also had to share three points with González for finishing fourth in the Belgian Grand Prix, which explains his unusual looking total of 24⁹⁄₁₄ points.

Points scoring
1st – 8 pts; 2nd – 6 pts; 3rd – 4 pts; 4th – 3 pts; 5th – 2 pts; fastest lap – 1 pt.
Best five results only to count. Shared fastest laps to receive shared points. Drivers sharing drives received half points.

1955

The number of championship rounds was scheduled to increase from nine to eleven but sadly only seven were completed because 1955 was a year of tragedy.

Firstly Alberto Ascari lost his life while testing at Monza just four days after surviving a dip in the harbour at Monte Carlo. That tragedy was followed by the sport's worst disaster when more than 80 people lost their lives at Le Mans when Pierre Levagh's Mercedes flew into the crowd during the 24-hour race. This tragedy resulted in the cancellation of the French, German, Swiss and Spanish Grands Prix. To this day motor racing has not returned to Switzerland.

Away from the tragedies, Fangio and his Mercedes continued to reign supreme. The Argentinian won four rounds of the championship while teammate Stirling Moss won the British Grand Prix at Aintree. The only other round (excepting Indianapolis) was won by Ferrari's Maurice Trintignant.

DRIVERS

Pts	Driver (Nationality)	Car
40 (41)	Juan Manuel Fangio (Arg)	Mercedes-Benz
23	Stirling Moss (GB)	Mercedes-Benz
12	Eugenio Castellotti (Ita)	Lancia/Ferrari
11	Maurice Trintignant (Fra)	Ferrari
10⅓	Giuseppe Farina (Ita)	Ferrari
9	Piero Taruffi (Ita)	Mercedes-Benz
8	Bob Sweikert (USA)	Kurtis Kraft-Offenhauser
7	Roberto Mieres (Arg)	Maserati
6	Jean Behra (Fra)	Maserati
6	Luigi Musso (Ita)	Maserati
5	Karl Kling (FRG)	Mercedes-Benz
4	Jimmy Davies (USA)	Kurtis Kraft-Offenhauser
3	Paul Frére (Bel)	Ferrari
3	Johnny Thompson (USA)	Kuzma-Offenhauser
3	Tony Bettenhausen (USA)	Kurtis Kraft-Offenhauser
3	Paul Russo (USA)	Kurtis Kraft-Offenhauser
2	José Froilán González (Arg)	Ferrari
2	Cesare Perdisa (Ita)	Maserati
2	Luigi Villoresi (Ita)	Lancia
2	Carlos Menditeguy (Arg)	Maserati
1⅓	Umberto Maglioli (Ita)	Ferrari
1	Hans Herrmann (FRG)	Mercedes-Benz
1	Walt Faulkner (USA)	Kurtis Kraft-Offenhauser
1	Bill Homeier (USA)	Kurtis Kraft-Offenhauser
1	Bill Vukovich (USA)	Kurtis Kraft-Offenhauser

Points scoring

1st – 8 pts; 2nd – 6 pts; 3rd – 4 pts; 4th – 3 pts; 5th – 2 pts; fastest lap – 1 pt.
  Best five results only to count. Shared fastest laps to receive shared points. Drivers sharing drives received half points.

1956

Mercedes came and conquered. They had achieved what they set out to do and at the end of 1955 announced they were pulling out of Grand Prix racing. That left the door open for the Italians to regain their supremacy and they did just that as Enzo Ferrari modified the Lancia D50 which went on to provide Fangio with his fourth world title. But chasing him all the way was Britain's Stirling Moss in his Maserati 250F.

With the exception of the two Indy cars, seven of the first nine places in the championship were occupied by either Lancia-Ferrari or Maserati drivers.

DRIVERS

Pts	Driver (Nationality)	Car
30 (33)	Juan Manuel Fangio (Arg)	Lancia-Ferrari
27 (28)	Stirling Moss (GB)	Maserati
25	Peter Collins (GB)	Lancia-Ferrari
22	Jean Behra (Fra)	Maserati
8	Pat Flaherty (USA)	Watson-Offenhauser
7½	Eugenio Castellotti (Ita)	Lancia-Ferrari
6	Paul Frére (Bel)	Lancia-Ferrari
6	Sam Hanks (USA)	Kurtis Kraft-Offenhauser
6	Francisco Godia (Spa)	Maserati
5	Jack Fairman (GB)	Connaught
4	Luigi Musso (Ita)	Lancia-Ferrari
4	Mike Hawthorn (GB)	Maserati
4	Ron Flockhart (GB)	Connaught
4	Don Freeland (USA)	Phillips-Offenhauser
3	Cesare Perdisa (Ita)	Maserati
3	Harry Schell (USA)	Vanwall
3	Alfonso de Portago (Spa)	Lancia-Ferrari
3	Johnnie Parsons (USA)	Kuzma-Offenhauser
2	Olivier Gendebien (Bel)	Lancia-Ferrari
2	Hernando da Silva Ramos (Bra)	Gordini
2	Luigi Villoresi (Ita)	Maserati
2	Horace Gould (GB)	Maserati
2	Louis Rosier (Fra)	Maserati

The drivers' title was not resolved until the last race of the season at Monza. Fangio took the title after coming home second in Peter Collins' Lancia-Ferrari. Collins had a chance of taking the title himself but, with Fangio seemingly out of the race, insisted that the Argentinian continue in his car to secure the necessary points.

1957

The 1957 season was a memorable one for the British manufacturers; when Stirling Moss took over Tony Brooks' Vanwall during the British Grand Prix at Aintree he went on to win the race and thus give a British manufacturer its first world championship success.

Moss went on to win two more races in the green Vanwall before the season was out but again he had to play second string to Fangio who won four races in his Maserati on his way to his fifth and last world title. In winning at the Nürburgring the Argentinian had the finest drive of his career, breaking the lap record no fewer than ten times within 22 laps before going on to win his 24th and last Grand Prix.

The championship was scheduled for 11 rounds but the Belgian, Dutch and Spanish races were cancelled.

2	Dick Rathmann (USA)	Kurtis Kraft-Offenhauser
1½	Chico Landi (Bra)	Maserati
1½	Gerino Gerini (Ita)	Maserati
1	Paul Russo (USA)	Kurtis Kraft-Novi

Fangio had a shared drive with Collins (2nd) and Castellotti (4th) in the Monaco Grand Prix but only received half points for finishing second.

Points scoring

1st – 8 pts; 2nd – 6 pts; 3rd – 4 pts; 4th – 3 pts; 5th – 2 pts; fastest lap – 1 pt.
   Best five results only to count. Shared fastest laps to receive shared points. Drivers sharing drives received half points.

DRIVERS

Pts	Driver (Nationality)	Car
40 (46)	Juan Manuel Fangio (Arg)	Maserati
25	Stirling Moss (GB)	Maserati/Vanwall
16	Luigi Musso (Ita)	Lancia-Ferrari
13	Mike Hawthorn (GB)	Lancia-Ferrari
11	Tony Brooks (GB)	Vanwall
10	Masten Gregory (USA)	Maserati
8	Harry Schell (USA)	Maserati
8	Sam Hanks (USA)	Epperly-Offenhauser
8	Peter Collins (GB)	Lancia-Ferrari
8	Jean Behra (Fra)	Maserati
7	Jim Rathmann (USA)	Epperly-Offenhauser
5	Stuart Lewis-Evans (GB)	Connaught/Vanwall
5	Maurice Trintignant (Fra)	Lancia-Ferrari
4	Wolfgang von Trips (FRG)	Lancia-Ferrari
4	Carlos Menditeguy (Arg)	Maserati
4	Jimmy Bryan (USA)	Kuzma-Offenhauser
3	Paul Russo (USA)	Kurtis Kraft-Novi
2	Roy Salvadori (GB)	Cooper-Climax
2	Andy Linden (USA)	Kurtis Kraft-Offenhauser
1	Giorgio Scarlatti (Ita)	Maserati
1	José Froilán González (Arg)	Lancia-Ferrari
1	Alfonso de Portago (Spa)	Lancia-Ferrari

Points scoring

1st – 8 pts; 2nd – 6 pts; 3rd – 4 pts; 4th – 3 pts; 5th – 2 pts; fastest lap – 1 pt.
   Best five results only to count. Shared fastest laps to receive shared points. Drivers sharing drives received half points.

Stirling Moss in the 1957 Vanwall which showed it could compete with the overseas manufacturers for the first time.

1958

For the first time since the championship started in 1950 it looked as though there would be a British breakthrough with either Moss or Brooks triumphing in the Vanwall. The British car was certainly competitive enough and when Fangio announced his retirement after the French Grand Prix the door was open for Moss to claim his first title.

Moss won four races but still lost the championship by one point despite winning the last race of the season at Casablanca and also gaining the extra point for the fastest lap. His rival, fellow Briton Mike Hawthorn, driving a Ferrari, managed to come home second in that race and take enough points to snatch the title. He had won only one race all season.

For the first time more than 10 rounds (there were 11) made up the championship. A con-

Britain's Mike Hawthorn poses for the cameras shortly after agreeing to join the successful Ferrari team.

structors' championship was also launched and to make up for the disappointment of not winning the drivers' championship Vanwall captured the new title. Sadly, the season was marred by the deaths of three drivers: the Italian Luigi Musso at Reims, and the British pair of Peter Collins, at the Nürburgring, and Stuart Lewis-Evans at Casablanca.

DRIVERS

Pts	Driver (Nationality)	Car
42 (49)	Mike Hawthorn (GB)	Ferrari
41	Stirling Moss (GB)	Cooper-Climax/Vanwall
24	Tony Brooks (GB)	Vanwall
15	Roy Salvadori (GB)	Cooper-Climax
14	Peter Collins (GB)	Ferrari
14	Harry Schell (USA)	BRM
12	Maurice Trintignant (Fra)	Cooper-Climax
12	Luigi Musso (Ita)	Ferrari
11	Stuart Lewis-Evans (GB)	Vanwall
9	Phil Hill (USA)	Ferrari
9	Wolfgang von Trips (FRG)	Ferrari
9	Jean Behra (Fra)	BRM
8	Jimmy Bryan (USA)	Epperly-Offenhauser
7	Juan Manuel Fangio (Arg)	Maserati
6	George Amick (USA)	Epperly-Offenhauser
4	Johnny Boyd (USA)	Kurtis Kraft-Offenhauser
4	Tony Bettenhausen (USA)	Epperly-Offenhauser
3	Jack Brabham (Aus)	Cooper-Climax
3	Cliff Allison (GB)	Lotus-Climax
3	Jo Bonnier (Swe)	BRM
2	Jim Rathmann (USA)	Epperly-Offenhauser

Points scoring
1st – 8 pts; 2nd – 6 pts; 3rd – 4 pts; 4th – 3 pts; 5th – 2 pts; fastest lap – 1 pt.
 Best six results only to count. Shared fastest laps to receive shared points. Drivers sharing cars were no longer awarded points, they had to be in charge of the car throughout the entire race to qualify for points.

CONSTRUCTORS

Pts	Car
48	Vanwall
40	Ferrari
31	Cooper-Climax
18	BRM
9	Maserati
3	Lotus-Climax

Points scoring
1st – 8 pts; 2nd – 6 pts; 3rd – 4 pts; 4th – 3 pts; 5th – 2 pts.
 Highest-placed car in each race only to be considered for points. Best six results only to count. Indianapolis 500 excluded from the constructors' championship.

Previous page *The story of the 1991 season: Ayrton Senna's McLaren is chased at Monza by the Williams of Nigel Mansell and Riccardo Patrese.*

Left Senna first, the rest nowhere . . . Out in front, the Brazilian heads for victory – and the drivers' title – in the Canadian Grand Prix, 1988.

Right A spin at the first corner produces a crowded racetrack at Monaco, 1990.

Above *A perfect view of the action for these deckchair enthusiasts at Spa-Francorchamps as the 1987 Belgian Grand Prix unfolds below them.*

Right *Spray from Nelson Piquet's Lotus and umbrellas in the crowd – a classic scene of motor racing in wet conditions at*

Mansell the hero – Britain's number one driver cruises to victory in the Williams at the 1991 British Grand Prix (right) and acknowledges the cheers of his supporters (above) at Silverstone.

Left *A superb view from the cockpit shows the open road in front of Alain Prost's McLaren-Honda at Silverstone.*

Below *Fans and photographers surround the winner's rostrum at Paul Ricard as Prost celebrates a victory on home soil, 1990.*

Below *A study in concentration, determination and will to win – Ayrton Senna, three times world champion between 1988 and 1991.*

Right *Mechanics swarm around Nelson Piquet's Brabham during a pit-stop at the 1983 French Grand Prix.*

Below *McLaren versus McLaren was the story for most of 1988 as Alain Prost and Ayrton Senna dominated the championship. Prost (11) was the eventual winner of this encounter at Paul Ricard; Senna took the title.*

Above *Sparks fly from Gerhard Berger's Ferrari at Monza, 1989. Berger had led a Ferrari 1–2 the previous year at the Italian Grand Prix but the Italian fans had to settle for second place for Berger's Ferrari this time around.*

Right *Berger stares out from the cockpit before the 1988 Brazilian Grand Prix.*

Left *The dramatic dash through the famous tunnel at Monaco.*

A dramatic reminder of the danger each driver must live with in motor racing. Nelson Piquet's Brabham (7) and Riccardo Patrese's Alfa Romeo crash spectacularly at Monaco, 1985.

At the 1991 British Grand Prix, Nigel Mansell famously stopped on his victory lap to give the unfortunate Ayrton Senna, now out of the race, a lift back to the Silverstone pits.

1959

As a result of the death of Stuart Lewis-Evans following an accident during the last race of the 1958 season, and owing to founder Tony Vandervell's ill health, Vanwall announced their decision to quit Grand Prix racing and their famous green *marque* was absent in 1959.

Mike Hawthorn's 1958 championship success also marked the end of an era. He was to be the last world champion in a front-engined car. Furthermore, Hawthorn was never to find out who his successor would be because he was killed in a car accident on the Guildford by-pass three months after winning the world title.

Vanwall might have disappeared, but that was not the end of the British challenge to the Italians. It was as strong as ever thanks to the Cooper-Climax and BRM teams. And it was the Australian Jack Brabham, in a Cooper, who won the first of his three world titles. But as in 1958, the championship was not decided until the last round at Sebring, and again Stirling Moss was in with a chance of that elusive title.

However, transmission failure to his Rob Walker Cooper on lap five put paid to the Briton's chances of the title and it was left to the Australasian pair of Brabham and Bruce McLaren, also in a Cooper, to battle it out for the chequered flag. Brabham had the race won but one kilometre from the finish he ran out of petrol and McLaren shot past to win. Brabham pushed his car over the line to finish an exhausted fourth. But with it came the world title.

DRIVERS

Pts	Driver (Nationality)	Car
31 (34)	Jack Brabham (Aus)	Cooper-Climax
27	Tony Brooks (GB)	Ferrari
25½	Stirling Moss (GB)	Cooper-Climax/BRM
20	Phil Hill (USA)	Ferrari
19	Maurice Trintignant (Fra)	Cooper-Climax
16½	Bruce McLaren (NZ)	Cooper-Climax
13	Dan Gurney (USA)	Ferrari
10	Jo Bonnier (Swe)	BRM
10	Masten Gregory (USA)	Cooper-Climax
8	Rodger Ward (USA)	Watson-Offenhauser
6	Jim Rathmann (USA)	Watson-Offenhauser
5	Harry Schell (USA)	BRM
5	Innes Ireland (GB)	Lotus-Climax
5	Johnny Thomson (USA)	Lesovsky-Offenhauser
3	Olivier Gendebien (Bel)	Ferrari
3	Tony Bettenhausen (USA)	Epperly-Offenhauser
2	Cliff Allison (GB)	Ferrari
2	Jean Behra (Fra)	Ferrari
2	Paul Goldsmith (USA)	Epperly-Offenhauser

Points scoring
1st – 8 pts; 2nd – 6 pts; 3rd – 4 pts; 4th – 3 pts; 5th – 2 pts; fastest lap – 1 pt.
Best five results only to count. Shared fastest laps to receive shared points.

CONSTRUCTORS

40	Cooper-Climax
32	Ferrari
18	BRM
5	Lotus-Climax

Points scoring
1st – 8 pts; 2nd – 6 pts; 3rd – 4 pts; 4th – 3 pts; 5th – 2 pts
Highest-placed car in each race only to be considered for points. Best five results only to count.

1960

The 1960 season saw the end of the point awarded to drivers for the fastest lap. Instead, the extra point was awarded to the driver occupying sixth place in a race. The season also saw the Indianapolis 500 form part of the World Championship for the last time. The title belonged to Australian Jack Brabham for the second successive year as the rear-engine revolution really took control.

Brabham won five consecutive races mid-season to capture the title from his fellow Australasian Bruce McLaren by nine points, with Britain's Stirling Moss a long way behind in third place in his Climax-powered Lotus 18. Moss missed half the season following an accident at Spa in June.

On a sad note, Britons Chris Bristow and Alan Stacey both lost their lives during the Belgian Grand Prix at Spa.

DRIVERS

Pts	Driver (Nationality)	Car
43	Jack Brabham (Aus)	Cooper-Climax
34 (37)	Bruce McLaren (NZ)	Cooper-Climax
19	Stirling Moss (GB)	Lotus-Climax
18	Innes Ireland (GB)	Lotus-Climax
16	Phil Hill (USA)	Ferrari
10	Olivier Gendebien (Bel)	Cooper-Climax
10	Wolfgang von Trips (FRG)	Ferrari
8	Jim Rathmann (USA)	Watson-Offenhauser
8	Richie Ginther (USA)	Ferrari
8	Jim Clark (GB)	Lotus-Climax
7	Tony Brooks (GB)	Cooper-Climax
6	Cliff Allison (GB)	Ferrari
6	John Surtees (GB)	Lotus-Climax
6	Rodger Ward (USA)	Watson-Offenhauser
4	Graham Hill GB)	BRM
4	Willy Mairesse (Bel)	Ferrari
4	Paul Goldsmith (USA)	Epperly-Offenhauser
4	Jo Bonnier (Swe)	BRM
3	Carlos Menditeguy (Arg)	Cooper-Maserati
3	Henry Taylor (GB)	Cooper-Climax
3	Giulio Cabianca (Ita)	Cooper-Castellotti
3	Don Branson (USA)	Phillips-Offenhauser
2	Johnny Thomson (USA)	Lesovsky-Offenhauser
1	Lucien Bianchi (Bel)	Cooper-Climax
1	Ron Flockhart (GB)	Lotus-Climax
1	Hans Herrmann (FRG)	Porsche
1	Eddie Johnson (USA)	Trevis-Offenhauser

Points scoring

1st – 8 pts; 2nd – 6 pts; 3rd – 4 pts; 4th – 3 pts; 5th – 2 pts; 6th – 1 pt.
  The point for the fastest lap was no longer awarded. Best six results only to count.

CONSTRUCTORS

Pts	
48 (58)	Cooper-Climax
34 (37)	Lotus-Climax
26 (27)	Ferrari
8	BRM
3	Cooper-Maserati
3	Cooper-Ferrari
1	Porsche

Points scoring

1st – 8 pts; 2nd – 6 pts; 3rd – 4 pts;
4th – 3 pts; 5th – 2 pts; 6th – 1 pt.
  Highest-placed car in each race only to be considered for points. Best six results only to count. Indianapolis 500 excluded.

1961

A giant like Ferrari never sleeps for long and after allowing the British manufacturers a couple of glory years the Italians came back with a vengeance in 1961, the first year of the new 1.5 litre formula.

Only eight rounds constituted the championship and five of them were won by Ferrari thanks to the American Phil Hill, the German Wolfgang von Trips and the Italian Giancarlo Baghetti. Hill and von Trips always occupied first and second places in the championship but any chance the German had of capturing the title ended in tragedy at Monza when his car flew off the track at the Parabolica, killing him and 15 spectators. It was a tragic end to a season which saw Ferrari well and truly back in the forefront of Grand Prix racing.

DRIVERS

Pts	Driver (Nationality)	Car
34 (38)	Phil Hill (USA)	Ferrari
33	Wolfgang von Trips (FRG)	Ferrari
21	Stirling Moss (GB)	Lotus-Climax
21	Dan Gurney (USA)	Porsche
16	Richie Ginther (USA)	Ferrari
12	Innes Ireland (GB)	Lotus-Climax
11	Jim Clark (GB)	Lotus-Climax
11	Bruce McLaren (NZ)	Cooper-Climax
9	Giancarlo Baghetti (Ita)	Ferrari
6	Tony Brooks (GB)	BRM-Climax
4	Jack Brabham (Aus)	Cooper-Climax
4	John Surtees (GB)	Cooper-Climax
3	Olivier Gendebien (Bel)	Ferrari
3	Jo Bonnier (Swe)	Porsche
3	Jack Lewis (GB)	Cooper-Climax
3	Graham Hill (GB)	BRM-Climax
2	Roy Salvadori (GB)	Cooper-Climax

Points scoring

1st – 9pts; 2nd – 6 pts; 3rd – 4 pts; 4th – 3 pts; 5th – 2 pts; 6th – 1 pt.
  Best five results only to count.

CONSTRUCTORS

40 (50)	Ferrari
32	Lotus-Climax
22 (23)	Porsche
14 (18)	Cooper-Climax
7	BRM-Climax

Points scoring

1st – 8 pts; 2nd – 6 pts; 3rd – 4 pts; 4th – 3 pts; 5th – 2 pts; 6th – 1 pt.
  Highest-placed car in each race only to be considered for points. Best five results only to count.

1962

Ferrari's return to the top was brief. After their successful 1961 season, the team was disrupted by internal problems the following season and that paved the way for the British teams to take over again. For the first time the world champion was a Briton driving a British car.

That honour fell to Graham Hill in a BRM. But close behind was the genial Scot Jim Clark who won his first Grand Prix at Spa in the Colin Chapman produced Lotus-Climax. That win was to herald the start of one of the most successful combinations in the history of Formula One.

The 1962 season saw the end of Stirling Moss' Grand Prix career. The finest driver never to win the world title, he was badly injured in a crash at Goodwood on Easter Monday. Mercifully his life was saved – but his career was ended.

DRIVERS

Pts	Driver (Nationality)	Car
42 (52)	Graham Hill (GB)	BRM
30	Jim Clark (GB)	Lotus-Climax
27 (30)	Bruce McLaren (NZ)	Cooper-Climax
19	John Surtees (GB)	Lola-Climax
15	Dan Gurney (USA)	Porsche
14	Phil Hill (USA)	Ferrari
13	Tony Maggs (SAf)	Cooper-Climax
10	Richie Ginther (USA)	BRM
9	Jack Brabham (Aus)	Lotus-Climax/ Brabham-Climax
6	Trevor Taylor (GB)	Lotus-Climax
5	Giancarlo Baghetti (Ita)	Ferrari
4	Lorenzo Bandini (Ita)	Ferrari
4	Ricardo Rodriguez (Mex)	Ferrari
3	Willy Mairesse (Bel)	Ferrari
3	Jo Bonnier (Swe)	Porsche
2	Innes Ireland (GB)	Lotus-Climax
2	Carel Godin de Beaufort (Hol)	Porsche
1	Masten Gregory (USA)	Lotus-BRM
1	Neville Lederle (SAf)	Lotus-Climax

Points scoring

1st – 9 pts; 2nd – 6 pts; 3rd – 4 pts; 4th – 3 pts; 5th – 2 pts; 6th – 1 pt.
  Best five results only to count.

CONSTRUCTORS

42 (56)	BRM	
36 (38)	Lotus-Climax	
29 (37)	Cooper-Climax	
19	Lola-Climax	
18	Ferrari	
18 (19)	Porsche	
6	Brabham-Climax	
1	Lotus-BRM	

Points scoring

1st – 9 pts; 2nd – 6 pts; 3rd – 4 pts;
4th – 3 pts; 5th – 2 pts; 6th – 1 pt.
  Best five results only to count.
  Highest-placed car in each race only considered for points.

1963

The announcement that the 1.5 litre formula would be extended by a further two seasons gave the opportunity for Jim Clark and Lotus to set up a championship-winning season. Clark's enormous talent was evident as he won seven of the ten rounds and inevitably the championship by a massive 25 points ahead of defending champion Graham Hill. In the three races he didn't win, Clark finished 8th, 2nd and 3rd. The monocoque chassis of the Lotus 25, complete with its powerful Coventry-Climax engine was too good for its rivals. And with Clark behind the wheel there was no stopping the powerful team.

Britain's John Surtees switched from the Lola team to Ferrari in 1963 and enjoyed the first Grand Prix success of his career at the Nürburgring with Clark second.

DRIVERS

Pts	Driver (Nationality)	Car
54 (73)	Jim Clark (GB)	Lotus-Climax
29	Graham Hill (GB)	BRM
29 (34)	Richie Ginther (USA)	BRM
22	John Surtees (GB)	Ferrari
19	Dan Gurney (USA)	Brabham-Climax
17	Bruce McLaren (NZ)	Cooper-Climax
14	Jack Brabham (Aus)	Brabham-Climax
9	Tony Maggs (SAf)	Cooper-Climax
6	Innes Ireland (GB)	BRP-BRM
6	Lorenzo Bandini (Ita)	BRM/Ferrari
6	Jo Bonnier (Swe)	Cooper-Climax
3	Gerhard Mitter (FRG)	Porsche
3	Jim Hall (USA)	Lotus-BRM
2	Carel Godin de Beaufort (Hol)	Porsche
1	Trevor Taylor (GB)	Lotus-Climax
1	Ludovico Scarfiotti (Ita)	Ferrari
1	Jo Siffert (Swi)	Lotus-BRM

Points scoring
1st – 9 pts; 2nd – 6 pts; 3rd – 4 pts; 4th – 3 pts; 5th – 2 pts; 6th – 1 pt.
    Best six results only to count.

CONSTRUCTORS

54 (74)	Lotus-Climax
36 (45)	BRM
28 (30)	Brabham-Climax
26	Ferrari
25 (26)	Cooper-Climax
6	BRP-BRM
5	Porsche
4	Lotus-BRM

Points scoring
1st – 9 pts; 2nd – 6 pts; 3rd – 4 pts;
4th – 3 pts; 5th – 2 pts; 6th – 1 pt.
    Best six results only to count.
Highest-placed car in each race only
considered for points.

1964

The season reached an exciting climax at Mexico City on 25 October. Graham Hill led the table with 39 points, John Surtees, the former motor-cycling world champion, was on 34, and reigning champion Jim Clark was on 30 points.

During the race, first Hill, then Clark, and ultimately Surtees, each looked in turn as though they were going to take the world title. In the event, Hill was out of the points at the chequered flag, Surtees was second and collected six points, while Clark could only pick up two points for finishing fifth; and so Surtees became the first and only man to win world titles on two and four wheels.

Surtees' six points also ensured the Constructors' Cup went back to Ferrari for the first time since 1961. The notorious Nürburgring claimed yet another life in 1964, that of the Dutch driver Carel Godin de Beaufort.

DRIVERS

Pts	Driver (Nationality)	Car
40	John Surtees (GB)	Ferrari
39 (41)	Graham Hill (GB)	BRM
32	Jim Clark (GB)	Lotus-Climax
23	Lorenzo Bandini (Ita)	Ferrari
23	Richie Ginther (USA)	BRM
19	Dan Gurney (USA)	Brabham-Climax
13	Bruce McLaren (NZ)	Cooper-Climax
11	Jack Brabham (Aus)	Brabham-Climax
11	Peter Arundell (GB)	Lotus-Climax
7	Jo Siffert (Swi)	Brabham-BRM
5	Bob Anderson (GB)	Brabham-Climax
4	Tony Maggs (SAf)	BRM
4	Mike Spence (GB)	Lotus-Climax
4	Innes Ireland (GB)	BRP-BRM
3	Jo Bonnier (Swe)	Cooper-Climax/Brabham-Climax
2	Chris Amon (NZ)	Lotus-BRM
2	Walt Hansgen (USA)	Lotus-Climax
2	Maurice Trintignant (Fra)	BRM
1	Trevor Taylor (GB)	BRP-BRM
1	Mike Hailwood (GB)	Lotus-BRM
1	Phil Hill (USA)	Cooper-Climax
1	Pedro Rodriguez (Mex)	Ferrari

Points scoring
1st – 9 pts; 2nd – 6 pts; 3rd – 4 pts; 4th – 3 pts; 5th – 2 pts; 6th – 1 pt.
    Best six results only to count.

CONSTRUCTORS

45 (49)	Ferrari
42 (51)	BRM
37 (40)	Lotus-Climax
30	Brabham-Climax
16	Cooper-Climax
7	Brabham-BRM
5	BRP-BRM
3	Lotus-BRM

Points scoring
1st – 9 pts; 2nd – 6 pts; 3rd – 4 pts;
4th – 3 pts; 5th – 2 pts; 6th – 1 pt.
    Best six results only to count.
Highest-placed car in each race only
considered for points.

1965

Being the last year of the 1.5 litre formula, 1965 saw most teams going through a period of technological change. But Jim Clark and Lotus were, yet again, virtually unstoppable. Despite picking up points in nine of the ten rounds, Graham Hill was still 14 points adrift of the Scot at the end of the season. Clark assured himself of the title by winning six of the first seven races. The Italian Grand Prix at Monza saw the first victory for Jackie Stewart, the next great British champion after Clark.

DRIVERS

Pts	Driver (Nationality)	Car
54	Jim Clark (GB)	Lotus-Climax
40 (47)	Graham Hill (GB)	BRM
33 (34)	Jackie Stewart (GB)	BRM
25	Dan Gurney (USA)	Brabham-Climax
17	John Surtees (GB)	Ferrari
13	Lorenzo Bandini (Ita)	Ferrari
11	Richie Ginther (USA)	Honda
10	Mike Spence (GB)	Lotus-Climax
10	Bruce McLaren (NZ)	Cooper-Climax
9	Jack Brabham (Aus)	Brabham-Climax
5	Denny Hulme (NZ)	Brabham-Climax
5	Jo Siffert (Swi)	Brabham-BRM
4	Jochen Rindt (Aut)	Cooper-Climax
2	Pedro Rodriguez (Mex)	Ferrari
2	Ron Bucknum (USA)	Honda
2	Dickie Attwood (GB)	Lotus-BRM

Points scoring

1st – 9 pts; 2nd – 6 pts; 3rd – 4 pts; 4th – 3 pts; 5th – 2 pts; 6th – 1 pt.
  Best six results only to count.

CONSTRUCTORS

54 (58)	Lotus-Climax
45 (61)	BRM
27 (31)	Brabham-Climax
26 (27)	Ferrari
14	Cooper-Climax
11	Honda
5	Brabham-BRM
2	Lotus-BRM

Points scoring

1st – 9 pts; 2nd – 6 pts; 3rd – 4 pts; 4th – 3 pts; 5th – 2 pts; 6th – 1 pt.
  Best six results only to count.
Highest-placed car in each race only considered for points.

Two legends of motor racing: Colin Chapman (left), the man who founded the Lotus empire, and Jim Clark, unquestionably the finest driver of all time.

1966

After five years of the 1.5 litre formula it was back to the big engines in 1966 with a limit of 3 litres for unsupercharged cars and 1.5 litres for supercharged engines. British teams were thrown into a state of chaos following Climax's withdrawal from Formula One. Cooper turned to Maserati for their power supply while Lotus used the BRM engine. But the most successful change was that of the Brabham team who used the Australian-made Repco engine. They secured their first constructors' championship and team boss Jack Brabham won his third drivers' title, uniquely doing so in a car bearing his own name.

John Surtees, runner-up to Brabham, had the rare distinction of winning races for different manufacturers in one season, first with Ferrari and then as a member of the Cooper-Maserati team. The Nürburgring claimed yet another life, that of Britain's John Taylor, and the first world champion Giuseppe Farina was killed in a car accident at the age of 59.

DRIVERS

Pts	Driver (Nationality)	Car
42 (45)	Jack Brabham (Aus)	Brabham-Repco
28	John Surtees (GB)	Ferrari/Cooper-Maserati
22 (24)	Jochen Rindt (Aut)	Cooper-Maserati
18	Denny Hulme (NZ)	Brabham-Repco
17	Graham Hill (GB)	BRM
16	Jim Clark (GB)	Lotus-Climax/Lotus-BRM
14	Jackie Stewart (GB)	BRM
12	Mike Parkes (GB)	Ferrari
12	Lorenzo Bandini (Ita)	Ferrari
9	Ludovico Scarfiotti (Ita)	Ferrari
5	Richie Ginther (USA)	Cooper-Maserati/Honda
4	Mike Spence (GB)	Lotus-BRM
4	Dan Gurney (USA)	Eagle-Climax
3	Bob Bondurant (USA)	BRM
3	Jo Siffert (Swi)	Cooper-Maserati
3	Bruce McLaren (NZ)	McLaren-Serenissima/McLaren-Ford
1	John Taylor (GB)	Brabham-BRM
1	Bob Anderson (GB)	Brabham-Climax
1	Peter Arundell (GB)	Lotus-Climax
1	Jo Bonnier (Swe)	Cooper-Maserati

Points scoring
1st – 9 pts; 2nd – 6 pts; 3rd – 4 pts; 4th – 3 pts; 5th – 2 pts; 6th – 1 pt.
   Best five results only to count.

CONSTRUCTORS

Pts	Car
42 (49)	Brabham-Repco
31 (32)	Ferrari
30 (35)	Cooper-Maserati
22	BRM
13	Lotus-BRM
8	Lotus-Climax
4	Eagle-Climax
3	Honda
2	McLaren-Ford
1	Brabham-BRM
1	Brabham-Climax
1	McLaren-Serenissima

Points scoring
1st – 9 pts; 2nd – 6 pts; 3rd – 4 pts;
4th – 3 pts; 5th – 2 pts; 6th – 1 pt.
   Best five results only to count.
Highest-placed car in each race only considered for points.

1967

The Brabham team continued with the Repco engine in 1967, and so did their success. This time they occupied first and second places in the drivers' championship with New Zealander Denny Hulme taking top spot. Had Jack Brabham not used his own car for testing new ideas, he could well have taken the title ahead of Hulme in the old but reliable car. The title was not decided until the last race of the season when Hulme got the third place necessary to prevent 'the boss' from retaining his title.

Colin Chapman's Lotus team struggled to find a satisfactory engine. But after using the BRM and then an old Climax unit they switched to the new Ford-Cosworth power unit and on its debut at Zandvoort Jim Clark powered the car to victory as the most successful engine in Formula One history won the first of its 150-plus races.

Pedro Rodriguez and Denny Hulme both enjoyed the first wins of their career but Hulme's success at Monaco was overshadowed by the tragic accident to Lorenzo Bandini on the 82nd lap when his car overturned in flames after hitting a barrier. Bandini died of his injuries three days later.

DRIVERS

Pts	Driver (Nationality)	Car
51	Denny Hulme (NZ)	Brabham-Repco
46 (48)	Jack Brabham (Aus)	Brabham-Repco
41	Jim Clark (GB)	Lotus-Ford
20	John Surtees (GB)	Honda
20	Chris Amon (NZ)	Ferrari
15	Pedro Rodriguez (Mex)	Cooper-Maserati
15	Graham Hill (GB)	Lotus-BRM/Lotus-Ford
13	Dan Gurney (USA)	Eagle-Weslake
10	Jackie Stewart (GB)	BRM
9	Mike Spence (GB)	BRM
6	John Love (SRho)	Cooper-Climax
6	Jochen Rindt (Aut)	Cooper-Maserati
6	Jo Siffert (Swi)	Cooper-Maserati
3	Bruce McLaren (NZ)	McLaren-BRM
3	Jo Bonnier (Swe)	Cooper-Maserati
2	Chris Irwin (GB)	BRM
2	Mike Parkes (GB)	Ferrari
2	Bob Anderson (GB)	Brabham-Climax
1	Guy Ligier (Fra)	Brabham-Repco
1	Ludovico Scarfiotti (Ita)	Ferrari
1	Jacky Ickx (Bel)	Cooper-Maserati

Points scoring

1st – 9 pts; 2nd – 6 pts; 3rd – 4 pts; 4th – 3 pts; 5th – 2 pts; 6th – 1 pt.

Best five results from first six races and best four results from remaining five races to count.

CONSTRUCTORS

Pts	
63 (67)	Brabham-Repco
44	Lotus-Ford
28	Cooper-Maserati
20	Honda
20	Ferrari
17	BRM
13	Eagle-Weslake
6	Cooper-Climax
6	Lotus-BRM
3	McLaren-BRM
2	Brabham-Climax

Points scoring

1st – 9 pts; 2nd – 6 pts; 3rd – 4 pts; 4th – 3 pts; 5th – 2 pts; 6th – 1 pt.

Best five results from first six races and best four results from remaining five races to count. Highest-placed car in each race only considered for points.

1968

Three teams used the Cosworth engine in 1968: Lotus, McLaren and the new Matra team. Those teams filled the first three places in the constructors' championship, thus highlighting the reliability and power of the engine.

Lotus were top manufacturers again and one of their drivers, Graham Hill, was the world champion. But they were the only bits of good news in an otherwise gloomy season for the team, and the entire motor racing world.

Jim Clark, unquestionably the greatest driver of the era, lost his life in a Formula Two race at Hockenheim on 6 April. His death shocked the motor racing world and suddenly it made drivers realise that motor racing was dangerous, because the one man they never thought would lose his life behind the wheel had done so.

DRIVERS

Pts	Driver (Nationality)	Car
48	Graham Hill (GB)	Lotus-Ford
36	Jackie Stewart (GB)	Matra-Ford
33	Denny Hulme (NZ)	McLaren-BRM/ McLaren-Ford
27	Jacky Ickx (Bel)	Ferrari
22	Bruce McLaren (NZ)	McLaren-Ford
18	Pedro Rodriguez (Mex)	BRM
12	Jo Siffert (Swi)	Lotus-Ford
12	John Surtees (GB)	Honda
11	Jean-Pierre Beltoise (Fra)	Matra/Matra-Ford
10	Chris Amon (NZ)	Ferrari
9	Jim Clark (GB)	Lotus-Ford
8	Jochen Rindt (Aut)	Brabham-Repco
6	Dickie Attwood (GB)	BRM
6	Johnny Servoz-Gavin (Fra)	Matra-Ford
6	Jackie Oliver (GB)	Lotus-Ford
6	Ludovico Scarfiotti (Ita)	Cooper-BRM
5	Lucien Bianchi (Bel)	Cooper-BRM
5	Vic Elford (GB)	Cooper-BRM
4	Brian Redman (GB)	Cooper-BRM
4	Piers Courage (GB)	BRM
3	Dan Gurney (USA)	McLaren-Ford
3	Jo Bonnier (Swe)	McLaren-BRM/Honda
2	Silvio Moser (Swi)	Brabham-Repco
2	Jack Brabham (Aus)	Brabham-Repco

Points scoring

1st – 9 pts; 2nd – 6 pts; 3rd – 4 pts; 4th – 3 pts; 5th – 2 pts; 6th – 1 pt.

Best five results from first six races and best five results from remaining six races to count.

After Clark's death the remainder of the season was played out in an atmosphere of numbness and Hill's championship success, although good for the team, seemed a hollow victory.

CONSTRUCTORS

62	Lotus-Ford
49	McLaren-Ford
45	Matra-Ford
32	Ferrari
28	BRM
14	Cooper-BRM
14	Honda
10	Brabham-Repco
8	Matra
3	McLaren-BRM

Points scoring
1st – 9 pts; 2nd – 6 pts; 3rd – 4 pts; 4th – 3 pts; 5th – 2 pts; 6th – 1 pt.
   Best five results from first six races, and best five results from remaining six races to count. Highest-placed car in each race only considered for points.

1969

The two-part championship continued. But it mattered little to the Ford-powered cars how the championship was constituted; they just kept on winning.

After winning 11 of the 12 championship rounds in 1968 they went on to win 11 more in 1969. The French/British Matra team was one of the supporters of the Cosworth engine and they won both the constructors' and drivers' titles with Jackie Stewart capturing the latter for the first time.

CONSTRUCTORS

66	Matra-Ford
49 (51)	Brabham-Ford
47	Lotus-Ford
38 (40)	McLaren-Ford
7	BRM
7	Ferrari

Points scoring
1st – 9 pts; 2nd – 6 pts; 3rd – 4 pts; 4th – 3 pts; 5th – 2 pts; 6th – 1 pt.
   Best five results from first six races and best four results from remaining five races to count. Highest-placed car in each race only considered for points.

DRIVERS

Pts	Driver (Nationality)	Car
63	Jackie Stewart (GB)	Matra-Ford
37	Jacky Ickx (Bel)	Brabham-Ford
26	Bruce McLaren (NZ)	McLaren-Ford
22	Jochen Rindt (Aut)	Lotus-Ford
21	Jean-Pierre Beltoise (Fra)	Matra-Ford
20	Denny Hulme (NZ)	McLaren-Ford
19	Graham Hill (GB)	Lotus-Ford
16	Piers Courage (GB)	Brabham-Ford
15	Jo Siffert (Swi)	Lotus-Ford
14	Jack Brabham (Aus)	Brabham-Ford
6	John Surtees (GB)	BRM
4	Chris Amon (NZ)	Ferrari
3	Dickie Attwood (GB)	Lotus-Ford
3	Pedro Rodriguez (Mex)	Ferrari
3	Vic Elford (GB)	McLaren-Ford
1	Johnny Servoz-Gavin (Fra)	Matra-Ford
1	Silvio Moser (Swi)	Brabham-Ford
1	Jackie Oliver (GB)	BRM

Points scoring
1st – 9 pts; 2nd – 6 pts; 3rd – 4 pts; 4th – 3 pts; 5th – 2 pts; 6th – 1 pt.
   Best five results from first six races and best four results from remaining five races to count.

1970

Jackie Stewart could not maintain his challenge in 1970 with, firstly, the new March team, and then with Ken Tyrrell's own Formula One team. That opened the door for Lotus to re-emerge as a major force.
   Their top driver was the likeable Austrian Jochen Rindt. He won four races in the first

CONSTRUCTORS

59	Lotus-Ford
52 (55)	Ferrari
48	March-Ford
35	Brabham-Ford
35	McLaren-Ford
23	Matra-Simca
23	BRM
3	Surtees-Ford

Points scoring
1st – 9 pts; 2nd – 6 pts; 3rd – 4 pts; 4th – 3 pts; 5th – 2 pts; 6th – 1 pt.
   Best six results from first seven races and best five results from remaining six races to count. Highest-placed car in each race only considered for points.

half of the season and in the first race of the second half, at Hockenhem, he won again. Two races later Rindt was dead, following an accident at Monza. Ten weeks earlier Britain's Piers

Courage had been killed at Zandvoort, and a tragedy-riddled season also saw the death of Bruce McLaren in a testing accident at Goodwood.

Before his death, however, Rindt had done enough to secure the championship and he thus became the first and only posthumous world champion. The death of Rindt was yet another blow to the Lotus team.

Jochen Rindt celebrates victory in the 1970 British Grand Prix.

DRIVERS

Pts	Driver (Nationality)	Car
45	Jochen Rindt (Aut)	Lotus-Ford
40	Jacky Ickx (Bel)	Ferrari
33	Clay Regazzoni (Swi)	Ferrari
27	Denny Hulme (NZ)	McLaren-Ford
25	Jack Brabham (Aus)	Brabham-Ford
25	Jackie Stewart (GB)	March-Ford
23	Pedro Rodriguez (Mex)	BRM
23	Chris Amon (NZ)	March-Ford
16	Jean-Pierre Beltoise (Fra)	Matra-Simca
12	Emerson Fittipaldi (Bra)	Lotus-Ford
10	Rolf Stommelen (FRG)	Brabham-Ford
8	Henri Pescarolo (Fra)	Matra-Simca
7	Graham Hill (GB)	Lotus-Ford
6	Bruce McLaren (NZ)	McLaren-Ford
4	Mario Andretti (USA)	March-Ford
4	Reine Wisell (Swe)	Lotus-Ford
3	Ignazio Giunti (Ita)	Ferrari
3	John Surtees (GB)	McLaren-Ford/ Surtees-Ford
2	John Miles (GB)	Lotus-Ford
2	Johnny Servoz-Gavin (Fra)	March-Ford
2	Jackie Oliver (GB)	BRM
1	Dan Gurney (USA)	McLaren-Ford
1	François Cevert (Fra)	March-Ford
1	Peter Gethin (GB)	McLaren-Ford
1	Derek Bell (GB)	Surtees-Ford

Points scoring

1st – 9 pts; 2nd – 6 pts; 3rd – 4 pts; 4th – 3 pts; 5th – 2 pts; 6th – 1 pt.

Best six results from first seven races and best five results from remaining six races to count.

1971

With a new designer, Ferrari were expected to do well in 1971 but it was the Cosworth-powered Tyrrell of Jackie Stewart that swept to the championship, brushing aside all opposition. Stewart registered six wins from 11 races as he won the title by nearly 30 points and was crowned champion driver for the second time. Team-mate François Cevert occupied third place.

Another of the sport's great partnerships: Ken Tyrrell (right) gives Jackie Stewart final instructions before the 1971 Italian Grand Prix.

DRIVERS

Pts	Driver (Nationality)	Car
62	Jackie Stewart (GB)	Tyrrell-Ford
33	Ronnie Peterson (Swe)	March-Ford
26	François Cevert (Fra)	Tyrrell-Ford
19	Jacky Ickx (Bel)	Ferrari
19	Jo Siffert (Swi)	BRM
16	Emerson Fittipaldi (Bra)	Lotus-Ford
13	Clay Regazzoni (Swi)	Ferrari
12	Mario Andretti (USA)	Ferrari
9	Peter Gethin (GB)	BRM
9	Pedro Rodriguez (Mex)	BRM
9	Chris Amon (NZ)	Matra-Simca
9	Reine Wisell (Swe)	Lotus-Ford
9	Denny Hulme (NZ)	McLaren-Ford
5	Tim Schenken (Aus)	Brabham-Ford
5	Howden Ganley (NZ)	BRM
4	Henri Pescarolo (Fra)	March-Ford
4	Mark Donohue (USA)	McLaren-Ford
3	Mike Hailwood (GB)	Surtees-Ford
3	Rolf Stommelen (FRG)	Surtees-Ford
3	John Surtees (GB)	Surtees-Ford
2	Graham Hill (GB)	Brabham-Ford
1	Jean-Pierre Beltoise (Fra)	Matra-Simca

Points scoring

1st – 9 pts; 2nd – 6 pts; 3rd – 4 pts; 4th – 3 pts; 5th – 2 pts; 6th – 1 pt.
  Best five results from first six races and best four results from remaining five races to count.

CONSTRUCTORS

73	Tyrrell-Ford
36	BRM
33	Ferrari
33 (34)	March-Ford
21	Lotus-Ford
10	McLaren-Ford
9	Matra-Simca
8	Surtees-Ford
5	Brabham-Ford

Points scoring

1st – 9 pts; 2nd – 6 pts; 3rd – 4 pts;
4th – 3 pts; 5th – 2 pts; 6th – 1 pt.
  Best five results from first six races
and best four results from remaining
five races to count. Highest-placed
car in each race only considered for
points.

1972

Colin Chapman's Lotus team took on a new look as the red and gold livery of the Gold Leaf brand name disappeared and was replaced by the famous black of the John Player name. The change of livery also brought about a change of luck as the team regained the Constructors' Cup, winning it for the fifth time.

Emerson Fittipaldi drove the John Player Lotus to five wins which carried him to the drivers' title. He became the first Brazilian to win it and remains, at 25, the youngest ever world champion. Despite winning four races, Jackie Stewart's Tyrrell was not quite good enough to compete with Lotus.

DRIVERS

Pts	Driver (Nationality)	Car
61	Emerson Fittipaldi (Bra)	Lotus-Ford
45	Jackie Stewart (GB)	Tyrrell-Ford
39	Denny Hulme (NZ)	McLaren-Ford
27	Jacky Ickx (Bel)	Ferrari
23	Peter Revson (USA)	McLaren-Ford
15	François Cevert (Fra)	Tyrrell-Ford
15	Clay Regazzoni (Swi)	Ferrari
13	Mike Hailwood (GB)	Surtees-Ford
12	Ronnie Peterson (Swe)	March-Ford
12	Chris Amon (NZ)	Matra-Simca
9	Jean-Pierre Beltoise (Fra)	BRM
4	Mario Andretti (USA)	Ferrari
4	Howden Ganley (NZ)	BRM
4	Brian Redman (GB)	McLaren-Ford
4	Graham Hill (GB)	Brabham-Ford
3	Andrea de Adamich (Ita)	Surtees-Ford
3	Carlos Reutemann (Arg)	Brabham-Ford
3	Carlos Pace (Bra)	March-Ford
2	Tim Schenken (Aus)	Surtees-Ford
1	Arturo Merzario (Ita)	Ferrari
1	Peter Gethin (GB)	BRM

Points scoring

1st – 9 pts; 2nd – 6 pts; 3rd – 4 pts; 4th – 3 pts; 5th – 2 pts; 6th – 1 point.
  Best five results from first six races and best five results from remaining six races to count.

CONSTRUCTORS

61	Lotus-Ford
51	Tyrrell-Ford
47 (49)	McLaren-Ford
33	Ferrari
18	Surtees-Ford
15	March-Ford
14	BRM
12	Matra-Simca
7	Brabham-Ford

Points scoring

1st – 9 pts; 2nd – 6 pts; 3rd – 4 pts; 4th – 3 pts; 5th – 2 pts; 6th – 1 pt.
　Best five results from first six races and best five results from remaining six races to count. Highest-placed car in each race only considered for points.

1973

Jackie Stewart bowed out of Grand Prix racing in 1973 as world champion for the third time. After 99 races, he withdrew from race 100 as a measure of respect for his team-mate François Cevert who was killed during practice for the final race of the season at Watkins Glen. Stewart already had the drivers' title sewn up because he was well clear of his nearest rival Emerson Fittipaldi.

　Stewart's last Grand Prix win was at the old Nürburgring on 5 August. It was his 27th win, a

François Cevert, team-mate of world champion Jackie Stewart, was killed at Watkins Glen during practice for the final race of the season.

DRIVERS

Pts	Driver (Nationality)	Car
71	Jackie Stewart (GB)	Tyrrell-Ford
55	Emerson Fittipaldi (Bra)	Lotus-Ford
52	Ronnie Peterson (Swe)	Lotus-Ford
47	François Cevert (Fra)	Tyrrell-Ford
38	Peter Revson (USA)	McLaren-Ford
26	Denny Hulme (NZ)	McLaren-Ford
16	Carlos Reutemann (Arg)	Brabham-Ford
14	James Hunt (GB)	March-Ford
12	Jacky Ickx (Bel)	Ferrari/McLaren-Ford
9	Jean-Pierre Beltoise (Fra)	BRM
7	Carlos Pace (Bra)	Surtees-Ford
6	Arturo Merzario (Ita)	Ferrari
5	George Follmer (USA)	Shadow-Ford
4	Jackie Oliver (GB)	Shadow-Ford
3	Andrea de Adamich (Ita)	Brabham-Ford
3	Wilson Fittipaldi (Bra)	Brabham-Ford
2	Niki Lauda (Aut)	BRM
2	Clay Regazzoni (Swi)	BRM
1	Chris Amon (NZ)	Tecno
1	Gijs van Lennep (Hol)	Williams-Ford
1	Howden Ganley (NZ)	Williams-Ford

Points scoring

1st – 9 pts; 2nd – 6 pts; 3rd – 4 pts; 4th – 3 pts; 5th – 2 pts; 6th – 1 pt.
　Best seven results from first eight races and best six results from remaining seven races to count.

CONSTRUCTORS

92 (96)	Lotus-Ford
82 (86)	Tyrrell-Ford
58	McLaren-Ford
22	Brabham-Ford
14	March-Ford
12	Ferrari
12	BRM
9	Shadow-Ford
7	Surtees-Ford
2	Williams-Ford
1	Tecno

Points scoring

1st – 9 pts; 2nd – 6 pts; 3rd – 4 pts; 4th – 3 pts; 5th – 2 pts; 6th – 1 pt.
　Best seven results from first eight races and best six results from remaining seven races to count. Highest-placed car in each race only considered for points.

record that stood until surpassed by Alain Prost in 1987.

Another death saddened the motor racing world in 1973 when Briton Roger Williamson perished in his blazing car at Zandvoort despite the desperate and brave effort of his good friend David Purley to release him.

1974

At one stage there were fears that the 1974 championship would not be allowed to get under way because of the global fuel crisis. But happily such action was thwarted and racing fans were treated to a closely-fought championship.

Ferrari, with Clay Regazzoni and Niki Lauda, were ready to attack the British manufacturers again and when it came to the last race of the season at Watkins Glen, Regazzoni and Emerson Fittipaldi (McLaren) were level on 52 points. Jody Scheckter of Tyrrell was also in with a chance of the title, albeit a slim one.

Scheckter's chance disappeared 15 laps from the end when he was forced out of the race with fuel problems. Regazzoni finished out of the points and Fittipaldi came home fourth to clinch his second world title and thus fend off the Ferrari challenge.

There was yet another tragedy in 1974: Peter Revson was killed while practising for the South African Grand Prix.

DRIVERS

Pts	Driver (Nationality)	Car
55	Emerson Fittipaldi (Bra)	McLaren-Ford
52	Clay Regazzoni (Swi)	Ferrari
45	Jody Scheckter (SAf)	Tyrrell-Ford
38	Niki Lauda (Aut)	Ferrari
35	Ronnie Peterson (Swe)	Lotus-Ford
32	Carlos Reutemann (Arg)	Brabham-Ford
20	Denny Hulme (NZ)	McLaren-Ford
15	James Hunt (GB)	Hesketh-Ford
14	Patrick Depailler (Fra)	Tyrrell-Ford
12	Jacky Ickx (Bel)	Lotus-Ford
12	Mike Hailwood (GB)	McLaren-Ford
11	Carlos Pace (Bra)	Surtees-Ford/ Brabham-Ford
10	Jean-Pierre Beltoise (Fra)	BRM
6	Jean-Pierre Jarier (Fra)	Shadow-Ford
6	John Watson (GB)	Brabham-Ford
5	Hans-Joachim Stuck (FRG)	March-Ford
4	Arturo Merzario (Ita)	Williams-Ford
1	Vittorio Brambilla (Ita)	March-Ford
1	Graham Hill (GB)	Lola-Ford
1	Tom Pryce (GB)	Shadow-Ford

Points scoring
1st – 9 pts; 2nd – 6 pts; 3rd – 4 pts; 4th – 3 pts; 5th – 2 pts; 6th – 1 pt.
  Best seven results from first eight races and best six results from remaining seven races to count.

CONSTRUCTORS

Pts	
73 (75)	McLaren-Ford
65	Ferrari
52	Tyrrell-Ford
42	Lotus-Ford
35	Brabham-Ford
15	Hesketh-Ford
10	BRM
7	Shadow-Ford
6	March-Ford
4	Williams-Ford
3	Surtees-Ford
1	Lola-Ford

Points scoring
1st – 9 pts; 2nd – 6 pts; 3rd – 4 pts; 4th – 3 pts; 5th – 2 pts; 6th – 1 pt.
  Best seven results from first eight races and best six results from remaining seven races to count. Highest-placed car in each race only considered for points.

1975

Sadly, 1975 is remembered all too well for its disasters.

First, three officials and a photographer were killed when Rolf Stommelen's car went out of control during the Spanish Grand Prix at Montjuich. Seven months later the entire motor racing world, and many outside the sport, were devastated when they heard of the death of Graham Hill.

He was killed, along with other members of his newly formed team, when their plane crashed on its way home from a testing session in France. Hill had retired from racing just a few months earlier and at Brazil at the beginning of the season he made the last of his record 176 starts.

Prior to the Hill tragedy Niki Lauda had helped fulfil the promise shown by Ferrari a year earlier by capturing the first of his three world titles, winning five races (including three in succession) in the process.

DRIVERS

Pts	Driver (Nationality)	Car
64½	Niki Lauda (Aut)	Ferrari
45	Emerson Fittipaldi (Bra)	McLaren-Ford
37	Carlos Reutemann (Arg)	Brabham-Ford
33	James Hunt (GB)	Hesketh-Ford
25	Clay Regazzoni (Swi)	Ferrari
24	Carlos Pace (Bra)	Brabham-Ford
20	Jody Scheckter (SAf)	Tyrrell-Ford
20	Jochen Mass (FRG)	McLaren-Ford
12	Patrick Depailler (Fra)	Tyrrell-Ford
8	Tom Pryce (GB)	Shadow-Ford
6½	Vittorio Brambilla (Ita)	March-Ford
6	Jacques Laffite (Fra)	Williams-Ford
6	Ronnie Peterson (Swe)	Lotus-Ford
5	Mario Andretti (USA)	Parnelli-Ford
5	Mark Donohue (USA)	Penske-Ford/March-Ford
3	Jacky Ickx (Bel)	Lotus-Ford
2	Alan Jones (Aus)	Hill-Ford
1½	Jean-Pierre Jarier (Fra)	Shadow-Ford
1	Tony Brise (GB)	Hill-Ford
1	Gijs van Lennep (Hol)	Ensign-Ford
½	Lella Lombardi (Ita)	March-Ford

Points scoring

1st – 9 pts; 2nd – 6 pts; 3rd – 4 pts; 4th – 3 pts; 5th – 2 pts; 6th – 1 pt.
 Best seven results from first eight races and best five results from remaining six races to count.

CONSTRUCTORS

72½	Ferrari
54 (56)	Brabham-Ford
53	McLaren-Ford
33	Hesketh-Ford
25	Tyrrell-Ford
9½	Shadow-Ford
9	Lotus-Ford
7½	March-Ford
6	Williams-Ford
5	Parnelli-Ford
3	Hill-Ford
2	Penske-Ford
1	Ensign-Ford

Points scoring

1st – 9 pts; 2nd – 6 pts; 3rd – 4 pts;
4th – 3 pts; 5th – 2 pts; 6th – 1 pt.
 Best seven results from first eight races and best five results from remaining six races to count. Highest-placed car in each race only considered for points.

1976

After a couple of years without any significant technical advances, Ken Tyrrell certainly made a mark in 1976 when he launched his revolutionary six-wheeled project 34 car.

Britain's James Hunt lost his sponsor, Lord Hesketh, in 1975, but was soon snapped up by McLaren, And what a debut season the new pairing had. It was the first championship to be contested over as many as 16 rounds and Niki Lauda in his Ferrari dominated the first half of what turned out to be a controversial season.

First, Hunt's car was disqualified from first place in the Spanish Grand Prix because it was too wide. Several weeks later the points were reinstated following an appeal. Then two months after winning the British Grand Prix Hunt was disqualified yet again, this time because he illegally received

DRIVERS

Pts	Driver (Nationality)	Car
69	James Hunt (GB)	McLaren-Ford
68	Niki Lauda (Aut)	Ferrari
49	Jody Scheckter (SAf)	Tyrrell-Ford
39	Patrick Depailler (Fra)	Tyrrell-Ford
31	Clay Regazzoni (Swi)	Ferrari
22	Mario Andretti (USA)	Parnelli-Ford/Lotus-Ford
20	John Watson (GB)	Penske-Ford
20	Jacques Laffite (Fra)	Ligier-Matra
19	Jochen Mass (FRG)	McLaren-Ford
11	Gunnar Nilsson (Swe)	Lotus-Ford
10	Ronnie Peterson (Swe)	March-Ford
10	Tom Pryce (GB)	Shadow-Ford
8	Hans-Joachim Stuck (FRG)	March-Ford
7	Carlos Pace (Bra)	Brabham-Alfa Romeo
7	Alan Jones (Aus)	Surtees-Ford
3	Carlos Reutemann (Arg)	Brabham-Alfa Romeo
3	Emerson Fittipaldi (Bra)	Fittipaldi-Ford
2	Chris Amon (NZ)	Ensign-Ford
1	Rolf Stommelen (FRG)	Brabham-Alfa Romeo
1	Vittorio Brambilla (Ita)	March-Ford

Points scoring

1st – 9 pts; 2nd – 6 pts; 3rd – 4 pts; 4th – 3 pts; 5th – 2 pts; 6th – 1 pt.
 Best seven results from first eight races and best seven results from remaining eight races to count.

repairs to his car before the restart after a shunt at the original start.

Amidst all that, Lauda had a near-fatal accident at the Nür-

burgring but made a remarkable comeback just as Hunt seemed to be coasting towards the title. It all came down to the last race of the season at rain-sodden Fuji, in Japan. Lauda pulled out of the race after two laps because the conditions were too dangerous and he valued his life, he said, more highly than the World Championship. Hunt went on to pick up the points necessary to win the title and he became the first Englishman since Graham Hill to be crowned world champion.

CONSTRUCTORS

83	Ferrari
74 (75)	McLaren-Ford
71	Tyrrell-Ford
29	Lotus-Ford
20	Ligier-Matra
20	Penske-Ford
19	March-Ford
10	Shadow-Ford
9	Brabham-Alfa Romeo
7	Surtees-Ford
3	Fittipaldi-Ford
2	Ensign-Ford
1	Parnelli-Ford

Points scoring

1st – 9 pts; 2nd – 6 pts; 3rd – 4 pts; 4th – 3 pts; 5th – 2 pts; 6th – 1 pt.

Best seven results from first eight races and best seven results from remaining eight races to count. Highest-placed car in each race only considered for points.

1977

Niki Lauda confirmed in 1977 what many had suspected the previous year: that he would have retained his world title had it not been for his accident in Germany. A season of consistent driving in 1977 helped him towards regaining the title and in the process he helped Ferrari to their third successive constructors' title.

Another six-wheeler appeared in 1977. This time it was the turn of March, but their car had four wheels at the back unlike the project 34 of Tyrrell which had the four at the front.

It was a memorable season for the South African Jody Scheckter in the Wolf-Ford. He won the opening race at Buenos Aires to make Wolf one of only three manufacturers to win their first ever Grand Prix (Alfa Romeo in 1950 and Mercedes-Benz in 1954 are the other two). Scheckter went on to finish second in the drivers' championship.

All eyes were focused on the new Renault RS01 which made its debut at the British Grand Prix. The car was powered by a 1.5 litre turbocharged engine – the first turbo car. The turbo charger, however, let the engine down on lap 17 and the doubting pundits celebrated. But the last laugh was on them. The Renault became a winner and within a few years nearly all Formula One teams were running turbo-powered cars.

DRIVERS

Pts	Driver (Nationality)	Car
72	Niki Lauda (Aut)	Ferrari
55	Jody Scheckter (SAf)	Wolf-Ford
47	Mario Andretti (USA)	Lotus-Ford
42	Carlos Reutemann (Arg)	Ferrari
40	James Hunt (GB)	McLaren-Ford
25	Jochen Mass (FRG)	McLaren-Ford
22	Alan Jones (Aus)	Shadow-Ford
20	Gunnar Nilsson (Swe)	Lotus-Ford
20	Patrick Depailler (Fra)	Tyrrell-Ford
18	Jacques Laffite (Fra)	Ligier-Matra
12	Hans-Joachim Stuck (FRG)	Brabham-Alfa Romeo
11	Emerson Fittipaldi (Bra)	Fittipaldi-Ford
9	John Watson (GB)	Brabham-Alfa Romeo
7	Ronnie Peterson (Swe)	Tyrrell-Ford
6	Carlos Pace (Bra)	Brabham-Alfa Romeo
6	Vittorio Brambilla (Ita)	Surtees-Ford
5	Clay Regazzoni (Swi)	Ensign-Ford
5	Patrick Tambay (Fra)	Ensign-Ford
1	Jean-Pierre Jarier (Fra)	Penske-Ford
1	Renzo Zorzi (Ita)	Shadow-Ford
1	Riccardo Patrese (Ita)	Shadow-Ford

Points scoring

1st – 9 pts; 2nd – 6 pts; 3rd – 4 pts; 4th – 3 pts; 5th – 2 pts; 6th – 1 pt.

Best eight results from first nine races and best seven results from remaining eight races to count.

CONSTRUCTORS

95 (97)	Ferrari
62	Lotus-Ford
60	McLaren-Ford
55	Wolf-Ford
27	Brabham-Alfa Romeo
27	Tyrrell-Ford
23	Shadow-Ford
18	Ligier-Matra
11	Fittipaldi-Ford
10	Ensign-Ford
6	Surtees-Ford
1	Penske-Ford

Points scoring

1st – 9 pts; 2nd – 6 pts; 3rd – 4 pts; 4th – 3 pts; 5th – 2 pts; 6th – 1 pt.

Best eight results from first nine races and best seven results from remaining eight races to count. Highest-placed car in each race only considered for points.

1978

Despite winning more races than Ferrari the previous year, Lotus could only finish second in the constructors' championship. They were determined to wrest back the trophy and in 1978 they won eight of the 16 rounds to win the title by nearly 30 points.

John Player Lotus drivers dominated the drivers' championship as Mario Andretti became the second North American after Phil Hill to win the title with his team-mate Ronnie Peterson in second place. But the Swede was not to see the season out.

Shortly after the start of the Italian Grand Prix at Monza there was a massive pile-up and amidst it all Peterson was trapped in his blazing car. James Hunt and Clay Regazzoni attempted to pull him out. But the injuries were so severe that the likeable Swede lost his life in hospital the following day.

DRIVERS

Pts	Driver (Nationality)	Car
64	Mario Andretti (USA)	Lotus-Ford
51	Ronnie Peterson (Swe)	Lotus-Ford
48	Carlos Reutemann (Arg)	Ferrari
44	Niki Lauda (Aut)	Brabham-Alfa Romeo
34	Patrick Depailler (Fra)	Tyrrell-Ford
25	John Watson (GB)	Brabham-Alfa Romeo
24	Jody Scheckter (SAf)	Wolf-Ford
19	Jacques Laffite (Fra)	Ligier-Matra
17	Gilles Villeneuve (Can)	Ferrari
17	Emerson Fittipaldi (Bra)	Fittipaldi-Ford
11	Alan Jones (Aus)	Williams-Ford
11	Riccardo Patrese (Ita)	Arrows-Ford
8	James Hunt (GB)	McLaren-Ford
8	Patrick Tambay (Fra)	McLaren-Ford
7	Didier Pironi (Fra)	Tyrrell-Ford
4	Clay Regazzoni (Swi)	Shadow-Ford
3	Jean-Pierre Jabouille (Fra)	Renault
2	Hans-Joachim Stuck (FRG)	Shadow-Ford
1	Hector Rebaque (Mex)	Lotus-Ford
1	Vittorio Brambilla (Ita)	Surtees-Ford
1	Derek Daly (Ire)	Ensign-Ford

Points scoring
1st – 9 pts; 2nd – 6 pts; 3rd – 4 pts; 4th – 3 pts; 5th – 2 pts; 6th – 1 pt.
Best seven results from first eight races and best seven results from remaining eight races to count.

CONSTRUCTORS

Pts	Constructor
86	Lotus-Ford
58	Ferrari
53	Brabham-Alfa Romeo
38	Tyrrell-Ford
24	Wolf-Ford
19	Ligier-Matra
17	Fittipaldi-Ford
15	McLaren-Ford
11	Williams-Ford
11	Arrows-Ford
6	Shadow-Ford
3	Renault
1	Surtees-Ford
1	Ensign-Ford

Points scoring
1st – 9 pts; 2nd – 6 pts; 3rd – 4 pts;
4th – 3 pts; 5th – 2 pts; 6th – 1 pt.
Best seven results from first eight races and best seven results from remaining eight races to count. Highest-placed car in each race only considered for points.

1979

The Frenchman Jean-Pierre Jabouille picked up only nine points in 1979, all for winning his home Grand Prix at Dijon. But the win was a significant one: it was the first ever Grand Prix success for a turbo-powered car. Renault team-mate René Arnoux was in third place after a great battle with Gilles Villeneuve in the Ferrari. And so was born the turbo revolution.

But the overall glory went to Ferrari once more. Their 312T was too good for the rest of the field as South African Jody Scheckter and the French-Canadian Villeneuve stormed the championship with first and second places while the team easily won the constructors' title.

Runner-up to Ferrari was the Williams team, newly expanded thanks to finances from Saudi Princes. Williams' performances in 1979 gave an indication of the prominent part they were to play in Grand Prix racing in future years. There was a welcome return to Formula One, after an absence of 28 years, for

Jody Scheckter, the only South African to succeed in Formula One.

the Alfa Romeo *marque*. But unlike their predecessors they were not to enjoy anything like the same success.

CONSTRUCTORS

113	Ferrari
75	Williams-Ford
61	Ligier-Ford
39	Lotus-Ford
28	Tyrrell-Ford
26	Renault
15	McLaren-Ford
7	Brabham-Alfa Romeo
5	Arrows-Ford
3	Shadow-Ford
2	ATS-Ford
1	Fittipaldi-Ford

Points scoring
1st – 9 pts; 2nd – 6 pts; 3rd – 4 pts; 4th – 3 pts; 5th – 2 pts; 6th – 1 pt.

All races to count and for the first time more than one car per race could obtain points.

DRIVERS

Pts	Driver (Nationality)	Car
51 (60)	Jody Scheckter (SAf)	Ferrari
47 (53)	Gilles Villeneuve (Can)	Ferrari
40 (43)	Alan Jones (Aus)	Williams-Ford
36	Jacques Laffite (Fra)	Ligier-Ford
29 (32)	Clay Regazzoni (Swi)	Williams-Ford
20 (22)	Patrick Depailler (Fra)	Ligier-Ford
20 (25)	Carlos Reutemann (Arg)	Lotus-Ford
17	René Arnoux (Fra)	Renault
15	John Watson (GB)	McLaren-Ford
14	Didier Pironi (Fra)	Tyrrell-Ford
14	Jean-Pierre Jarier (Fra)	Tyrrell-Ford
14	Mario Andretti (USA)	Lotus-Ford
9	Jean-Pierre Jabouille (Fra)	Renault
4	Niki Lauda (Aut)	Brabham-Alfa Romeo
3	Nelson Piquet (Bra)	Brabham-Alfa Romeo
3	Elio de Angelis (Ita)	Shadow-Ford
3	Jacky Ickx (Bel)	Ligier-Ford
3	Jochen Mass (FRG)	Arrows-Ford
2	Riccardo Patrese (Ita)	Arrows-Ford
2	Hans-Joachim Stuck (FRG)	ATS-Ford
1	Emerson Fittipaldi (Bra)	Fittipaldi-Ford

Points scoring
1st – 9 pts; 2nd – 6 pts; 3rd – 4 pts; 4th – 3 pts; 5th – 2 pts; 6th – 1 pt.

Best four results from first seven races and best four results from remaining eight races to count.

1980

Having registered four wins in five races in the second half of 1979, the Williams team were more than ready for the new season. They started where they left off, with a win in Argentina, and went on to win five more championship races which was enough to clinch the constructors' title and for Australian Alan Jones to take the drivers' title which he captured when his nearest challenger Nelson Piquet's engine blew up on the 24th lap of the season's penultimate race at Montreal.

Controversies and disputes had become very much a part of Grand Prix racing in the 1970s, and it was no different as the sport went into the 80s. Alan Jones would have added to his total of wins had his success in the Spanish Grand Prix been allowed to stand. However, the race was declared illegal follow-

DRIVERS

Pts	Driver (Nationality)	Car
67 (71)	Alan Jones (Aus)	Williams-Ford
54	Nelson Piquet (Bra)	Brabham-Ford
42 (51)	Carlos Reutemann (Arg)	Williams-Ford
34	Jacques Laffite (Fra)	Ligier-Ford
32	Didier Pironi (Fra)	Ligier-Ford
29	René Arnoux (Fra)	Renault
13	Elio de Angelis (Ita)	Lotus-Ford
9	Jean-Pierre Jabouille (Fra)	Renault
7	Riccardo Patrese (Ita)	Arrows-Ford
6	Keke Rosberg (Fin)	Fittipaldi-Ford
6	Derek Daly (Ire)	Tyrrell-Ford
6	John Watson (GB)	McLaren-Ford
6	Jean-Pierre Jarier (Fra)	Tyrrell-Ford
6	Gilles Villeneuve (Can)	Ferrari
5	Emerson Fittipaldi (Bra)	Fittipaldi-Ford
5	Alain Prost (Fra)	McLaren-Ford
4	Jochen Mass (FRG)	Arrows-Ford
4	Bruno Giacomelli (Ita)	Alfa Romeo
2	Jody Scheckter (SAf)	Ferrari
1	Hector Rebaque (Mex)	Brabham-Ford
1	Mario Andretti (USA)	Lotus-Ford

Points scoring
1st – 9 pts; 2nd – 6 pts; 3rd – 4 pts; 4th – 3 pts; 5th – 2 pts; 6th – 1 pt.

Best five results from first seven races and best five results from remaining seven races to count.

ing a rift between FISA and FOCA as a result of certain drivers not paying fines imposed on them by FISA.

Grand Prix racing was saddened by the death of Frenchman Patrick Depailler in 1980. Shortly after returning to action following a hang-gliding accident he was killed while testing an Alfa Romeo at Hockenheim.

CONSTRUCTORS

120	Williams-Ford		11	Arrows-Ford
66	Ligier-Ford		11	Fittipaldi-Ford
55	Brabham-Ford		11	McLaren-Ford
38	Renault		8	Ferrari
14	Lotus-Ford		4	Alfa Romeo
12	Tyrrell-Ford			

Points scoring

1st – 9 pts; 2nd – 6 pts; 3rd – 4 pts; 4th – 3 pts; 5th – 2 pts; 6th – 1 pt.
All races to count.

1981

The authorities' wrangling continued into 1981 and following a further rift between FISA and FOCA, the South African Grand Prix was organised by FOCA, and won by Carlos Reutemann in a Williams, but it was not officially recognised as a World Championship race. Despite the power struggle between the ruling bodies, the battle on the track was as intense as ever.

Argentinian Reutemann had been chasing the drivers' title relentlessly since 1972 and as the 1981 championship went into its last round at Las Vegas he had his best ever chance to capture the title. Lying one point ahead of Nelson Piquet the Argentinian had to stay in front of the Brazilian to win the title. But he could only finish 8th while Piquet finished 5th and snatched the title by one point. At 28, Piquet became one of the youngest world champions.

For the first time since 1966 the championship was not split into two halves. It was based on the best 10 results from 15 rounds.

DRIVERS

Pts	Driver (Nationality)	Car
50	Nelson Piquet (Bra)	Brabham-Ford
49	Carlos Reutemann (Arg)	Williams-Ford
46	Alan Jones (Aus)	Williams-Ford
44	Jacques Laffite (Fra)	Talbot-Matra
43	Alain Prost (Fra)	Renault
27	John Watson (GB)	McLaren-Ford
25	Gilles Villeneuve (Can)	Ferrari
14	Elio de Angelis (Ita)	Lotus-Ford
11	René Arnoux (Fra)	Renault
11	Hector Rebaque (Mex)	Brabham-Ford
10	Riccardo Patrese (Ita)	Arrows-Ford
10	Eddie Cheever (USA)	Tyrrell-Ford
9	Didier Pironi (Fra)	Ferrari
8	Nigel Mansell (GB)	Lotus-Ford
7	Bruno Giacomelli (Ita)	Alfa Romeo
4	Marc Surer (Swi)	Ensign-Ford
3	Mario Andretti (USA)	Alfa Romeo
1	Patrick Tambay (Fra)	Theodore-Ford
1	Andrea de Cesaris (Ita)	McLaren-Ford
1	Slim Borgudd (Swe)	ATS-Ford
1	Eliseo Salazar (Chi)	Ensign-Ford

Points scoring

1st – 9 pts; 2nd – 6 pts; 3rd – 4 pts; 4th – 3 pts; 5th – 2 pts; 6th – 1 pt.
Best 10 results from 15 races to count.

CONSTRUCTORS

95	Williams-Ford		10	Arrows-Ford
61	Brabham-Ford		10	Alfa Romeo
54	Renault		10	Tyrrell-Ford
44	Talbot-Matra		5	Ensign-Ford
34	Ferrari		1	Theodore-Ford
28	McLaren-Ford		1	ATS-Ford
22	Lotus-Ford			

Points scoring

1st – 9 pts; 2nd – 6 pts; 3rd – 4 pts; 4th – 3 pts; 5th – 2 pts; 6th – 1 pt.
All races to count.

1982

Keke Rosberg's first Grand Prix win was the 1982 Swiss Grand Prix at Dijon. At the end of the season he still had only that one win to his credit. Nevertheless, he was crowned world champion. Consistent driving in the reliable Williams helped the Swedish-born Finn to his one and only title.

The championship went 'to the wire' with any one of three men, Rosberg, John Watson or Didier Pironi capable of winning the title before the final race around the car park of Caesar's Palace, but the showman Rosberg held off the challenge of his rivals.

There were two tragedies in 1982. First Gilles Villeneuve was killed when his car left the track during practice for the Belgian Grand Prix at Zolder. The ever-increasing use of 'skirts', which reduced suspension, was blamed for the accident and at the end of the season they were banned. A month after Villeneuve's death the young Italian Ricardo Paletti lost his life on the start line of the Canadian Grand Prix.

DRIVERS

Pts	Driver (Nationality)	Car
44	Keke Rosberg (Fin)	Williams-Ford
39	John Watson (GB)	McLaren-Ford
39	Didier Pironi (Fra)	Ferrari
34	Alain Prost (Fra)	Renault
30	Niki Lauda (Aut)	McLaren-Ford
28	René Arnoux (Fra)	Renault
25	Michele Alboreto (Ita)	Tyrrell-Ford
25	Patrick Tambay (Fra)	Ferrari
23	Elio de Angelis (Ita)	Lotus-Ford
21	Riccardo Patrese (Ita)	Brabham-Ford/ Brabham-BMW
20	Nelson Piquet (Bra)	Brabham-BMW
15	Eddie Cheever (USA)	Talbot-Matra
8	Derek Daly (Ire)	Williams-Ford
7	Nigel Mansell (GB)	Lotus-Ford
6	Carlos Reutemann (Arg)	Williams-Ford
6	Gilles Villeneuve (Can)	Ferrari
5	Andrea de Cesaris (Ita)	Alfa Romeo
5	Jacques Laffite (Fra)	Talbot-Matra
4	Mario Andretti (USA)	Ferrari
3	Jean-Pierre Jarier (Fra)	Osella-Ford
3	Marc Surer (Swi)	Arrows-Ford
2	Manfred Winkelhock (FRG)	ATS-Ford
2	Eliseo Salazar (Chi)	ATS-Ford
2	Bruno Giacomelli (Ita)	Alfa Romeo
2	Mauro Baldi (Ita)	Arrows-Ford
1	Chico Serra (Bra)	Fittipaldi-Ford

Points scoring

1st – 9 pts; 2nd – 6 pts; 3rd – 4 pts; 4th – 3 pts; 5th – 2 pts; 6th – 1 pt.
  Best 11 results from 16 races to count.

Didier Pironi and Gilles Villeneuve pulled off a Ferrari 1–2 at the San Marino Grand Prix. Tragically, it would be Villeneuve's last race.

An unhappy season was made even worse in November when one of the sport's greatest innovators, Colin Chapman, died following a heart attack. He was only 54. The Lotus team had endured so many setbacks over the years. Each time it had bounced back from adversity; would it be able to haul itself back after losing its mentor?

1983

Nelson Piquet emulated fellow Brazilian Emerson Fittipaldi and won the world title for a second time in 1983. Like his first triumph two years earlier, Piquet waited until the very last race of the season before snatching the title. This time it was Alain Prost, bidding to become the first French world champion, who was to lose out as Piquet leapfrogged above him in the last race at Kyalami to win the title by two points.

With turbo-power taking control, many manufacturers were looking to replace the Cosworth engine. With over 150 wins to its credit, the Ford unit had now become dated. Even one of its most loyal supporters, Lotus, turned to the Renault turbo in 1983. Honda returned to Formula One as supplier of engines to the Frank Williams team, However, perhaps predictably, the Constructors' Cup went to Ferrari for the 8th time.

CONSTRUCTORS

74	Ferrari	20	Talbot-Matra
69	McLaren-Ford	19	Brabham-Ford
62	Renault	7	Alfa Romeo
58	Williams-Ford	5	Arrows-Ford
30	Lotus-Ford	4	ATS-Ford
25	Tyrrell-Ford	3	Osella-Ford
22	Brabham-BMW	1	Fittipaldi-Ford

Points scoring
1st – 9 pts; 2nd – 6 pts; 3rd – 4 pts; 4th – 3 pts; 5th – 2 pts; 6th – 1 pt.
All races to count.

DRIVERS

Pts	Driver (Nationality)	Car
59	Nelson Piquet (Bra)	Brabham-BMW
57	Alain Prost (Fra)	Renault
49	René Arnoux (Fra)	Ferrari
40	Patrick Tambay (Fra)	Ferrari
27	Keke Rosberg (Fin)	Williams-Ford/ Williams-Honda
22	John Watson (GB)	McLaren-Ford
22	Eddie Cheever (USA)	Renault
15	Andrea de Cesaris (Ita)	Alfa Romeo
13	Riccardo Patrese (Ita)	Brabham-BMW
12	Niki Lauda (Aut)	McLaren-Ford
11	Jacques Laffite (Fra)	Williams-Ford
10	Michele Alboreto (Ita)	Tyrrell-Ford
10	Nigel Mansell (GB)	Lotus-Ford/ Lotus-Renault
9	Derek Warwick (GB)	Toleman-Hart
4	Marc Surer (Swi)	Arrows-Ford
3	Mauro Baldi (Ita)	Alfa Romeo
2	Elio de Angelis (Ita)	Lotus-Renault
2	Danny Sullivan (USA)	Tyrrell-Ford
1	Johnny Cecotto (Ven)	Theodore-Ford
1	Bruno Giacomelli (Ita)	Toleman-Hart

Points scoring
1st – 9 pts; 2nd – 6 pts; 3rd – 4 pts; 4th – 3 pts; 5th – 2 pts; 6th – 1 pt.
Best 11 results from 15 races to count.

CONSTRUCTORS

89	Ferrari	11	Lotus-Renault
79	Renault	10	Toleman-Hart
72	Brabham-BMW	4	Arrows-Ford
36	Williams-Ford	2	Williams-Honda
34	McLaren-Ford	1	Theodore-Ford
18	Alfa Romeo	1	Lotus-Ford
12	Tyrrell-Ford		

Points scoring
1st – 9 pts; 2nd – 6 pts; 3rd – 4 pts; 4th – 3 pts; 5th – 2 pts; 6th – 1 pt.
All races to count.

1984

With the turbo revolution in full flow, the Porsche engine proved to be the most reliable as it helped power the McLarens of Niki Lauda (out of retirement) and Alain Prost to a championship 1–2. Sadly for Prost, he once more missed out on his ambition to become the first French world champion when his team-mate pipped him by half a point to win his third title.

The title was decided in Portugal in the final race of the season. Lauda had to finish within sight of the Frenchman, but if Prost won the race then the Austrian had to finish second to take the title. Prost took the lead and on lap 28 Lauda was lying fifth. The Frenchman had the championship in his sights. However, the Austrian gradually pulled himself into second place and stayed there to clinch the title by the narrowest of margins.

DRIVERS

Pts	Driver (Nationality)	Car
72	Niki Lauda (Aut)	McLaren-Porsche
71½	Alain Prost (Fra)	McLaren-Porsche
34	Elio de Angelis (Ita)	Lotus-Renault
30½	Michele Alboreto (Ita)	Ferrari
29	Nelson Piquet (Bra)	Brabham-BMW
27	René Arnoux (Fra)	Ferrari
23	Derek Warwick (GB)	Renault
20½	Keke Rosberg (Fin)	Williams-Honda
13	Nigel Mansell (GB)	Lotus-Renault
13	Ayrton Senna (Bra)	Toleman-Hart
11	Patrick Tambay (Fra)	Renault
9	Teo Fabi (Ita)	Brabham-BMW
8	Riccardo Patrese (Ita)	Alfa Romeo
5	Jacques Laffite (Fra)	Williams-Honda
5	Thierry Boutsen (Bel)	Arrows-Ford/ Arrows-BMW
3	Eddie Cheever (USA)	Alfa Romeo
3	Andrea de Cesaris (Ita)	Ligier-Renault
3	Stefan Johansson (Swe)	Toleman-Hart
2	Piercarlo Ghinzani (Ita)	Osella-Alfa Romeo
1	Marc Surer (Swi)	Arrows-BMW

Points scoring

1st – 9 pts; 2nd – 6 pts; 3rd – 4 pts; 4th – 3 pts; 5th – 2 pts; 6th – 1 pt.
Best 11 results from 16 races to count.

The 1984 championship race between Niki Lauda (8) and Alain Prost was as close as this action from Portugal, in the final race of the season, suggests.

Had the Monaco Grand Prix not been shortened due to adverse weather conditions, Prost would surely have been champion. He won the race but half-points only were awarded, and instead of getting nine he only collected 4½.

The 1984 season was a troubled one for Ken Tyrrell and his team. After Martin Brundle finished second at Detroit it was found that his fuel tank contained lead pellets which would effectively increase the octane level of the fuel above the permitted level. Brundle lost his championship points and all those gained by Tyrrell and their drivers were deducted because the team was banned from the 1984 championship. However, Ken Tyrrell successfully cleared his name via the courts and the team was reinstated in 1985.

CONSTRUCTORS

143½	McLaren-Porsche	16	Toleman-Hart
57½	Ferrari	11	Alfa Romeo
47	Lotus-Renault	3	Arrows-BMW
38	Brabham-BMW	3	Arrows-Ford
34	Renault	3	Ligier-Renault
25½	Williams-Honda	2	Osella-Alfa.

Points scoring

1st – 9 pts; 2nd – 6 pts; 3rd – 4 pts; 4th – 3 pts; 5th – 2 pts; 6th – 1 pt.
All races to count.

1985

After two close encounters, Alain Prost eventually fulfilled his ambition by winning the world title in 1985, and he won it with plenty of points to spare; there was no close finish this time. The McLaren was as reliable as ever with the new TAG power unit. They won six rounds of the championship, with Prost behind the wheel on five occasions.

Not having had a world champion since 1976, British fans were looking for their next hero to emerge. And he did, in the European Grand Prix at Brands Hatch in the latter part of the season. The new hero was Nigel Mansell. Twelve months later he was to challenge for that world crown. Mansell wasn't the only first-time winner in 1985; in the rain at Estoril, Ayrton Senna drove magnificently to win his first race.

DRIVERS

Pts	Driver (Nationality)	Car
73 (76)	Alain Prost (Fra)	McLaren-TAG
53	Michele Alboreto (Ita)	Ferrari
40	Keke Rosberg (Fin)	Williams-Honda
38	Ayrton Senna (Bra)	Lotus-Renault
33	Elio de Angelis (Ita)	Lotus-Renault
31	Nigel Mansell (GB)	Williams-Honda
26	Stefan Johansson (Swe)	Ferrari
21	Nelson Piquet (Bra)	Brabham-BMW
16	Jacques Laffite (Fra)	Ligier-Renault
14	Niki Lauda (Aut)	McLaren-TAG
11	Patrick Tambay (Fra)	Renault
11	Thierry Boutsen (Bel)	Arrows-BMW
5	Derek Warwick (GB)	Renault
5	Marc Surer (Swi)	Brabham-BMW
4	Philippe Streiff (Fra)	Ligier-Renault
4	Stefan Bellof (FRG)	Tyrrell-Ford
3	René Arnoux (Fra)	Ferrari
3	Andrea de Cesaris (Ita)	Ligier-Renault
3	Gerhard Berger (Aut)	Arrows-BMW
3	Ivan Capelli (Ita)	Tyrrell-Renault

Points scoring

1st – 9 pts; 2nd – 6 pts; 3rd – 4 pts; 4th – 3 pts; 5th – 2 pts; 6th – 1 pt.
Best 11 results from 16 races to count.

CONSTRUCTORS

90	McLaren-TAG
82	Ferrari
71	Williams-Honda
71	Lotus-Renault
26	Brabham-BMW
23	Ligier-Renault
16	Renault
14	Arrows-BMW
4	Tyrrell-Ford
3	Tyrrell-Renault

Points scoring

1st – 9 pts; 2nd – 6 pts; 3rd – 4 pts; 4th – 3 pts; 5th – 2 pts; 6th – 1 pt.
All races to count.

1986

Teams had been given notice that from 1989 turbo-powered engines would be banned. So 1986 was the last full season of turbo cars. Renault no longer had a team, but continued supplying engines to Ligier, Lotus and Tyrrell. But it was the Honda-powered Williams that was the 'car of the year' and won nine of the 16 rounds. But their two drivers, Nelson Piquet and Britain's Nigel Mansell, had to be content as 'bridesmaids' to Alain Prost who retained his world title. But how agonising it was for Mansell in his quest to become Britain's first world champion since James Hunt.

Mansell needed to finish third or better in final race at Adelaide to win the title. But on lap 63 he burst a tyre coming down the Brabham straight at 200 mph. A disaster was averted, but Mansell was out of the race and could only watch as Prost took the chequered flag and the title.

DRIVERS

Pts	Driver (Nationality)	Car
72 (74)	Alain Prost (Fra)	McLaren-TAG
70 (72)	Nigel Mansell (GB)	Williams-Honda
69	Nelson Piquet (Bra)	Williams-Honda
55	Ayrton Senna (Bra)	Lotus-Renault
23	Stefan Johansson (Swe)	Ferrari
22	Keke Rosberg (Fin)	McLaren-TAG
17	Gerhard Berger (Aut)	Benetton-BMW
14	Michele Alboreto (Ita)	Ferrari
14	René Arnoux (Fra)	Ligier-Renault
14	Jacques Laffite (Fra)	Ligier-Renault
8	Martin Brundle (GB)	Tyrrell-Renault
4	Alan Jones (Aus)	Lola-Ford
3	Johnny Dumfries (GB)	Lotus-Renault
3	Philippe Streiff (Fra)	Tyrrell-Renault
2	Teo Fabi (Ita)	Benetton-BMW
2	Patrick Tambay (Fra)	Lola-Ford
2	Riccardo Patrese (Ita)	Brabham-BMW
1	Christian Danner (FRG)	Arrows-BMW
1	Philippe Alliot (Fra)	Ligier-Renault

Points scoring
1st – 9 pts; 2nd – 6 pts; 3rd – 4 pts; 4th – 3 pts; 5th – 2 pts; 6th – 1 pt.
Best 11 results from 16 races to count.

CONSTRUCTORS

141	Williams-Honda		19	Benetton-BMW
96	McLaren-TAG		11	Tyrrell-Renault
58	Lotus-Renault		6	Lola-Ford
37	Ferrari		2	Brabham-BMW
29	Ligier-Renault		1	Arrows-BMW

Points scoring
1st – 9 pts; 2nd – 6 pts; 3rd – 4 pts; 4th – 3 pts; 5th – 2 pts; 6th – 1 pt.
All races to count.

1987

With the phasing out of the turbo, the FIA introduced two championships for drivers and two for constructors in 1987. In addition to the usual competitions there were two new trophies for non-turbo (normally aspirated) cars. The Colin Chapman Cup (for constructors) was won by Tyrrell with their Cosworth engine. One of their drivers, Jonathan Palmer, won the Jim Clark Cup, the non-turbo drivers' title.

The Williams-Honda turbo combination was again too strong for the rest of the field and for the second year running won nine of the 16 championship rounds. Britain's Nigel

DRIVERS (Turbo)

Pts	Driver (Nationality)	Car
73 (76)	Nelson Piquet (Bra)	Williams-Honda
61	Nigel Mansell (GB)	Williams-Honda
57	Ayrton Senna (Bra)	Lotus-Honda
46	Alain Prost (Fra)	McLaren-TAG
36	Gerhard Berger (Aut)	Ferrari
30	Stefan Johansson (Swe)	McLaren-TAG
17	Michele Alboreto (Ita)	Ferrari
16	Thierry Boutsen (Bel)	Benetton-Ford
12	Teo Fabi (Ita)	Benetton-Ford
8	Eddie Cheever (USA)	Arrows-Megatron
7	Satoru Nakajima (Jap)	Lotus-Honda
7	Jonathan Palmer (GB)	Tyrrell-Ford
6	Riccardo Patrese (Ita)	Brabham-BMW
4	Andrea de Cesaris (Ita)	Brabham-BMW
4	Philippe Streiff (Fra)	Tyrrell-Ford
3	Derek Warwick (GB)	Arrows-Megatron
3	Philippe Alliot (Fra)	Lola-Ford
2	Martin Brundle (GB)	Zakspeed
1	René Arnoux (Fra)	Ligier-Megatron
1	Ivan Capelli (Ita)	March-Ford
1	Roberto Moreno (Bra)	AGS-Ford

Mansell was again in contention for the title but a shunt at Suzuka, Japan, in the penultimate round of the championship damaged his back, and dented his hopes once more as team-mate Nelson Piquet went on to win his third world title and join such greats as Jack Brabham, Jackie Stewart and Niki Lauda as three-times world champions. Alain Prost also put his name in the record books when he surpassed Jackie Stewart's long standing record of 27 Grand Prix wins.

CONSTRUCTORS
(Colin Chapman Trophy)

169	Tyrrell-Ford
43	Lola-Ford
39	AGS-Ford
38	March-Ford

DRIVERS (Jim Clark Trophy)

Pts	Driver (Nationality)	Car
87 (95)	Jonathan Palmer (GB)	Tyrrell-Ford
74	Philippe Streiff (Fra)	Tyrrell-Ford
43	Philippe Alliot (Fra)	Lola-Ford
38	Ivan Capelli (Ita)	March-Ford
35	Pascal Fabre (Fra)	AGS-Ford
4	Roberto Moreno (Bra)	AGS-Ford

Points scoring
1st – 9 pts; 2nd – 6 pts; 3rd – 4 pts; 4th – 3 pts; 5th – 2 pts; 6th – 1 pt.
  Best 11 results from 16 races to count.

CONSTRUCTORS (Turbo)

137	Williams-Honda	10	Brabham-BMW
76	McLaren-TAG	3	Lola-Ford
64	Lotus-Honda	2	Zakspeed
53	Ferrari	1	Ligier-Megatron
28	Benetton-Ford	1	March-Ford
11	Arrows-Megatron	1	AGS-Ford
11	Tyrrell-Ford		

Points scoring
1st – 9 pts; 2nd – 6 pts; 3rd – 4 pts; 4th – 3 pts; 5th – 2 pts; 6th – 1 pt.
  All races to count.

1988

If 1986 and 1987 belonged to the Williams team then 1988 belonged to the Marlboro-McLaren team. Fastest in practice in virtually every race entered, they were also fastest in the races themselves and won a staggering 15 rounds of the 16-race championship. They did not suffer their first defeat until the 12th race of the season when Ayrton Senna collided with Jean-Louis Schlesser at Monza and Ferrari went on to take first and second places on 'home' soil, the success coming just a month after Enzo Ferrari's death.

A lot of McLaren's success was due not only to top class drivers in Prost and Senna, but to the Honda turbo engine, the Japanese manufacturer having switched allegiance from Williams. Frank Williams had early season problems with his new Judd engine before making something of a revival towards the end of the season.

The Constructors' Cup was a formality, but which one of the two McLaren drivers would win the drivers' title remained unresolved until the last race of the season in Australia. Prost took the final chequered flag of a keenly fought season but second place was good enough to give his Brazilian team-mate the title.

Alain Prost and Ayrton Senna dominated the championship in 1988 – but their rivalry was as keen as ever.

DRIVERS

Pts	Driver (Nationality)	Car
90 (94)	Ayrton Senna (Bra)	McLaren-Honda
87 (105)	Alain Prost (Fra)	McLaren-Honda
41	Gerhard Berger (Aut)	Ferrari
27	Thierry Boutsen (Bel)	Benetton-Ford
24	Michele Alboreto (Ita)	Ferrari
20	Nelson Piquet (Bra)	Lotus-Honda
17	Ivan Capelli (Ita)	March-Judd
17	Derek Warwick (GB)	Arrows-Megatron
12	Nigel Mansell (GB)	Williams-Judd
12	Alessandro Nannini (Ita)	Benetton-Ford
8	Riccardo Patrese (Ita)	Williams-Judd
6	Eddie Cheever (USA)	Arrows-Megatron
5	Mauricio Gugelmin (Bra)	March-Judd
5	Jonathan Palmer (GB)	Tyrrell-Ford
3	Andrea de Cesaris (Ita)	Rial-Ford
1	Pierluigi Martini (Ita)	Minardi-Ford
1	Satoru Nakajima (Jap)	Lotus-Honda

Points scoring
1st – 9 pts; 2nd – 6 pts; 3rd – 4 pts; 4th – 3 pts; 5th – 2 pts; 6th – 1 pt.
 Best 11 results from 16 races to count.

Right Prost (2) and Senna collide at Suzuka in 1989. The shunt cost Senna the title; the following year he would return the compliment.

CONSTRUCTORS

199	McLaren-Honda
65	Ferrari
39	Benetton-Ford
23	Lotus-Honda
23	Arrows-Megatron
22	March-Judd
20	Williams-Judd
5	Tyrrell-Ford
3	Rial-Ford
1	Minardi-Ford

Points scoring
1st – 9 pts; 2nd – 6 pts; 3rd – 4 pts;
4th – 3 pts; 5th – 2 pts; 6th – 1 pt.
 All races to count.

1989

It was back to normally-aspirated engines in 1989; the turbocharger had been, conquered, and gone. Nigel Mansell opened the season with a win for his new team, Ferrari, and gave hope to British racing fans that they would have their first champion driver since 1976. It also gave hope to fans of the Italian manufacturer. But their early promise soon gave way to the McLarens of Prost and Senna who again dominated, winning 10 of the 16 rounds.

Prost and Senna, although team-mates, were the deadliest of rivals and certainly weren't on each other's Christmas card list. The tension in their relationship came to a head at Suzuka when they were involved in a shunt. Senna was able to get going again and went on to take the chequered flag but FISA disqualified him for taking an illegal track during the shunt with his team-mate and Prost was handed his third championship. Halfway through the season, and while leading the championship, Prost announced he was quitting McLaren and teaming up with Nigel Mansell at Ferrari for the 1990 season.

DRIVERS

Pts	Driver (Nationality)	Car
76 (81)	Alain Prost (Fra)	McLaren-Honda
60	Ayrton Senna (Bra)	McLaren-Honda
40	Riccardo Patrese (Ita)	Williams-Renault
38	Nigel Mansell (GB)	Ferrari
37	Thierry Boutsen (Bel)	Williams-Renault
32	Alessandro Nannini (Ita)	Benetton-Ford
21	Gerhard Berger (Aut)	Ferrari
12	Nelson Piquet (Bra)	Lotus-Judd
8	Jean Alesi (Fra)	Tyrrell-Ford
7	Derek Warwick (GB)	Arrows-Ford
6	Stefan Johansson (Swe)	Onyx-Ford
6	Michele Alboreto (Ita)	Tyrrell-Ford
6	Eddie Cheever (USA)	Arrows-Ford
5	Johnny Herbert (GB)	Benetton-Ford
5	Pierluigi Martini (Ita)	Minardi-Ford
4	Andrea de Cesaris (Ita)	Dallara-Ford
4	Mauricio Gugelmin (Bra)	March-Judd
4	Stefano Modena (Ita)	Brabham-Judd
4	Alex Caffi (Ita)	Dallara-Ford
4	Martin Brundle (GB)	Brabham-Judd
3	Christian Danner (FRG)	Rial-Ford
3	Satoru Nakajima (Jap)	Lotus-Judd
2	René Arnoux (Fra)	Ligier-Ford
2	Emanuele Pirro (Ita)	Benetton-Ford
2	Jonathan Palmer (GB)	Tyrrell-Ford
1	Gabriele Tarquini (Ita)	AGS-Ford
1	Philippe Alliot (Fra)	Lola-Lamborghini
1	Olivier Grouillard (Fra)	Ligier-Ford
1	Luis Sala (Spa)	Minardi-Ford

Points scoring
1st – 9 pts; 2nd – 6 pts; 3rd – 4 pts; 4th – 3 pts; 5th – 2 pts; 6th – 1 pt.
 Best 11 results from 16 races to count.

CONSTRUCTORS

141	McLaren-Honda	13	Arrows-Ford	3	Ligier-Ford		
77	Williams-Renault	8	Dallara-Ford	3	Rial-Ford		
59	Ferrari	8	Brabham-Judd	1	AGS-Ford		
39	Benetton-Ford	6	Onyx-Ford	1	Lola-Lamborghini		
16	Tyrrell-Ford	6	Minardi-Ford				
15	Lotus-Judd	4	March-Judd				

Points scoring

1st – 9 pts; 2nd – 6 pts; 3rd – 4 pts; 4th – 3 pts; 5th – 2 pts; 6th – 1 pt.
  All races to count.

1990

Ayrton Senna started the 1990 campaign determined to regain the world title he was deprived of a year earlier. He set the early pace and was at the top of the table after the seventh race, the French Grand Prix at Paul Ricard, which saw Prost power the Ferrari to the 100th Grand Prix win of its career. After the next race, the British Grand Prix, the Frenchman had taken a two point lead in the championship. British fans were shocked when Nigel Mansell announced his decision to quit the sport at the end of the season. Three months later, he announced a turnaround in his plans: he would be returning to drive for Williams in 1991.

Back on the track, Senna regained his championship lead after the next race, in Germany,

DRIVERS

Pts	Driver (Nationality)	Car
78	Ayrton Senna (Bra)	McLaren-Honda
71 (73)	Alain Prost (Fra)	Ferrari
43 (44)	Nelson Piquet (Bra)	Benetton-Ford
43	Gerhard Berger (Aut)	McLaren-Honda
37	Nigel Mansell (GB)	Ferrari
34	Thierry Boutsen (Bel)	Williams-Renault
23	Riccardo Patrese (Ita)	Williams-Renault
21	Alessandro Nannini (Ita)	Benetton-Ford
13	Jean Alesi (Fra)	Tyrrell-Ford
6	Roberto Moreno (Bra)	Benetton-Ford
6	Ivan Capelli (Ita)	Leyton House-Judd
6	Aguri Suzuki (Jap)	Lola-Lamborghini
5	Eric Bernard (Fra)	Lola-Lamborghini
3	Derek Warwick (GB)	Lotus-Lamborghini
3	Satoru Nakajima (Jap)	Tyrrell-Ford
2	Alex Caffi (Ita)	Arrows-Ford
2	Stefano Modena (Ita)	Brabham-Judd
1	Mauricio Gugelmin (Bra)	Leyton House-Judd

Points scoring

1st – 9 pts; 2nd – 6 pts; 3rd – 4 pts; 4th – 3 pts; 5th – 2 pts; 6th – 1 pt.
  Best 11 results from 16 races to count.

and held on to it for the remainder of the season. But there was more controversy to follow. Again it involved Senna and Prost, and again it was at Suzuka.

Senna was in pole position with Prost alongside him on the front row of the grid. Getting a nose in front was essential at the first bend, a right-hander, and as they approached it, Senna was on the inside. He caught Prost's car and took both of them out of the race, thus clinching the championship without completing a lap. A year later, following an outburst aimed at the former FISA president Jean-Marie Balestre, Senna admitted he had deliberately taken Prost out at the first bend in order to win the championship. He subsequently denied it, saying his comments had been taken out of context.

CONSTRUCTORS

121	McLaren-Honda		7	Leyton House-Judd
110	Ferrari		3	Lotus-Lamborghini
71	Benetton-Ford		2	Brabham-Judd
57	Williams-Renault		2	Arrows-Ford
16	Tyrrell-Ford			

The Larrousse Lola-Lambourghini team obtained 11 points but had them all deducted from them after the end of the season because FISA discovered they had made a false declaration on their entry form. They said their car was built by SEPO-Larrousse when, in fact, it was built by Lola.

Points scoring
1st – 9 pts; 2nd – 6 pts; 3rd – 4 pts; 4th – 3 pts; 5th – 2 pts; 6th – 1 pt.
All races to count.

1991

Ayrton Senna looked like being the runaway champion, particularly after becoming the first man to win the opening four races of the season. But his run was ended at Montreal when Nelson Piquet took the chequered flag. But how sad it was for Nigel Mansell, who had the flag in his sights when his car ground to a halt.

However, the Briton registered the 17th win of his career at Magny Cours and became the most successful English driver. He followed it with successive wins at Silverstone and Hockenheim, getting to within eight points of Senna. But that was to be as close as Mansell got to the Brazilian, who returned to winning ways in Hungary and went on to win the title in Japan when he finished second with Mansell out of the race and the points.

For the first time since 1980 Alain Prost failed to win a Grand Prix and before the final race of the season Ferrari announced that the two were parting company. Ten points were awarded to each race winner for the first time.

DRIVERS

Pts	Driver (Nationality)	Car
96	Ayrton Senna (Bra)	McLaren-Honda
72	Nigel Mansell (GB)	Williams-Renault
53	Riccardo Patrese (Ita)	Williams-Renault
43	Gerhard Berger (Aut)	McLaren-Honda
34	Alain Prost (Fra)	Ferrari
26½	Nelson Piquet (Bra)	Benetton-Ford
21	Jean Alesi (Fra)	Ferrari
10	Stefano Modena (Ita)	Tyrrell-Honda
9	Andrea de Cesaris (Ita)	Jordan-Ford
8	Roberto Moreno (Bra)	Minardi-Ferrari
6	Pierluigi Martini (Ita)	Minardi-Ferrari
4	JJ Lehto (Fin)	Dallara-Ford
4	Bertrand Gachot (Bel)	Jordan-Ford
4	Michael Schumacher (Ger)	Benetton-Ford
2	Miki Hakkinen (Fin)	Lotus-Judd
2	Martin Brundle (GB)	Brabham-Yamaha
2	Satoru Nakajima (Jap)	Tyrrell-Honda
1	Julian Bailey (GB)	Lotus-Judd
1	Eric Bernard (Fra)	Lola-Ford
1	Ivan Capelli (Ita)	Leyton House-Ilmor
1	Aguri Suzuki (Jap)	Lola-Ford
1	Emanuele Pirro (Ita)	Dallara-Judd
1	Mark Blundell (GB)	Brabham-Yamaha
½	Gianni Morbidelli (Ita)	Ferrari

Points scoring
1st – 10 pts; 2nd – 6 pts; 3rd – 4 pts; 4th – 3 pts; 5th – 2 pts; 6th – 1 pt.
All 16 races to count.

CONSTRUCTORS

139	McLaren-Honda		6	Minardi-Ferrari
125	Williams-Renault		5	Dallara-Judd
55½	Ferrari		3	Brabham-Yamaha
38½	Benetton-Ford		3	Lotus-Judd
13	Jordan-Ford		2	Lola-Ford
12	Tyrrell-Honda		1	Leyton House-Ilmor

Points scoring
1st – 10 pts; 2nd – 6 pts; 3rd – 4 pts; 4th – 3 pts; 5th – 2 pts; 6th – 1 pt.
All 16 races to count.

DRIVERS

WORLD TITLES

5 Juan Manuel Fangio (Arg) 1951, 1954–7

3 Jack Brabham (Aus) 1959–60, 1966; Jackie Stewart (GB) 1969, 1971, 1973; Niki Lauda (Aut) 1975, 1977, 1984; Nelson Piquet (Bra) 1981, 1983, 1987; Alain Prost (Fra) 1985–6, 1989; Ayrton Senna (Bra) 1988, 1990–1

2 Alberto Ascari (Ita) 1952–3; Jim Clark (GB) 1963, 1965; Graham Hill (GB) 1962, 1968; Emerson Fittipaldi (Bra) 1972, 1974

1 Giuseppe Farina (Ita) 1950; Mike Hawthorn (GB) 1958; Phil Hill (USA) 1961; John Surtees (GB) 1964; Denny Hulme (NZ) 1967; Jochen Rindt (Aut) 1970; James Hunt (GB) 1976; Mario Andretti (USA) 1978; Jody Scheckter (SAf) 1979; Alan Jones (Aus) 1980; Keke Rosberg (Fin) 1982

RUNNERS-UP

4 Stirling Moss (GB) 1955–8*; Alain Prost (Fra) 1983–4, 1988, 1990

3 Graham Hill (GB) 1963–5; Nigel Mansell (GB) 1986–7, 1991*

2 Juan Manuel Fangio (Arg) 1950, 1953; Jacky Ickx (Bel) 1969–70*; Jackie Stewart (GB) 1968, 1972; Emerson Fittipaldi (Bra) 1973, 1975; Ronnie Peterson (Swe) 1971, 1978*;

1 Alberto Ascari (Ita) 1951; Giuseppe Farina (Ita) 1952; José Froilán González (Arg) 1954*; Tony Brooks (GB) 1959*; Bruce McLaren (NZ) 1960*; Wolfgang von Trips (FRG) 1961*; Jim Clark (GB) 1962; Richie Ginther (USA) 1963*; John Surtees (GB) 1966; Jack Brabham (Aus) 1967; Clay Regazzoni (Swi) 1974*; Niki Lauda (Aut) 1976; Jody Scheckter (SAf) 1977; Gilles Villeneuve (Can) 1979*; Nelson Piquet (Bra) 1980; Carlos Reutemann (Arg)* 1981; John Watson (GB) 1982*; Didier Pironi (Fra) 1982*; Michele Alboreto (Ita) 1985*; Ayrton Senna (Bra) 1989

* Indicates never won the title

YOUNGEST WORLD CHAMPIONS

25 yr 10 mths	Emerson Fittipaldi (1972)
26 yr 7 mths	Niki Lauda (1975)
27 yr 7 mths	Jim Clark (1963)
28 yr 6 mths	Jochen Rindt (1970)
28 yr 7 mths	Ayrton Senna (1988)
29 yr 2 mths	James Hunt (1976)
29 yr 2 mths	Nelson Piquet (1981)
29 yr 6 mths	Mike Hawthorn (1958)
29 yr 8 mths	Jody Scheckter (1979)

Emerson Fittipaldi, who started the 'Brazilian Revolution'.

MOST WINS IN A YEAR

8 Ayrton Senna (1988)
7 Jim Clark (1963)
7 Alain Prost (1984) [1]
7 Ayrton Senna (1991)
6 Alberto Ascari (1952)
6 Juan Manuel Fangio (1954)
6 Jim Clark (1965)
6 Jackie Stewart (1969)
6 Jackie Stewart (1971)
6 James Hunt (1976)
6 Mario Andretti (1978)
6 Nigel Mansell (1987) [1]
6 Ayrton Senna (1989) [1]
6 Ayrton Senna (1990)
[1] Not *that season's* world champion

OLDEST WORLD CHAMPIONS

46 yr 2 mths	Juan Manuel Fangio (1957)
43 yr 11 mths	Giuseppe Farina (1950)
40 yr 6 mths	Jack Brabham (1966)
39 yr 9 mths	Graham Hill (1968)
38 yr 8 mths	Mario Andretti (1978)
35 yr 8 mths	Niki Lauda (1984)
35 yr 3 mths	Nelson Piquet (1987)
35 yr 1 mth	Alberto Ascari (1953)

RACE WINS

44 Alain Prost (Fra)
33 Ayrton Senna (Bra)
27 Jackie Stewart (GB)
25 Jim Clark (GB); Niki Lauda (Aut)
24 Juan Manuel Fangio (Arg)
23 Nelson Piquet (Bra)
21 Nigel Mansell (GB)
16 Stirling Moss (GB)
14 Jack Brabham (Aus); Emerson Fittipaldi (Bra); Graham Hill (GB)
13 Alberto Ascari (Ita)
12 Mario Andretti (USA); Alan Jones (Aus); Carlos Reutemann (Arg)
10 James Hunt (GB); Ronnie Peterson (Swe); Jody Scheckter (SAf)
8 Denny Hulme (NZ); Jacky Ickx (Bel)
7 René Arnoux (Fra)
6 Gerhard Berger (Aut); Tony Brooks (GB); Jacques Laffite (Fra); Jochen Rindt (Aut); John Surtees (GB); Gilles Villeneuve (Can)
5 Michele Alboreto (Ita); Giuseppe Farina (Ita); Riccardo Patrese (Ita); Clay Regazzoni (Swi); Keke Rosberg (Fin); John Watson (GB)
4 Dan Gurney (USA); Bruce McLaren (NZ)

3 Thierry Boutsen (Bel); Peter Collins (GB); Mike Hawthorn (GB); Phil Hill (USA); Didier Pironi (Fra)
2 Elio de Angelis (Ita); Patrick Depailler (Fra); José Froilán González (Arg); Jean-Pierre Jabouille (Fra); Peter Revson (USA); Pedro Rodriguez (Mex); Jo Siffert (Swi); Patrick Tambay (Fra); Maurice Trintignant (Fra); Wolfgang von Trips (FRG); Bill Vukovich (USA)
1 Giancarlo Baghetti (Ita); Lorenzo Bandini (Ita); Jean-Pierre Beltoise (Fra); Jo Bonnier (Swe); Vittorio Brambilla (Ita); Jimmy Bryan (USA); François Cevert (Fra); Luigi Fagioli (Ita); Pat Flaherty (USA); Peter Gethin (GB); Richie Ginther (USA); Innes Ireland (GB); Jochen Mass (FRG); Luigi Musso (Ita); Alessandro Nannini (Ita); Gunnar Nilsson (Swe); Carlos Pace (Bra); Johnnie Parsons (USA); Jim Rathmann (USA); Troy Ruttman (USA); Ludovico Scarfiotti (Ita); Bob Sweikert (USA); Piero Taruffi (Ita); Lee Wallard (USA); Rodger Ward (USA)

WINS BY NATIONALITY

Great Britain (138)
27 Jackie Stewart **25** Jim Clark **21** Nigel Mansell **16** Stirling Moss **14** Graham Hill **10** James Hunt **6** Tony Brooks, John Surtees **5** John Watson **3** Peter Collins, Mike Hawthorn **1** Peter Gethin, Innes Ireland

Brazil (71)
33 Ayrton Senna **23** Nelson Piquet **14** Emerson Fittipaldi **1** Carlos Pace

France (70)
44 Alain Prost **7** René Arnoux **6** Jacques Laffite **3** Didier Pironi **2** Patrick Depailler, Jean-Pierre Jabouille, Patrick Tambay, Maurice Trintignant **1** Jean-Pierre Beltoise, François Cevert

Argentina (38)
24 Juan Manuel Fangio **12** Carlos Reutemann **2** José Froilán González

Italy (38)
13 Alberto Ascari **5** Michele Alboreto, Giuseppe Farina, Riccardo Patrese **2** Elio de Angelis **1** Giancarlo Baghetti, Lorenzo Bandini, Vittorio Brambilla, Luigi Fagioli, Luigi Musso, Ludovico Scarfiotti, Alessandro Nannini, Piero Taruffi

Austria (37)
25 Niki Lauda **6** Jochen Rindt, Gerhard Berger

United States (33)
12 Mario Andretti **4** Dan Gurney **3** Phil Hill **2** Peter Revson, Bill Vukovich **1** Jimmy Bryan, Pat Flaherty, Richie Ginther, Sam Hanks, Johnnie Parsons, Jim Rathmann, Troy Ruttman, Lee Wallard, Rodger Ward, Bob Sweikert

Australia (26)
14 Jack Brabham **12** Alan Jones

Sweden (12)
10 Ronnie Peterson **1** Jo Bonnier, Gunnar Nilsson

New Zealand (12)
8 Denny Hulme **4** Bruce McLaren

Belgium (11)
8 Jacky Ickx **3** Thierry Boutsen

South Africa (10)
10 Jody Scheckter

Switzerland (7)
5 Clay Regazzoni **2** Jo Siffert

Canada (6)
6 Gilles Villeneuve

Finland (5)
5 Keke Rosberg

Germany (3)
2 Wolfgang von Trips **1** Jochen Mass

Mexico (2)
2 Pedro Rodriguez

Alain Prost, the most successful driver of all time, celebrates win number 44 at Jerez in 1990.

Jackie Stewart is one of eight British drivers to have won the British Grand Prix.

WINNERS OF GRAND PRIX IN THEIR OWN COUNTRY

Argentina
Juan Manuel Fangio 1954, 1955, 1956[1], 1957
Austria
Niki Lauda 1984
Brazil
Emerson Fittipaldi 1973, 1974
Carlos Pace 1975
Nelson Piquet 1983, 1986
Ayrton Senna 1991
Great Britain
Stirling Moss 1955, 1957[1]
Tony Brooks 1957[1]
Peter Collins 1958
Jim Clark 1962, 1963, 1964, 1965, 1967
Jackie Stewart 1969, 1971
James Hunt 1977
John Watson 1981
Nigel Mansell 1985 [2],1986, 1987, 1991
Canada
Gilles Villeneuve 1978
France
Jean-Pierre Jabouille 1979
Alain Prost 1981, 1983, 1988, 1989, 1990
René·Arnoux 1982
Italy
Giuseppe Farina 1950
Alberto Ascari 1951, 1952
Ludovico Scarfiotti 1966
South Africa
Jody Scheckter 1975
United States
Mario Andretti 1977
[1] *Shared drive*
[2] *European Grand Prix, held at Brands Hatch*
The Italians Elio de Angelis (1985) and Riccardo Patrese (1990) both won the San Marino Grand Prix; San Marino being a republic within Italy

NATIONS PROVIDING THE MOST DRIVERS TO WIN RACES

15	United States	3	Austria	2	Switzerland
13	Great Britain	3	Sweden	1	Canada
13	Italy	2	Australia	1	Finland
10	France	2	Belgium	1	Mexico
4	Brazil	2	Germany	1	South Africa
3	Argentina	2	New Zealand		

EACH NATION'S FIRST GRAND PRIX WINNER

Argentina: Juan Manuel Fangio, Alfa Romeo, Monaco GP 1950
Australia: Jack Brabham, Cooper-Climax, Monaco GP 1959
Austria: Jochen Rindt, Lotus-Ford, United States GP 1969
Belgium: Jacky Ickx, Ferrari, French GP 1968
Brazil: Emerson Fittipaldi, Lotus-Ford, United States GP 1970
Canada: Gilles Villeneuve, Ferrari, Canadian GP 1978
Finland: Keke Rosberg, Williams-Ford, Swiss GP 1982
France: Maurice Trintignant, Ferrari, Monaco GP 1955
Germany: Wolfgang von Trips, Ferrari, Dutch GP 1961
Great Britain: Mike Hawthorn, Ferrari, French GP 1953
Italy: Giuseppe Farina, Alfa Romeo, British GP 1950
Mexico: Pedro Rodriguez, Cooper-Maserati, South African GP 1967
New Zealand: Bruce McLaren, Cooper-Climax, United States GP 1959
South Africa: Jody Scheckter, Tyrrell-Ford, Swedish GP 1974
Sweden: Jo Bonnier, BRM, Dutch GP 1959
Switzerland: Jo Siffert, Lotus-Ford, British GP 1968
United States: Johnnie Parsons, Wynn's Friction Proof, Indianapolis 1950
(The first non-Indianapolis 500 winner was Phil Hill, Italian GP 1960)

WINNERS OF RACES IN THREE OR MORE DIFFERENT MAKES OF CAR

(Figures in brackets indicate number of wins for each manufacturer)
5 Stirling Moss (Mercedes-Benz 1, Maserati 2, Vanwall 6, Cooper 3, Lotus 4)
4 Juan Manuel Fangio (Alfa Romeo 6, Maserati 7, Mercedes-Benz 8, Lancia-Ferrari 3)
Jackie Stewart (BRM 2, Matra 9, March 1, Tyrrell 15)
3 Dan Gurney (Porsche 1, Brabham 2, Eagle 1)
John Surtees (Ferrari 4, Cooper 1, Honda 1)
Jody Scheckter (Tyrrell 4, Wolf 3, Ferrari 3)
Niki Lauda (Ferrari 15, Brabham 2, McLaren 3)
Carlos Reutemann (Brabham 4, Ferrari 5, Williams 3)
Nelson Piquet (Brabham 13, Williams 7, Benetton 3)
Alain Prost (Renault 9, McLaren 30, Ferrari 5)
Gerhard Berger (Benetton 1, Ferrari 4, McLaren 1)

MOST WINS FOR ONE MANUFACTURER

Wins	Driver	Manufacturer	Wins	Driver	Manufacturer
30	Alain Prost	McLaren	11	Alan Jones	Williams
27	Ayrton Senna	McLaren	10	Graham Hill	BRM
25	Jim Clark	Lotus	9	Jackie Stewart	Matra
18	Nigel Mansell	Williams	9	James Hunt	McLaren
15	Jackie Stewart	Tyrrell	9	Ronnie Peterson	Lotus
15	Niki Lauda	Ferrari	9	Emerson Fittipaldi	Lotus
13	Alberto Ascari	Ferrari	9	Alain Prost	Renault
13	Nelson Piquet	Brabham	8	Juan Manuel Fangio	Mercedes-Benz
11	Mario Andretti	Lotus	8	Niki Lauda	McLaren

LONGEST GAP BETWEEN 1st AND 2nd GRAND PRIX WINS

5 yr 232 days   Mario Andretti (6 Mar 1971–24 Oct 1976)
4 yr 339 days   John Watson (15 Aug 1976–18 Jul 1981)
3 yr 332 days   Clay Regazzoni (6 Sep 1970–4 Aug 1974)
3 yr 156 days   Pedro Rodriguez (2 Jan 1967–7 Jun 1970)
3 yr 26 days   Jo Siffert (20 Jul 1968–15 Aug 1971)
3 yr 3 days   José Froilán González (14 Jul 1951–17 Jul 1954)

LONGEST GAP BETWEEN 1st AND LAST GRAND PRIX WINS

11 yr 119 days   Niki Lauda (28 Apr 1974–25 Aug 1985)
11 yr 64 days   Nelson Piquet (30 Mar 1980–2 Jun 1991)
10 yr 301 days   Jack Brabham (10 May 1959–7 Mar 1970)
9 yr 311 days   Clay Regazzoni (6 Sep 1970–14 Jul 1979)
9 yr 122 days   Riccardo Patrese (23 May 1982–22 Sep 1991)
9 yr 87 days   Alain Prost (5 Jul 1981–30 Sep 1990)
8 yr 180 days   Bruce McLaren (12 Dec 1959–9 Jun 1968)

MOST SUCCESSIVE WINS

(Indianapolis 500 excluded)
9 Alberto Ascari (1952/1953)
5 Jack Brabham (1960)
5 Jim Clark (1965)
4 Juan Manuel Fangio (1953/1954)
4 Jim Clark (1963)
4 Jack Brabham (1966)
4 Jochen Rindt (1970)
4 Ayrton Senna (1988)
4 Ayrton Senna (1991)[1]
3 Juan Manuel Fangio (1954)
3 Stirling Moss (1957/1958)
3 Juan Manuel Fangio (1957)
3 Jim Clark (1967/1968)
3 Jackie Stewart (1969)
3 Jackie Stewart (1971)
3 Niki Lauda (1975)
3 Niki Lauda (1975/1976)
3 Alan Jones (1979)
3 Alan Jones (1980/1981)
3 Alain Prost (1984/1985)
3 Ayrton Senna (1989)
3 Alain Prost (1990)
3 Nigel Mansell (1991)
[1] *The first four races of the season*

MOST RACES WITHOUT A WIN

165 Andrea de Cesaris (1980–91)
136 Jean-Pierre Jarier (1971–83)
132 Eddie Cheever (1978–89)
131 Derek Warwick (1981–91)
96 Chris Amon (1963–76)
93 Philippe Alliot (1984–90)
83 Martin Brundle (1984–91)
82 Marc Surer (1979–86)
82 Jonathan Palmer (1983–9)
79 Stefan Johansson (1983–91)
78 Ivan Capelli (1985–91)
74 Hans-Joachim Stuck (1974–9)
74 Satoru Nakajima (1987–91)
71 Piercarlo Ghinzani (1981–9)
70 Pierluigi Martini (1985–91)
69 Bruno Giacomelli (1977–90)
64 Teo Fabi (1982–7)
59 Mauricio Gugelmin (1988–91)
58 Stefano Modena (1987–91)
57 Henri Pescarolo (1968–76)
57 Arturo Merzario (1972–9)
56 Harry Schell (1950–60)
56 Alex Caffi (1986–91)
54 Rolf Stommelen (1969–78)
54 Philippe Streiff (1984–8)
52 Jean Behra (1952–9)
50 Mike Hailwood (1963–74)
50 Jackie Oliver (1967–77)

MOST SEASONS IN WHICH WINS WERE GAINED

10 Alain Prost (1981–90)
10 Nelson Piquet (1980–91)
8 Jackie Stewart (1965–73)
8 Niki Lauda (1974–85)
7 Juan Manuel Fangio (1950–7)
7 Stirling Moss (1955–61)
7 Jim Clark (1962–8)
7 Ayrton Senna (1985–91)
6 Graham Hill (1962–9)
6 Denny Hulme (1967–74)
6 Carlos Reutemann (1974–81)
6 Nigel Mansell (1985–91)

MOST CONSECUTIVE SEASONS IN WHICH WINS WERE GAINED

10 Alain Prost (1981–90)
8 Nelson Piquet (1980–7)
7 Stirling Moss (1955–61)
7 Jim Clark (1962–8)
7 Ayrton Senna (1985–91)
6 Jackie Stewart (1968–73)
5 Juan Manuel Fangio (1953–7)
5 Jacky Ickx (1968–72)
5 Niki Lauda (1974–8)

WINNERS OF THEIR FIRST WORLD CHAMPIONSHIP GRAND PRIX

Giuseppe Farina, 1950 British Grand Prix [1]

Giancarlo Baghetti, 1961 French GP

[1] *The very first world championship race*

Right *Giancarlo Baghetti (50) in the privately entered Ferrari won the 1961 French Grand Prix in his first ever race.*

STARTS

224 Riccardo Patrese (Ita)
204 Nelson Piquet (Bra)
183 Alain Prost (Fra)
176 Jacques Laffite (Fra); Graham Hill (GB)
171 Niki Lauda (Aut)
165 Nigel Mansell (GB); Andrea de Cesaris (Ita)
153 Michele Alboreto (Ita)
152 John Watson (GB)
149 René Arnoux (Fra)
146 Carlos Reutemann (Arg)
144 Emerson Fittipaldi (Bra)
137 Thierry Boutsen (Bel)
136 Jean-Pierre Jarier (Fra)
132 Clay Regazzoni (Swi); Eddie Cheever (USA)
131 Derek Warwick (GB)
128 Mario Andretti (USA)
126 Jack Brabham (Aus); Ayrton Senna (Bra)
123 Ronnie Peterson (Swe)
116 Alan Jones (Aus); Jacky Ickx (Bel)
115 Gerhard Berger (Aut)
114 Keke Rosberg (Fin); Patrick Tambay (Fra)
112 Denny Hulme (NZ); Jody Scheckter (SAf)
111 John Surtees (GB)
108 Elio de Angelis (Ita)
105 Jochen Mass (FRG)
104 Jo Bonnier (Swe)
101 Bruce McLaren (NZ)
 99 Jackie Stewart (GB)
 96 Chris Amon (NZ); Jo Siffert (Swi)
 95 Patrick Depailler (Fra)
 93 Philippe Alliot (Fra)
 92 James Hunt (GB)
 86 Jean-Pierre Beltoise (Fra); Dan Gurney (USA)
 83 Martin Brundle (GB)
 82 Maurice Trintignant (Fra);

Jonathan Palmer (GB); Marc Surer (Swi)
 79 Stefan Johansson (Swe)
 78 Ivan Capelli (Ita)
 77 Alessandro Nannini (Ita)
 74 Hans-Joachim Stuck (FRG); Vittorio Brambilla (Ita); Satoru Nakajima (Jap)
 72 Carlos Pace (Bra); Jim Clark (GB)
 71 Piercarlo Ghinzani (Ita)
 70 Didier Pironi (Fra); Pierluigi Martini (Ita)
 69 Bruno Giacomelli (Ita)
 67 Gilles Villeneuve (Can)
 66 Stirling Moss (GB)
 60 Jochen Rindt (Aut)
 59 Mauricio Gugelmin (Bra)
 58 Stefano Modena (Ita)
 57 Henri Pescarolo (Fra); Arturo Merzario (Ita)
 56 Alex Caffi (Ita); Harry Schell (USA)
 55 Pedro Rodriguez (Mex)
 54 Philippe Streiff (Fra); Rolf Stommelen (FRG)
 52 Jean Behra (Fra); Richie Ginther (USA)
 51 Juan Manuel Fangio (Arg)
 50 Mike Hailwood (GB); Innes Ireland (GB); Jackie Oliver (GB)
 49 Jean-Pierre Jabouille (Fra); Derek Daly (Ire)
 48 Phil Hill (USA)
 47 François Cevert (Fra); Manfred Winkelhock (FRG); Roy Salvadori (GB)
 45 Mike Hawthorn (GB)
 42 Tom Pryce (GB); Lorenzo Bandini (Ita)
 41 Hector Rebaque (Mex)
 39 Jean Alesi (Fra)
 38 Louis Rosier (Fra); Tony Brooks (GB); Masten Gregory (USA)
 37 Emanuele Pirro (Ita)
 36 Wilson Fittipaldi (Bra); Mike

Spence (GB); Mauro Baldi (Ita)
 35 Howden Ganley (NZ)
 34 Tim Schenken (Aus); Christian Danner (FRG)
 33 Giuseppe Farina (Ita)
 32 Peter Collins (GB); Alberto Ascari (Ita)
 31 Eric Bernard (Fra); Luigi Villoresi (Ita); Gunnar Nilsson (Swe)
 30 Peter Gethin (GB); Andrea de Adamich (Ita); Peter Revson (USA)
 29 Aguri Suzuki (Jap)
 28 Robert Manzon (Fra); Piers Courage (GB); Carel Godin de Beaufort (Hol)
 27 Wolfgang von Trips (FRG); Trevor Taylor (GB)
 26 José Froilán González (Arg); Luis Sala (Spa)
 25 Olivier Grouillard (Fra); Bob Anderson (GB); Tony Maggs (SAf)
 24 Roberto Moreno (Bra); Eliseo Salazar (Chi); Luigi Musso (Ita); Gabriele Tarquini (Ita)
 23 JJ Lehto (Fin)
 22 Reine Wisell (Swe); Emmanuel de Graffenried (Swi)
 21 Giancarlo Baghetti (Ita)
 20 Stefan Bellof (FRG)
 19 Gianni Morbidelli (Ita); 'B Bira' (Siam)
 18 Chico Serra (Bra); Hans Herrmann (FRG); Piero Taruffi (Ita); Johnny Cecotto (Ven)
 17 Roberto Mieres (Arg); Lucien Bianchi (Bel); Dick Attwood (GB)
 16 Cliff Allison (GB)
 15 Bertrand Gachot (Bel); Miki Hakkinen (Fin); Johnny Dumfries (GB); Johnny Herbert (GB); Ken Wharton (GB); Felice Bonetto (Ita); Louis Chiron (Mon); Danny Sullivan (USA)

Riccardo Patrese has competed in more Formula One Grand Prix races than any other driver.

14 Olivier Gendebien (Bel); Mark Blundell (GB); Horace Gould (GB); Stuart Lewis-Evans (GB); Eugenio Castellotti (Ita); Mark Donohue (USA)

13 Yves Giraud-Cabantous (Fra); Vic Elford (GB); Ron Flockhart (GB); Francisco Godia (Spa)

12 Willy Mairesse (Bel); Philippe Etancelin (Fra); Guy Ligier (Fra); Johnny Servoz-Gavin (Fra); Jack Fairman (GB); John Miles (GB); Brian Redman (GB); Lella Lombardi (Ita); Giorgio Scarlatti (Ita); Silvio Moser (Swi); George Follmer (USA); Rodger Ward (USA)

11 Onofre Marimon (Arg); Paul Frére (Bel); Karl Kling (FRG); Peter Arundell (GB); Tony Bettenhausen (USA); Ron Bucknum (USA); Jim Hall (USA)

10 Carlos Menditeguy (Arg); Tony Brise (GB); Chris Irwin (GB); Peter Whitehead (GB); Umberto Maglioli (Ita); Ludovico Scarfiotti (Ita); Slim Borgudd (Swe); Jim Rathmann (USA)

9 André Pilette (Bel); Derek Bell (GB); Jack Lewis (GB); John Love (SRho); Bob Bondurant (USA); Jimmy Bryan (USA); Eddie Johnson (USA); Johnnie Parsons (USA)

8 Alan Brown (GB); Henry Taylor (GB); Gijs van Lennep (Hol); Freddie Agabashian (USA); Duane Carter (USA); Don

Freeland (USA); Sam Hanks (USA); Paul Russo (USA); Troy Ruttman (USA); Johnny Thomson (USA)

7 Hernando da Silva Ramos (Bra); Elie Bayol (Fra); Julian Bailey (GB); Luigi Fagioli (Ita); Sergio Mantovani (Ita); Cesare Perdisa (Ita); Renzo Zorzi (Ita); Rudi Fischer (Swi); Andy Linden (USA)

6 Chico Landi (Bra); Michael Schumacher (Ger); Mike Parkes (GB); Reg Parnell (GB); Teo Fabi (Ita); Gerino Gerini (Ita); Johnny Boyd (USA); Pat Flaherty (USA); Jack McGrath (USA)

5 Raymond Sommer (Fra); Gerhard Mitter (FRG); John Taylor (GB); Consalvo Sanesi (Ita); Ricardo Rodriguez (Mex); Alfonso de Portago (Spa); Jimmy Davies

(USA); Walt Faulkner (USA); Dick Rathmann (USA); Bob Sweikert (USA); Bill Vukovich (USA)

4 Ignazio Giunti (Ita); Manny Ayulo (USA); Art Cross (USA)

3 Eugene Chaboud (Fra); Giulio Cabianca (Ita); Paul Goldsmith (USA); Bill Homeier (USA); Mike Nazaruk (USA)

2 Hermann Lang (FRG); Dennis Poore (GB); Bobby Ball (USA); Don Branson (USA); Cecil Green (USA); Walt Hansgen (USA); Bill Holland (USA); Mauri Rose (USA); Lee Wallard (USA)

1 Oscar Galvez (Arg); Eric Thompson (GB); Dorino Serafini (Ita); Neville Lederle (SAf); George Amick (USA); Joie Chitwood (USA)

LONGEST CAREERS

16 yr 8 mths	Graham Hill, May 1958–Jan 1975
15 yr 3 mths	Jack Brabham, Jul 1955–Oct 1970
14 yr 9 mths	Jo Bonnier, Jan 1957–Oct 1971
14 yr 6 mths	Riccardo Patrese, May 1977–Nov 1991
14 yr 4 mths	Maurice Trintignant, May 1950–Sep 1964
14 yr 3 mths	Niki Lauda, Aug 1971–Nov 1985
13 yr 11 mths	Mario Andretti, Oct 1968–Sep 1982
13 yr 4 mths	Nelson Piquet, Jul 1978–Nov 1991
13 yr 2 mths	Jacky Ickx, Aug 1966–Oct 1979
13 yr 2 mths	Chris Amon, Jun 1963–Aug 1976

Graham Hill in 1975, his last season. His career of more than 16 years is the longest in the sport.

TOTAL POINTS

699½	Alain Prost (Fra)
491	Ayrton Senna (Bra)
485½	Nelson Piquet (Bra)
420½	Niki Lauda (Aut)
361	Nigel Mansell (GB)
360	Jackie Stewart (GB)
310	Carlos Reutemann (Arg)
289	Graham Hill (GB)
281	Emerson Fittipaldi (Bra)
277¹⁄₇	Juan Manuel Fangio (Arg)
274	Jim Clark (GB)
261	Jack Brabham (Aus)
255	Jody Scheckter (SAf)
248	Denny Hulme (NZ)
228	Jacques Laffite (Fra)
212	Clay Regazzoni (Swi)
206	Alan Jones (Aus); Ronnie Peterson (Swe)
205	Riccardo Patrese (Ita)
204	Gerhard Berger (Aut)
196½	Bruce McLaren (NZ)
186⁹⁄₁₄	Stirling Moss (GB)
181	Jacky Ickx (Bel); René Arnoux (Fra)
180	John Surtees (GB); Mario Andretti (USA)
179½	Michele Alboreto (Ita)
179	James Hunt (GB)
169	John Watson (GB)
159½	Keke Rosberg (Fin)
141	Patrick Depailler (Fra)
140⁹⁄₁₄	Alberto Ascari (Ita)
133	Dan Gurney (USA)
130	Thierry Boutsen (Bel)
127⁹⁄₁₄	Mike Hawthorn (GB)
127⅓	Giuseppe Farina (Ita)
122	Elio de Angelis (Ita)
109	Jochen Rindt (Aut)
107	Gilles Villeneuve (Can); Richie Ginther (USA)
103	Patrick Tambay (Fra)
101	Didier Pironi (Fra)
98	Phil Hill (USA)
89	François Cevert (Fra)
88	Stefan Johansson (Swe)
83	Chris Amon (NZ)
77⁹⁄₁₄	José Froilán González (Arg)
77	Jean-Pierre Beltoise (Fra)
75	Tony Brooks (GB)
72⅓	Maurice Trintignant (Fra)
71	Jochen Mass (FRG); Pedro Rodriguez (Mex)
70	Eddie Cheever (USA)
68	Jo Siffert (Swi)
67	Derek Warwick (GB)
65	Alessandro Nannini (Ita)
61	Peter Revson (USA)
58	Carlos Pace (Bra); Lorenzo Bandini (Ita)
56	Wolfgang von Trips (FRG)
53¹⁄₇	Jean Behra (Fra)
49	Luigi Villoresi (Ita)

47	Peter Collins (GB); Innes Ireland (GB); Andrea de Cesaris (Ita)
44	Luigi Musso (Ita)
42	Jean Alesi (Fra)
41	Piero Taruffi (Ita)
39	Jo Bonnier (Swe)
32	Luigi Fagioli (Ita)
31½	Jean-Pierre Jarier (Fra)
31	Gunnar Nilsson (Swe)
30	Harry Schell (USA)
29	Hans-Joachim Stuck (FRG); Mike Hailwood (GB); Jim Rathmann (USA)
28	Ivan Capelli (Ita)
27	Mike Spence (GB)
26	Tony Maggs (SAf)
23	Teo Fabi (Ita)
21	Jean-Pierre Jabouille (Fra); Masten Gregory (USA)
20	Piers Courage (GB); Sam Hanks (USA)
19½	Eugenio Castellotti (Ita)
19	Tom Pryce (GB); Roy Salvadori (GB); Bill Vukovich (USA)
18	Olivier Gendebien (Bel); Louis Rosier (Fra); Jimmy Bryan (USA)
17½	Felice Bonetto (Ita)
17	Karl Kling (FRG); Ludovico Scarfiotti (Ita); Marc Surer (Swi)
16	Robert Manzon (Fra); Martin Brundle (GB); Stuart Lewis-Evans (GB); Stefano Modena (Ita); Satoru Nakajima (Jap)
15½	Vittorio Brambilla (Ita)
15	Roberto Moreno (Bra); Derek Daly (Ire); Rodger Ward (USA)
14	Rolf Stommelen (FRG); Jonathan Palmer (GB); Mike Parkes (GB); Giancarlo Baghetti (Ita); Bruno Giacomelli (Ita)
13	Roberto Mieres (Arg); Jackie Oliver (GB); Hector Rebaque (Mex); Reine Wisell (Swe)
12	Henri Pescarolo (Fra); Peter Arundell (GB); Pierluigi Martini (Ita); Johnnie Parsons (USA)
11	Paul Frére (Bel); Philippe Streiff (Fra); Cliff Allison (GB); Dick Attwood (GB); Peter Gethin (GB); Arturo Merzario (Ita); Tony Bettenhausen (USA)
10	Mauricio Gugelmin (Bra); Hans Herrmann (FRG); Howden Ganley (NZ); Rudi Fischer (Swi); Johnny Thomson (USA)
9½	Troy Ruttman (USA)

9	Carlos Menditeguy (Arg); Johnny Servoz-Gavin (Fra); Reg Parnell (GB); Emmanuel de Graffenried (Swi); Jack McGrath (USA)
8½	Paul Russo (USA)
8¹⁄₇	Onofre Marimon (Arg)
8	Bob Anderson (GB); Vic Elford (GB); Brian Redman (GB); Trevor Taylor (GB); 'B Bira' (Siam); Art Cross (USA); Mark Donohue (USA); Pat Flaherty (USA); Mike Nazaruk (USA); Bob Sweikert (USA); Lee Wallard (USA)·
7	Tim Schenken (Aus); Willy Mairesse (Bel); Aguri Suzuki (Jap)
6½	Duane Carter (USA)
6	Lucien Bianchi (Bel); Eric Bernard (Fra); Andrea de Adamich (Ita); Alex Caffi (Ita); John Love (SRho); Francisco Godia (Spa); George Amick (USA); Paul Goldsmith (USA); Bill Holland (USA)
5	Philippe Alliot (Fra); Yves Giraud-Cabantous(Fra); Jack Fairman (GB); Ron Flockhart (GB); Johnny Herbert (GB); Mauro Baldi (Ita); Cesare Perdisa (Ita); George Follmer (USA); Andy Linden (USA)
4	Bertrand Gachot (Bel); JJ Lehto (Fin); Stefan Bellof (FRG); Christian Danner (FRG); Michael Schumacher (Ger); Peter Whitehead (GB); Carel Godin de Beaufort (Hol); Sergio Mantovani (Ita); Ricardo Rodriguez (Mex); Louis Chiron (Mon); Alfonso de Portago (Spa); Johnny Boyd (USA); Jimmy Davies (USA); Don Freeland (USA); Mauri Rose (USA)
3⅓	Umberto Maglioli (Ita)
3	Wilson Fittipaldi (Bra); Eliseo Salazar (Chi); Philippe Etancelin (Fra); Raymond Sommer (Fra); Gerhard Mitter (FRG); Johnny Dumfries (GB); Jack Lewis (GB); Dennis Poore (GB); Henry Taylor (GB); Ken Wharton (GB); Giulio Cabianca (Ita); Ignazio Giunti (Ita); Emanuele Pirro (Ita); Consalvo Sanesi (Ita); Dorino Serafini (Ita); Silvio Moser (Swi); Bob Bondurant (USA); Don Branson (USA); Cecil Green (USA); Jim Hall (USA)

2   Oscar Galvez (Arg); André Pilette (Bel); Hernando da Silva Ramos (Bra); Miki Hakkinen (Fin); Elie Bayol (Fra); Hermann Lang (FRG); Manfred Winkelhock (FRG); Alan Brown (GB); Horace Gould (GB); Chris Irwin (GB); John Miles (GB); Eric Thompson (GB); Gijs van Lennep (Hol); Piercarlo Ghinzani (Ita); Manny Ayulo (USA); Bobby Ball (USA); Ron Bucknum (USA); Walt Hansgen (USA); Dick Rathmann (USA); Danny Sullivan (USA)

1½   Chico Landi (Bra); Gerino Gerini (Ita); Freddie Agabashian (USA)

1   Chico Serra (Bra); Eugene Chaboud (Fra); Olivier Grouillard (Fra); Guy Ligier (Fra); Julian Bailey (GB); Derek Bell (GB); Mark Blundell (GB); Tony Brise (GB); John Taylor (GB); Giorgio Scarlatti (Ita); Gabriele Tarquini (Ita); Renzo Zorzi (Ita); Neville Lederle (SAf); Luis Sala (Spa); Slim Borgudd (Swe); Joie Chitwood (USA); Walt Faulkner (USA); Bill Homeier (USA); Eddie Johnson (USA); Johnny Cecotto (Ven)

0½   Lella Lombardi (Ita); Gianni Morbidelli (Ita)

> Giuseppe Farina
> obtained points in each
> of the first six seasons of
> the world championship,
> 1950–5

Italy's Lella Lombardi, the first woman to obtain a championship point – or rather half of one!

MOST RACES WITHOUT GAINING A POINT

40 Nicola Larini (Ita) 1987–91
34 Brett Lunger (USA) 1975–8
28 Mike Beuttler (GB) 1971–3
26 Huub Rothengatter (Hol) 1984–6
25 Rupert Keegan (GB) 1977–82

23 John Claes (Bel) 1950–5
23 Raul Boesel (Bra) 1982–3
21 Jan Lammers (Hol) 1979–82
21 Roberto Guerrero (Col) 1982–3
21 Yannick Dalmas (Fra) 1987–90

NATIONS PROVIDING THE MOST DRIVERS TO HAVE OBTAINED WORLD CHAMPIONSHIP POINTS

51 Great Britain
50 United States
41 Italy
27 France
11 Germany
10 Brazil
8 Belgium
7 Argentina
6 Sweden
6 Switzerland
4 New Zealand
3 Australia
3 Austria

3 Finland
3 Mexico
3 South Africa
3 Spain
2 Holland
2 Japan
1 Canada
1 Chile
1 Reublic of Ireland
1 Monaco
1 Southern Rhodesia
1 Siam
1 Venezuela

POLE POSITIONS

60 Ayrton Senna (Bra)
33 Jim Clark (GB)
28 Juan Manuel Fangio (Arg)
24 Niki Lauda (Aut); Nelson Piquet (Bra)
20 Alain Prost (Fra)
18 René Arnoux (Fra); Mario Andretti (USA)
17 Nigel Mansell (GB); Jackie Stewart (GB)
16 Stirling Moss (GB)
14 Ronnie Peterson (Swe); James Hunt (GB); Alberto Ascari (Ita)
13 Jacky Ickx (Bel); Jack Brabham (Aus); Graham Hill (GB);
10 Jochen Rindt (Aut)
8 John Surtees (GB); Gerhard Berger (Aut)
7 Jacques Laffite (Fra); Riccardo Patrese (Ita)
6 Emerson Fittipaldi (Bra); Carlos Reutemann (Arg); Alan

Jones (Aus); Phil Hill (USA); Jean-Pierre Jabouille (Fra)
5 Patrick Tambay (Fra); Keke Rosberg (Fin); Clay Regazzoni (Swi); Giuseppe Farina (Ita); Chris Amon (NZ)
4 Mike Hawthorn (GB); Didier Pironi (Fra)
3 Jody Scheckter (SAf); Jean-Pierre Jarier (Fra); Elio de Angelis (Ita); Tony Brooks (GB); Teo Fabi (Ita); José Froilán González (Arg); Dan Gurney (USA)
2 Michele Alboreto (Ita); John Watson (GB); Stuart Lewis-Evans (GB); Jo Siffert (Swi); Gilles Villeneuve (Can)
1 Wolfgang von Trips (FRG); Walt Faulkner (USA); Vittorio Brambilla (Ita); Tom Pryce (GB); Peter Revson (USA); Peter Collins (GB); Patrick Depailler (Fra); Pat Flaherty (USA); Mike Parkes (GB); Lorenzo Bandini (Ita);

Ayrton Senna at Monza in 1991. He again claimed pole position, for the 60th time in his career.

Johnny Thomson (USA); Jack McGrath (USA); Freddie Agabashian (USA); Eugenio Castellotti (Ita); Dick Rathmann (USA); Carlos Pace (Bra); Bruno Giacomelli (Ita); Bill Vukovich (USA); Thierry Boutsen (Bel); Jo Bonnier (Swe); Denny Hulme (NZ); Andrea de Cesaris (Ita)

MOST CONSECUTIVE POLE POSITIONS

8 Ayrton Senna (1988/1989)
7 Ayrton Senna (1990/1991)
6 Stirling Moss (1959/1960)
6 Ayrton Senna (1988)
6 Ayrton Senna (1989)
5 Juan Manuel Fangio (1950/51)
5 Alberto Ascari (1952/53)
5 Juan Manuel Fangio (1955/1956)
5 Phil Hill (1961)

FASTEST LAPS

35 Alain Prost (Fra)
28 Jim Clark (GB)
24 Niki Lauda (Aut)
23 Nelson Piquet (Bra); Juan Manuel Fangio (Arg)
22 Nigel Mansell (GB)
19 Stirling Moss (GB)
17 Ayrton Senna (Bra)
15 Jackie Stewart (GB); Clay Regazzoni (Swi)
14 Jacky Ickx (Bel); Gerhard Berger (Aut)
13 Alberto Ascari (Ita); Alan Jones (Aus)
12 René Arnoux (Fra); Jack Brabham (Aus)
11 John Surtees (GB)
10 Riccardo Patrese (Ita); Mario Andretti (USA); Graham Hill (GB)

9 Ronnie Peterson (Swe); Denny Hulme (NZ)
8 James Hunt (GB); Gilles Villeneuve (Can)
6 Phil Hill (USA); Mike Hawthorn (GB); José Froilán González (Arg); Jacques Laffite (Fra); Emerson Fittipaldi (Bra); Dan Gurney (USA); Carlos Reutemann (Arg)
5 Michele Alboreto (Ita); John Watson (GB); Jody Scheckter (SAf); Giuseppe Farina (Ita); Didier Pironi (Fra); Carlos Pace (Bra)
4 Patrick Depailler (Fra); Jo Siffert (Swi); Jean-Pierre Beltoise (Fra)
3 Tony Brooks (GB); Richie Ginther (USA); Keke Rosberg (Fin); Jochen Rindt (Aut); Jean-Pierre Jarier (Fra); Chris Amon (NZ); Bruce McLaren (NZ); Bill Vukovich (USA)
2 Teo Fabi (Ita); Patrick Tambay (Fra); Lorenzo Bandini (Ita); Jochen Mass (Ger); Jim Rathmann (USA); François Cevert (Fra); Derek Warwick (GB); Alessandro Nannini (Ita)
1 Vittorio Brambilla (Ita); Tony Bettenhausen (USA); Thierry Boutsen (Bel); Satoru Nakajima (Jap); Roberto Moreno (Bra); Roberto Mieres (Arg); Piero Taruffi (Ita); Pedro Rodriguez (Mex); Paul Russo (USA); Onofre Marimon (Arg); Mike Hailwood (GB); Maurice Trintignant (Fra); Marc Surer (Swi); Luigi Villoresi (Ita); Luigi Musso (Ita); Ludovico Scarfiotti (Ita); Lee Wallard (USA); Karl Kling (FRG); Jonathan Palmer (GB); Johnny Thomson (USA); Jean Behra (Fra); Jean Alesi (Fra); Jackie Oliver (GB); Jack McGrath (USA); Innes Ireland (GB); Henri Pescarolo (Fra); Hans Herrmann (FRG); Gunnar Nilsson (Swe); Giancarlo Baghetti (Ita); Dick Attwood (GB); Bill Holland (USA); Bertrand Gachot (Bel); Andrea de Cesaris (Ita)

GRAND PRIX MILESTONES

100th Grand Prix
6 August 1961, German GP,
Nürburgring
won by Stirling Moss (GB) Lotus-Climax

200th Grand Prix
23 May 1971, Monaco GP, Monte Carlo,
won by Jackie Stewart (GB) Tyrrell-Ford

250th Grand Prix
6 October 1974 United States GP, Watkins Glen,
won by Carlos Reutemann (Arg) Brabham-Ford

300th Grand Prix
4 March 1978, South African GP, Kyalami,
won by Ronnie Peterson (Swe) Lotus-Ford

400th Grand Prix
19 August 1984, Austrian GP, Österreichring,
won by Niki Lauda (Aut) McLaren-Porsche

500th Grand Prix
4 November 1990, Australian GP, Adelaide,
won by Nelson Piquet (Bra) Benetton-Ford

EARLIEST START TO A SEASON

1 January (1965) South African GP, East London,
won by Jim Clark (GB) Lotus-Climax
1 January (1968) South African GP, Kyalami,
won by Jim Clark (GB) Lotus-Ford

LATEST START TO A SEASON

27 May (1951) Swiss GP, Bremgarten,
won by Juan Manuel Fangio (Arg) Alfa Romeo

LATEST FINISH TO A SEASON

29 December (1962) South African GP, East London,
won by Graham Hill (GB) BRM

EARLIEST FINISH TO A SEASON

2 September (1956) Italian GP, Monza,
won by Stirling Moss, Maserati

After two seasons without a win, Nelson Piquet won successive races in 1990 in Japan and Australia (above).

LONGEST SEASON

10 months 2 days from 1 January to 3 November 1968

SHORTEST SEASON

3 months 20 days from 18 May to 7 September 1952. It was one day shorter than the championship's inaugural season, 1950.

MANUFACTURERS

CONSTRUCTORS' CUP WINNERS

8 Ferrari (1961, 1964, 1975–7, 1979, 1982–3)
7 Lotus (1965, 1968, 1970, 1972–3, 1978); McLaren (1974, 1984–5, 1988–91)
4 Williams (1980–1, 1986–7)
2 Cooper (1959–60); Brabham (1966–7)
1 Vanwall (1958); BRM (1962); Matra (1969); Tyrrell (1971)

CARS PROVIDING THE MOST WORLD CHAMPION DRIVERS

9 Ferrari *(Ascari 2, Fangio, Hawthorn, P Hill, Surtees, Lauda 2, Scheckter)*
9 McLaren *(Fittipaldi, Hunt, Lauda, Prost 3, Senna 3)*
6 Lotus *(Clark 2, G Hill, Rindt, Fittipaldi, Andretti)*
4 Brabham *(Brabham, Hulme, Piquet 2)*
3 Williams *(Jones, Rosberg, Piquet)*
2 Alfa Romeo *(Farina, Fangio)*
2 Mercedes-Benz *(Fangio 2)*
2 Cooper *(Brabham 2)*
2 Tyrrell *(Stewart 2)*
1 Maserati *(Fangio)*
1 BRM *(G Hill)*
1 Matra *(Stewart)*

RACE WINS

103 Ferrari
 94 McLaren
 39 McLaren-Honda
 30 McLaren-Ford
 25 McLaren-TAG/Porsche
 79 Lotus
 47 Lotus-Ford
 24 Lotus-Climax
 5 Lotus-Renault
 2 Lotus-Honda
 1 Lotus-BRM
 51 Williams
 23 Williams-Honda
 17 Williams-Ford
 11 Williams-Renault
 35 Brabham
 15 Brabham-Ford
 8 Brabham-Repco
 8 Brabham-BMW
 2 Brabham-Climax
 2 Brabham-Alfa Romeo
 23 Tyrrell
 23 Tyrrell-Ford
 17 BRM
 16 Cooper
 14 Cooper-Climax
 2 Cooper-Maserati

 15 Renault
 10 Alfa Romeo
 9 Mercedes-Benz
 9 Maserati
 9 Matra
 9 Matra-Ford
 9 Vanwall
 8 Ligier
 5 Ligier-Ford
 3 Ligier-Matra
 5 Benetton
 4 Benetton-Ford
 1 Benetton-BMW
 3 March
 3 March-Ford
 3 KK
 3 KK-Offenhauser[1]
 3 Watson
 3 Watson-Offenhauser[1]

 3 Wolf
 3 Wolf-Ford
 2 Epperly
 2 Epperly-Offenhauser[1]
 2 Honda
 2 Kurtis Kraft
 2 Kurtis Kraft-Offenhauser[1]
 1 Eagle
 Eagle-Weslake
 1 Hesketh
 Hesketh-Ford
 1 Kuzma
 Kuzma-Offenhauser[1]
 1 Penske
 Penske-Ford
 1 Porsche
 1 Shadow
 Shadow-Ford
 [1]Indianapolis 500 winners

> Stirling Moss was behind the wheel when Vanwall, Cooper, and Lotus had their first championship success. Dan Gurney (Porsche, Brabham and Eagle) and Jackie Stewart (Matra, March and Tyrrell) also drove three different cars to their debut wins

MOST WINS IN ONE YEAR

15 McLaren-Honda (1988)
12 McLaren-Porsche (1984)
10 McLaren-Honda (1989)
 9 Williams-Honda (1986)
 9 Williams-Honda (1987)
 8 Lotus-Ford (1978)
 8 McLaren-Honda (1991)
 7 Ferrari (1952)
 7 Ferrari (1973)
 7 Lotus-Climax (1963)
 7 Lotus-Ford (1973)
 7 Williams-Renault (1991)

MOST SUCCESSIVE WINS

14 Ferrari (1952/1953)
11 McLaren-Honda (1988)[1]
 9 Alfa Romeo (1950/1951)
 8 McLaren-Porsche/TAG (1984/ 1985)
 5 Cooper-Climax (1960)
 5 Lotus-Climax (1965)
 5 Lotus-Ford (1967/1968)
 5 Ferrari (1975/1976)
[1] First 11 races of the season

Another Ferrari 1–2 with Alain Prost (right) taking the spoils ahead of team-mate Gerhard Berger at Jerez in 1990.

MANUFACTURERS WHO WON THEIR FIRST WORLD CHAMPIONSHIP GRAND PRIX

1950 Alfa Romeo (British GP)[1]
1954 Mercedes-Benz (French GP)

1977 Wolf-Ford (Argentine GP)
[1] *The first ever world championship race*

POINTS

1730½	Ferrari	13	Dallara
1690½	McLaren	13	Jordan
1343	Lotus	13	Minardi
1062½	Williams	11	BRP-BRM
864	Brabham	9	Maserati
588	Tyrrell	8	ATS
433	BRM	8	Leyton
342	Cooper		House
312	Renault	6	Onyx
307	Ligier	6	Parnelli
234½	Benetton	5	Osella
170½	March	4	Rial
163	Matra	3	Larrousse
116	Arrows		Lola
79	Wolf	2	AGS
67½	Shadow	2	Theodore
57	Vanwall	2	Zakspeed
53	Surtees	1	Tecno
50	Alfa Romeo		
48	Hesketh		
48	Honda		
47	Porsche		
44	Fittipaldi		
32	Lola		
26	Toleman		
22	Penske		
19	Ensign		
17	Eagle		

Eddie Cheever, who went a then-record 132 races without a win between 1978 and 1989, contributing 46 to Arrows' winless total of 207.

MOST RACES CONTESTED

489	Ferrari	136	Osella
443	Lotus	129	Cooper
391	Brabham	123	Renault
362	McLaren	118	Surtees
316	Tyrrell	114	Lola
282	Williams	112	Alfa Romeo
245	Ligier	108	Minardi
207	Arrows	104	Fittipaldi
197	BRM	104	Shadow
184	March		

MOST RACES WITHOUT A WIN

(Figures in brackets indicate best finish)

207	Arrows (2nd)	99	ATS (5th)
136	Osella (4th)	99	Ensign (4th)
118	Surtees (2nd)	62	Dallara (3rd)
114	Lola (2nd)	57	Toleman (2nd)
108	Minardi (4th)	54	Zakspeed (5th)
104	Fittipaldi (2nd)	51	AGS (6th)

FASTEST RACES

Speed mph/kph	Race (Venue)	Winner (Car)
150.75/246.62	1971 Italian GP (Monza)	Peter Gethin (BRM)
149.94/241.31	1970 Belgian GP (Spa)	Pedro Rodriguez (BRM)
147.14/236.80	1968 Belgian GP (Spa)	Bruce McLaren (McLaren)
147.11/236.75	1991 Italian GP (Monza)	Nigel Mansell (Williams)
147.08/236.70	1970 Italian GP (Monza)	Clay Regazzoni (Ferrari)
147.00/236.57	1990 Italian GP (Monza)	Ayrton Senna (McLaren)
146.97/236.52	1969 Italian GP (Monza)	Jackie Stewart (Matra)
146.28/235.42	1985 British GP (Silverstone)	Alain Prost (McLaren)
146.28/235.42	1987 Austrian GP (Österreichring)	Nigel Mansell (Williams)
146.21/235.30	1987 British GP (Silverstone)	Nigel Mansell (Williams)

Since the World Championship started in 1950 more than 630 drivers have sought to win a Grand Prix. Only 68 of them have enjoyed the thrill of taking the chequered flag and only 251 of them have actually obtained World Championship points.

The following is a list of those 251 chronicled according to nationality and including details of their Formula One career. Figures in brackets after a driver's name indicate the years he was an active driver.

ARGENTINA

Juan Manuel FANGIO (1950-8)

Races:	51
Wins:	24
	1950 Monaco, Belgian, French (Alfa Romeo)
	1951 Swiss, French, Spanish (Alfa Romeo)
	1953 Italian (Maserati)
	1954 Argentine, Belgian (Maserati), French, German, Swiss, Italian (Mercedes-Benz)
	1955 Argentine, Belgian, Dutch, Italian (Mercedes-Benz)
	1956 Argentine (shared), British, German (Lancia-Ferrari)
	1957 Argentine, Monaco, French, German (Maserati)
Points:	277½
Pole:	28[1]
Fastest laps:	23

[1] At the 1956 French GP Fangio had the fastest practice speed but Peter Collins (GB) was inadvertently given pole position

Oscar GALVEZ (1953)

Races:	1
Wins:	0 Best finish: 5th
Points:	2
Pole:	0
Fastest laps:	0

José Froilán GONZÁLEZ (1950-60)

Races:	26
Wins:	2
	1951 British (Ferrari)
	1954 British (Ferrari)
Points:	77⁹/₁₄
Pole:	3
Fastest laps:	6

Onofre MARIMON (1951-4)

Races:	11
Wins:	0 Best finish: 3rd
Points:	8½
Pole:	0
Fastest laps:	1

Carlos MENDITEGUY (1953-60)

Races:	10
Wins:	0 Best finish: 3rd
Points:	9
Pole:	0
Fastest laps:	0

Roberto MIERES (1953-5)

Races:	17
Wins:	0 Best finish: 4th
Points:	13
Pole:	0
Fastest laps:	1

Carlos REUTEMANN (1972-82)

Races:	146
Wins:	12
	1974 South African, Austrian, United States (Brabham)
	1975 German (Brabham)
	1977 Brazilian (Ferrari)
	1978 Brazilian, United States (West), British, United States (Ferrari)
	1980 Monaco (Williams)
	1981 Brazilian, Belgian (Williams)
Points:	310
Pole:	6
Fastest laps:	6

Carlos Reutemann.

CHAMPION DRIVERS

Juan Manuel Fangio

Born: Balcarce, Argentina, 24 June 1911

Juan Manuel Fangio is one of the few drivers who can rightly claim to be one of the giants of motor racing. His record of five world titles is unsurpassed and his total of 24 Grand Prix wins remained unbeaten until the arrival of Jim Clark in the 1960s.

Fangio, however, didn't have youth on his side like the next breed of Grand Prix drivers; he was already 39 when the World Championship was launched and when he won his record-breaking fifth title he was 46 years of age. He began his career in 1928 as a travelling mechanic but his driving did not develop until 1933 when he started driving model-A Fords and Chevrolets.

His first trip to Europe in 1948 saw him driving one of the famous blue and yellow Maseratis but he teamed up with the more powerful Alfa team for the first World Championship. Despite winning three races, matching Giuseppe Farina, the Argentinian had to be happy with the runners-up position behind the Italian. A year later he was champion for the first time.

Then in 1952 he was forced to return to Maserati when Alfa pulled out of the sport and a bad accident meant he missed a large part of the season. He was runner-up to Ascari in 1953 but the following year he won the first of four successive world titles, with Mercedes in 1954 and 1955, with Lancia-Ferrari in 1956, and finally with Maserati in his last championship-winning season, 1957.

His last race was the 1958 French Grand Prix as he announced his retirement after 51 races. He bowed out with the

finest record the sport had seen at the time and his total of five world titles remains a record. To this day, Juan Manuel Fangio is still idolised in his native Argentina.

AUSTRALIA

Jack BRABHAM (1955–70)

Races:	126
Wins:	14
	1959 Monaco, British *(Cooper)*
	1960 Dutch, Belgian, French, British, Portuguese *(Cooper)*
	1966 French, British, Dutch, German *(Brabham)*
	1967 French, Canadian *(Brabham)*
	1970 South African *(Brabham)*
Points:	261
Pole:	13
Fastest laps:	12

Alan JONES (1975–86)

Races:	116
Wins:	12
	1977 Austrian *(Shadow)*
	1979 German, Austrian, Dutch, Canadian *(Williams)*
	1980 Argentine, French, British, Canadian, United States *(Williams)*
	1981 United States (West), Las Vegas *(Williams)*
Points:	206
Pole:	6
Fastest laps:	13

Tim SCHENKEN (1970–4)

Races:	34		
Wins:	0	Best finish:	3rd
Points:	7		
Pole:	0	Fastest laps:	0

HAMPION DRIVERS

Jack Brabham

Born: Sydney, Australia, 2 April 1926

Jack Brabham's contribution to Grand Prix racing is two-fold. He made his mark initially as Australia's first world champion, and then as an outstanding engineer he formed his own Brabham team and holds the distinction of being the only world champion to capture the title in one of his own cars.

After establishing himself as a top-class driver in Australia, Brabham came to England in 1955 and tried his luck in the British Grand Prix at Aintree, but his Cooper-Bristol was no match for the powerful Mercedes and Maseratis. He returned to Australia but realised that if he was going to make any real impact in the sport he had to return to the World Championship circuit. He came back to England in 1957 and joined the Cooper team.

Brabham was to spearhead their new rear-engined attack on the customary front-engined machines and in 1959 he duly became the first world champion in a rear-engined car. The following year both Brabham and Cooper retained their respective titles.

He quit Cooper at the end of 1961 and the following season he and his designer Ron Tauranac introduced the new Brabham Grand Prix car. Four years later Jack captured his third world title, and that same year he was awarded the OBE for his services to the sport.

Jack Brabham quit racing in 1970 but the name lives on through the Brabham team. Jack himself has nothing to do with it anymore, and his sons Gary, David and Geoff are all carving out successful careers for themselves in motor racing on both sides of the Atlantic.

Alan Jones

Born: Melbourne, Australia, 2 November 1946

No man has worked harder at achieving his aim of the world drivers' title than Australia's Alan Jones. Totally dedicated to the sport, he rose through the ranks of Formula Three, Formula Atlantic and Formula 5000 before getting his break and a much sought-after Formula One drive.

That came in 1975 when, at the age of 29, he drove a privately entered Hesketh. But he was hit with the blow of his sponsor pulling out and it looked as though he would be out of Formula One until the Graham Hill team offered him one of their cars. But, of course, the Hill team was to come to a sudden and tragic end at the end of 1975.

Jones got a drive with Surtees in 1976 and the following year replaced the late Tom Pryce in the Shadow team. It was in the rain at the Österreichring in 1977 that he won his first race. But a move to Williams in 1978 was to herald the start of his march towards the World Championship.

Third behind Scheckter and Villeneuve in 1979 – despite winning more races than each of the Ferrari men – he took the championship by storm in 1980. He won five races in the FW07 and took the title by 13 points ahead of Nelson Piquet. Jones retired in 1981 whilst still at the top and returned to Australia to run a cattle farm. But he was lured out of retirement by Jackie Oliver, who wanted him for the Arrows team in 1983. A further retirement followed but he made a second comeback with Lola in 1985. The next year he quit; this time for good.

AUSTRIA

Gerhard BERGER (1984–91)

Races:	115
Wins:	6
	1986 Mexican *(Benetton)*
	1987 Japanese, Australian *(Ferrari)*
	1988 Italian *(Ferrari)*
	1989 Portuguese *(Ferrari)*
	1991 Japanese *(McLaren)*
Points:	204
Pole:	8
Fastest laps:	13

Niki LAUDA (1971–85)

Races:	171
Wins:	25
	1974 Spanish, Dutch *(Ferrari)*
	1975 Monaco, Belgian, Swedish, French, United States *(Ferrari)*
	1976 Brazilian, South African, Belgian, Monaco, British *(Ferrari)*
	1977 South Africa, German, Dutch *(Ferrari)*
	1978 Swedish, Italian *(Brabham)*
	1982 United States (West), British *(McLaren)*
	1984 South African, French, British, Austrian, Italian *(McLaren)*
	1985 Dutch *(McLaren)*
Points:	420½
Pole:	24
Fastest laps:	24

Gerhard Berger will be hoping to emulate fellow Austrians Lauda and Rindt with a world title win.

Jochen RINDT (1964–70)

Races:	60
Wins:	6
	1969 United States *(Lotus)*
	1970 Monaco, Dutch, French, British, German *(Lotus)*
Points:	109
Pole:	10
Fastest laps:	3

CHAMPION DRIVERS

Jochen Rindt

Born: Mainz, Germany, 18 April 1942
Died: Monza, Italy, 5 September 1970

Jochen Rindt is the only man to win the world title posthumously because he lost his life when his Lotus swerved into a guardrail during practice for the 1970 Italian Grand Prix at Monza. He led the World Championship by 20 points at the time and the gap was too big for Jack Brabham to make up and so Rindt was proclaimed champion.

Although born in Germany, he was actually brought up over the border in Austria by his grandparents after his own parents were killed when he was only a year old. His racing career started with saloon cars in 1962 but within two years he was in Formula One with Brabham.

He was given regular rides by the Rob Walker Cooper team in 1965 but he did not enjoy his first taste of Formula One success until teaming up with Lotus in 1969. He had, however, enjoyed the sweet smell of success by winning the 1965 Le Mans with Masten Gregory in a Ferrari. But it was in the Lotus 72 in 1970 that Rindt was to enjoy his most successful spell in Formula One. He won five of the first eight rounds, including four in succession, but victory at Hockenheim was to prove to be the last of Rindt's career. Two races later he was dead.

CHAMPION DRIVERS

Niki Lauda

Born: Vienna, Austria, 22 February 1949

Austria's Niki Lauda has three world titles to his credit. Had it not been for a bad accident at the notorious Nürburgring in 1976 that total would surely have been increased by one, putting him just one behind Juan Manuel Fangio's all-time record. But although he surrendered his crown to Britain's James Hunt in 1976, the bravery displayed by Lauda in coming back just weeks after nearly losing his life is one of motor racing's true stories of courage.

The son of a paper mill owner, Lauda started racing in 1968 and three years later was driving in Formula One for March. He became a member of the BRM team in 1973 but the car was not good enough for Lauda's talents. Enzo Ferrari was quick to spot the Austrian's ability, though, and Lauda joined his team the following year. His first ever win came at Jarama in his debut season at Ferrari.

In 1975 he ran away with the drivers' title and when in contention to retain it a year later he had his accident in Germany. Lauda suffered serious burns and was given the Last Rites. Remarkably, six weeks later he was driving again. But in the end he lost the title to Hunt by just one point.

Lauda was back to his brilliant best in 1977 and recaptured the title by 17 points ahead of Jody Scheckter. He moved to Brabham the following season but announced his retirement in 1980. McLaren tempted him back into the sport in 1982 and two years later he was world champion for a third time. He eventually retired for good in 1985 to spend more time on developing his airline company, Lauda Air.

BELGIUM

Lucien BIANCHI (1960–8)

Races:	17
Wins:	0 Best finish: 3rd
Points:	6
Pole:	0
Fastest laps:	0

Thierry BOUTSEN (1983–91)

Races:	137
Wins:	3
	1989 Canadian, Australian *(Williams)*
	1990 Hungarian *(Williams)*
Points:	130

Pole:	1
Fastest laps:	1

Paul FRÉRE (1952–6)

Races:	11
Wins:	0 Best finish: 2nd
Points:	11
Pole:	0
Fastest laps:	0

Bertrand GACHOT (1989–91)

Races:	15
Wins:	0 Best finish: 5th
Points:	4
Pole:	0
Fastest laps:	1

Olivier GENDEBIEN (1956–61)

Races: 14
Wins: 0 Best finish: 2nd
Points: 18
Pole: 0
Fastest laps: 0

Jacky ICKX (1966–79)

Races: 116
Wins: 8
1968 French (Ferrari)
1969 German, Canadian (Brabham)
1970 Austrian, Canadian, Mexican
(Ferrari)
1971 Dutch (Ferrari)
1972 German (Ferrari)
Points: 181

Pole: 13
Fastest laps: 14

Willy MAIRESSE (1960–63)

Races: 12
Wins: 0 Best finish: 3rd
Points: 7
Pole: 0
Fastest laps: 0

André PILETTE (1951–64)

Races: 9
Wins: 0 Best finish: 5th
Points: 2
Pole: 0
Fastest laps: 0

BRAZIL

Emerson FITTIPALDI (1970–80)

Races: 144
Wins: 14
1970 United States (Lotus)
1972 Spanish, Belgian, British, Austrian,
Italian (Lotus)
1973 Argentine, Brazilian, Spanish (Lotus)
1974 Brazilian, Belgian, Canadian
(McLaren)
1975 Argentine, British (McLaren)
Points: 281
Pole: 6
Fastest laps: 6

Wilson FITTIPALDI (1972–5)

Races: 36
Wins: 0 Best finish: 5th
Points: 3
Pole: 0
Fastest laps: 0

Mauricio GUGELMIN (1988–91)

Races: 59
Wins: 0 Best finish: 3rd
Points: 10
Pole: 0
Fastest laps: 0

Chico LANDI (1951–6)

Races: 6
Wins: 0 Best finish: 4th
Points: 1½
Pole: 0
Fastest laps: 0

The Fittipaldi brothers, Emerson (left) and Wilson.

Roberto MORENO (1987–91)

Races: 24
Wins: 0 Best finish: 2nd
Points: 15
Pole: 0
Fastest laps: 1

Carlos PACE (1972–7)

Races: 72
Wins: 1
1975 Brazilian (Brabham)
Points: 58
Pole: 1
Fastest laps: 5

CHAMPION DRIVERS

Nelson Piquet

Born: Rio de Janeiro, Brazil, 17 August 1952

Nelson Piquet became the second Brazilian world champion when he captured the title in 1981. He went on to win two more titles, and in an age when the sport is as competitive as it has ever been, that is a tremendous feat.

Piquet gave up a potentially successful lawn tennis career to take up Kart racing in 1970. But his natural talent behind the wheel indicated that he had made the right decision and in 1972 he was the Brazilian Kart champion. In 1976 he was his country's Super Vee champion and in 1977 he came to Europe to challenge for the Formula Three title.

The following year he had his first Formula One drive in an Ensign at the German Grand Prix. He also had drives for McLaren and Brabham before the 1978 season was out. He was to spend seven years at Brabham and during his spell there he captured two of his world titles and won 13 races, the first of which was at Long Beach in 1980. He won three races the following year as he snatched the title by one point from his fellow South American Carlos Reutemann.

When Piquet won his next title in 1983 it was, again, a close affair, as he won by two points from Alain Prost. Piquet joined Williams in 1986 and in his second season with his new team became world champion for the third time when he took the title ahead of team-mate Nigel Mansell who was forced to miss the last two races of the season through injury. But his time at Williams was not a particularly happy one because of unpleasantness between himself and Mansell, and in 1988 the Brazilian moved to Lotus.

In 1990 he moved on to Benetton and returned to winning ways by capturing the last two races of the season before enjoying further success in 1991 when he won the Canadian Grand Prix. However, Benetton announced that they were releasing Piquet at the end of the 1991 season and the three times world champion was forced to look for another team.

Emerson Fittipaldi

Born: São Paulo, Brazil, 12 December 1946

Brazil has produced three outstanding world champions who have won eight world titles between them. The first was Emerson Fittipaldi who captured the title in 1972 and again in 1974.

The son of a racing journalist, Emerson started in Kart racing before progressing to Formula One via Formula Vee, Formula Ford, Formula Three and Formula Two. He was given his first Formula One drive in the Lotus 49 in 1970 and finished 8th in the British Grand Prix from the back row of the grid.

Before the season was out he found himself as team leader following Jochen Rindt's death and won his first race, at Watkins Glen. Two years later, at the age of 25, Fittipaldi became the youngest ever world champion, a record which remains unsurpassed.

He joined McLaren in 1974 and won his second world title in their M23. He joined his brother Wilson's Copersucar team in 1976 but the car was not good enough for Emerson's skills. He quit racing in 1980 and returned to Brazil, but made a comeback and has enjoyed a successful second career in North America, in 1989 becoming the first non-American winner of the Indianapolis 500 since Britain's Graham Hill in 1966.

Nelson PIQUET (1978–91)

Races:	204
Wins:	23
	1980 United States (West), Dutch, Italian (Brabham)
	1981 Argentine, San Marino, Germany (Brabham)
	1982 Canadian (Brabham)
	1983 Brazilian, Italian, European (Brabham)
	1984 Canadian, Detroit (Brabham)
	1985 French (Brabham)
	1986 Brazilian, German, Hungarian, Italian (Williams)
	1987 German, Hungarian, Italian (Williams)
	1990 Japanese, Australian (Benetton)
	1991 Canadian (Benetton)
Points:	485½
Pole:	24
Fastest laps:	23

Ayrton SENNA (1984–91)

Races:	126
Wins:	33
	1985 Portuguese, Belgian (Lotus)
	1986 Spanish, Detroit (Lotus)
	1987 Monaco, United States (Lotus)
	1988 San Marino, Canadian, United States, British, German, Hungarian, Belgian, Japanese (McLaren)
	1989 San Marino, Monaco, Mexican, German, Belgian, Spanish (McLaren)
	1990 United States, Monaco, Canadian, German, Belgian, Italian (McLaren)
	1991 United States, Brazilian, San Marino, Monaco, Hungarian, Belgian, Australian (McLaren)
Points:	491
Pole:	60
Fastest laps:	17

Chico SERRA (1981–3)

Races:	18
Wins:	0 Best finish: 6th
Points:	1
Pole:	0
Fastest laps:	0

Hernando da SILVA RAMOS (1955–6)

Races:	7
Wins:	0 Best finish: 5th
Points:	2
Pole:	0
Fastest laps:	0

CANADA

Gilles VILLENEUVE (1977–82)

Races:	67
Wins:	6
	1978 Canadian (Ferrari)
	1979 South African, United States (West), United States (Ferrari)
	1981 Monaco, Spanish (Ferrari)
Points:	107
Pole:	2
Fastest laps:	8

CHILE

Eliseo SALAZAR (1981–3)

Races:	24
Wins:	0 Best finish: 5th
Points:	3
Pole:	0
Fastest laps:	0

FINLAND

Miki HAKKINEN (1991)

Races:	15
Wins:	0 Best finish: 5th
Points:	2
Pole:	0
Fastest laps:	0

Jirki Jarvi 'J J' LEHTO (1989–91)

Races:	23
Wins:	0 Best finish: 3rd
Points:	4
Pole:	0
Fastest laps:	0

Keke ROSBERG (1978–86)

Races:	114
Wins:	5
	1982 Swiss (Williams)
	1983 Monaco (Williams)
	1984 Dallas (Williams)
	1985 Detroit, Australian (Williams)
Points:	159½
Pole:	5
Fastest laps:	3

CHAMPION DRIVERS

Ayrton Senna

Born: São Paulo, Brazil, 21 March 1960

The extremely talented Ayrton Senna first attracted attention in 1983 when he won a staggering 12 rounds of the British Formula Three championship, including the first nine races of the season, taking the title from Britain's Martin Brundle. He was the hottest property around and started his Formula One career with the Toleman team, making his debut in his home Grand Prix in 1984.

His first points came in the next race, in South Africa, when he finished sixth. Then, despite driving a car that was inferior to the leading cars he pushed it into second place in the rain at Monaco, and his tremendous skill became obvious. Understandably, he was snapped up by one of the bigger teams and in 1985 he joined Lotus. He had his first win in the Portuguese Grand Prix in his first season with his new team.

Senna spent three years at Lotus and, despite not lifting the world title, was an obvious champion in the making with the right car. That chance improved when he moved to McLaren in 1988 and his first season with the new team reaped immediate results as he took the crown from team-mate Alain Prost. Senna won a record eight races during the season. He was runner-up to Prost in 1989, when it was apparent that relations between the two McLaren drivers were strained, to say the least. Prost moved on to Ferrari in 1990 and Senna recaptured the world title. But the animosity between the two continued, on and off the track.

Senna won his third world title in 1991 after winning the first four races of the season. His McLaren team have been ensuring he has the machinery to fit his enormous natural talent, and providing they can keep on producing the right car then there is every chance that Senna will catch, and possibly overtake, the record of five World Championship wins held by that first great South American driver, Juan Manuel Fangio.

Keke Rosberg

Born: Stockholm, Sweden, 6 December 1948

Like Mike Hawthorn 24 years earlier, Keke Rosberg captured the world title in 1982 by winning just one race. And like Hawthorn, Rosberg was also one of motor racing's showmen. Although born in Sweden he was brought up in Finland and started his career Kart racing; in 1971 he was the Scandinavian and Finnish Kart champion. He came through the other branches of the sport before eventually getting his first Formula One drive with Theodore in 1978. He also drove for ATS and Wolf that season.

Another season at Wolf was followed by two at Fittipaldi before he teamed up with the Frank Williams outfit in 1982. He enjoyed his first win in the Swiss Grand Prix at Dijon. But that one win, together with a season of consistent driving, was good enough to give him the drivers' title. He spent three more seasons at Williams and had four more wins before his last season in Formula One, with McLaren in 1986.

FRANCE

Jean ALESI (1989–91)

Races: 39
Wins: 0 Best finish: 2nd
Points: 42
Pole: 0
Fastest laps: 1

Philippe ALLIOT (1984–90)

Races: 93
Wins: 0 Best finish: 6th
Points: 5
Pole: 0
Fastest laps: 0

René ARNOUX (1978–89)

Races: 149
Wins: 7
 1980 Brazilian, South African (Renault)
 1982 French, Italian (Renault)
 1983 Canadian, German, Dutch (Ferrari)
Points: 181
Pole: 18
Fastest laps: 12

Elie BAYOL (1952–6)

Races: 7
Wins: 0 Best finish: 5th
Points: 2
Pole: 0
Fastest laps: 0

Jean BEHRA (1952–9)

Races: 52
Wins: 0 Best finish: 2nd
Points: 53½
Pole: 0
Fastest laps: 1

Jean-Pierre BELTOISE (1966–74)

Races: 86
Wins: 1
 1972 Monaco (BRM)
Points: 77
Pole: 0
Fastest laps: 4

Eric BERNARD (1989–91)

Races: 31
Wins: 0 Best finish: 4th
Points: 6
Pole: 0
Fastest laps: 0

François CEVERT (1969–73)

Races: 47
Wins: 1
 1971 United States (Tyrrell)
Points: 89
Pole: 0
Fastest laps: 2

Eugene CHABOUD (1950–1)

Races: 3
Wins: 0 Best finish: 5th
Points: 1
Pole: 0
Fastest laps: 0

Patrick DEPAILLER (1972–80)

Races: 95
Wins: 2
 1978 Monaco (Tyrrell)
 1979 Spanish (Ligier)
Points: 141
Pole: 1
Fastest laps: 4

Philippe ETANCELIN (1950–2)

Races: 12
Wins: 0 Best finish: 5th
Points: 3
Pole: 0
Fastest laps: 0

Yves GIRAUD-CABANTOUS (1950–3)

Races: 13
Wins: 0 Best finish: 4th
Points: 5
Pole: 0
Fastest laps: 0

Olivier GROUILLARD (1989–91)

Races: 25
Wins: 0 Best finish: 6th
Points: 1
Pole: 0
Fastest laps: 0

Jean-Pierre JABOUILLE (1975–81)

Races: 49
Wins: 2
 1979 French (Renault)
 1980 Austrian (Renault)
Points: 21
Pole: 6
Fastest laps: 0

Jean-Pierre JARIER (1971–83)

Races: 136
Wins: 0 Best finish: 3rd

Points: 31½
Pole: 3
Fastest laps: 3

Jacques LAFFITE (1974–86)

Races: 176
Wins: 6
1977 Swedish (*Ligier*)
1979 Argentine, Brazilian (*Ligier*)
1980 German (*Ligier*)
1981 Austrian, Canadian (*Talbot*)
Points: 228
Pole: 7
Fastest laps: 6

Guy LIGIER (1966–7)

Races: 12
Wins: 0 **Best finish:** 6th
Points: 1
Pole: 0
Fastest laps: 0

Robert MANZON (1950–6)

Races: 28
Wins: 0 **Best finish:** 3rd
Points: 16
Pole: 0
Fastest laps: 0

Henri PESCAROLO (1968–76)

Races: 57
Wins: 0 **Best finish:** 3rd
Points: 12
Pole: 0
Fastest laps: 1

Didier PIRONI (1978–82)

Races: 70
Wins: 3
1980 Belgian (*Ligier*)
1982 San Marino, Dutch (*Ferrari*)
Points: 101
Pole: 4
Fastest laps: 5

Alain PROST (1980–91)

Races: 183
Wins: 44
1981 French, Dutch, Italian (*Renault*)
1982 South African, Brazilian (*Renault*)
1983 French, Belgian, British, Austrian
(*Renault*)
1984 Brazilian, San Marino, Monaco,
German, Dutch, European,
Portuguese (*McLaren*)
1985 Brazilian, Monaco, British, Austrian,
Italian (*McLaren*)
1986 San Marino, Monaco, Austrian,
Australian (*McLaren*)
1987 Brazilian, Belgian, Portuguese
(*McLaren*)
1988 Brazilian, Monaco, Mexican, French,
Portuguese, Spanish, Australian
(*McLaren*)
1989 United States, French, British, Italian
(*McLaren*)
1990 Brazilian, Mexican, French, British,
Spanish (*Ferrari*)
Points: 699½
Pole: 20
Fastest laps: 35

Louis ROSIER (1950–6)

Races: 38
Wins: 0 **Best finish:** 3rd
Points: 18
Pole: 0
Fastest laps: 0

Johnny SERVOZ-GAVIN (1967–70)

Races: 12
Wins: 0 **Best finish:** 2nd
Points: 9
Pole: 0
Fastest laps: 0

Raymond SOMMER (1950)

Races: 5
Wins: 0 **Best finish:** 4th
Points: 3
Pole: 0
Fastest laps: 0

Philippe STREIFF (1984–8)

Races: 54
Wins: 0 **Best finish:** 3rd
Points: 11
Pole: 0
Fastest laps: 0

Didier Pironi survived a career in Formula One only to lose his life in his next sporting venture, powerboat racing.

CHAMPION DRIVERS

Alain Prost

Born: St Chamond, nr St Etienne, France, 24 February 1955

Considering that France is regarded as the 'home' of motor racing she had to wait a very long time for her first world champion, and it was not until the arrival of Alain Prost that the country ever looked like producing one. But even Prost had to suffer two agonising near misses before eventually getting his hands on the title.

Prost could have enjoyed a successful career as a footballer but chose motor racing instead and in 1976 he attracted a lot of attention by winning 12 of the 13 rounds of the French Formula Renault championship. He was the 1979 European Formula Three champion and the following year he was John Watson's partner in the McLaren Formula One team. In his first ever Grand Prix, at Buenos Aires, he picked up his first point.

He joined the French Renault team in 1981 and appropriately enjoyed his first win on home soil, in the French Grand Prix at Dijon. That was to be the first of a record 44 wins for the Frenchman whose calculated approach to the sport has earned him the nickname 'The Professor'. He was runner-up, by two points, to Nelson Piquet in the 1983 championship and the following year, after returning to McLaren, he lost out by a mere half a point when team-mate Niki Lauda captured his third world title.

The elusive title finally came the Frenchman's way the following year when he won five races to win comfortably from Michele Alboreto. He retained the title in 1986 when he took advantage of Nigel Mansell's misfortune in Australia. But the following year he could only finish fourth in the championship despite three race wins.

The 1988 season was dominated by McLaren as Prost and his team-mate Ayrton Senna, not the best of friends, won 15 of the 16 rounds. The title went to the Brazilian. Prost recaptured the championship in 1989 and in 1990 moved to Ferrari but could only finish runner-up, again to Senna.

In 1991, for the first time since 1980, Alain Prost failed to win a world championship race. Furthermore, his fifth place in the championship was his lowest since 1981. Ferrari announced they were parting company with the former champion and he was replaced for the last race of the season.

Patrick TAMBAY (1977–86)

Races:	114
Wins:	2
	1982 German (Ferrari)
	1983 San Marino (Ferrari)
Points:	103
Pole:	5
Fastest laps:	2

Maurice TRINTIGNANT (1950–64)

Races:	82
Wins:	2
	1955 Monaco (Ferrari)
	1958 Monaco (Cooper)
Points:	72⅓
Pole:	0
Fastest laps:	1

GERMANY

Stefan BELLOF (1984–5)

Races:	20
Wins:	0 Best finish: 4th
Points:	4
Pole:	0
Fastest laps:	0

Christian DANNER (1985–9)

Races:	34
Wins:	0 Best finish: 4th
Points:	4
Pole:	0
Fastest laps:	0

Hans HERRMANN (1953–66)

Races: 18
Wins: 0 Best finish: 3rd
Points: 10
Pole: 0
Fastest laps: 1

Karl KLING (1954–5)

Races: 11
Wins: 0 Best finish: 2nd
Points: 17
Pole: 0
Fastest laps: 1

Hermann LANG (1953–4)

Races: 2
Wins: 0 Best finish: 5th
Points: 2
Pole: 0
Fastest laps: 0

Jochen MASS (1973–82)

Races: 105
Wins: 1
 1975 Spanish *(McLaren)*
Points: 71
Pole: 0
Fastest laps: 2

Gerhard MITTER (1963–7)

Races: 5
Wins: 0 Best finish: 4th
Points: 3
Pole: 0
Fastest laps: 0

Michael SCHUMACHER (1991)

Races: 6
Wins: 0 Best finish: 5th
Points: 4
Pole: 0
Fastest laps: 0

Rolf STOMMELEN (1969–78)

Races: 54
Wins: 0 Best finish: 3rd
Points: 14
Pole: 0
Fastest laps: 0

Hans-Joachim STUCK (1974–9)

Races: 74
Wins: 0 Best finish: 3rd
Points: 29
Pole: 0
Fastest laps: 0

Michael Schumacher burst onto the Formula One scene in 1991 – Germany's great hope for the future.

Wolfgang von TRIPS (1957–61)

Races: 27
Wins: 2
                 1961 Dutch, British *(Ferrari)*
Points: 56
Pole: 1
Fastest laps: 0

Manfred WINKELHOCK (1982–5)

Races: 47
Wins: 0 **Best finish:** 5th
Points: 2
Pole: 0
Fastest laps: 0

GREAT BRITAIN

Cliff ALLISON (1958–61)

Races: 16
Wins: 0 **Best finish:** 2nd
Points: 11
Pole: 0
Fastest laps: 0

Bob ANDERSON (1963–7)

Races: 25
Wins: 0 **Best finish:** 3rd
Points: 8
Pole: 0
Fastest laps: 0

Peter ARUNDELL (1964–6)

Races: 11
Wins: 0 **Best finish:** 3rd
Points: 12
Pole: 0
Fastest laps: 0

Dick ATTWOOD (1965–9)

Races: 17
Wins: 0 **Best finish:** 2nd
Points: 11
Pole: 0
Fastest laps: 1

Julian BAILEY (1988–91)

Races: 7
Wins: 0 **Best finish:** 6th
Points: 1
Pole: 0
Fastest laps: 0

Derek Bell scored just one point in Formula One but excelled in the world of sports car racing.

Derek BELL (1968–74)

Races: 9
Wins: 0 **Best finish:** 6th
Points: 1
Pole: 0
Fastest laps: 0

Mark BLUNDELL (1991)

Races: 14
Wins: 0 **Best finish:** 6th
Points: 1
Pole: 0
Fastest laps: 0

Tony BRISE (1975)

Races: 10
Wins: 0 **Best finish:** 6th
Points: 1
Pole: 0
Fastest laps: 0

Delight for Stirling Moss (right) and Tony Brooks after their shared drive gave them victory in the 1957 British Grand Prix at Aintree.

Tony BROOKS (1956–61)

Races: 38
Wins: 6
    1957 British (shared) *(Vanwall)*
    1958 Belgian, German, Italian *(Vanwall)*
    1959 French, German *(Ferrari)*
Points: 75
Pole: 3
Fastest laps: 3

Alan BROWN (1952–3)

Races: 8
Wins: 0 **Best finish:** 5th
Points: 2
Pole: 0
Fastest laps: 0

Martin BRUNDLE (1984–91)

Races: 83
Wins: 0 **Best finish:** 4th
Points: 16
Pole: 0
Fastest laps: 0

Jim CLARK (1960–8)

Races: 72
Wins: 25
    1962 Belgian, British, United States *(Lotus)*
    1963 Belgian, Dutch, French, British,
    Italian, Mexican, South African
    (Lotus)
    1964 Dutch, Belgian, British *(Lotus)*

    1965 South African, Belgian, French,
    British, Dutch, German *(Lotus)*
    1966 United States *(Lotus)*
    1967 Dutch, British, United States,
    Mexican *(Lotus)*
    1968 South African *(Lotus)*
Points: 274
Pole: 33
Fastest laps: 28

Peter COLLINS (1952–8)

Races: 32
Wins: 3
    1956 Belgian, French *(Lancia-Ferrari)*
    1958 British *(Ferrari)*
Points: 47
Pole: 1*
Fastest laps: 0
* Collins started from pole position in the 1956 French Grand Prix but shouldn't have done because Fangio's practice time was better than Collins' but was incorrectly read by officials

Piers COURAGE (1966–70)

Races: 28
Wins: 0 **Best finish:** 2nd
Points: 20
Pole: 0
Fastest laps: 0

Johnny DUMFRIES (1986)

Races: 15
Wins: 0 **Best finish:** 5th

CHAMPION DRIVERS

Jim Clark

Born: Fife, Scotland, 4 March 1936
Died: Hockenheim, Germany, 7 April 1968

Jim Clark was the ultimate professional who was totally dedicated to motor racing, and when he died at Hockenheim in 1968 it sent shock waves through the sport. Clark was the one man they never thought would lose his life behind the wheel of a racing car: suddenly the other drivers felt vulnerable.

Clark's death deprived the sport of one of its most talented drivers. The son of a Fife farmer, he started driving around his

father's farm at an early age but was 20 when he made his debut in saloon car racing. That was in 1956; two years later he met Colin Chapman and the finest partnership in Formula One was about to develop.

Clark spent all his Formula One career at Lotus, won 25 races and captured two world titles. More would surely have followed had it not been for his untimely death. In his first world championship year,

1963, the Scot won a staggering seven races. When he won his second title two years later he won six races and was 14 points clear of his closest rival Graham Hill. To make it a memorable season Clark also became the first non-American winner of the Indianapolis 500.

At the time of his accident at Hockenheim, Clark had taken part in 72 Formula One Grands Prix. Ironically, he was killed in a Formula Two race.

Points: 3
Pole: 0
Fastest laps: 0

Vic ELFORD (1968–71)

Races: 13
Wins: 0 Best finish: 4th
Points: 8
Pole: 0
Fastest laps: 0

Jack FAIRMAN (1953–61)

Races: 12
Wins: 0 Best finish: 4th
Points: 5
Pole: 0
Fastest laps: 0

Ron FLOCKHART (1954–60)

Races: 13
Wins: 0 Best finish: 3rd
Points: 5
Pole: 0
Fastest laps: 0

Peter GETHIN (1970–4)

Races: 30
Wins: 1
               1971 Italian (BRM)
Points: 11
Pole: 0
Fastest laps: 0

Horace GOULD (1954–8)

Races: 14
Wins: 0 Best finish: 5th
Points: 2
Pole: 0
Fastest laps: 0

Mike HAILWOOD (1963–74)

Races: 50
Wins: 0 Best finish: 2nd
Points: 29
Pole: 0
Fastest laps: 1

Mike HAWTHORN (1952–8)

Races: 45
Wins: 3
               1953 French (Ferrari)
               1954 Spanish (Ferrari)
               1958 French (Ferrari)
Points: 127⁹/₁₄
Pole: 4
Fastest laps: 6

Johnny HERBERT (1989–91)

Races: 15
Wins: 0 Best finish: 4th
Points: 5
Pole: 0
Fastest laps: 0

Graham HILL (1958–75)

Races: 176
Wins: 14
               1962 Dutch, German, Italian, South African
                    (BRM)
               1963 Monaco, United States (BRM)
               1964 Monaco, United States (BRM)
               1965 Monaco, United States (BRM)
               1968 Spanish, Monaco, Mexican (Lotus)
               1969 Monaco (Lotus)
Points: 289
Pole: 13
Fastest laps: 10

James HUNT (1973–9)

Races: 92
Wins: 10
               1975 Dutch (Hesketh)
               1976 Spanish, French, German, Dutch,
                    Canadian, United States (McLaren)
               1977 British, United States, Japanese
                    (McLaren)
Points: 179
Pole: 14
Fastest laps: 8

Innes IRELAND (1959–66)

Races: 50
Wins: 1
               1961 United States (Lotus)
Points: 47
Pole: 0
Fastest laps: 1

Just one win for Innes Ireland, the 1961 US Grand Prix in a Lotus-Climax.

CHAMPION DRIVERS

Mike Hawthorn

Born: Mexborough, Yorkshire, England, 10 April 1929
Died: Guildford, Surrey, England, 22 January 1959

Mike Hawthorn enjoyed life to the full and was one of Grand Prix racing's flamboyant stars. He made an immediate impact on the motor racing world with his handling of the Formula Two Cooper-Bristols in 1952 and within no time was invited to Italy to test drive for Ferrari who subsequently offered him a place in the team.

Had there been suitable British manufacturers at the time, the very British Hawthorn would have remained loyal. But it was off to Ferrari, and he spent all but a brief spell of his Formula One career with the legendary Italian manufacturer. His debut season in Formula One was 1953 and before the season was out he had carved himself a place in history as the first British winner of a World Championship race when he won the French Grand Prix.

He moved to Vanwall in 1955 and that year won the ill-fated Le Mans 24-hour race in a Jaguar with co-driver Ivor Bueb. Hawthorn returned to Ferrari in 1957 and a year later, despite winning just one championship race, he pipped Stirling Moss to the title by a single point. But it was to be his last season. Following the death of his Ferrari team-mate Peter Collins he announced his decision to quit racing at the end of the season. Three months later Mike Hawthorn, one of motor racing's great characters, was killed following an accident in his Jaguar on the Guildford by-pass.

Graham Hill

Born: London, England, 15 February 1929
Died: Hendon, England, 29 November 1975

When Graham Hill was killed in a plane crash on a golf course in North London, motor racing lost a great friend and a charismatic personality. Twice world champion, in 1962 and 1968, Hill's career spanned 17 years and a then record 176 races.

Most of his career was spent with two of Britain's top manufacturers of the day, Lotus and BRM. Formerly a mechanic, he was part of Colin Chapman's Lotus team when they entered Formula One in 1958 but two years later switched to the BRM team and it was for them that he won his first world title.

He won the Indianapolis 500 in 1966, returned to Lotus the following year and in 1968, in the wake of Jim Clark's death, captured his second world title. A bad injury towards the end of 1969 meant Graham was no longer the force he had been in Grand Prix racing but his versatility was evident when he won the Le Mans 24-hour race with Henri Pescarolo in 1972.

He formed his own Embassy-Hill team in 1975 but his tragic death a few months later in an accident which also claimed the lives of other team members, left motor racing without one of its great personalities.

James Hunt

Born: Epsom, Surrey, England, 29 August 1947

Despite the efforts of Nigel Mansell in the 1980s, James Hunt remains Britain's most recent world champion, having captured the title in the rain at Fuji, Japan, in 1976 after a season-long battle with Niki Lauda (and the sport's governing body). In the end, the Briton was world champion by just one point.

Hunt started racing in 1967 and came through the ranks before eventually breaking into Formula One. It was during his days in Formula Ford that he was involved in several accidents which earned him the unfortunate nickname of 'Hunt the Shunt'.

He was given his chance in Formula One by Lord Hesketh in 1973. Hunt drove a March in his first season but Hesketh launched his own team the following year and in 1975 Hunt powered the car to its debut victory at Zandvoort. It was the first of his 10 Grand Prix successes.

He was offered the number one job at McLaren in 1976 upon Emerson Fittipaldi's departure and was now showing signs of being a potential world champion. Sure enough, in his first year with his new team he lifted the title for Britain. He spent two more seasons with McLaren but never came close to winning the title again. He joined the Wolf team in 1979 but quit before the season was out and took up a career alongside Murray Walker in the BBC television commentary box.

Chris IRWIN (1966–7)

Races:	10
Wins:	0 **Best finish:** 5th
Points:	2
Pole:	0
Fastest laps:	0

Jack LEWIS (1961–2)

Races:	9
Wins:	0 **Best finish:** 4th
Points:	3
Pole:	0
Fastest laps:	0

Stuart LEWIS-EVANS (1957–8)

Races:	14
Wins:	0 **Best finish:** 3rd
Points:	16
Pole:	2
Fastest laps:	0

Nigel MANSELL (1980–91)

Races:	165
Wins:	21
	1985 European, South African *(Williams)*
	1986 Belgian, Canadian, French, British, Portuguese *(Williams)*
	1987 San Marino, French, British, Austrian, Spanish, Mexican *(Williams)*
	1989 Brazilian, Hungarian *(Ferrari)*
	1990 Portuguese *(Ferrari)*
	1991 French, British, German, Italian, Spanish *(Williams)*
Points:	361
Pole:	17
Fastest laps:	22

John MILES (1969–70)

Races:	12
Wins:	0 **Best finish:** 5th
Points:	2
Pole:	0
Fastest laps:	0

Stirling MOSS (1951–61)

Races:	66
Wins:	16
	1955 British *(Mercedes-Benz)*
	1956 Monaco, Italian *(Maserati)*
	1957 British (shared), Pescara, Italian *(Vanwall)*
	1958 Argentine *(Cooper)*, Dutch, Portuguese, Moroccan *(Vanwall)*
	1959 Portuguese, Italian *(Cooper)*
	1960 Monaco, United States *(Lotus)*
	1961 Monaco, German *(Lotus)*
Points:	186⁹⁄₁₄
Pole:	16
Fastest laps:	19

Jackie OLIVER (1967–77)

Races: 50
Wins: 0 Best finish: 3rd
Points: 13
Pole: 0
Fastest laps: 1

Jonathan PALMER (1983–9)

Races: 82
Wins: 0 Best finish: 4th
Points: 14
Pole: 0
Fastest laps: 1

Mike PARKES (1966–7)

Races: 6
Wins: 0 Best finish: 2nd
Points: 14
Pole: 1
Fastest laps: 0

Reg PARNELL (1950–4)

Races: 6
Wins: 0 Best finish: 3rd
Points: 9
Pole: 0
Fastest laps: 0

Dennis POORE (1952)

Races: 2
Wins: 0 Best finish: 4th
Points: 3
Pole: 0
Fastest laps: 0

Tom PRYCE (1974–7)

Races: 42
Wins: 0 Best finish: 3rd
Points: 19
Pole: 1
Fastest laps: 0

Brian REDMAN (1968–74)

Races: 12
Wins: 0 Best finish: 3rd
Points: 8
Pole: 0
Fastest laps: 0

Roy SALVADORI (1952–62)

Races: 47
Wins: 0 Best finish: 2nd
Points: 19
Pole: 0
Fastest laps: 0

Mike SPENCE (1963–8)

Races: 36
Wins: 0 Best finish: 3rd
Points: 27
Pole: 0
Fastest laps: 0

Jackie STEWART (1965–73)

Races: 99
Wins: 27
    1965 Italian *(BRM)*
    1966 Monaco *(BRM)*
    1968 Dutch, German, United States
      (Matra)
    1969 South African Spanish, Dutch,
      French, British, Italian *(Matra)*
    1970 Spanish *(March)*
    1971 Spanish, Monaco, French, British,
      German, Canadian *(Tyrrell)*
    1972 Argentine, French, Canadian, United
      States *(Tyrrell)*
    1973 South African, Belgian, Monaco,
      Dutch, German *(Tyrrell)*
Points: 360
Pole: 17
Fastest laps: 15

John SURTEES (1960–72)

Races: 111
Wins: 6
    1963 German *(Ferrari)*
    1964 German, Italian *(Ferrari)*
    1966 Belgian *(Ferrari)*, Mexican *(Cooper)*
    1967 Italian *(Honda)*
Points: 180
Pole: 8
Fastest laps: 11

Henry TAYLOR (1959–61)

Races: 8
Wins: 0 Best finish: 4th
Points: 3
Pole: 0
Fastest laps: 0

John TAYLOR (1964–6)

Races: 5
Wins: 0 Best finish: 6th
Points: 1
Pole: 0
Fastest laps: 0

Trevor TAYLOR (1961–6)

Races: 27
Wins: 0 Best finish: 2nd
Points: 8
Pole: 0
Fastest laps: 0

CHAMPION DRIVERS

Jackie Stewart

Born: Dumbarton, Scotland, 11 June 1939

It is interesting that two of Britain's greatest ever drivers should both come from Scotland and Jackie Stewart certainly carried on where fellow Scot Jim Clark left off as he went on to win 27 races, which stood as a record for 14 years until surpassed by Frenchman Alain Prost in 1987.

Stewart had his first taste of competitive racing at Oulton Park in 1964 and two years later he teamed up with Ken Tyrrell to form a partnership that was to be reminiscent of the Clark-Chapman combination. After racing Formula Three and Formula Two cars for Tyrrell, Stewart was recruited by the BRM

Formula One team in 1965. He celebrated his first season with a win at Monza and ended the season in third place in the championship behind Clark and BRM team-mate Graham Hill.

Ken Tyrrell came into Formula One in 1968 with the Matra team and Stewart was soon recruited. He was second in the championship but the following year captured the title, as well as the Constructors' Cup for Matra. Tyrrell ran the new March team in 1970 and again had Jackie as the number one driver. But the following year Ken Tyrrell ran his own Formula One team and it was to

prove a winning combination for driver and car as Stewart took his second world title.

His third title was in 1973 and he should have crowned the season by competing in his 100th Grand Prix in the last race of the season at Watkins Glen. But as a measure of respect for team-mate François Cevert, who was killed in practice, he pulled out of the race. Stewart never raced again despite countless offers to come out of retirement. But he has remained in contact with the sport and can regularly be heard behind a microphone giving his expert comments.

Eric THOMPSON (1952)

Races: 1
Wins: 0 Best finish: 5th
Points: 2
Pole: 0
Fastest laps: 0

Derek WARWICK (1981–91)

Races: 131
Wins: 0 Best finish: 2nd
Points: 67
Pole: 0
Fastest laps: 2

John WATSON (1973–85)

Races: 152
Wins: 5
    1976 Austrian *(Penske)*
    1981 British *(McLaren)*
    1982 Belgian, Detroit *(McLaren)*
    1983 United States (West) *(McLaren)*
Points: 169
Pole: 2
Fastest laps: 5

Derek Warwick.

Ken WHARTON (1952–5)

Races: 15
Wins: 0 Best finish: 4th
Points: 3
Pole: 0
Fastest laps: 0

John Surtees

Born: Westerham, Kent, England, 11 February 1934

Over the years the likes of Mike Hailwood and Johnny Cecotto have attempted to make the transition from Grand Prix motorcycling to Formula One car racing. But while they enjoyed their brief moments of success, no one has matched the achievement of John Surtees, the only man to win world titles on both two and four wheels.

His motorcycle racing career in fact started on *three* wheels, with John as a passenger for his father in sidecar races in 1949. But seven years later John won the first of his seven solo world titles when he captured the 500cc crown on an MV Agusta. He turned to four wheels in 1960 and dovetailed his two careers, driving for the Lotus Formula One team when his motorcycling commitments permitted.

The following year he con-centrated on cars full-time and joined the Cooper team, but a year later he was driving for Lola. In 1963 he was invited to join the Ferrari team. He had his first Grand Prix success that year and the following season saw him capture the world title in a gripping climax at Mexico City.

A second world title was on the horizon in 1966 but he fell out with Ferrari mid-season and returned to Cooper. He ended the season as runner-up to Jack Brabham and had subsequent spells at Honda and BRM before racing his own cars. He quit driving in 1972 but kept his team in Formula One until 1978. They never registered a win in 111 starts.

Surtees guides the Ferrari to victory at Monza in 1964, his championship season.

Peter WHITEHEAD (1950–4)

Races: 10
Wins: 0 **Best finish:** 3rd
Points: 4
Pole: 0
Fastest laps: 0

HOLLAND

Carel Godin de BEAUFORT (1957–64)

Races: 28
Wins: 0 **Best finish:** 6th
Points: 4
Pole: 0
Fastest laps: 0

Gijs van LENNEP (1971–5)

Races: 8
Wins: 0 **Best finish:** 6th
Points: 2
Pole: 0
Fastest laps: 0

Republic of IRELAND

Derek DALY (1978–82)

Races: 49
Wins: 0 **Best finish:** 4th
Points: 15
Pole: 0
Fastest laps: 0

ITALY

Andrea de ADAMICH (1968–73)

Races: 30
Wins: 0 **Best finish:** 4th
Points: 6
Pole: 0
Fastest laps: 0

Michele ALBORETO (1981–91)

Races: 153
Wins: 5
           1982 Las Vegas *(Tyrrell)*
           1983 Detroit *(Tyrrell)*
           1984 Belgian *(Ferrari)*
           1985 Canadian, German *(Ferrari)*
Points: 179½
Pole: 2
Fastest laps: 5

Elio de ANGELIS (1979–86)

Races: 108
Wins: 2
           1982 Austrian *(Lotus)*
           1985 San Marino *(Lotus)*
Points: 122
Pole: 3
Fastest laps: 0

Alberto ASCARI (1950–5)

Races: 32
Wins: 13
           1951 German, Italian *(Ferrari)*
           1952 Belgian, French, British, German,
                Dutch, Italian *(Ferrari)*
           1953 Argentine, Dutch, Belgian, British,
                Swiss *(Ferrari)*
Points: 140⁹⁄₁₄
Pole: 14
Fastest laps: 13

Giancarlo BAGHETTI (1961–7)

Races: 21
Wins: 1
           1961 French *(Ferrari)*
Points: 14
Pole: 0
Fastest laps: 1

Mauro BALDI (1982–5)

Races: 36
Wins: 0 Best finish: 5th
Points: 5
Pole: 0
Fastest laps: 0

Lorenzo BANDINI (1961–7)

Races: 42
Wins: 1
           1964 Austrian *(Ferrari)*
Points: 58
Pole: 1
Fastest laps: 2

Felice BONETTO (1950–3)

Races: 15
Wins: 0 Best finish: 3rd
Points: 17½
Pole: 0
Fastest laps: 0

Vittorio BRAMBILLA (1974–80)

Races: 74
Wins: 1
           1975 Austrian *(March)*
Points: 15½
Pole: 1
Fastest laps: 1

Giulio CABIANCA (1958–60)

Races: 3
Wins: 0 Best finish: 4th
Points: 3
Pole: 0
Fastest laps: 0

Alex CAFFI (1986–91)

Races: 56
Wins: 0 Best finish: 4th
Points: 6
Pole: 0
Fastest laps: 0

Ivan CAPELLI (1985–91)

Races: 78
Wins: 0 Best finish: 2nd
Points: 28
Pole: 0
Fastest laps: 0

Eugenio CASTELLOTTI (1955–7)

Races: 14
Wins: 0 Best finish: 2nd
Points: 19½
Pole: 1
Fastest laps: 0

Andrea de CESARIS (1980–91)

Races: 165
Wins: 0 Best finish: 2nd
Points: 47
Pole: 1
Fastest laps: 1

Teo FABI (1982–7)

Races: 64
Wins: 0 Best finish: 3rd
Points: 23
Pole: 3
Fastest laps: 2

CHAMPION DRIVERS

Alberto Ascari

Born: Milan, Italy, 13 July 1918
Died: Monza, Italy, 26 May 1955

It was during the Formula Two days of the World Championship, in 1952 and 1953, that Alberto Ascari and his Ferrari 500 were almost unbeatable as he captured successive world crowns and in doing so won no fewer than 11 races.

Ascari started his motor sport career riding motorcycles but in 1947 switched to the four-wheeled scene. He started driving Maseratis and captured the 1949 Argentine Grand Prix, his first major success. In 1951 he moved to Ferrari and enjoyed his first World Championship win that year at the Nürburgring.

The following year he started one of motor sport's most amazing sequences by winning the first of nine consecutive races which took him to his two world titles. He agreed to switch to the new Lancia team in 1954 but his new car was not ready until the season was nearly at its end and a third successive championship was ruled out.

In 1955, just four days after surviving an accident which saw him dumped in the harbour at Monte Carlo, Alberto Ascari died while testing a new Ferrari sports car at Monza. His father also lost his life on the track and both men left wives and two young children.

Ascari, the first man to win successive world titles (1952 and 1953).

Giuseppe Farina

Born: Turin, Italy, 30 October 1906
Died: Aiguebelle, France, 30 June 1966

Dr Giuseppe Farina holds a special place in Formula One history as both the winner of the first World Championship race, at Silverstone on 13 May 1950, and as the sport's first world champion ahead of Argentina's Juan Manuel Fangio.

'Nino', as he was affectionately known, started racing as a hill-climber in 1933 and his obvious skills were soon spotted by Enzo Ferrari who signed him for his Scuderia Ferrari team which raced Alfa Romeos at the time. Farina's first major victory came in the Alfa 159 in the 1940 Tripoli Grand Prix. He continued racing during the war but announced his retirement in 1946.

However, he made a comeback with Maserati two years later and by the time the World Championship started, Farina had returned to Alfa. He moved back to Ferrari in 1952 after Alfa quit Formula One. But he was never to recapture the world crown. He was involved in a horrific accident at Buenos Aires during the 1953 Argentine Grand Prix when his car hurtled into the crowd killing 15 spectators. Farina himself escaped with minor injuries.

A year later he was involved in another bad accident during the *Mille Miglia*; he never recovered sufficiently and announced his retirement in 1955. Ironically, after surviving those two accidents, the sport's first world champion was to lose his life behind the wheel of his Lotus Cortina in the French Alps whilst on his way to the 1966 French Grand Prix at Reims.

Luigi FAGIOLI (1950–1)

Races:	7
Wins:	1
	1951 French (shared) *(Alfa Romeo)*
Points:	32
Pole:	0
Fastest laps:	0

Giuseppe FARINA (1950–5)

Races:	33
Wins:	5
	1950 British, Swiss, Italian *(Alfa Romeo)*
	1951 Belgian *(Alfa Romeo)*
	1953 German *(Ferrari)*
Points:	127⅓
Pole:	5
Fastest laps:	5

Gerino GERINI (1956–8)

Races:	6
Wins:	0 Best finish: 4th
Points:	1½
Pole:	0
Fastest laps:	0

Piercarlo GHINZANI (1981–9)

Races:	71
Wins:	0 Best finish: 5th
Points:	2
Pole:	0
Fastest laps:	0

Bruno GIACOMELLI (1977–90)

Races:	69
Wins:	0 Best finish: 3rd
Points:	14
Pole:	1
Fastest laps:	0

Ignazio GIUNTI (1970)

Races:	4
Wins:	0 Best finish: 4th
Points:	3
Pole:	0
Fastest laps:	0

Lella LOMBARDI (1975–6)

Races:	12
Wins:	0 Best finish: 6th
Points:	½
Pole:	0
Fastest laps:	0

Umberto MAGLIOLI (1953–7)

Races:	10
Wins:	0 Best finish: 3rd
Points:	3⅓

Pole:	0
Fastest laps:	0

Sergio MANTOVANI (1953–5)

Races:	7
Wins:	0 Best finish: 5th
Points:	4
Pole:	0
Fastest laps:	0

Pierluigi MARTINI (1985–91)

Races:	70
Wins:	0 Best finish: 4th
Points:	12
Pole:	0
Fastest laps:	0

Arturo MERZARIO (1972–9)

Races:	57
Wins:	0 Best finish: 4th
Points:	11
Pole:	0
Fastest laps:	0

Stefano MODENA (1987–91)

Races:	58
Wins:	0 Best finish: 2nd
Points:	16
Pole:	0
Fastest laps:	0

Gianni MORBIDELLI (1990–1)

Races:	19
Wins:	0 Best finish: 6th
Points:	½
Pole:	0
Fastest laps:	0

Luigi MUSSO (1953–8)

Races:	24
Wins:	1
	1956 Argentine (shared) *(Lancia-Ferrari)*
Points:	44
Pole:	0
Fastest laps:	1

Alessandro NANNINI (1986–90)

Races:	77
Wins:	1
	1989 Japanese *(Benetton)*
Points:	65
Pole:	0
Fastest laps:	2

Riccardo PATRESE (1977–91)

Races:	224
Wins:	5

1982 Monaco *(Brabham)*
1983 South African *(Brabham)*
1990 San Marino *(Williams)*
1991 Mexican, Portuguese *(Williams)*

Points: 205
Pole: 7
Fastest laps: 10

Cesare PERDISA (1955–7)

Races: 7
Wins: 0 Best finish: 3rd
Points: 5
Pole: 0
Fastest laps: 0

Emanuele PIRRO (1989–91)

Races: 37
Wins: 0 Best finish: 5th
Points: 3
Pole: 0
Fastest laps: 0

Consalvo SANESI (1950–1)

Races: 5
Wins: 0 Best finish: 4th
Points: 3
Pole: 0
Fastest laps: 0

Ludovico SCARFIOTTI (1963–8)

Races: 10
Wins: 1
               1966 Italian *(Ferrari)*
Points: 17
Pole: 0
Fastest laps: 1

Giorgio SCARLATTI (1956–61)

Races: 12
Wins: 0 Best finish: 5th
Points: 1
Pole: 0
Fastest laps: 0

Dorino SERAFINI (1950)

Races: 1
Wins: 0 Best finish: 2nd
Points: 3
Pole: 0
Fastest laps: 0

Piero TARUFFI (1950–6)

Races: 18
Wins: 1
               1952 Swiss *(Ferrari)*
Points: 41
Pole: 0
Fastest laps: 1

Gabriele TARQUINI (1987–91)

Races: 24
Wins: 0 Best finish: 6th
Points: 1
Pole: 0
Fastest laps: 0

Luigi VILLORESI (1950–6)

Races: 31
Wins: 0 Best finish: 2nd
Points: 49
Pole: 0
Fastest laps: 1

Renzo ZORZI (1975–7)

Races: 7
Wins: 0 Best finish: 6th
Points: 1
Pole: 0
Fastest laps: 0

JAPAN

Satoru NAKAJIMA (1987–91)

Races: 74
Wins: 0 Best finish: 4th
Points: 16
Pole: 0
Fastest laps: 1

Aguri SUZUKI (1988–91)

Races: 29
Wins: 0 Best finish: 3rd
Points: 7
Pole: 0
Fastest laps: 0

MEXICO

Hector REBAQUE (1977-81)

Races: 41
Wins: 0 Best finish: 4th
Points: 13
Pole: 0
Fastest laps: 0

Pedro RODRIGUEZ (1963-71)

Races: 55
Wins: 2
               1967 South African *(Cooper)*
               1970 Belgian *(BRM)*

Points: 71
Pole: 0
Fastest laps: 1

Ricardo RODRIGUEZ (1961-2)

Races: 5
Wins: 0 Best finish: 4th
Points: 4
Pole: 0
Fastest laps: 0

MONACO

Louis CHIRON (1950-5)

Races: 15
Wins: 0 Best finish: 3rd
Points: 4
Pole: 0
Fastest laps: 0

NEW ZEALAND

Chris AMON (1963-76)

Races: 96
Wins: 0 Best finish: 2nd
Points: 83
Pole: 5
Fastest laps: 3

Howden GANLEY (1971-4)

Races: 35
Wins: 0 Best finish: 4th
Points: 10
Pole: 0
Fastest laps: 0

Denny HULME (1965-74)

Races: 112
Wins: 8

1967 Monaco, German (*Brabham*)
1968 Italian, Canadian (*McLaren*)
1969 Mexican (*McLaren*)
1972 South African (*McLaren*)
1973 Swedish (*McLaren*)

CHAMPION DRIVERS

Denny Hulme

Born: Te Puke, New Zealand, 18 June 1936

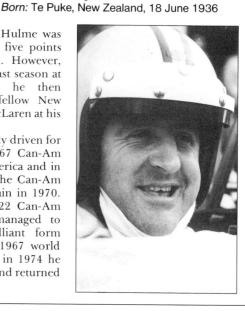

Denny Hulme came to Britain in 1960 with the aid of a scholarship and carried on the Formula Two career he had started in his home country by driving Formula Two Coopers. The following year he became a mechanic at the new Brabham team and at Brands Hatch on Boxing Day that year, 1961, he drove a Brabham to victory in the Formula Junior race. It was a significant win because it was the first ever victory for a Brabham car.

Hulme had his first Formula One drive in 1965 and in 1966 became the team's number two driver behind Jack Brabham. He finished fourth in the championship won by Brabham but the following year Hulme was champion himself, five points clear of 'the boss'. However, that was to be his last season at Brabham because he then teamed up with fellow New Zealander Bruce McLaren at his new team in 1968.

Denny had already driven for McLaren in the 1967 Can-Am series in North America and in 1968 he captured the Can-Am title, winning it again in 1970. He won a record 22 Can-Am races but never managed to recapture the brilliant form that won him the 1967 world drivers' crown and in 1974 he quit Formula One and returned to New Zealand.

1974 Argentine *(McLaren)*

Points: 248
Pole: 1
Fastest laps: 9

Bruce McLAREN (1958–70)

Races: 101
Wins: 4
  1959 United States *(Cooper)*
  1960 Argentine *(Cooper)*
  1962 Monaco *(Cooper)*
  1968 Belgian *(McLaren)*
Points: 196½
Pole: 0
Fastest laps: 3

Bruce McLaren, founder of the highly successful team of constructors which bears his name.

RHODESIA (Now Zimbabwe)

John LOVE (1962–72)

Races: 9
Wins: 0 Best finish: 2nd
Points: 6
Pole: 0
Fastest laps: 0

SIAM (Now Thailand)

Prince Birabongse of Siam who raced under the pseudonym of 'B Bira'.

'B BIRA' (Prince Birabongse) (1950–4)

Races: 19
Wins: 0 Best finish: 4th
Points: 8
Pole: 0
Fastest laps: 0

SOUTH AFRICA

Neville LEDERLE (1962)

Races: 1
Wins: 0 Best finish: 6th
Points: 1
Pole: 0
Fastest laps: 0

CHAMPION DRIVERS

Jody Scheckter

Born: East London, South Africa, 29 January 1950

Jody Scheckter came close to winning the world title in his first full season, 1974. But he had to wait five years before eventually lifting Formula One's most coveted prize.

Hailing from East London, the one-time home of the South African Grand Prix, Scheckter got the taste for motor racing at a very early age. He came to Europe in 1971 and the following year joined the McLaren Formula Two team.

He had his first taste of Formula One at Watkins Glen in the final race of the 1972 season before teaming up with Tyrrell for his first full season. His first success came in the Cosworth-powered 007 in the Swedish Grand Prix of 1974 and he finished third behind Emerson Fittipaldi and Clay Regazzoni in that year's championship. Only one win in 1975 put him out of contention but he was third behind Hunt and Lauda the following year when he drove the six-wheeled Project 34 Tyrrell to its first ever victory.

He joined the new Wolf team in 1977 and powered the car to victory in its first ever race, in Argentina. Scheckter was again a championship contender but had to be content with second place to Niki Lauda. The Wolf was uncompetitive in 1978 and Scheckter moved to Ferrari where in 1979 the 312s of Scheckter and Gilles Villeneuve proved invincible, the South African just pipping his team-mate to the title. His 1980 Ferrari was nowhere near as competitive and Scheckter announced his retirement at the end of the season, just 12 months after taking the world title.

Tony MAGGS (1961–5)

Races:	25
Wins:	0 Best finish: 2nd
Points:	26
Pole:	0
Fastest laps:	0

Jody SCHECKTER (1972–80)

Races:	112
Wins:	10
	1974 Swedish, British *(Tyrrell)*
	1975 South African *(Tyrrell)*
	1976 Swedish *(Tyrrell)*
	1977 Argentine, Monaco, Canadian *(Wolf)*
	1979 Belgian, Monaco, Italian *(Ferrari)*
Points:	255
Pole:	3
Fastest laps:	5

SPAIN

Francisco GODIA (1951–8)

Races:	13
Wins:	0 Best finish: 4th
Points:	6

Pole:	0
Fastest laps:	0

Alfonso de PORTAGO (1956–7)

Races:	5
Wins:	0 Best finish: 2nd
Points:	4
Pole:	0
Fastest laps:	0

Luis SALA (1988–9)

Races:	26
Wins:	0 Best finish: 6th
Points:	1
Pole:	0
Fastest laps:	0

SWEDEN

Jo BONNIER (1956–71)

Races:	104
Wins:	1
	1959 Dutch *(BRM)*
Points:	39
Pole:	1
Fastest laps:	0

Slim BORGUDD (1981–2)

Races: 10
Wins: 0 **Best finish:** 6th
Points: 1
Pole: 0
Fastest laps: 0

Stefan JOHANSSON (1983–91)

Races: 79
Wins: 0 **Best finish:** 2nd
Points: 88
Pole: 0
Fastest laps: 0

Gunnar NILSSON (1976–7)

Races: 31
Wins: 1
1977 Belgian *(Lotus)*
Points: 31
Pole: 0
Fastest laps: 1

Ronnie PETERSON (1970–8)

Races: 123
Wins: 10
1973 French, Austrian, Italian, United
States *(Lotus)*
1974 Monaco, French, Italian *(Lotus)*
1976 Italian *(March)*
1978 South African, Austrian *(Lotus)*
Points: 206
Pole: 14
Fastest laps: 9

Reine WISELL (1970–4)

Races: 22
Wins: 0 **Best finish:** 3rd
Points: 13
Pole: 0
Fastest laps: 0

SWITZERLAND

Rudi FISCHER (1951–2)

Races: 7
Wins: 0 **Best finish:** 2nd
Points: 10
Pole: 0
Fastest laps: 0

Emmanuel de GRAFFENRIED (1950–6)

Races: 22
Wins: 0 **Best finish:** 4th
Points: 9
Pole: 0
Fastest laps: 0

Silvio MOSER (1967–71)

Races: 12
Wins: 0 **Best finish:** 5th
Points: 3
Pole: 0
Fastest laps: 0

Above *Stefan Johansson still awaits his first win.*

Right *Another of the sport's nice guys whose life ended tragically – Ronnie Peterson.*

Clay REGAZZONI (1970–80)

Races: 132
Wins: 5
          1970 Italian *(Ferrari)*
          1974 German *(Ferrari)*
          1975 Italian *(Ferrari)*
          1976 United States (West) *(Ferrari)*
          1979 British *(Williams)*
Points: 212
Pole: 5
Fastest laps: 15

Jo SIFFERT (1962–71)

Races: 96
Wins: 2
          1968 British *(Lotus)*
          1971 Austrian *(BRM)*
Points: 68
Pole: 2
Fastest laps: 4

Marc SURER (1979–86)

Races: 82
Wins: 0 **Best finish:** 4th
Points: 17
Pole: 0
Fastest laps: 1

UNITED STATES

Freddie AGABASHIAN (1950–7)

Races: 8
Wins: 0 **Best finish:** 4th
Points: 1½
Pole: 1
Fastest laps: 0

George AMICK (1958)

Races: 1
Wins: 0 **Best finish:** 2nd
Points: 6
Pole: 0
Fastest laps: 0

Mario ANDRETTI (1968–82)

Races: 128
Wins: 12
          1971 South African *(Ferrari)*
          1976 Japanese *(Lotus)*
          1977 United States (West), Spanish,
                  French, Italian *(Lotus)*

          1978 Argentine, Belgian, Spanish, French,
                  German, Dutch *(Lotus)*
Points: 180
Pole: 18
Fastest laps: 10

Manny AYULO (1951–4)

Races: 4
Wins: 0 **Best finish:** 3rd
Points: 2
Pole: 0
Fastest laps: 0

Bobby BALL (1951–2)

Races: 2
Wins: 0 **Best finish:** 5th
Points: 2
Pole: 0
Fastest laps: 0

Tony BETTENHAUSEN (1950–60)

Races: 11
Wins: 0 **Best finish:** 2nd
Points: 11
Pole: 0
Fastest laps: 1

Bob BONDURANT (1965–6)

Races: 9
Wins: 0 **Best finish:** 4th
Points: 3
Pole: 0
Fastest laps: 0

Johnny BOYD (1955–60)

Races: 6
Wins: 0 **Best finish:** 3rd
Points: 4
Pole: 0
Fastest laps: 0

Don BRANSON (1959–60)

Races: 2
Wins: 0 **Best finish:** 4th
Points: 3
Pole: 0
Fastest laps: 0

Jimmy BRYAN (1952–60)

Races: 9
Wins: 1
          1958 Indianapolis 500 *(Epperly-*
                  Offenhauser)
Points: 18
Pole: 0
Fastest laps: 0

Ron BUCKNUM (1964–6)

Races:	11
Wins:	0 Best finish: 5th
Points:	2
Pole:	0
Fastest laps:	0

Eddie CHEEVER (1978–89)

Races:	132
Wins:	0 Best finish: 2nd
Points:	70
Pole:	0
Fastest laps:	0

Duane CARTER (1950–60)

Races:	8
Wins:	0 Best finish: 3rd
Points:	6½
Pole:	0
Fastest laps:	0

Joie CHITWOOD (1950)

Races:	1
Wins:	0 Best finish: 5th
Points:	1
Pole:	0
Fastest laps:	0

CHAMPION DRIVERS

Mario Andretti

Born: Montona, Italy, 28 February 1940

Although born in Italy, Mario Andretti moved to the United States as a youngster and is regarded as the second North American world champion after Phil Hill.

He was brought up in Pisa and every year the famous *Mille Miglia* would travel through the town. It was the thrill of watching the race that inspired the youngster to eventually choose a career in the sport. On his arrival in the States as a teenager Andretti started racing midget cars and in 1964 had his first drive in a single-seater. He soon established himself as a top driver and was three times the USAC champion.

He got his first chance to race in Formula One in 1968 when Colin Chapman gave him a drive in one of his Lotuses at the 1968 United States Grand Prix. He took the car to the front row of the grid and, in the race, powered his way to the front before eventually having to pull out. But he had given an indication of his ability to drive in the world of Formula One.

After winning the 1969 Indianapolis 500 he joined the March Formula One team the following year and in 1971 moved to Ferrari and had his first Grand Prix win, at Kyalami. After a spell with the Parnelli team he rejoined Lotus towards the end of 1976 and the following season finished third in the World Championship.

But 1978 was to be the great year for the Lotus pair of Andretti and Ronnie Peterson. They dominated the championship with the American taking the title ahead of his team-mate. That was to be Andretti's Formula One swansong. He never recaptured that form again but he returned to the Indy scene and continued racing beyond his 50th birthday.

Words of encouragement for a young Mario Andretti from Lotus boss Colin Chapman.

America's Mark Donohue looked as though he might make the transition from American racing to Formula One, but was tragically killed following an accident while warming-up for the 1975 Austrian Grand Prix.

Art CROSS (1952–5)

Races: 4
Wins: 0 **Best finish:** 2nd
Points: 8
Pole: 0
Fastest laps: 0

Jimmy DAVIES (1950–5)

Races: 5
Wins: 0 **Best finish:** 3rd
Points: 4
Pole: 0
Fastest laps: 0

Mark DONOHUE (1971–5)

Races: 14
Wins: 0 **Best finish:** 3rd
Points: 8
Pole: 0
Fastest laps: 0

Walt FAULKNER (1950–5)

Races: 5
Wins: 0 **Best finish:** 5th
Points: 1
Pole: 1
Fastest laps: 0

Pat FLAHERTY (1950–9)

Races: 6
Wins: 1
                1956 Indianapolis 500 *(Watson-Offenhauser)*
Points: 8
Pole: 1
Fastest laps: 0

George FOLLMER (1973)

Races: 12
Wins: 0 **Best finish:** 3rd
Points: 5
Pole: 0
Fastest laps: 0

Don FREELAND (1953–60)

Races: 8
Wins: 0 Best finish: 3rd
Points: 4
Pole: 0
Fastest laps: 0

Richie GINTHER (1960–6)

Races: 52
Wins: 1
1965 Mexican *(Honda)*
Points: 107
Pole: 0
Fastest laps: 3

Paul GOLDSMITH (1958–60)

Races: 3
Wins: 0 Best finish: 3rd
Points: 6
Pole: 0
Fastest laps: 0

Cecil GREEN (1950–1)

Races: 2
Wins: 0 Best finish: 4th
Points: 3
Pole: 0
Fastest laps: 0

Masten GREGORY (1957–65)

Races: 38
Wins: 0 Best finish: 2nd
Points: 21
Pole: 0
Fastest laps: 0

Dan GURNEY (1959–70)

Races: 86
Wins: 4
1962 French *(Porsche)*
1964 French, Mexican *(Brabham)*
1967 Belgian *(Eagle)*
Points: 133
Pole: 3
Fastest laps: 6

Jim HALL (1960–3)

Races: 11
Wins: 0 Best finish: 5th
Points: 3
Pole: 0
Fastest laps: 0

Sam HANKS (1950–7)

Races: 8
Wins: 1
1957 Indianapolis 500 *(Epperly-Offenhauser)*
Points: 20
Pole: 0
Fastest laps: 0

Walt HANSGEN (1961–4)

Races: 2
Wins: 0 Best finish: 5th
Points: 2
Pole: 0
Fastest laps: 0

Phil HILL (1958–64)

Races: 48
Wins: 3
1960 Italian *(Ferrari)*
1961 Belgian, Italian *(Ferrari)*
Points: 98
Pole: 6
Fastest laps: 6

Bill HOLLAND (1950–3)

Races: 2
Wins: 0 Best finish: 2nd
Points: 6
Pole: 0
Fastest laps: 1

Bill HOMEIER (1954–60)

Races: 3
Wins: 0 Best finish: 5th
Points: 1
Pole: 0
Fastest laps: 0

Eddie JOHNSON (1952–60)

Races: 9
Wins: 0 Best finish: 6th
Points: 1
Pole: 0
Fastest laps: 0

Andy LINDEN (1951–7)

Races: 7
Wins: 0 Best finish: 4th
Points: 5
Pole: 0
Fastest laps: 0

CHAMPION DRIVERS

Phil Hill

Born: Santa Monica, California, USA, 20 April 1927

America's Phil Hill is often the 'forgotten man' of motor racing because his 48-race Formula One career lasted only six years. But during that time he managed to capture the world title in 1961 ahead of his Ferrari teammate Wolfgang von Trips as he became North America's first world champion.

Before joining the Ferrari Formula One team in 1958, Hill had enjoyed success in the Italian manufacturer's sports cars and won that year's Le Mans. He came into their Grand Prix team after the deaths of Luigi Musso and Peter Collins earlier that season. Hill won his first race at Monza in 1960 and the following season it was at the Italian track that he clinched the title ahead of von Trips who, sadly, was killed at Monza.

However, that was to be Hill's last Formula One success and after spells at ATS and Cooper he concentrated on sports car racing once again. Twice more he won Le Mans before eventually retiring in 1967.

Jack McGRATH (1950–5)

Races: 6
Wins: 0 Best finish: 3rd
Points: 3
Pole: 1
Fastest laps: 1

Mike NAZARUK (1951–4)

Races: 3
Wins: 0 Best finish: 2nd
Points: 8
Pole: 0
Fastest laps: 0

Johnnie PARSONS (1950–8)

Races: 9
Wins: 1
1950 Indianapolis 500 (*Kurtis Kraft-Offenhauser*)
Points: 12
Pole: 0
Fastest laps: 0

Dick RATHMANN (1950–60)

Races: 5
Wins: 0 Best finish: 5th
Points: 2
Pole: 1
Fastest laps: 0

Jim RATHMANN (1950–60)

Races: 10
Wins: 1
1960 Indianapolis 500 (*Watson-Offenhauser*)
Points: 29
Pole: 0
Fastest laps: 2

Peter REVSON (1964–74)

Races: 30
Wins: 2
1973 British, Canadian (*McLaren*)
Points: 61
Pole: 1
Fastest laps: 0

Mauri ROSE (1950–1)

Races: 2
Wins: 0 Best finish: 3rd
Points: 4
Pole: 0
Fastest laps: 0

Paul RUSSO (1950–9)

Races: 8
Wins: 0 Best finish: 2nd
Points: 8½
Pole: 0
Fastest laps: 1

Troy RUTTMAN (1950–60)

Races:	8
Wins:	1
	1952 Indianapolis 500 (Kuzma-Offenhauser)
Points:	9½
Pole:	0
Fastest laps:	0

Harry SCHELL (1950–60)

Races:	56
Wins:	0 **Best finish:** 2nd
Points:	30
Pole:	0
Fastest laps:	0

Danny SULLIVAN (1983)

Races:	15
Wins:	0 **Best finish:** 5th
Points:	2
Pole:	0
Fastest laps:	0

Bob SWEIKERT (1952–6)

Races:	5
Wins:	1
	1955 Indianapolis 500 (Kurtis Kraft-Offenhauser)
Points:	8
Pole:	0
Fastest laps:	0

Johnny THOMSON (1953–60)

Races:	8
Wins:	0 **Best finish:** 3rd
Points:	10
Pole:	1
Fastest laps:	1

Bill VUKOVICH (1951–5)

Races:	5
Wins:	2
	1953 Indianapolis 500 (Kurtis Kraft-Offenhauser)
	1954 Indianapolis 500 (Kurtis Kraft-Offenhauser)
Points:	19
Pole:	1
Fastest laps:	3

Lee WALLARD (1950–1)

Races:	2
Wins:	1
	1951 Indianapolis 500 (Kurtis Kraft-Offenhauser)
Points:	8
Pole:	0
Fastest laps:	1

Rodger WARD (1951–63)

Races:	12
Wins:	1
	1959 Indianapolis 500 (Watson-Offenhauser)
Points:	15
Pole:	0
Fastest laps:	0

VENEZUELA

Johnny CECOTTO (1983–4)

Races:	18
Wins:	0 **Best finish:** 6th
Points:	1
Pole:	0
Fastest laps:	0

Johnny Cecotto was another former world motorcycling champion to venture into the four-wheeled branch of motor sport, but he failed to emulate John Surtees and become a double champion.

THE MANUFACTURERS

Over 120 manufacturers have invested large sums of money in the hope of producing a car capable of winning a World Championship Grand Prix. Only 24 have enjoyed that magical moment (29 if the Indi-anapolis 500 is included), and only about one third of the total have actually obtained World Championship points since the launch of the constructors' championship in 1958.

For most of them the flirta-tion with the world of Grand Prix racing was brief and expensive. The following is a potted World Championship history of every one of the teams who have obtained points.

AGS (1986–91)

Race wins: 0
Best finish: 6th
Races contested: 51
Points: 2

ALFA ROMEO (1950–85)

Known as Euroracing 1984-5
Race wins: 10
First win: 1950 British GP (Giuseppe Farina)
Latest win: 1951 Spanish GP (Juan Manuel Fangio)
World Champions:
1950 Giuseppe Farina (Ita)
1951 Juan Manuel Fangio (Arg)
Races contested: 112
Points: 50

BRM's world champion, Graham Hill.

ARROWS (1978–91)

Known as Footwork Arrows 1990-1
Race wins: 0
Best finish: 2nd
Races contested: 207
Points: 116

ATS (1977–84)

Race wins: 0
Best finish: 5th
Races contested: 99
Points: 8

BENETTON (1986–91)

Race wins: 5
First win: 1986 Mexican GP (Gerhard Berger)
Latest win: 1991 Canadian GP (Nelson Piquet)
Races contested: 96
Points: 234½

BRABHAM (1962–91)

Race wins: 35
First win: 1964 French GP (Dan Gurney)
Latest win: 1985 French GP (Nelson Piquet)
Constructors' Championship: 1966, 1967
World Champions:
1966 Jack Brabham (Aus)
1967 Denny Hulme (NZ)
1981 Nelson Piquet (Bra)
1983 Nelson Piquet (Bra)
Races contested: 391
Points: 864

BRM (1951–77)

Race wins: 17
First win: 1959 Dutch GP (Jo Bonnier)
Latest win: 1972 Monaco GP (Jean-Pierre Beltoise)
Constructors' Championship: 1962

World Champions:
1962 Graham Hill (GB)
Races contested: 197
Points: 433

BRP-BRM (1963–4)

Race wins: 0
Best finish: 4th
Races contested: 13
Points: 11

COOPER (1959–69)

Race wins: 16
First win: 1958 Argentine GP (Stirling
Moss)
Latest win: 1967 South African GP
(Pedro Rodriguez)
Constructors' Championship: 1959,
1960
World Champions:
1959 Jack Brabham (Aus)
1960 Jack Brabham (Aus)
Races contested: 129
Points: 342

DALLARA (1988–91)

Race wins: 0
Best finish: 3rd
Races contested: 62
Points: 13

EAGLE (1966–9)

Race wins: 1
1967 Belgian GP (Dan Gurney)
Races contested: 25
Points: 17

ENSIGN (1973–82)

Race wins: 0
Best finish: 4th
Races contested: 99
Points: 19

FERRARI (1950–91)

Lancia-Ferrari 1956–7
Race wins: 103
First win: 1951 British GP (José Froilán
González)
Latest win: 1990 Spanish GP (Alain
Prost)
Constructors' Championship: 1961,
1964, 1975, 1976, 1977, 1979, 1982,
1983
World Champions:
1952 Alberto Ascari (Ita)
1953 Alberto Ascari (Ita)
1956 Juan Manuel Fangio (Arg)
1958 Mike Hawthorn (GB)
1961 Phil Hill (USA)

*Lord Hesketh (left) with James Hunt and Mario Andretti. It was Hesketh
who gave Hunt his break into Formula One.*

1964 John Surtees (GB)
1975 Niki Lauda (Aut)
1977 Niki Lauda (Aut)
1979 Jody Scheckter (SAf)
Races contested: 489 (incl. one
Indianapolis 500)
Points: 1730½

FITTIPALDI (1975–82)

Race wins: 0
Best finish: 2nd
Races contested: 104
Points: 44

HESKETH (1974–8)

Race wins: 1
1975 Dutch GP (James Hunt)
Races contested: 52
Points: 48

HONDA (1964–8)

Race wins: 2
First win: 1965 Mexican GP (Richie
Ginther)
Latest win: 1967 Italian GP (John
Surtees)
Races contested: 35
Points: 48

JORDAN (1991)

Race wins: 0
Best finish: 4th
Races contested: 16
Points: 13

LARROUSSE LOLA (1990–1)

Race wins: 0
Best finish: 3rd
Races contested: 31
Points: 3
*The Larrouse Lola team scored 11
points in the 1990 championship but
had them deducted for making an
illegal declaration on their entry form.*

LEYTON HOUSE (1990–1)

Race wins: 0
Best finish: 2nd
Races contested: 30
Points: 8

LIGIER (1976–91)

Talbot-Ligier 1981–2
Race wins: 8
First win: 1977 Swedish GP (Jacques
Laffite)
Latest win: 1981 Canadian GP
(Jacques Laffite)
Races contested: 245
Points: 307

LOLA (1962–89)

See Larrouse Lola 1990–91
Race wins: 0
Best finish: 2nd
Races contested: 114
Points: 32

LOTUS (1958–91)

Race wins: 79
First win: 1960 Monaco GP (Stirling Moss)
Latest win: 1987 United States GP (Ayrton Senna)
Constructors' Championship: 1963, 1965, 1968, 1970, 1972, 1973, 1978
World Champions:
1963 Jim Clark (GB)
1965 Jim Clark (GB)
1968 Graham Hill (GB)
1970 Jochen Rindt (Aut)
1972 Emerson Fittipaldi (Bra)
1978 Mario Andretti (USA)
Races contested: 443
Points: 1343

McLAREN (1966–91)

Race wins: 94
First win: 1968 Belgian GP (Bruce McLaren)
Latest win: 1991 Australian GP (Ayrton Senna)
Constructors' Championship: 1974, 1984, 1985, 1988, 1989, 1990, 1991
World Champions:
1974 Emerson Fittipaldi (Bra)
1976 James Hunt (GB)
1984 Niki Lauda (Aut)
1985 Alain Prost (Fra)
1986 Alain Prost (Fra)
1988 Ayrton Senna (Bra)
1989 Alain Prost (Fra)

Ayrton Senna in 1988, the season which saw the first of four consecutive constructors' championship wins for McLaren.

1990 Ayrton Senna (Bra)
1991 Ayrton Senna (Bra)
Races contested: 362
Points: 1690½

MARCH (1970–89)

Race wins: 3
First win: 1970 Spanish GP (Jackie Stewart)
Latest win: 1976 Italian GP (Ronnie Peterson)
Races contested: 184
Points: 170½

MASERATI (1950–60)

Race wins: 9
First win: 1953 Italian GP (Juan Manuel Fangio)
Latest win: 1957 German GP (Juan Manuel Fangio)
World Champions:
1957 Juan Manuel Fangio (Arg)
Races contested: 70 (Incl. two Indianapolis 500s)
Points: 9

MATRA (1966–72)

Race wins: 9
First win: 1968 Dutch GP (Jackie Stewart)
Latest win: 1969 Italian GP (Jackie Stewart)
Constructors' Championship: 1969
World Champions:
1969 Jackie Stewart (GB)
Races contested: 62
Points: 163

MINARDI (1985–91)

Race wins: 0
Best finish: 4th
Races contested: 108
Points: 13

ONYX (1989–90)

Became Monteverdi midway through 1990 season
Race wins: 0
Best finish: 3rd
Races contested: 17
Points: 6

Jim Clark at the wheel of the famous Lotus-Climax.

The car which started the turbo revolution, the Renault RS01 in 1977.

Best finish: 2nd
Races contested: 118
Points: 53

TECNO (1969–73)

Race wins: 0
Best finish: 6th
Races contested: 11
Points: 1

THEODORE (1978–83)

Race wins: 0
Best finish: 6th
Races contested: 34
Points: 2

TOLEMAN (1981–5)

Race wins: 0
Best finish: 2nd
Races contested: 57
Points: 26

TYRRELL (1970–91)

Race wins: 23
First win: 1971 Spanish GP (Jackie Stewart)
Latest win: 1983 United States GP (Michele Alboreto)
Constructors' Championship: 1971
World Champions:
1971 Jackie Stewart (GB)
1973 Jackie Stewart (GB)
Races contested: 316
Points: 588

VANWALL (1954–60)

Race wins: 9
First win: 1957 British GP (Tony Brooks/Stirling Moss)
Latest win: 1958 Moroccan GP (Stirling Moss)
Constructors' Championship: 1958
Races contested: 28
Points: 57

WILLIAMS (1972–91)

Race wins: 51
First win: 1979 British GP (Clay Regazzoni)
Latest win: 1991 Spanish GP (Nigel Mansell)
Constructors' Championship: 1980, 1981, 1986, 1987

OSELLA (1980–91)

Became Fondmetal 1991
Race wins: 0
Best finish: 4th
Races contested: 136
Points: 5

PARNELLI (1974–6)

Race wins: 0
Best finish: 4th
Races contested: 16
Points: 6

PENSKE (1974–7)

Race wins: 1
1976 Austrian GP (John Watson)
Races contested: 32
Points: 22

PORSCHE (1957–64)

Race wins: 1
1962 French GP (Dan Gurney)
Races contested: 33
Points: 47

RENAULT (1977–85)

Race wins: 15
First win: 1979 French GP (Jean-Pierre Jabouille)
Latest win: 1983 Austrian GP (Alain Prost)
Races contested: 123
Points: 312

RIAL (1988–9)

Race wins: 0
Best finish: 4th
Races contested: 20
Points: 4

SHADOW (1973–80)

Race wins: 1
1977 Austrian GP (Alan Jones)
Races contested: 104
Points: 67½

SURTEES (1970–8)

Race wins: 0

One of the sport's great cars, the streamlined version of the Mercedes W196.

World Champions:
1980 Alan Jones (Aus)
1982 Keke Rosberg (Fin)
1987 Nelson Piquet (Bra)
Races contested: 282
Points: 1062½

WOLF (1977–9)

Race wins: 3
First win: 1977 Argentine GP (Jody
  Scheckter)
Latest win: 1977 Canadian GP (Jody
  Scheckter)
Races contested: 47
Points: 79

ZAKSPEED (1985–9)

Race wins: 0
Best finish: 5th
Races contested: 54
Points: 2

The following teams either won races in the days prior to the launch of the constructors' championship in 1958 or only in the Indianapolis 500, and consequently are not officially credited with any points.

EPPERLY (1955–60)

Race wins: 2
First win: 1957 Indianapolis 500 (Sam
  Hanks)
Latest win: 1958 Indianapolis 500
  (Jimmy Bryan)
Races contested: 5

KK (1950–60)

Race wins: 3
First win: 1953 Indianapolis 500 (Bill
  Vukovich)
Latest win: 1955 Indianapolis 500
  (Bob Sweikert)
Races contested: 11

KURTIS KRAFT (1950–60)

Race wins: 2
First win: 1950 Indianapolis 500
  (Johnny Parsons)
Latest win: 1951 Indianapolis 500
  (Lee Wallard)
Races contested: 12

KUZMA (1951–60)

Race wins: 1
Win: 1952 Indianapolis 500 (Troy
  Ruttman)
Races contested: 10

MERCEDES-BENZ (1954–5)

Race wins: 9
First win: 1954 French GP (Juan
  Manuel Fangio)
Latest win: 1955 Italian GP (Juan
  Manuel Fangio)
World Champions:
1954 Juan Manuel Fangio (Arg)
1955 Juan Manuel Fangio (Arg)
Races contested: 12

WATSON (1950–60)

Race wins: 3
First win: 1956 Indianapolis 500 (Pat
  Flaherty)
Latest win: 1960 Indianapolis 500 (Jim
  Rathmann)
Races contested: 9

TECHNICAL & SAFETY DEVELOPMENTS

The driver's safety must always be the foremost consideration in a sport as potentially dangerous as motor racing. Over the years the drivers themselves and the governing bodies have been mindful of these considerations, and whether it be with the introduction of safer circuits or safer cars, the driver's welfare has been the first and foremost priority.

Understandably, with a sport as competitive as motor racing, and with scientific advancements, the engineers have at times allowed their genius to take control and on occasions technical advancements have outweighed the safety precautions. But the sport has always been wise enough to curb, or control, advancements that are potentially dangerous.

From the early days of the motor car technical advances were rapid. Petrol-driven engines soon replaced those driven by liquid hydrocarbon, suspension was added, rubberised tyres were introduced, and so on. These are things that are now taken for granted with a motor car, but it wasn't always like that. Likewise, the Formula One racing car wasn't always the sophisticated computerised piece of machinery it is today, even if it was always the *crème de la crème* of its day.

From the early days of racing, organisers have tried to issue sets of rules, and early races divided cars into two categories, heavyweight and lightweight, with those weighing more than 400kg (882lb) falling into the first category.

But cars used for racing soon became bigger and developed larger and more powerful engines. Winning was a matter of such prestige that safety became a secondary consideration, but after a series of accidents during the 1903 Paris–Madrid race the racing of cars on open roads was discontinued and such racing was allowed only on closed circuits. This situation gave birth to the likes of Brooklands, a pioneer amongst purpose-built racing and testing tracks.

To try to make races safer, a weight limit of 1000kg (2204lb) was imposed by the Automobile Club of France in 1906. Further restrictions came the following year when cars entered for the French Grand Prix of 1907 were allowed to carry only 231 litres (50.8 gallons) of fuel. The organisers were now trying to make racing more scientific and eliminate the theory that the biggest car would win, a theory that still holds good to a certain extent today because a bad driver will not make a good car great and vice versa.

After the weight limit and fuel capacity restrictions, the next piece of legislation restricted piston size. This was followed by restrictions on body size, the banning of streamlining and so on. These restrictions all formed the early basis for the Formula One rules that were in force when the World Championship started in 1950.

At the time of the launch of the championship, supercharging was a popular form of boosting engine power by forcing a mixture of fuel and air into the cylinders under pressure. Cars with supercharged engines were therefore restricted to a maximum capacity of 1.5 litres while unsupercharged cars could have engine capacitites up to 4.5 litres.

This formula was in force for the first two years of the World Championship but manufacturers were given notice of changes for the 1952 season when all races were run to Formula Two regulations: supercharged cars had a capacity limit of 500cc while the unsupercharged engines were reduced to a 2 litre capacity.

This formula was a temporary one until the launch of the new Formula One 500cc/2.5 litre formula that came into force in 1954. Manufacturers have always had plenty of notice of these changes in formulae and consequently had time to get the engineers at work on developing the most powerful units within the regulations.

The 1959 season was significant in the world of Formula One because for the first time, the world champion, Jack Brabham of Australia, captured the title driving a rear-engined car, the Cooper-Climax. Previously all cars saw the driver seated behind the powerful engine. Now a revolution was on its way as the shape and look of the racing car changed.

Left *Emerson Fittipaldi in the new black John Player Lotus in 1972.*

Facing page *Those who mocked the turbo-powered Renault had to eat their words when Jean-Pierre Jabouille stormed to victory in the 1979 French Grand Prix.*

On 1 January 1961 the most sweeping changes to Formula One were launched. Superchargers had gone and a limit of 1.5 litres was imposed on all engines. Furthermore, to prevent manufacturers making a chassis that was too light for the powerful engines being produced, a *minimum* weight limit of 450kg (992lb) was introduced, along with further safety measures like the compulsory fitting of roll-over bars, self-starters and double braking, as well as an insistence that all fuel should be pump fuel. Further restrictions prevented oil being taken on board during a race, and none of the wheels of a vehicle were allowed to be enclosed within the chassis.

These were, indeed, sweeping new regulations. But with competitive racing becoming bigger business than ever before, the governing bodies were conscious that they had to protect the sport from overambitious manufacturers who now realised that motor racing contests started on the drawing board and not on the starting grid. The 1.5 litre formula was scheduled to last three years but the governing body, the *Commission Sportive Internationale* (CSI), extended it a further two years

until the end of the 1965 season.

It was during the 1.5 litre formula that Lotus boss Colin Chapman came up with the sport's greatest technological advance since the launch of the World Championship when he introduced the monocoque framed car. It was a simple idea that saw the driver seated between two frames instead of the multi-tubular framed chassis of the old cars. As a result of Chapman's invention, frames became lighter, the driver was seated nearer the ground, better suspension systems were fitted, there was improved roadholding and, consequently, cornering became easier. It was an innovation that other manufacturers were soon to follow. It was simple but very effective.

The new rules for 1966 allowed a 3 litre unsupercharged capacity with a 1.5 litre capacity for the reintroduced supercharged engines. Weight limits were also changed with a minimum weight limit of 500kg (1102lb), and race distances were restricted to a maximum of 400km/248 miles. On-board fire extinguishers were made compulsory in 1969 and safety fuel tanks were introduced in 1970.

The increasing use of aerody-

namic aids came in for close scrutiny and restrictions were imposed on them too in 1969, as was a 12 cylinder limit on all engines three years later. By the mid-seventies, Formula One cars were starting to take on the look of the car of today with the low chassis and rear aerofoils. But the biggest technical advance of the 1970s was launched at the 1977 British Grand Prix when Renault introduced their new turbocharged engine.

The turbocharger was more powerful than the supercharger and was a compressor which boosted the fuel/air mixture by utilising the engine's exhaust gasses. The turbocharger let the Renault down at the British Grand Prix but two years later the first turbocharged car won a Grand Prix when the Renault triumphed in France. That was to be the start of a revolution that lasted ten years until turbochargers were banned completely at the end of the 1988 season.

Meanwhile, Lotus led the way again in 1977 when they launched their 'wing' car, the Lotus 78, which, through its design, improved down thrust, kept the car closer to the track and thus had less air going under the car. Soon, other manufacturers latched on to the idea and by the end of the decade the advantages of cars with less air passing under them were obvious, chiefly the ability to corner at greater speed, and as a result, skirts were added to the chassis. But cornering at high speed rendered the sport potentially dan-

gerous and in 1981 sliding skirts were banned.

It would not be until 1987 that designers would find a way of increasing cornering speed and that was done with the introduction of the 'active' suspension system which took advantage of the very latest computer technology to control the height of a car off the ground under varying conditions, when cornering, braking and accelerating etc.

A fuel restriction was reimposed in 1984 at 220 litres (48.39 gallons), reduced to 150 litres (33 gallons) four years later. Turbocharged engines were restricted to a 1.5 litre capacity in 1986, and the following year normally-aspirated engines were allowed to have a maximum capacity of 3.5 litres. From 1989 all cars ran to the 3.5 litre capacity following the end

of the turbocharger revolution.

That is the formula to which the World Championship is currently run, but as designers find new ways to make cars go faster, the governing body, FISA, will continue to curb anything that is potentially dangerous. On-board computers are, however, very much part of the 1990s Formula One car and these contribute to its smooth and safe running.

It is not only the tightening up of engine and car design that has helped make motor racing a safer sport to participate in and watch. The circuits, too, have become safer places. How often do you see cars crash at high speed today only for the driver to be seen walking away unhurt with the steering wheel in hand? This is largely due to the high standard of the modern-day Grand Prix car, but is also

attributable to the safety precautions at circuits, with more run-off areas, well organised marshalling, and one of the best things to arrive in the world of high speed Grand Prix racing, the Armco safety barrier. These barriers give drivers that peace of mind they need when hurtling around a track at 150 mph.

Motor racing is essentially a safe sport. There have been, and there always will be, fatalities, but that applies to any sport. The people involved with motor racing, and in particular Formula One, are keen to utilise the best technology available to them. They do that very skilfully, but at the same time they do not let the computer simply tell them to do this or that, they query the safety aspect of new advances. Happily we are in an age were the two can go hand in glove.

A total of 58 circuits from 22 countries have been used as the home of a World Championship Grand Prix.

The following countries have all staged World Championship races. The figures indicate the number of different circuits each country has provided:

9	United States
7	France
5	Spain
3	Argentina, Belgium, Canada, Germany, Great Britain, Italy, Portugal
2	Austria, Brazil, Japan, South Africa
1	Australia, Holland, Hungary, Mexico, Monaco, Morocco, Sweden, Switzerland

The following is a list showing every circuit, when it has been used, its varying lengths, and the holder of its lap record. The figures in brackets indicate a circuit's length and the years used at that length.

ARGENTINA

BUENOS AIRES NO. 2
(3.912 km/2.431 miles: 1953–8, 1960)
Fastest Lap: 142.36kph/88.48mph Stirling Moss, Cooper-Climax, 1960
BUENOS AIRES NO. 9
(3.344 km/2.078 miles: 1972–3)
Fastest Lap: 169.1kph/105.08mph Emerson Fittipaldi, Lotus-Ford, 1973
BUENOS AIRES NO. 15
(5.967 km/3.708 miles: 1974–5, 1977–81)
Fastest Lap: 204.07kph/126.81mph Nelson Piquet, Brabham-Ford, 1981

AUSTRALIA

ADELAIDE
(3.779 km/2.348 miles: 1985–7)
Fastest Lap: 169.18kph/105.12mph Gerhard Berger, Ferrari, 1987
(3.780 km/2.349 miles: 1987–91)
Fastest Lap: 174.01kph/108.17mph Nigel Mansell, Ferrari, 1990

AUSTRIA

ZELTWEG
(3.199 km/1.988 miles: 1964)
Fastest Lap: 163.46kph/101.57mph Dan Gurney, Brabham-Climax
ÖSTERREICHRING
(5.911 km/3.673 miles: 1970–5)
Fastest Lap: 218.88kph/136.01mph Clay Regazzoni, Ferrari, 1974
(5.911 km/3.672 miles: 1976)
Fastest Lap: 221.81kph/137.83mph James Hunt, McLaren-Ford
(5.942 km/3.692 miles: 1977–87)
Fastest Lap: 242.21kph/150.50mph Nigel Mansell, Williams-Honda, 1987

BELGIUM

SPA-FRANCORCHAMPS
(14.120 km/8.774 miles: 1950–6)
Fastest Lap: 199.58kph/124.01mph Stirling Moss, Maserati, 1956
(14.099 km/8.761 miles: 1958, 1960–8, 1970)
Fastest Lap: 244.74kph/152.08mph Chris Amon, March-Ford, 1970
(6.949 km/4.318 miles: 1983)
Fastest Lap: 196.22kph/121.93mph Andrea de Cesaris, Alfa Romeo
(6.940 km/4.312 miles: 1985–91)
Fastest Lap: 217.09kph/134.89mph Alain Prost, Ferrari, 1990
NIVELLES-BAULERS
(3.724 km/2.314 miles: 1972, 1974)
Fastest Lap: 188.00kph/116.82mph Denny Hulme, McLaren-Ford, 1974
ZOLDER
(4.220 km/2.622 miles: 1973)
Fastest Lap: 177.85kph/110.51mph François Cevert, Tyrrell-Ford
(4.262 km/2.648 miles: 1975–82, 1984)
Fastest Lap: 193.50kph/120.24mph René Arnoux, Ferrari, 1984

BRAZIL

INTERLAGOS
(7.960 km/4.946 miles: 1973–7)
Fastest Lap: 185.88kph/115.50mph Jean-Pierre Jarier, Shadow-Ford, 1975
(7.875 km/4.893 miles: 1979–80)
Fastest Lap: 192.42kph/119.57mph René Arnoux, Renault, 1980
(4.324 km/2.687 miles: 1990–1)
Fastest Lap: 194.87kph/121.09mph Gerhard Berger, McLaren-Honda, 1990
RIO DE JANEIRO
(5.031 km/3.126 miles: 1978, 1981–9)
Fastest Lap: 195.79kph/121.65mph Riccardo Patrese, Williams-Renault, 1989

CIRCUIT FOCUS

Spa-Francorchamps

After Monza, Belgium's Spa-Francorchamps circuit in the Ardennes district, south of Liege, is the next fastest Grand Prix circuit. The original track, built in 1924, resembled a triangle and measured approximately 14km/8.75 miles but full-scale reconstruction in 1983 resulted in a major change and the current Spa circuit bears very little resemblance to the original track.

Because of the increase in speed of the Formula One cars, Spa became too dangerous in the early 1970s and was removed from the World Championship rota. It was not until its major reconstruction in 1983 that it regained its place and it is now very much part of the Grand Prix calendar once again.

CANADA

MOSPORT PARK
(93.957 km/2.459 miles: 1967, 1969, 1971–4, 1976–7)
Fastest Lap: 194.36kph/120.77mph Mario Andretti, Lotus-Ford, 1977
ST JOVITE
(4.265 km/2.650 miles: 1968, 1970)
Fastest Lap: 166.51kph/103.47mph Clay Regazzoni, Ferrari, 1970

MONTREAL
(4.410 km/2.740 miles: 1978–86)
Fastest Lap: 186.88kph/116.13mph Nelson Piquet, Williams-Honda, 1986
(4.390 km/2.728 miles: 1988–90)
Fastest Lap: 192.55kph/119.65mph Gerhard Berger, McLaren-Honda, 1990
(4.431 km/2.753 miles: 1991)
Fastest Lap: 193.58kph/120.28mph Nigel Mansell, Williams-Renault

THE GRAND PRIX CIRCUITS

FRANCE

REIMS
(7.817 km/4.857 miles: 1950–1)
Fastest Lap: 190.37kph/118.20mph Juan Manuel Fangio, Alfa Romeo, 1951
(8.348 km/5.187 miles: 1953)
Fastest Lap: 186.53kph/115.91mph Juan Manuel Fangio, Maserati, & Alberto Ascari, Ferrari
(8.303 km/5.159 miles: 1954, 1956, 1958–61, 1963, 1966)
Fastest Lap: 227.62kph/141.44mph Lorenzo Bandini, Ferrari, 1966

ROUEN-LES-ESSARTS
(5.100 km/3.169 miles: 1952)
Fastest Lap: 133.72kph/83.09mph Alberto Ascari, Ferrari
(6.542 km/4.065 miles: 1957, 1962, 1964, 1968)
Fastest Lap: 179.23kph/111.37mph Jack Brabham, Brabham-Climax, 1964

CLERMONT-FERRAND
(8.055 km/5.005 miles: 1965, 1969–70, 1972)
Fastest Lap: 166.75kph/103.61mph Chris Amon, Matra-Simca, 1972

LE MANS (Bugatti)
(4.422 km/2.748 miles: 1967)
Fastest Lap: 164.64kph/102.29mph Graham Hill, Lotus-Ford

PAUL RICARD
(5.810 km/3.610 miles: 1971, 1973, 1975–6, 1978, 1980, 1982–3, 1985)
Fastest Lap: 209.34kph/130.08mph Keke Rosberg, Williams-Honda, 1985
(3.813 km/2.369 miles: 1986–90)
Fastest Lap: 201.83kph/125.41mph Nigel Mansell, Ferrari, 1990

DIJON–PRENOIS
(3.289 km/2.044 miles: 1974)
Fastest Lap: 197.34kph/122.62mph Jody Scheckter, Tyrrell-Ford
(3.800 km/2.361 miles: 1977, 1979, 1981–2[1])
Fastest Lap: 202.74kph/125.98mph Alain Prost, Renault, 1982
(3.887 km/2.415 miles: 1984)
Fastest Lap: 214.43kph/133.25mph Alain Prost, McLaren-Porsche

NEVERS–MAGNY COURS
(4.271 km/2.654 miles: 1991)
Fastest Lap: 194.22kph/120.68mph Nigel Mansell, Williams-Renault

GERMANY

NÜRBURGRING
(22.809 km/14.173 miles: 1951–4, 1956–8, 1961–6)
Fastest Lap: 106.90kph/101.22mph Jim Clark, Lotus-Climax, 1965
(22.835 km/14.189 miles: 1967–9, 1971–6)
Fastest Lap: 192.79kph/119.80mph Clay Regazzoni, Ferrari, 1975
(4.542 km/2.822 miles: 1984–5[2])
Fastest Lap: 197.46kph/122.70mph Niki Lauda, McLaren-TAG, 1985

AVUS
(8.299 km/5.157 miles: 1959)
Fastest Lap: 240.00kph/149.13mph Tony Brooks, Ferrari

HOCKENHEIM
(6.788 km/4.218 miles: 1970, 1977–81)
Fastest Lap: 225.28kph/139.98mph Alan Jones, Williams-Ford, 1980

[1] *1982 Swiss Grand Prix*   [2] *1984 European Grand Prix*

A packed house at Hockenheim.

Paul Ricard

Between 1971 and 1990 the Paul Ricard circuit, adjacent to the Le Castellet aerodrome, near Marseille, was the home of the French Grand Prix on 14 occasions before being replaced by Magny Cours in 1991. Built in 1970 at the request of drinks magnate Paul Ricard, it was notable for its high-quality pits area and very high safety standards, both important requisites in Grand Prix racing in the 1970s.

While the circuit is flat it is popular with drivers and the back straight (Mistral Straight) is one of the fastest in Formula One with speeds of up to 320kph/200mph being attained.

This is followed by the Courbe de Signes, one of the toughest bends in Formula One, but one that can be taken at 275kph/170mph by the leading drivers. Paul Ricard is also popular as a testing circuit and its removal from the Grand Prix list in 1991 met with some objections from the Formula One teams.

Silverstone

Silverstone has been Britain's premier circuit since the launch of the World Championship in 1950, and it was at the Towcester circuit in Northamptonshire that the first ever World Championship race took place.

Built on a disused airfield, its arrival came at a time when Brooklands, for so long Britain's leading circuit, was facing its ultimate demise. The Northamptonshire track opened in 1948 and soon established itself as Britain's top venue.

Hangar Straight, Woodcote, Maggotts, Copse, Stowe, and Becketts are among the most famous landmarks on any Grand Prix circuit in the world.

(6.796 km/4.223 miles: 1982–4, 1986–9)
Fastest Lap: 232.44kph/144.43mph Ayrton Senna, McLaren-Honda, 1989
(6.803 km/4.227 miles: 1990–1)
Fastest Lap: 236.44kph/146.92mph Riccardo Patrese, Williams-Renault, 1991

GREAT BRITAIN

SILVERSTONE
(4.649 km/2.889 miles: 1950–1)
Fastest Lap: 160.92kph/99.99mph Giuseppe Farina, Alfa Romeo, 1951
(4.711 km/2.927 miles: 1952–4, 1956, 1958, 1960, 1963, 1965, 1967, 1969, 1971, 1973)
Fastest Lap: 215.75kph/134.06mph James Hunt, March-Ford, 1973
(4.719 km/2.932 miles: 1975, 1977, 1979, 1981, 1983, 1985)
Fastest Lap: 243.07kph/151.04mph Alain Prost, McLaren-TAG, 1985
(4.778 km/2.969 miles: 1987–90)
Fastest Lap: 241.36kph/149.98mph Nigel Mansell, Ferrari, 1990
(5.226 km/3.247 miles: 1991)
Fastest Lap: 217.78kph/135.33mph Nigel Mansell, Williams-Renault

AINTREE
(4.828 km/3.000 miles: 1955, 1957, 1959, 1961–2)
Fastest Lap: 151.14kph/93.91mph Jim Clark, Lotus-Climax, 1962

BRANDS HATCH
(4.265 km/2.650 miles: 1964, 1966, 1968, 1970, 1972, 1974)
Fastest Lap: 189.31kph/117.63mph Niki Lauda, Ferrari, 1974
(4.207 km/2.614 miles: 1976, 1978, 1980, 1982–6[3])
Fastest Lap: 217.60kph/135.22mph Nigel Mansell, Williams-Honda, 1986

HOLLAND

ZANDVOORT
(4.192 km/2.605 miles: 1952–3, 1955, 1958–71)
Fastest Lap: 190.52kph/118.38mph Jacky Ickx, Ferrari, 1970
(4.226 km/2.626 miles: 1973–9)
Fastest Lap: 191.52kph/119.00mph Gilles Villeneuve, Ferrari, 1979
(4.252 km/2.642 miles: 1980–5)
Fastest Lap: 199.99kph/124.27mph Alain Prost, McLaren-TAG, 1985
[3] *Venue for the 1983 and 1985 European Grands Prix*

HUNGARY

HUNGARORING
(4.014 km/2.494 miles: 1986-8)
Fastest Lap: 160.30kph/99.60mph Nelson Piquet, Williams-Honda, 1987
(3.967 km/2.465 miles: 1989-91)
Fastest Lap: 175.17kph/108.85mph Bertrand Gachot, Jordan-Ford, 1991

ITALY

MONZA
(6.301 km/3.915 miles: 1950-4)
Fastest Lap: 195.52kph/121.49mph Giuseppe Farina, Alfa Romeo, 1951
(10.000 km/6.214 miles: 1955-6, 1960-1)
Fastest Lap: 220.05kph/136.73mph Phil Hill, Ferrari, 1960
(5.750 km/3.573 miles: 1957-9, 1962-71)
Fastest Lap: 247.02kph/153.49mph Henri Pescarolo, March-Ford, 1971
(5.774 km/3.588 miles: 1972-3)
Fastest Lap: 218.15kph/135.55mph Jackie Stewart, Tyrrell-Ford, 1973
(5.781 km/3.592 miles: 1974-5)
Fastest Lap: 223.50kph/138.88mph Clay Regazzoni, Ferrari, 1975

(5.800 km/3.604 miles: 1976-9, 1981-91)
Fastest Lap: 242.62kph/150.76mph Ayrton Senna, McLaren-Honda, 1991

PESCARA
(25.579 km/15.894 miles: 1957[4])
Fastest Lap: 157.52kph/97.88mph Stirling Moss, Vanwall

IMOLA
(5.000 km/3.107 miles: 1980)
Fastest Lap: 187.33kph/116.40mph Alan Jones, Williams-Ford
(5.040 km/3.132 miles: 1981-91[5])
Fastest Lap: 210.26kph/130.65mph Alain Prost, McLaren-Honda, 1989

[4] *Pescara Grand Prix*   [5] *San Marino Grand Prix*

JAPAN

FUJI
(4.360 km/2.709 miles: 1976-7)
Fastest Lap: 211.20kph/131.24mph Jody Scheckter, Wolf-Ford, 1977

SUZUKA
(5.860 km/3.641 miles: 1987-91)
Fastest Lap: 207.48kph/128.92mph Ayrton Senna, McLaren-Honda, 1991

CIRCUIT FOCUS

Monza

Italy's Monza track can claim to be the fastest ever to have staged a World Championship Grand Prix because the 1971 Italian Grand Prix over the Milan circuit was the fastest race the championship has seen. The Monza autodrome was built in 1922 and is a purpose-built track constructed in the Royal Park. The park's perimeter roads were soon utilised and the circuit offered plenty of variety. The banked course was demolished in 1933 and in 1955 a demanding concrete bowl was constructed, but many felt it was far too dangerous and it was consequently not always incorporated into the Grand Prix circuit.

The full circuit has not been used since 1961. Because Monza was becoming too dangerous it was replaced by Imola in 1980, the one and only time the Italian Grand Prix has not been held at the Milan circuit. Nevertheless, Monza has staged more World Championship races than any other circuit.

Monte Carlo

The Monaco Grand Prix through the streets of Monte Carlo is the slowest of all World Championship races. But it is one of the best known and is a glittering and glamorous sporting occasion as thousands of people flock to the Principality every spring and the streets of the wealthy town come to life with the smell and roar of Formula One cars.

The nature of the circuit, winding its way through the hotels, shops, restaurants and apartments of Monte Carlo, make it a very demanding and, at times, uninteresting circuit.

But to see cars come out of the tunnel and along the harbour wall is a great sight as drivers get their one real chance of overtaking rivals. Other circuits have, over the years, tried to emulate Monaco; but none has managed to recreate the special atmosphere of Monte Carlo.

MEXICO

MEXICO CITY
(5.000 km/3.107 miles: 1963–70)
Fastest Lap: 174.67kph/108.54mph Jacky Ickx, Brabham-Ford, 1969
(4.421 km/2.747 miles: 1986–91)
Fastest Lap: 207.27kph/128.79mph Nigel Mansell, Williams-Renault, 1991

MONACO

MONTE CARLO
(3.180 km/1.976 miles: 1950)
Fastest Lap: 103.14kph/64.09mph Juan Manuel Fangio, Alfa Romeo
(3.145 km/1.954 miles: 1955–72)
Fastest Lap: 137.74kph/85.59mph Jackie Stewart, Tyrrell-Ford, 1971
(3.278 km/2.037 miles: 1973–5)
Fastest Lap: 134.25kph/83.42mph Ronnie Peterson, Lotus-Ford, 1974
(3.312 km/2.058 miles: 1976–85)
Fastest Lap: 144.28kph/89.65mph Michele Alboreto, Ferrari, 1985
(3.328 km/2.068 miles: 1986–91)
Fastest Lap: 142.01kph/88.24mph Alain Prost, Ferrari, 1991

MOROCCO

AIN DIAB (CASABLANCA)
(7.619 km/4.734 miles: 1958)
Fastest Lap: 192.46kph/119.59mph Stirling Moss, Vanwall

PORTUGAL

OPORTO
(7.406 km/4.602 miles: 1958, 1960)
Fastest Lap: 180.74kph/112.31mph John Surtees, Lotus-Climax, 1960
MONSANTO
(5.440 km/3.380 miles: 1959)
Fastest Lap: 156.58kph/97.30mph Stirling Moss, Cooper-Climax
ESTORIL
(4.350 km/2.703 miles: 1984–91)
Fastest Lap: 201.15kph/124.99mph Riccardo Patrese, Williams-Renault, 1990

SOUTH AFRICA

EAST LONDON
(3.920 km/2.436 miles: 1962–3, 1965)
Fastest Lap: 161.11kph/100.11mph Jim Clark, Lotus-Climax, 1965

The backdrop of the hotels, apartments, bars, restaurants and shops has made the Monaco Grand Prix motor racing's most glamorous and attractive event. This is the 1957 race won by Fangio.

KYALAMI
(4.094 km/2.544 miles: 1967)
Fastest Lap: 163.95kph/101.87mph Denny Hulme,
Brabham-Repco
(4.103 km/2.550 miles: 1968-80, 1982-5)
Fastest Lap: 216.80kph/134.71mph Keke Rosberg,
Williams-Honda, 1985

SPAIN

PEDRALBES
(6.317 km/3.925 miles: 1951, 1954)
Fastest Lap: 166.05kph/103.18mph Juan Manuel Fangio,
Alfa Romeo, 1951
JARAMA
(3.404 km/2.115 miles: 1968, 1970, 1972, 1974, 1976-9)
Fastest Lap: 160.31kph/99.61mph Gilles Villeneuve,
Ferrari, 1979
(3.312 km/2.058 miles: 1981)
Fastest Lap: 153.22kph/95.21mph Alan Jones, Williams-
Ford
MONTJUICH
(3.792 km/2.356 miles: 1969, 1971, 1973, 1975)
Fastest Lap: 162.86kph/101.20mph Ronnie Peterson,
Lotus-Ford, 1973

JEREZ
(4.218 km/2.621 miles: 1986-90)
Fastest Lap: 179.67kph/111.64mph Riccardo Patrese,
Williams-Renault, 1990
CATALUNYA
(4.746 km/2.949 miles: 1991)
Fastest Lap: 206.30kph/128.19mph Riccardo Patrese,
Williams-Renault

SWEDEN

ANDERSTORP
(4.019 km/2.497 miles: 1973-7)
Fastest Lap: 167.91kph/104.33mph Denny Hulme,
McLaren-Ford, 1973
(4.031 km/2.505 miles: 1978)
Fastest Lap: 171.06kph/106.29mph Niki Lauda, Brabham-
Alfa Romeo

SWITZERLAND

BREMGARTEN
(7.281 km/4.524 miles: 1950-4)
Fastest Lap: 164.10kph/101.97mph Juan Manuel Fangio,
Mercedes-Benz, 1954

The circuit at Catalunya near Barcelona became Spain's fifth World Championship circuit when first used in 1991.

CIRCUIT FOCUS

Indianapolis

While the Indianapolis 500 race formed a part of the Formula One World Championship for just 11 years, its home, the Indianapolis Raceway, is one of the great motor racing venues and, like Brooklands, was a purpose-built track. Built in 1910, the track was laid with thousands of bricks, the last one being a gold one. Not surprisingly, the circuit is affectionately known as 'The Brickyard'.

The bricks were taken up in 1930 and the circuit was asphalted. The track measures 2.5 miles/4.023km and is basic-ally a rectangle joined together by four slightly banked corners. Because all corners are left-handers, manufacturers have to modify their cars for the race allowing for the extra wear on tyres and suspension.

UNITED STATES

INDIANAPOLIS
(4.023 km/2.500 miles: 1950–60)
Fastest Lap: 235.16kph/146.13mph Jim Rathmann, Watson-Offenhauser, 1960
SEBRING
(8.369 km/5.200 miles: 1959)
Fastest Lap: 162.85kph/101.19mph Maurice Trintignant, Cooper-Climax
RIVERSIDE
(5.271 km/3.275 miles: 1960)
Fastest Lap: 163.15kph/101.38mph Jack Brabham, Cooper-Climax
WATKINS GLEN
(3.701 km/2.300 miles: 1961–70)
Fastest Lap: 212.39kph/131.97mph Jacky Ickx, Ferrari, 1970
(5.345 km/3.377 miles: 1971–80)
Fastest Lap: 207.99kph/129.24mph Alan Jones, Williams-Ford, 1980
LONG BEACH
(3.251 km/2.020 miles: 1976–81)
Fastest Lap: 146.60kph/91.09mph Nelson Piquet, Brabham-Ford, 1980
(3.428 km/2.130 miles: 1982)
Fastest Lap: 135.86kph/84.42mph Niki Lauda, McLaren-Ford

(3.275 km/2.035 miles: 1983)
Fastest Lap: 133.48kph/82.94mph Niki Lauda, McLaren-Ford
LAS VEGAS
(3.650 km/2.268 miles: 1981–2)
Fastest Lap: 164.99kph/102.52mph Michele Alboreto, Tyrrell-Ford, 1982
DETROIT
(4.012 km/2.493 miles: 1982)
Fastest Lap: 130.80kph/81.28mph Alain Prost, Renault
(4.023 km/2.500 miles: 1983–8)
Fastest Lap: 144.17kph/89.58mph Ayrton Senna, Lotus-Honda, 1987
DALLAS
(3.901 km/2.424 miles: 1984)
Fastest Lap: 133.30kph/82.83mph Niki Lauda, McLaren-Porsche
PHOENIX
(3.798 km/2.360 miles: 1989–90)
Fastest Lap: 150.17kph/93.31mph Gerhard Berger, McLaren-Honda, 1990
(3.721 km/2.312 miles: 1991)
Fastest Lap: 154.40kph/95.94mph Jean Alesi, Ferrari

Nürburgring

After the giant Pescara circuit, Germany's Old Nürburgring, at over 22km/14 miles, is the second longest circuit ever to be used for a World Championship Grand Prix. Set in the Eifel district of Germany near Koblenz, the tough circuit took in more than 70 twists and turns of tree-lined roads and made it a really demanding test for drivers.

The 'Ring' was built in the 1920s and staged its first German Grand Prix in 1927 when Otto Merz won in a Mercedes. Sadly, such was the nature and danger of the Old circuit that it is believed to have claimed the lives of more than 50 drivers over the years. Because of its dangers it was removed from the World Championship calendar in 1970 while some of the trees, rocks and fences which lined the roads were removed.

It returned after a year's absence and was certainly an improvement. The 14-plus mile circuit was last used in 1976, when Niki Lauda had his horrific accident and moves were made to design a new circuit in line with the shorter distances of other venues. In May 1984 the new, safer, and much smaller Nürburgring was opened. Some features of the old circuit were retained but a racing institution was gone.

LONGEST CIRCUITS

The following have been the longest circuits ever to be used for a World Championship Grand Prix. Where a circuit has been modified, its longest distance only is taken into consideration.

Km/miles	Circuit
25.579/15.894	Pescara (Ita)
22.835/14.189	Nürburgring (Ger)
14.120/8.774	Spa-Francorchamps (Bel)
10.000/6.214	Monza (Ita)
8.369/5.200	Sebring (USA)
8.348/5.187	Reims (Fra)
8.299/5.157	Avus (Ger)
8.055/5.005	Clermont-Ferrand (Fra)
7.960/4.946	Interlagos (Bra)
7.619/4.734	Ain Diab (Mor)
7.406/4.602	Oporto (Por)
7.281/4.524	Bremgarten (Swi)
6.803/4.227	Hockenheim (Ger)
6.542/4.065	Rouen-les-Essarts (Fra)

SHORTEST CIRCUITS

The following have been the shortest circuits ever to be used for a World Championship Grand Prix. Where a circuit has been modified, its shortest distance only is taken into consideration.

Km/miles	Circuit
3.145/1.954	Monte Carlo (Mon)
3.199/1.988	Zeltweg (Aut)
3.251/2.020	Long Beach (USA)
3.289/2.044	Dijon-Prenois (Fra)
3.312/2.058	Jarama (Spa)
3.344/2.078	Buenos Aires No. 9 (Arg)
3.650/2.268	Las Vegas (USA)
3.701/2.300	Watkins Glen (USA)
3.721/2.312	Phoenix (USA)
3.724/2.314	Nivelles-Baulers (Bel)
3.779/2.348	Adelaide (Aus)
3.792/2.356	Montjuich (Spa)
3.813/2.369	Paul Ricard (Fra)
3.901/2.424	Dallas (USA)
3.912/2.431	Buenos Aires No. 2 (Arg)
3.920/2.436	East London (SA)
3.957/2.459	Mosport Park (Can)
3.967/2.465	Hungaroring (Hun)
4.012/2.493	Detroit (USA)
4.019/2.497	Anderstorp (Swe)

MOST FREQUENTLY USED CIRCUITS

No. of times used	Circuit	Years first & last used
41	Monza (Ita)	1950–91
38	Monte Carlo (Mon)	1950–91
30	Zandvoort (Hol)	1952–85
26	Spa-Francorchamps (Bel)	1950–91
25	Silverstone (GB)	1950–91
24	Nürburgring (Ger)	1951–85
20	Watkins Glen (USA)	1961–80
18	Österreichring (Aut)	1970–87
18	Kyalami (SAf)	1967–85
15	Hockenheim (Ger)	1970–91
14	Paul Ricard (Fra)	1971–90
14	Brands Hatch (GB)	1964–86
14	Mexico City (Mex)	1963–91
13	Montreal (Can)	1978–91
12	Imola (Ita)	1980–91
11	Reims (Fra)	1950–66
11	Indianapolis (USA)	1950–60
10	Zolder (Bel)	1975–84
10	Rio de Janeiro (Bra)	1978–89
9	Interlagos (Bra)	1973–91
9	Jarama (Spa)	1968–81
8	Mosport Park (Can)	1967–77
8	Estoril (Por)	1984–91
8	Long Beach (USA)	1976–83
7	Buenos Aires No. 2 (Arg)	1953–60
7	Buenos Aires No. 15 (Arg)	1974–81
7	Adelaide (Aus)	1985–91
7	Detroit (USA)	1982–88
6	Dijon-Prenois (Fra)	1974–84
6	Hungaroring (Hun)	1986–91
6	Anderstorp (Swe)	1973–78
5	Rouen-les-Essarts (Fra)	1952–68
5	Aintree (GB)	1955–62
5	Suzuka (Jap)	1987–91
5	Jerez (Spa)	1986–90
5	Bremgarten (Swi)	1950–54

Monza has been the home of every Italian Grand Prix since 1950 with the exception of 1980 when the race was moved to Imola, which subsequently became the home of the San Marino Grand Prix.

The following circuits have been used on just one occasion each:

Pescara (Ita) 1957; Ain Diab (Mor) 1958; Avus (Ger) 1959; Monsanto (Por) 1959; Sebring (USA) 1959; Riverside (USA) 1960; Zeltweg (Aut) 1964; Le Mans Bugatti Circuit (Fra) 1967; Dallas (USA) 1984; Catalunya (Spa) 1991; Nevers-Magny Cours (Fra) 1991

LEADING LAP-RECORD HOLDERS

From the list of lap record holders at the various World Championship Grand Prix circuits, the following appear the most often:

9 Nigel Mansell (GB)

8 Alain Prost (Fra)

6 Niki Lauda (Aut)

5 Juan Manuel Fangio (Arg), Stirling Moss (GB), Riccardo Patrese (Ita)

4 Gerhard Berger (Aut), Alan Jones (Aus), Nelson Piquet (Bra), Clay Regazzoni (Swi), Ayrton Senna (Bra)

3 Jim Clark (GB), Denny Hulme (NZ), Jacky Ickx (Bel)

2 Michele Alboreto (Ita), Chris Amon (NZ), René Arnoux (Fra), Alberto Ascari (Ita), Jack Brabham (Aus), Giuseppe Farina (Ita), James Hunt (GB), Ronnie Peterson (Swe), Keke Rosberg (Fin), Jody Scheckter (SAf), Jackie Stewart (GB), Gilles Villeneuve (Can)

INDEX

Page references in italics denote illustrations.

Jack Brabham.

John Watson wins the 1981 British Grand Prix at Silverstone in his McLaren-Ford.